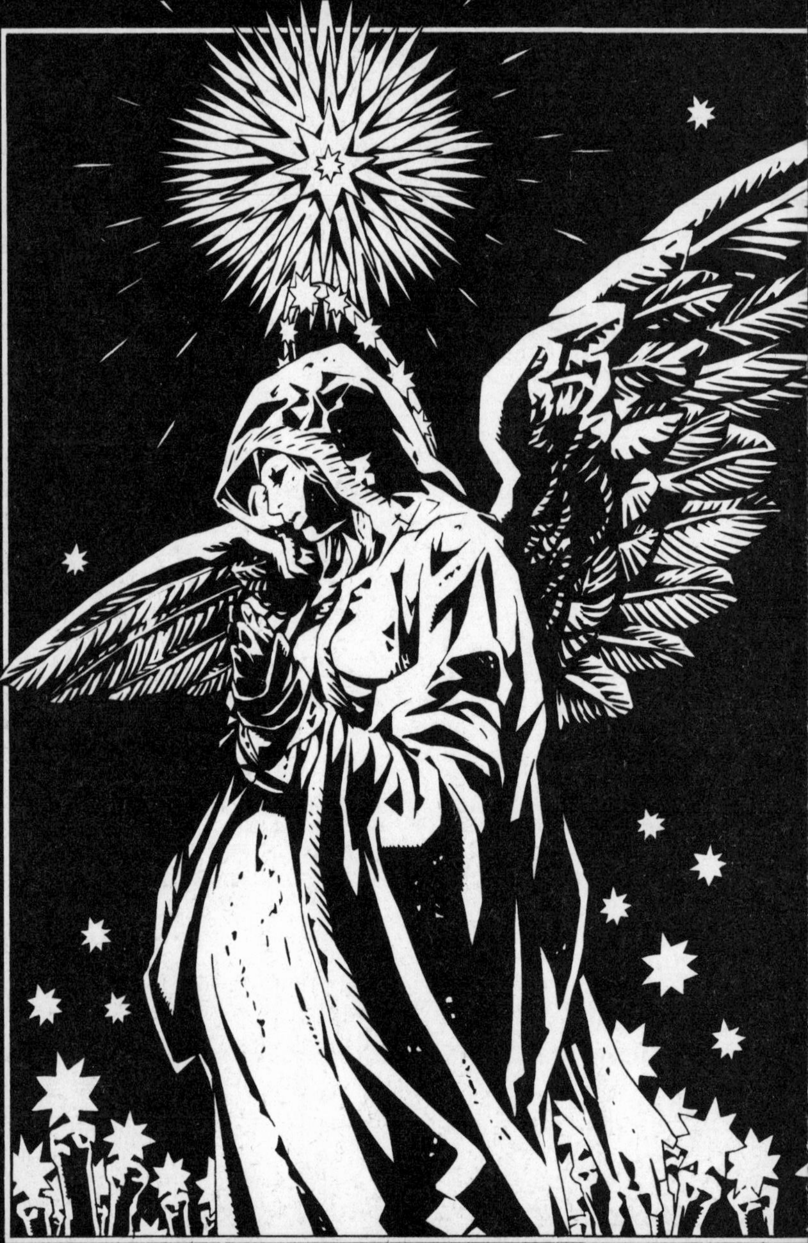

List of Characters

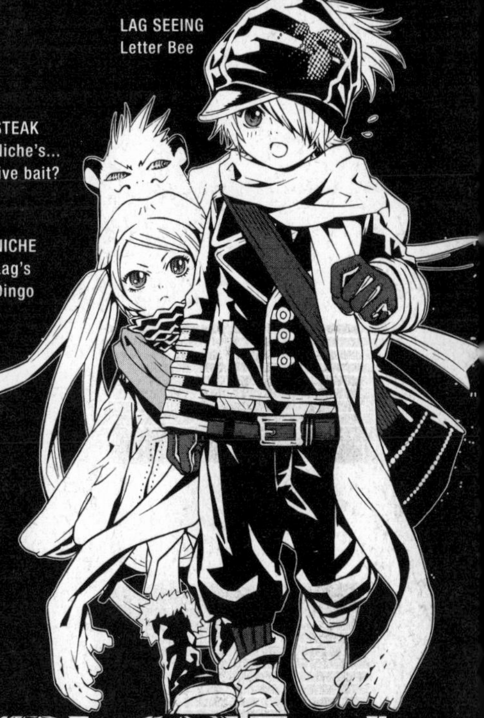

LAG SEEING
Letter Bee

STEAK
Niche's...
live bait?

NICHE
Lag's
Dingo

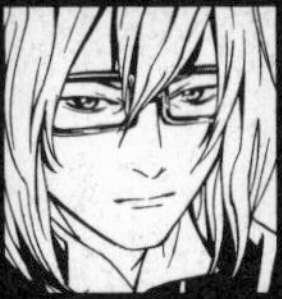

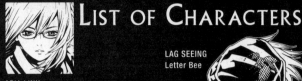

LARGO LLOYD
Beehive Director

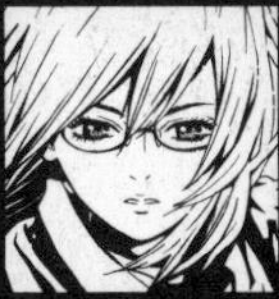

ARIA LINK
Beehive Assistant
Director

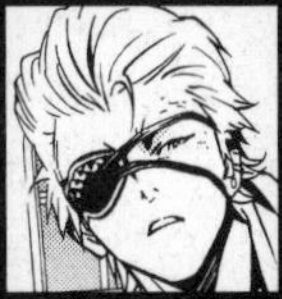

DR. THUNDERLAND, JR.
Member of the AG
Biological Science
Advisory Board,
Third Division and
head doctor at the
Beehive

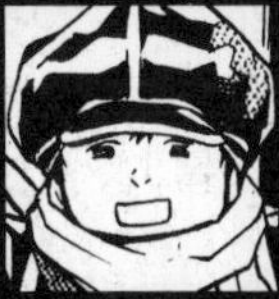

CONNOR KLUFF
Letter Bee

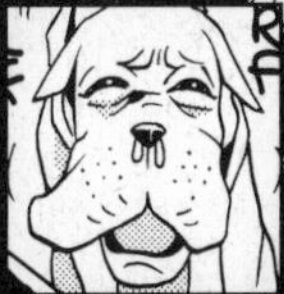

GUS
Connor's Dingo

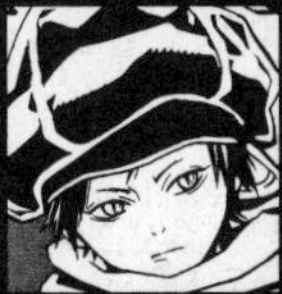

ZAZIE
Letter Bee

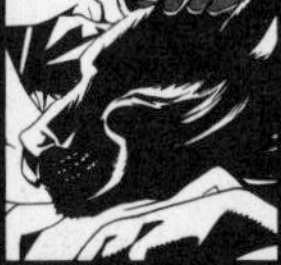

WASIOLKA
Zazie's Dingo

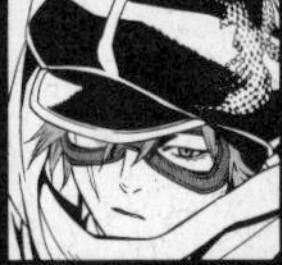

JIGGY PEPPER
Express Delivery
Letter Bee

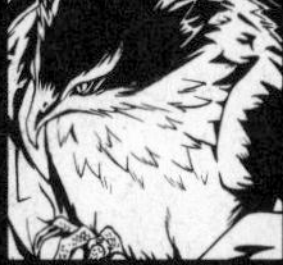

HARRY
Jiggy's Dingo

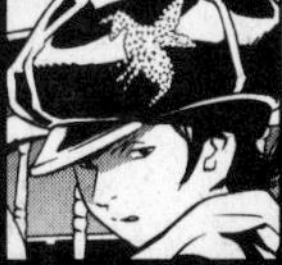

MOC SULLIVAN
Letter Bee

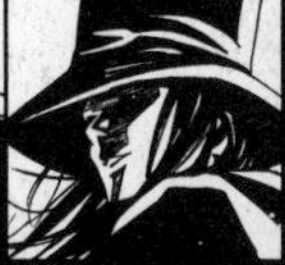

THE MAN WHO COULD
NOT BECOME SPIRIT
The ringleader of
Reverse

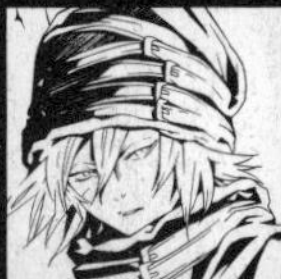

NOIR (FORMERLY
GAUCHE SUEDE)
Marauder for
Reverse and an
ex–Letter Bee

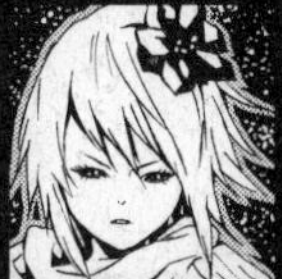

RODA
Noir's Dingo

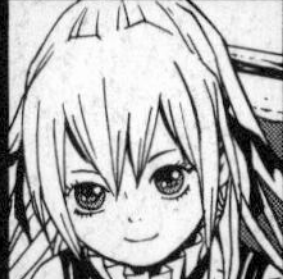

SYLVETTE SUEDE
Gauche's Sister

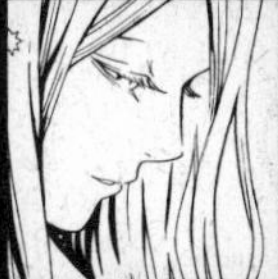

ANNE SEEING
Lag's Mother
(Missing)

Tegami Bachi
LETTER · BEE

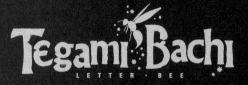

VOLUME 6

The Lighthouse in the Wasteland

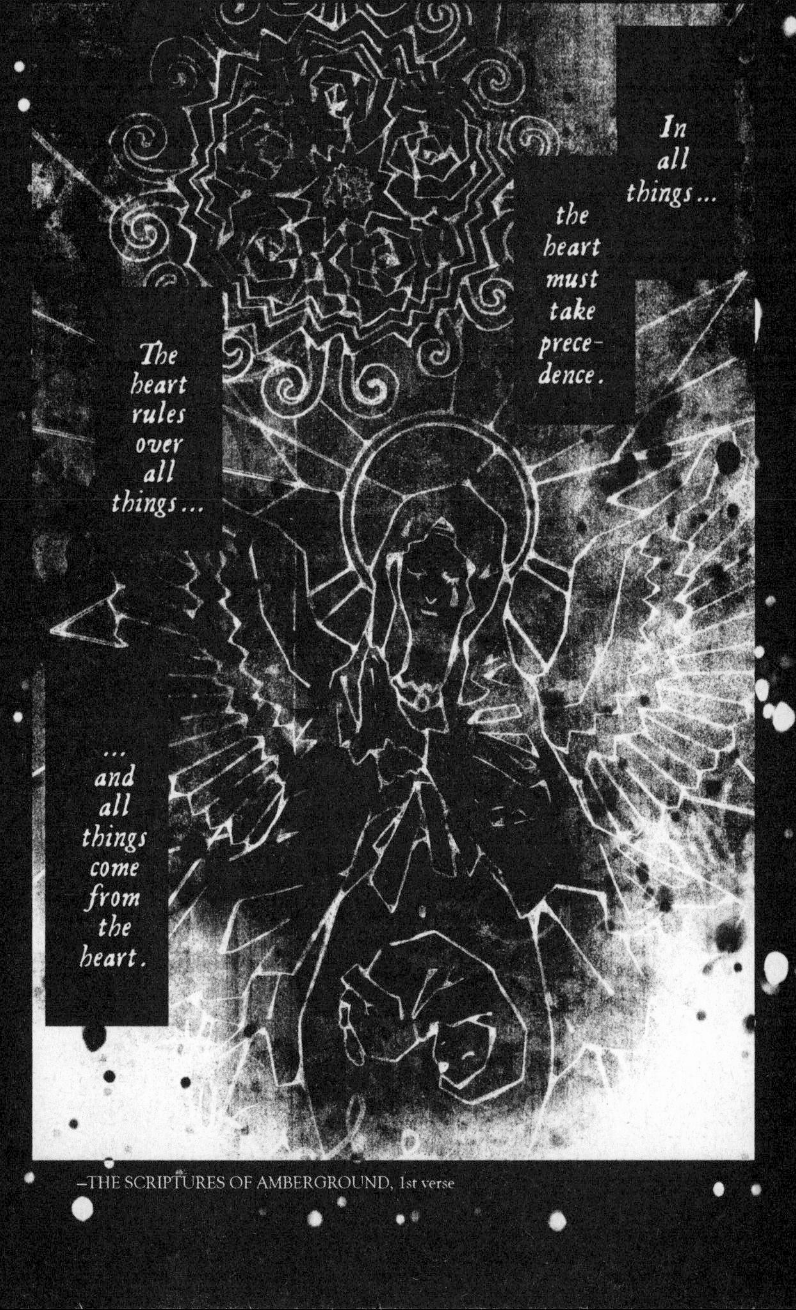
In all things...
the heart must take precedence.
The heart rules over all things...
... and all things come from the heart.
–THE SCRIPTURES OF AMBERGROUND, 1st verse

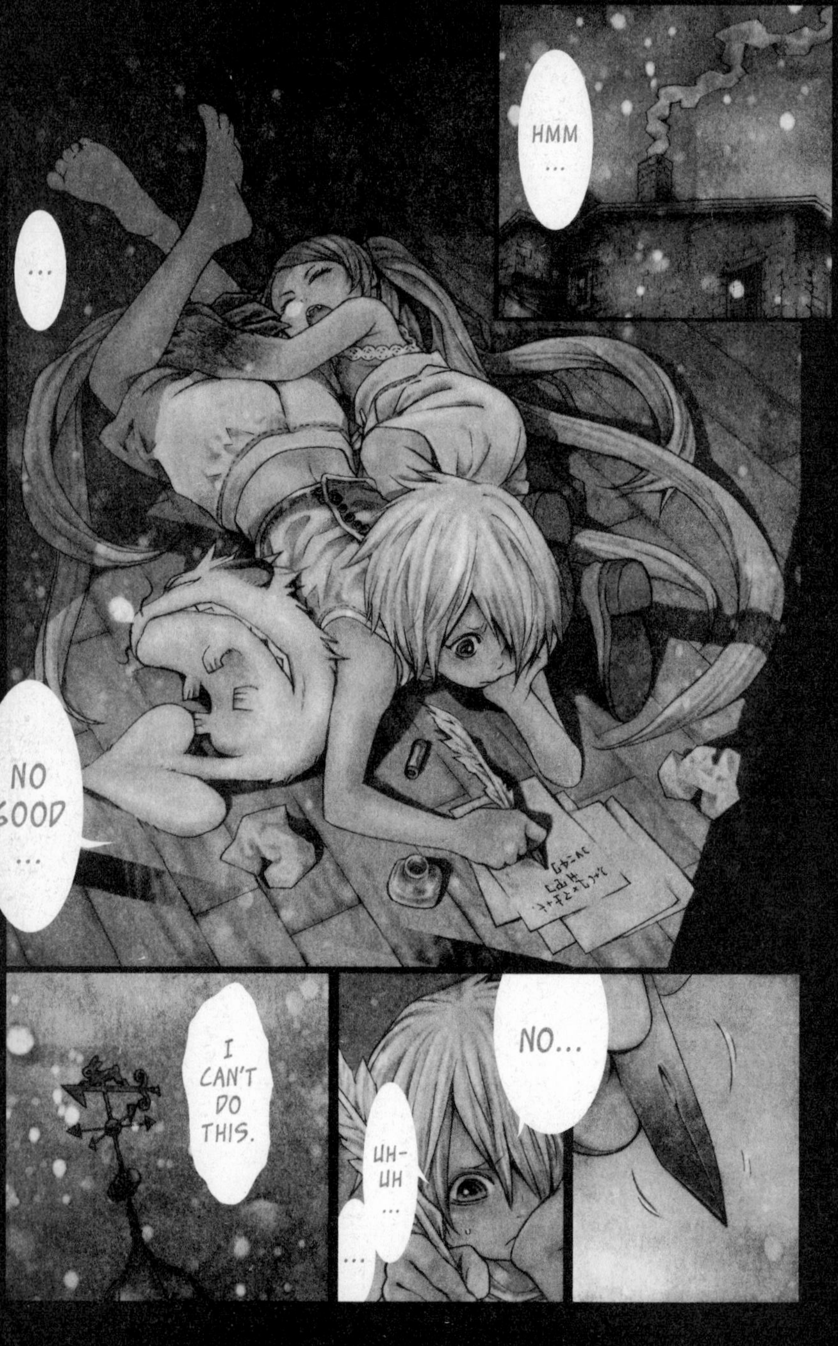
HMM ...
...
NO GOOD ...
NO...
UH-UH ...
...
I CAN'T DO THIS.

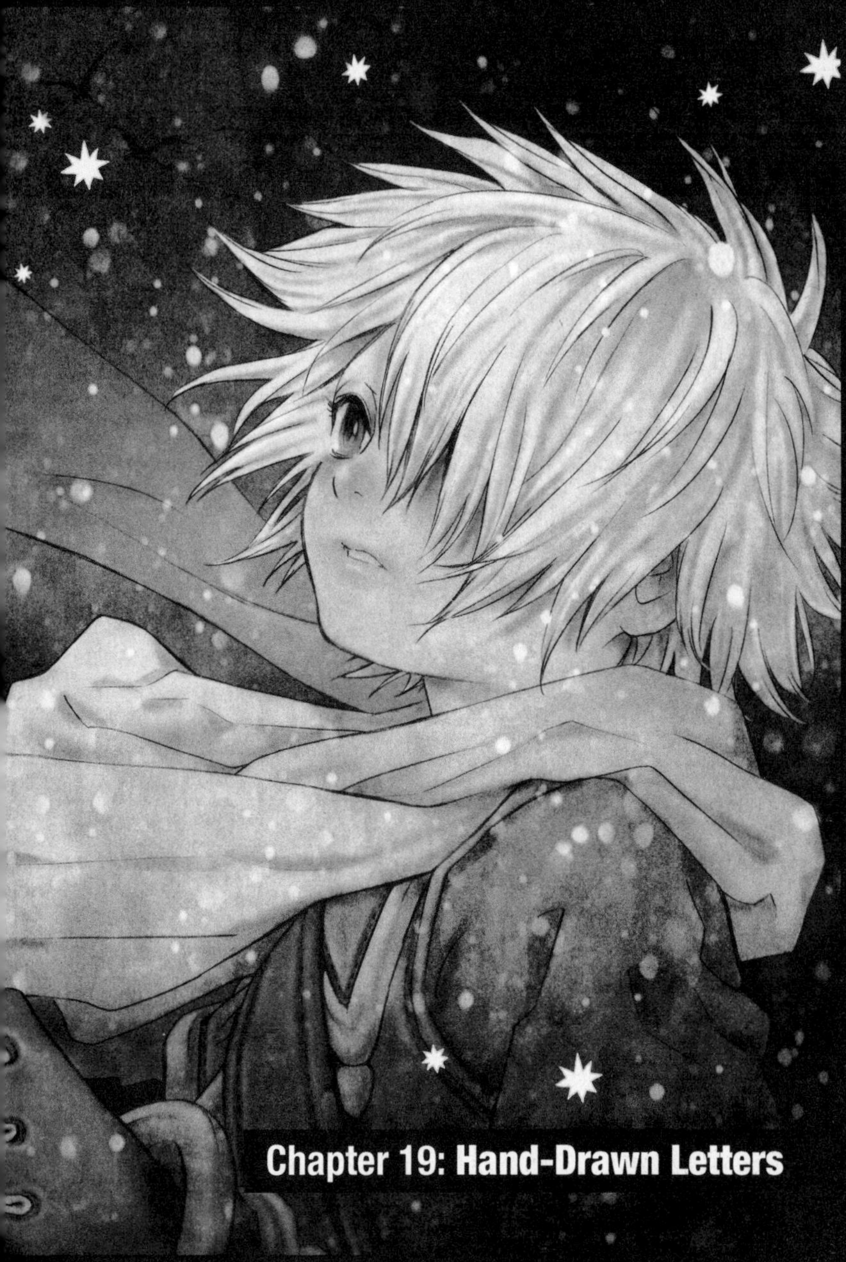

Chapter 19: Hand-Drawn Letters

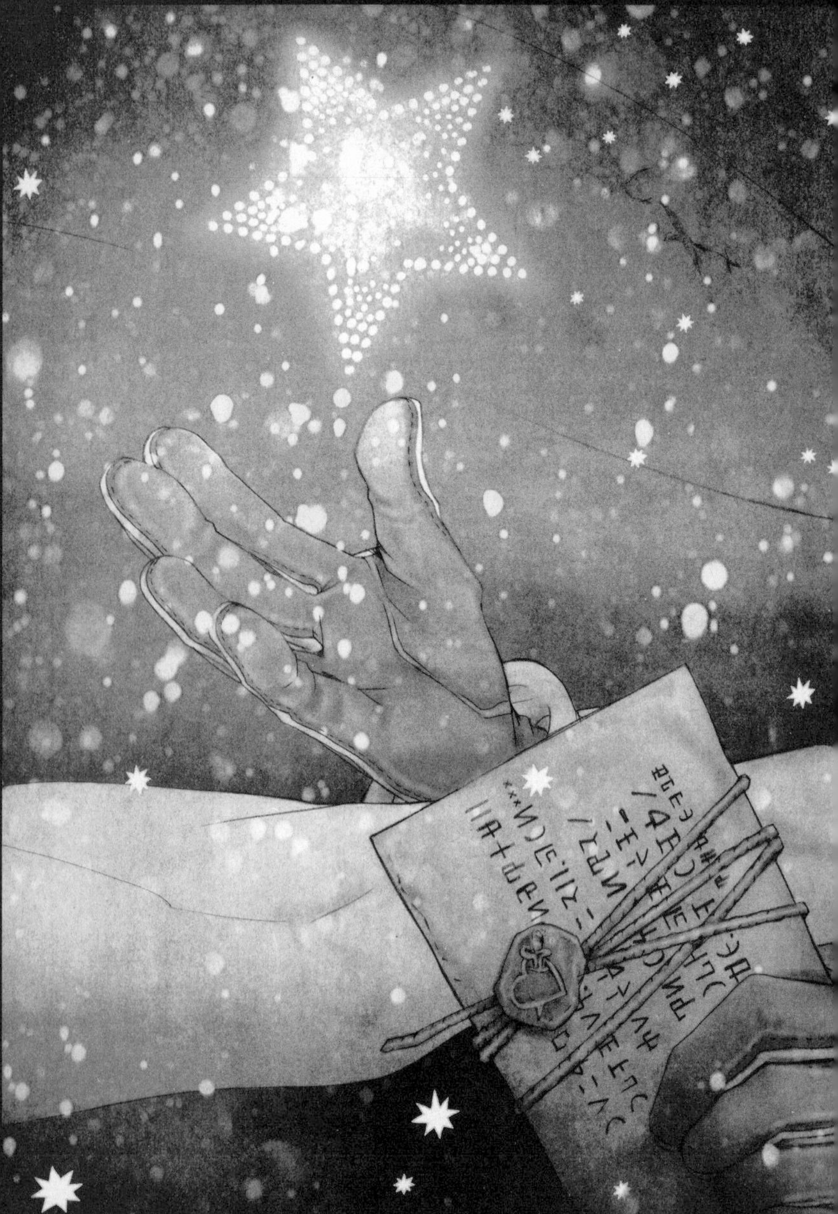

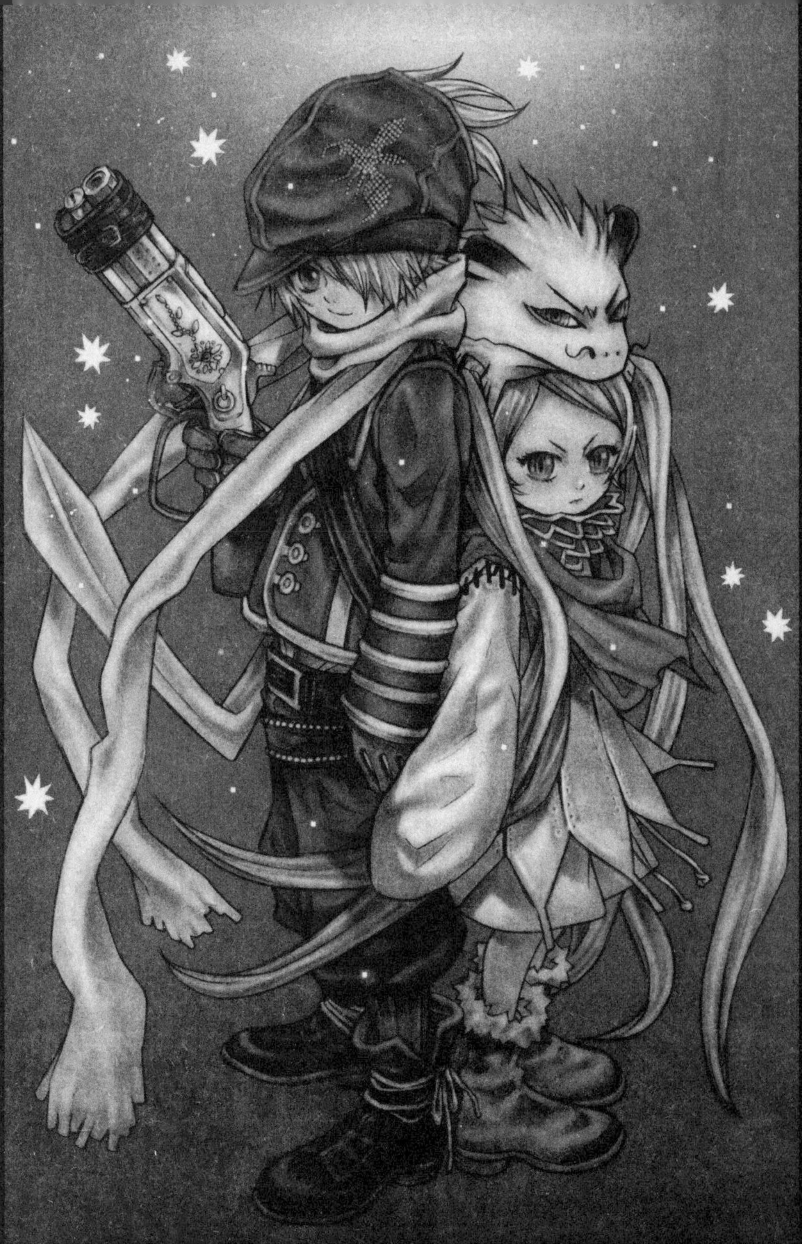

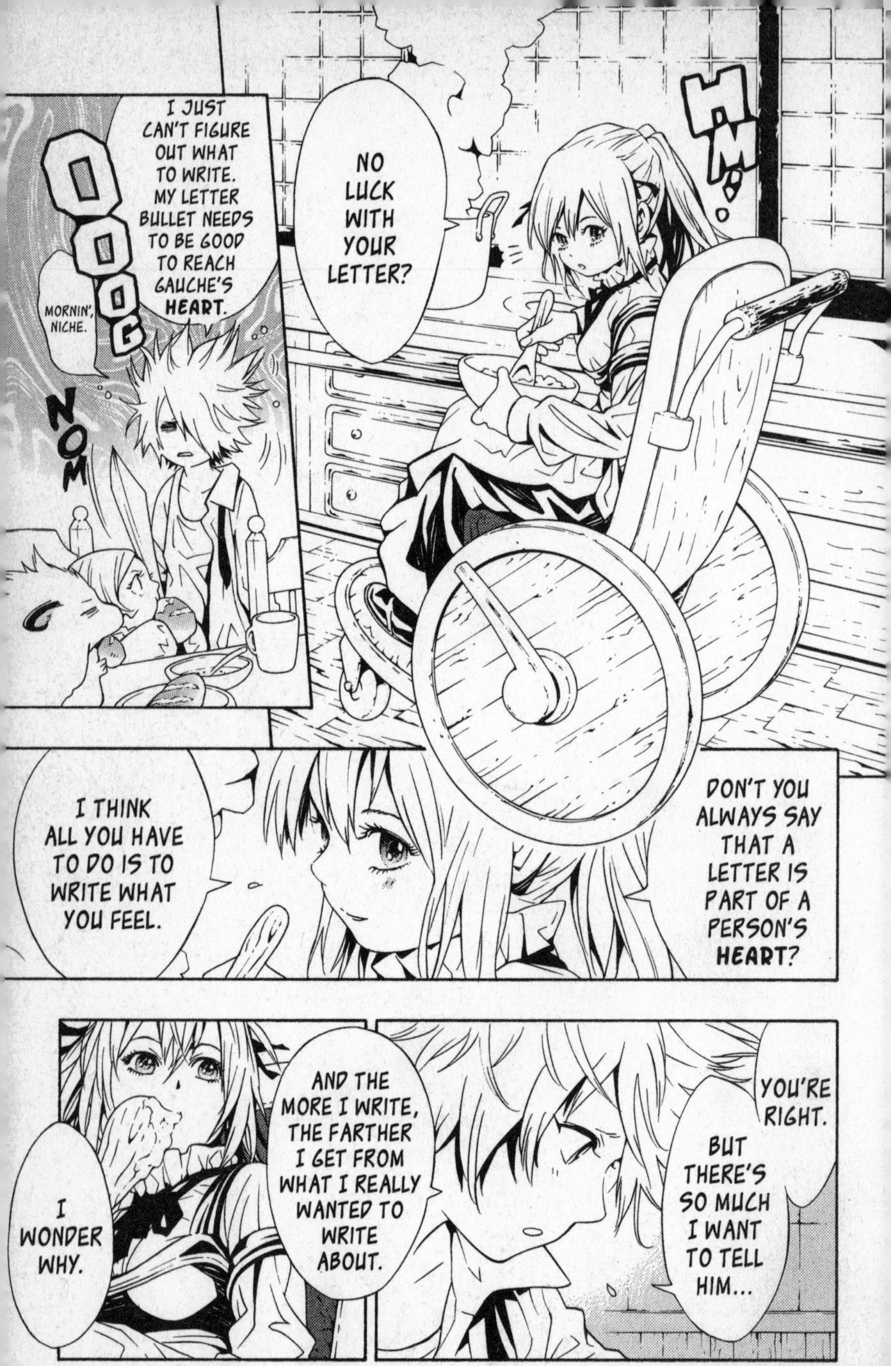
HM...
NO LUCK WITH YOUR LETTER?
I JUST CAN'T FIGURE OUT WHAT TO WRITE. MY LETTER BULLET NEEDS TO BE GOOD TO REACH GAUCHE'S **HEART**.
OOOG
MORNIN', NICHE.
NOM
DON'T YOU ALWAYS SAY THAT A LETTER IS PART OF A PERSON'S **HEART**?
I THINK ALL YOU HAVE TO DO IS TO WRITE WHAT YOU FEEL.
YOU'RE RIGHT.
BUT THERE'S SO MUCH I WANT TO TELL HIM...
AND THE MORE I WRITE, THE FARTHER I GET FROM WHAT I REALLY WANTED TO WRITE ABOUT.
I WONDER WHY.

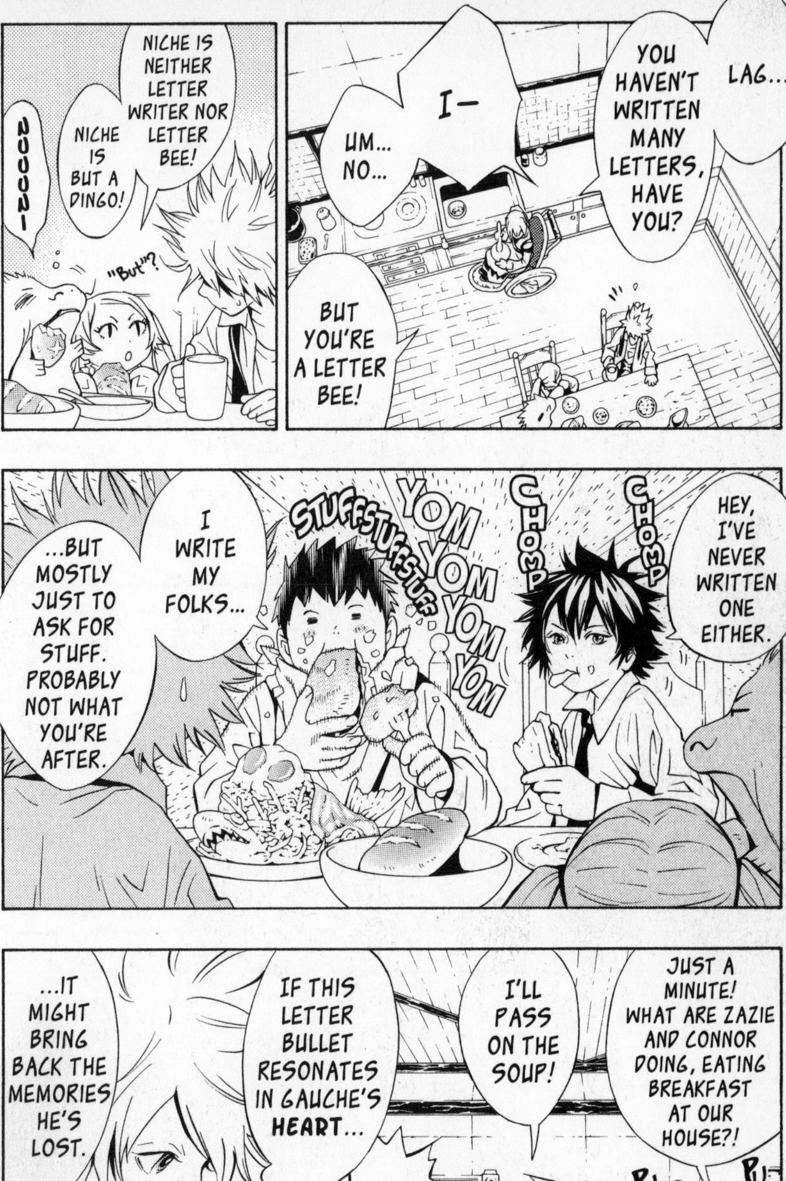
LAG...
YOU HAVEN'T WRITTEN MANY LETTERS, HAVE YOU?
I—
UM... NO...
BUT YOU'RE A LETTER BEE!
NICHE IS NEITHER LETTER WRITER NOR LETTER BEE!
NICHE IS BUT A DINGO!
NUUUNI
"But"?
HEY, I'VE NEVER WRITTEN ONE EITHER.
CHOMP
CHOMP
YOM YOM YOM YOM
STUFFSTUFFSTUFFSTUFF
I WRITE MY FOLKS...
...BUT MOSTLY JUST TO ASK FOR STUFF. PROBABLY NOT WHAT YOU'RE AFTER.
JUST A MINUTE! WHAT ARE ZAZIE AND CONNOR DOING, EATING BREAKFAST AT OUR HOUSE?!
PUFF
PUFF
I'LL PASS ON THE SOUP!
WHAT ?!
IF THIS LETTER BULLET RESONATES IN GAUCHE'S **HEART**...
...IT MIGHT BRING BACK THE MEMORIES HE'S LOST.

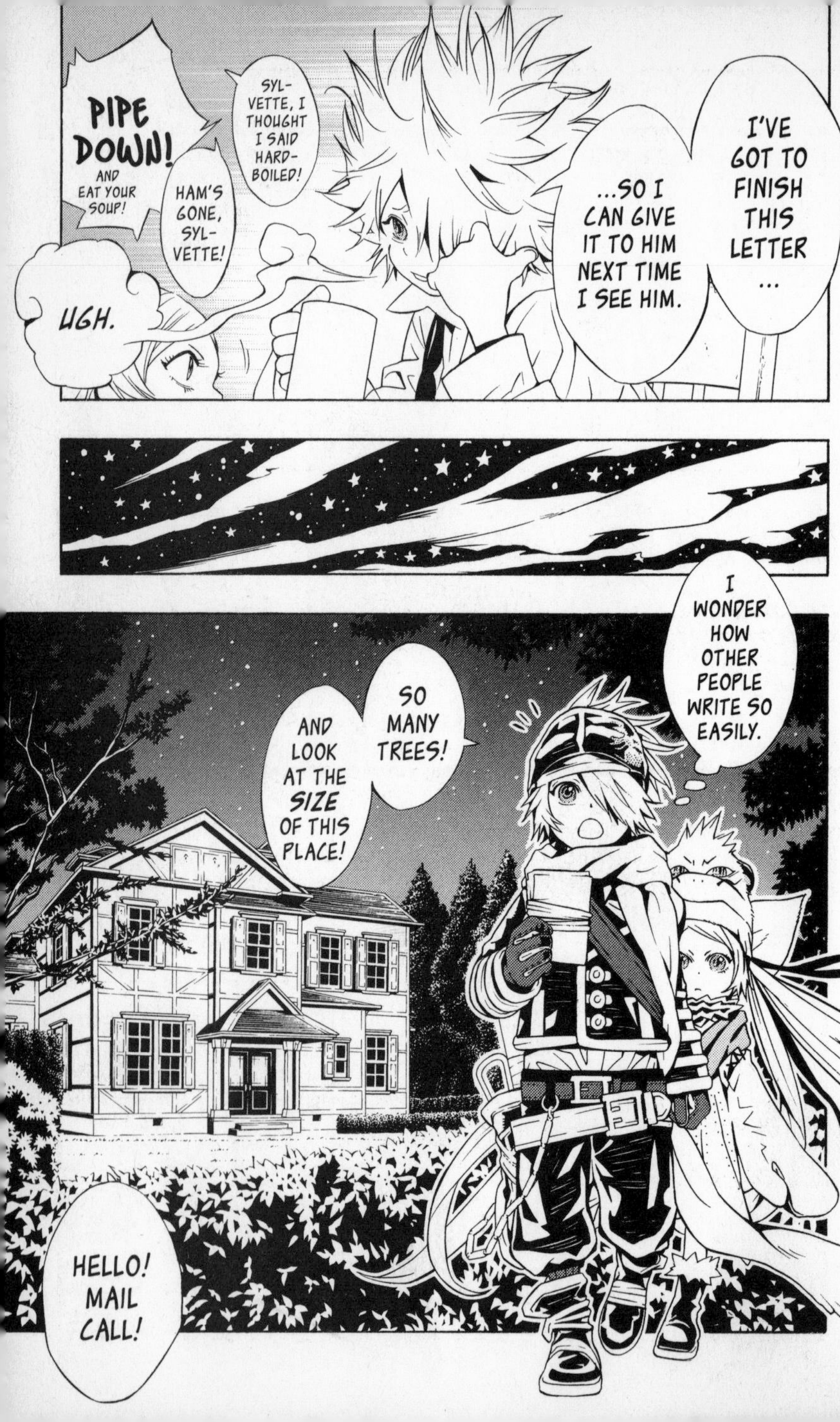
I'VE GOT TO FINISH THIS LETTER ...
...SO I CAN GIVE IT TO HIM NEXT TIME I SEE HIM.
SYL-VETTE, I THOUGHT I SAID HARD-BOILED!
HAM'S GONE, SYL-VETTE!
PIPE DOWN! AND EAT YOUR SOUP!
UGH.
I WONDER HOW OTHER PEOPLE WRITE SO EASILY.
SO MANY TREES!
AND LOOK AT THE SIZE OF THIS PLACE!
HELLO! MAIL CALL!

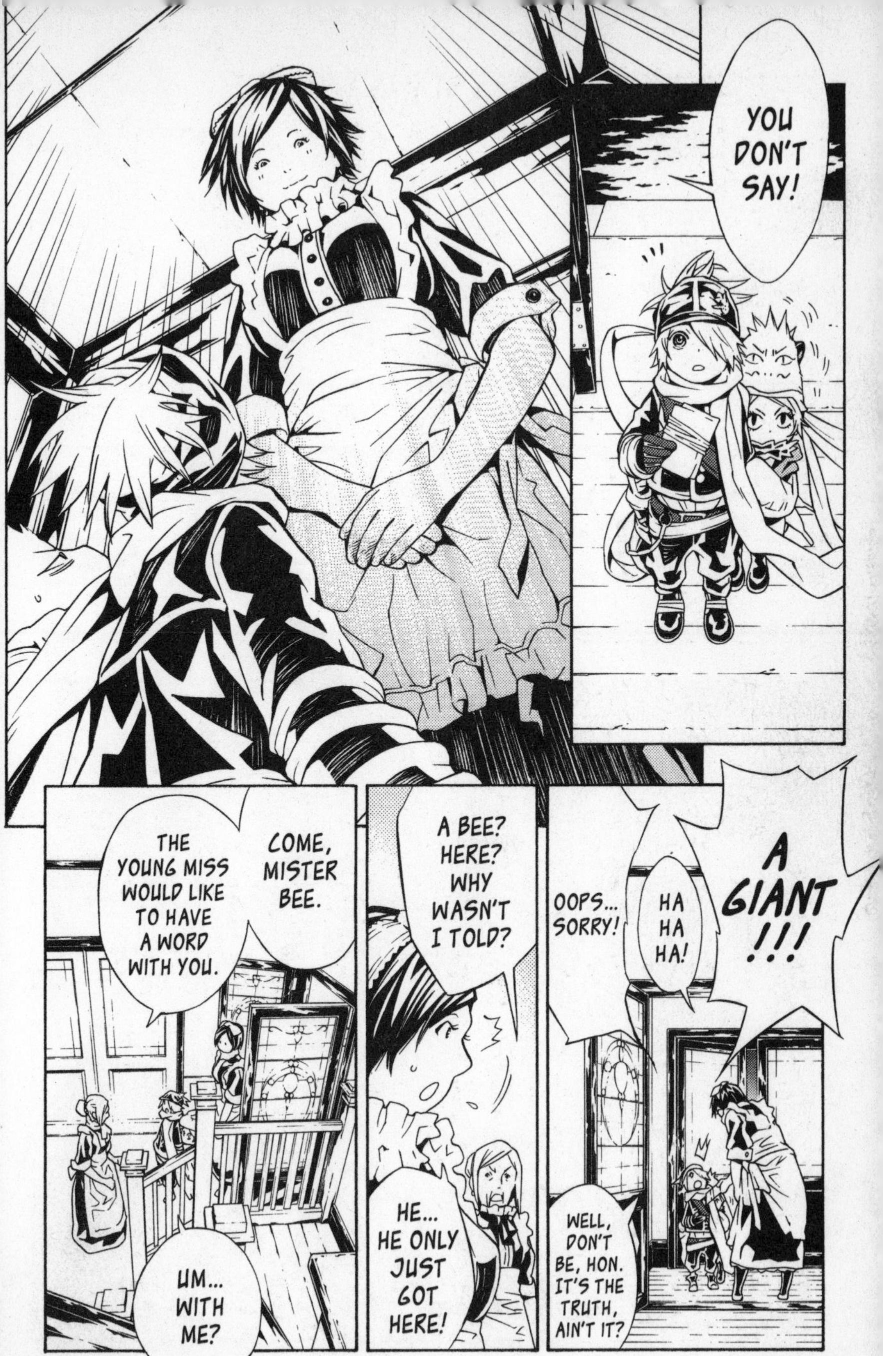
YOU DON'T SAY!
A GIANT!!!
HA HA HA!
OOPS... SORRY!
WELL, DON'T BE, HON. IT'S THE TRUTH, AIN'T IT?
A BEE? HERE? WHY WASN'T I TOLD?
HE... HE ONLY JUST GOT HERE!
COME, MISTER BEE.
THE YOUNG MISS WOULD LIKE TO HAVE A WORD WITH YOU.
UM... WITH ME?

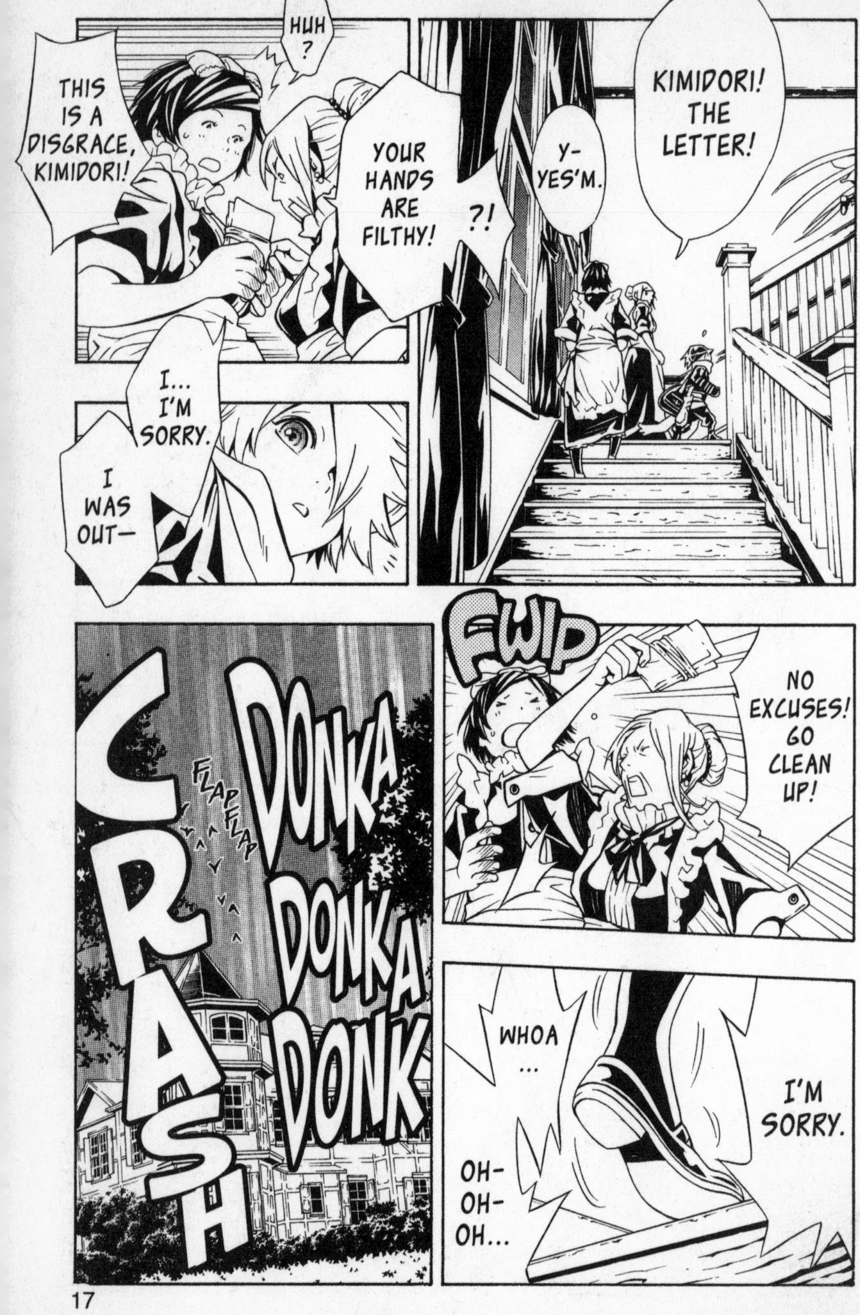
KIMIDORI! THE LETTER!
Y-YES'M.
HUH?
YOUR HANDS ARE FILTHY!
?!
THIS IS A DISGRACE, KIMIDORI!
I... I'M SORRY.
I WAS OUT—
FWIP
NO EXCUSES! GO CLEAN UP!
I'M SORRY.
WHOA...
OH-OH-OH...
DONKA DONKA DONK
FLAP FLAP
CRASH

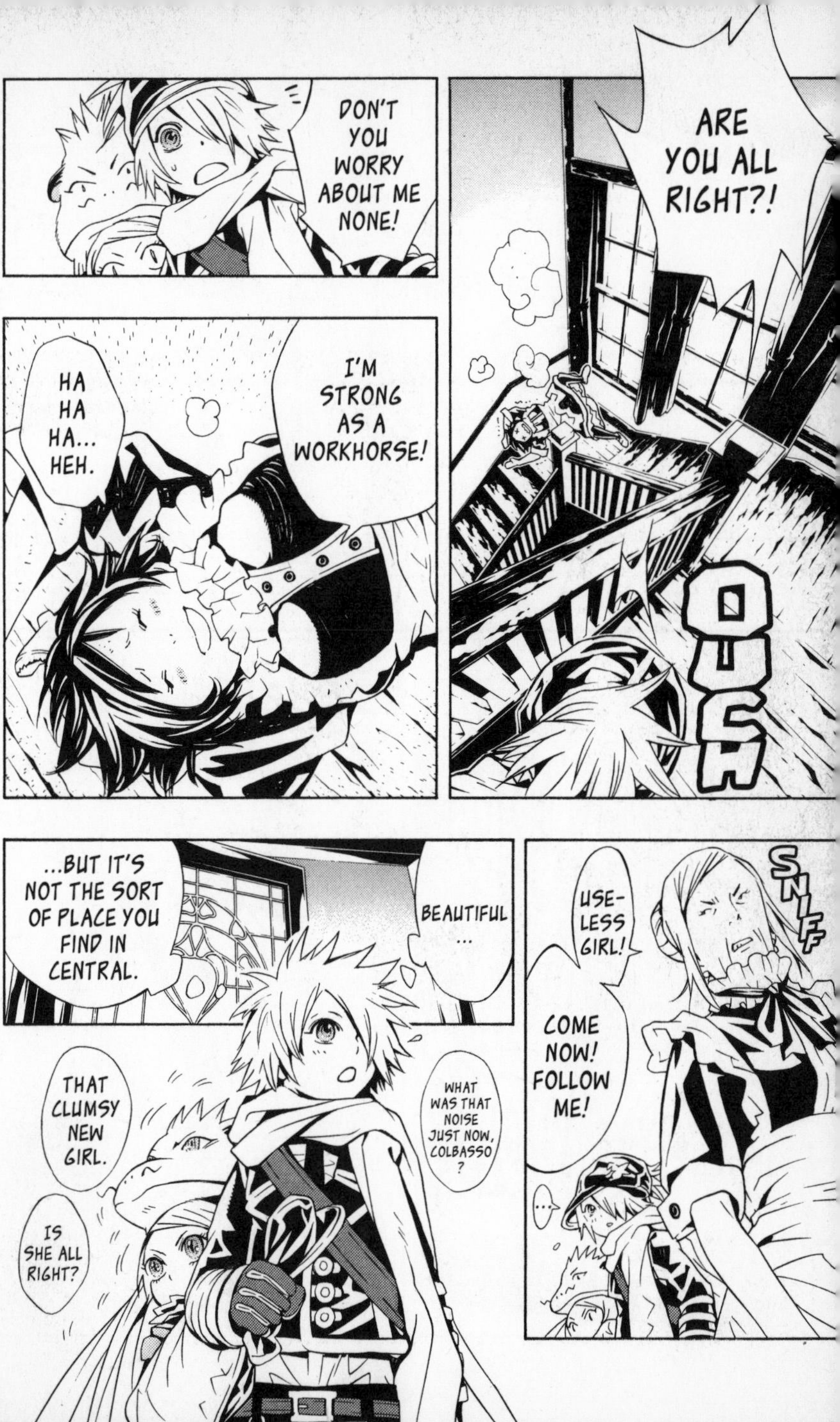
ARE YOU ALL RIGHT?!
OUCH
DON'T YOU WORRY ABOUT ME NONE!
I'M STRONG AS A WORKHORSE!
HA HA HA... HEH.
SNIFF
USE-LESS GIRL!
COME NOW! FOLLOW ME!
...
BEAUTIFUL...
...BUT IT'S NOT THE SORT OF PLACE YOU FIND IN CENTRAL.
WHAT WAS THAT NOISE JUST NOW, COLBASSO?
THAT CLUMSY NEW GIRL.
IS SHE ALL RIGHT?

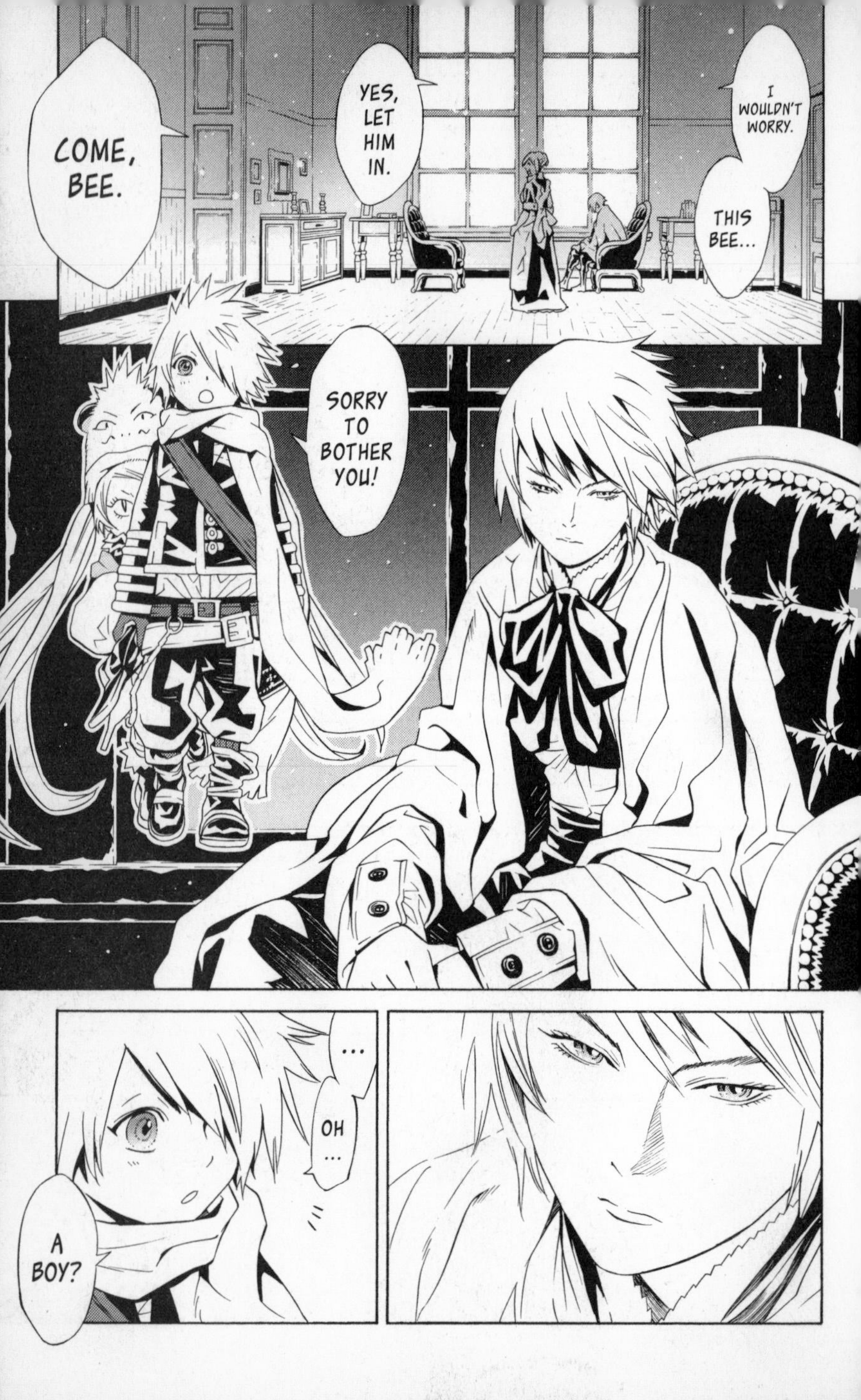
I WOULDN'T WORRY.
THIS BEE...
YES, LET HIM IN.
COME, BEE.
SORRY TO BOTHER YOU!
...
OH...
A BOY?

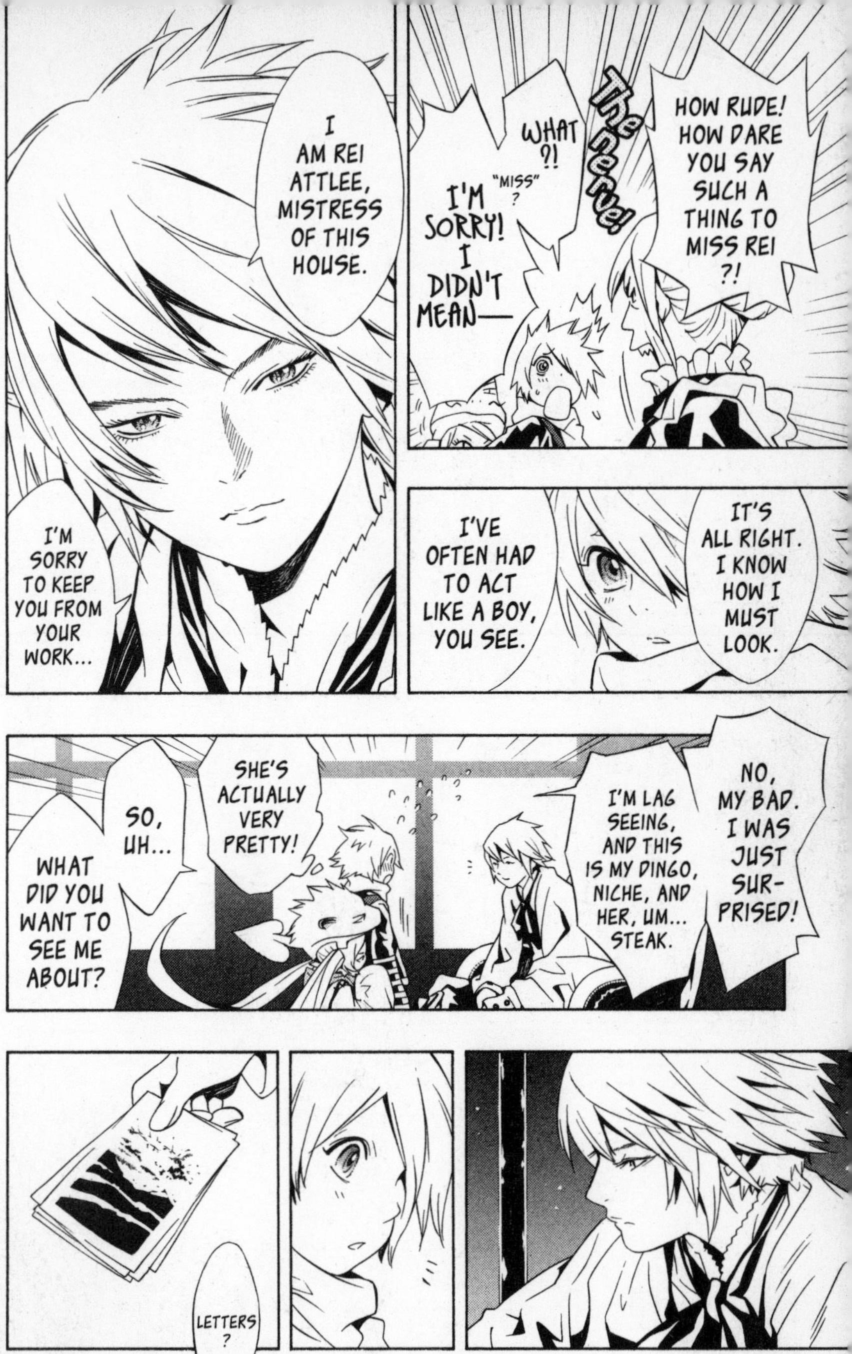
HOW RUDE! HOW DARE YOU SAY SUCH A THING TO MISS REI ?!
The nerve!
WHAT ?!
"MISS" ?
I'M SORRY! I DIDN'T MEAN—
IT'S ALL RIGHT. I KNOW HOW I MUST LOOK.
I'VE OFTEN HAD TO ACT LIKE A BOY, YOU SEE.
I AM REI ATTLEE, MISTRESS OF THIS HOUSE.
I'M SORRY TO KEEP YOU FROM YOUR WORK...
NO, MY BAD. I WAS JUST SUR-PRISED!
I'M LAG SEEING, AND THIS IS MY DINGO, NICHE, AND HER, UM... STEAK.
SHE'S ACTUALLY VERY PRETTY!
SO, UH...
WHAT DID YOU WANT TO SEE ME ABOUT?
LETTERS ?

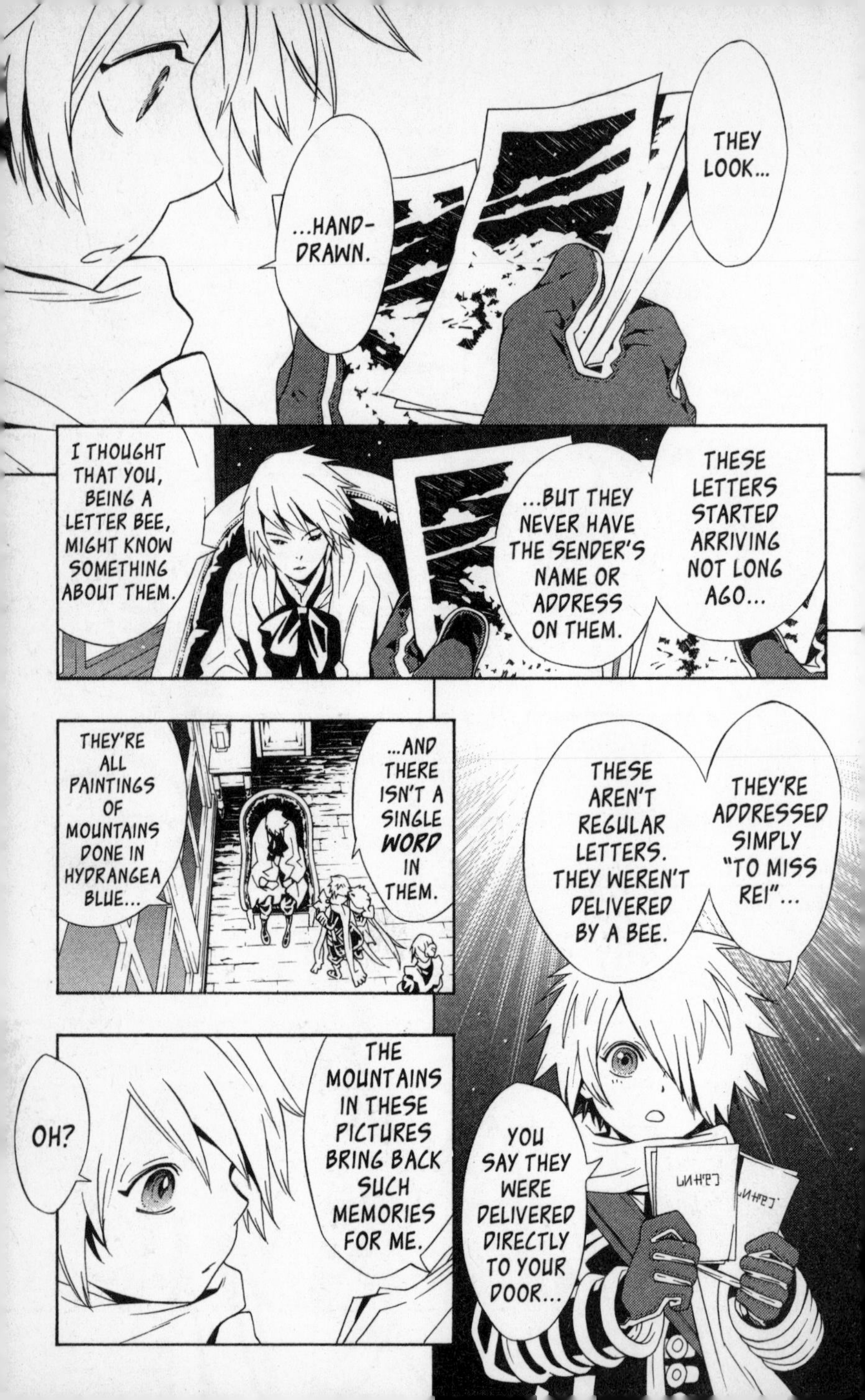
THEY LOOK...
...HAND-DRAWN.
THESE LETTERS STARTED ARRIVING NOT LONG AGO...
...BUT THEY NEVER HAVE THE SENDER'S NAME OR ADDRESS ON THEM.
I THOUGHT THAT YOU, BEING A LETTER BEE, MIGHT KNOW SOMETHING ABOUT THEM.
THEY'RE ADDRESSED SIMPLY "TO MISS REI"...
THESE AREN'T REGULAR LETTERS. THEY WEREN'T DELIVERED BY A BEE.
YOU SAY THEY WERE DELIVERED DIRECTLY TO YOUR DOOR...
...AND THERE ISN'T A SINGLE WORD IN THEM.
THEY'RE ALL PAINTINGS OF MOUNTAINS DONE IN HYDRANGEA BLUE...
THE MOUNTAINS IN THESE PICTURES BRING BACK SUCH MEMORIES FOR ME.
OH?

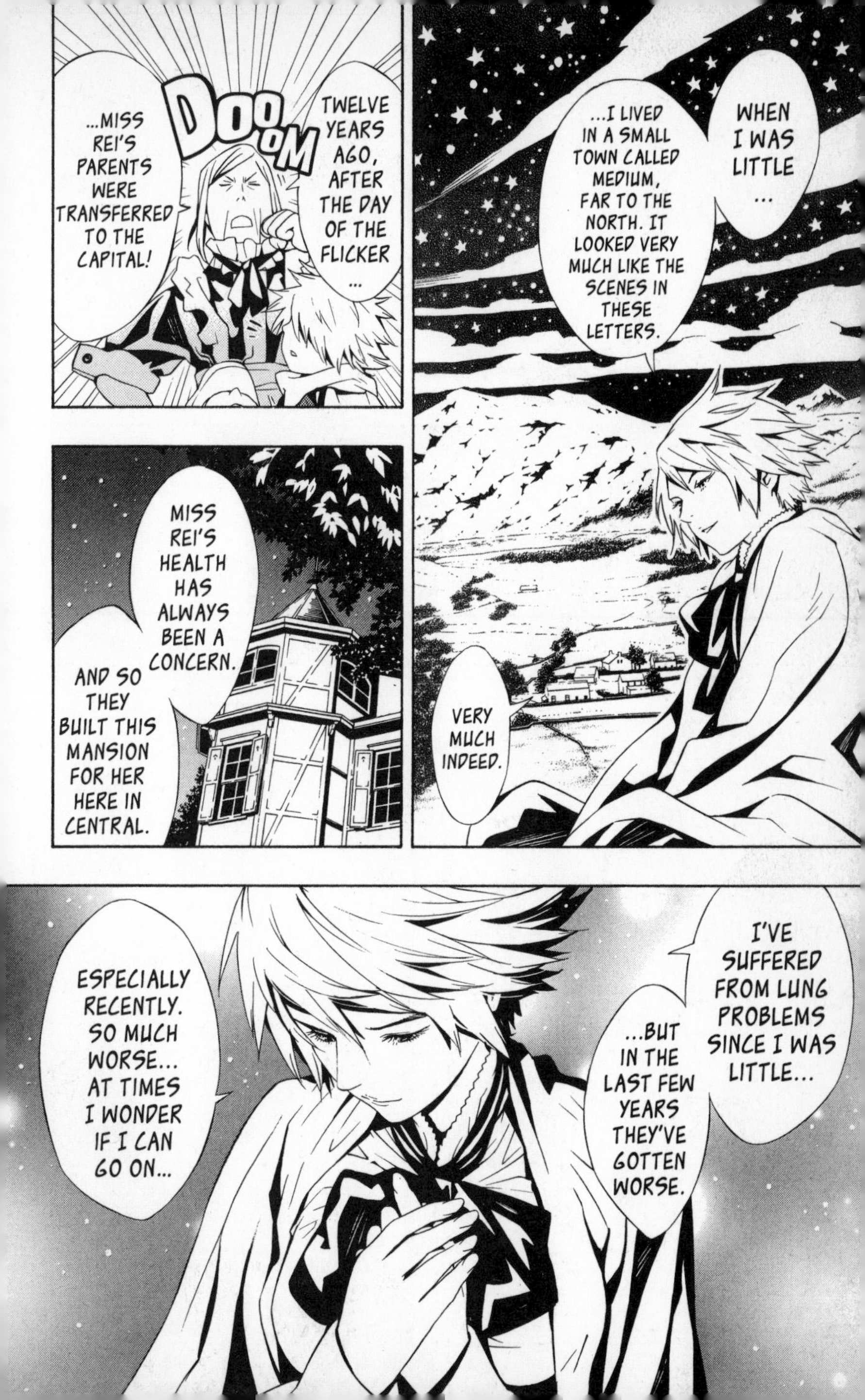
WHEN I WAS LITTLE ...
...I LIVED IN A SMALL TOWN CALLED MEDIUM, FAR TO THE NORTH. IT LOOKED VERY MUCH LIKE THE SCENES IN THESE LETTERS.
VERY MUCH INDEED.
TWELVE YEARS AGO, AFTER THE DAY OF THE FLICKER ...
DOOOM
...MISS REI'S PARENTS WERE TRANSFERRED TO THE CAPITAL!
MISS REI'S HEALTH HAS ALWAYS BEEN A CONCERN.
AND SO THEY BUILT THIS MANSION FOR HER HERE IN CENTRAL.
I'VE SUFFERED FROM LUNG PROBLEMS SINCE I WAS LITTLE...
...BUT IN THE LAST FEW YEARS THEY'VE GOTTEN WORSE.
ESPECIALLY RECENTLY. SO MUCH WORSE... AT TIMES I WONDER IF I CAN GO ON...

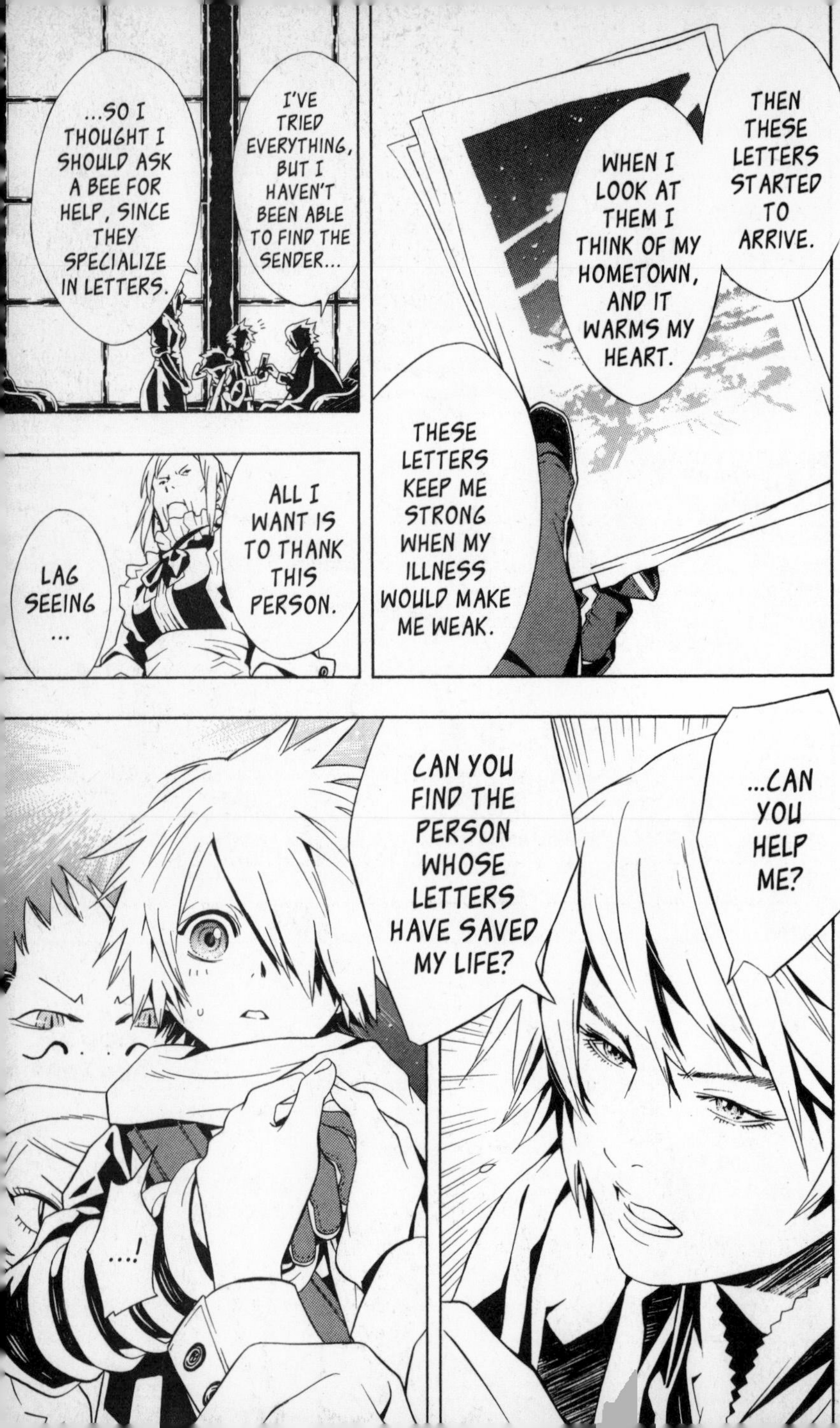
THEN THESE LETTERS STARTED TO ARRIVE.
WHEN I LOOK AT THEM I THINK OF MY HOMETOWN, AND IT WARMS MY HEART.
THESE LETTERS KEEP ME STRONG WHEN MY ILLNESS WOULD MAKE ME WEAK.
I'VE TRIED EVERYTHING, BUT I HAVEN'T BEEN ABLE TO FIND THE SENDER...
...SO I THOUGHT I SHOULD ASK A BEE FOR HELP, SINCE THEY SPECIALIZE IN LETTERS.
ALL I WANT IS TO THANK THIS PERSON.
LAG SEEING ...
...CAN YOU HELP ME?
CAN YOU FIND THE PERSON WHOSE LETTERS HAVE SAVED MY LIFE?
...!

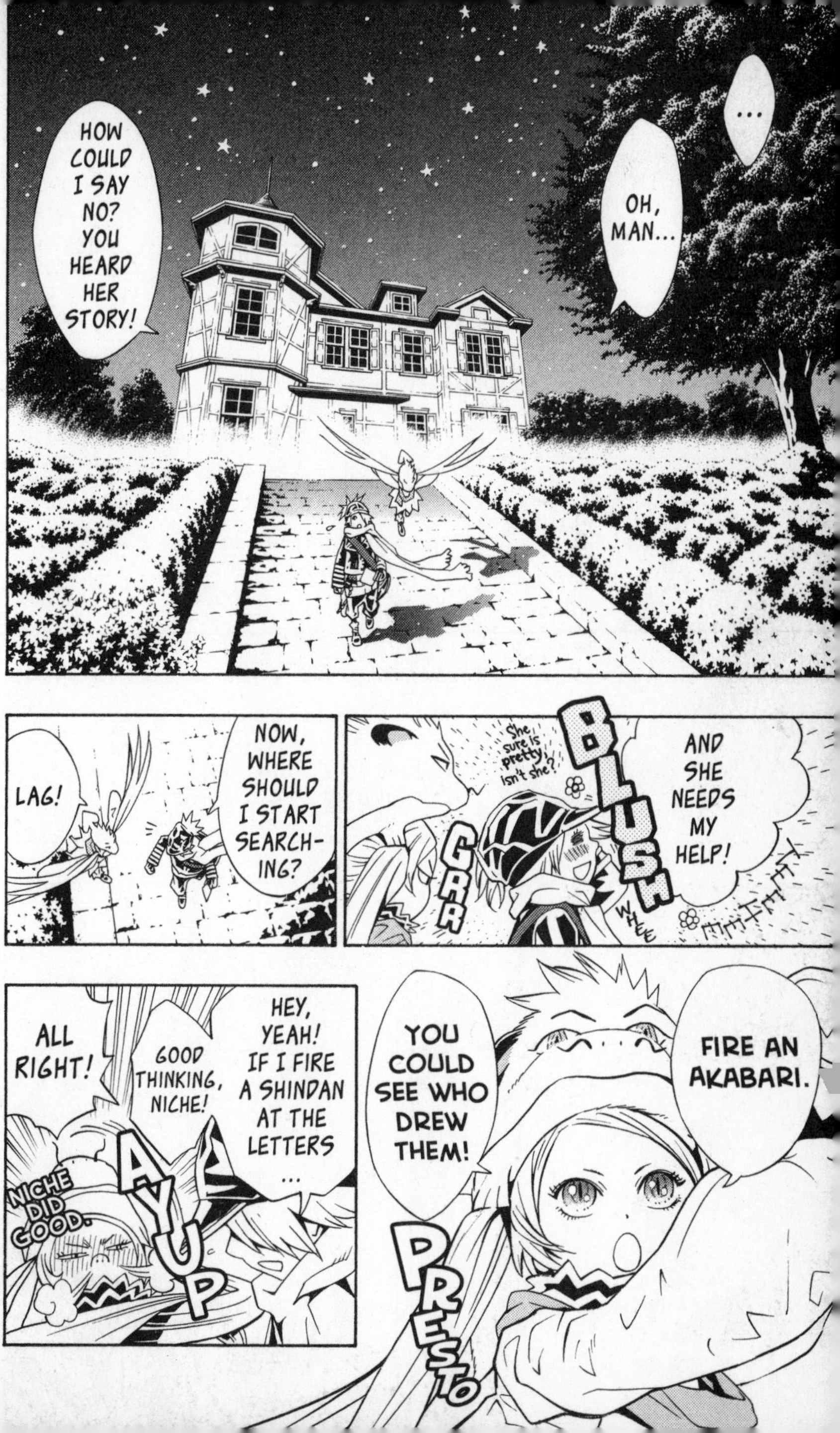
...
OH, MAN...
HOW COULD I SAY NO? YOU HEARD HER STORY!
AND SHE NEEDS MY HELP!
TEEHEE
BLUSH
She sure is pretty, isn't she?
GRR
WHEE
NOW, WHERE SHOULD I START SEARCHING?
LAG!
FIRE AN AKABARI.
YOU COULD SEE WHO DREW THEM!
PRESTO
HEY, YEAH! IF I FIRE A SHINDAN AT THE LETTERS ...
GOOD THINKING, NICHE!
ALL RIGHT!
AYUP
NICHE DID GOOD.

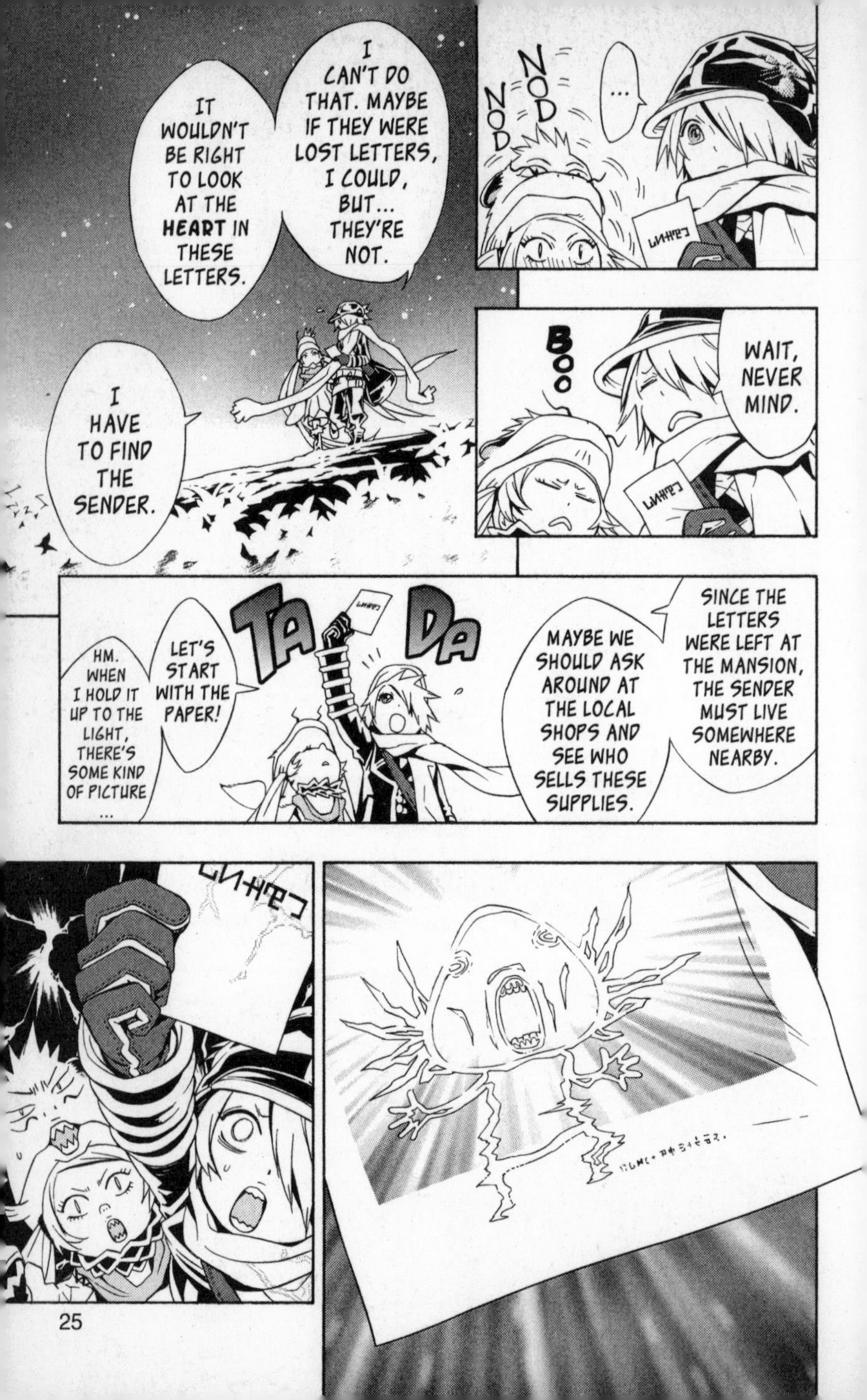
...
NOD NOD
WAIT, NEVER MIND.
BOO
I CAN'T DO THAT. MAYBE IF THEY WERE LOST LETTERS, I COULD, BUT... THEY'RE NOT.
IT WOULDN'T BE RIGHT TO LOOK AT THE **HEART** IN THESE LETTERS.
I HAVE TO FIND THE SENDER.
SINCE THE LETTERS WERE LEFT AT THE MANSION, THE SENDER MUST LIVE SOMEWHERE NEARBY.
MAYBE WE SHOULD ASK AROUND AT THE LOCAL SHOPS AND SEE WHO SELLS THESE SUPPLIES.
TA DA
LET'S START WITH THE PAPER!
HM. WHEN I HOLD IT UP TO THE LIGHT, THERE'S SOME KIND OF PICTURE ...

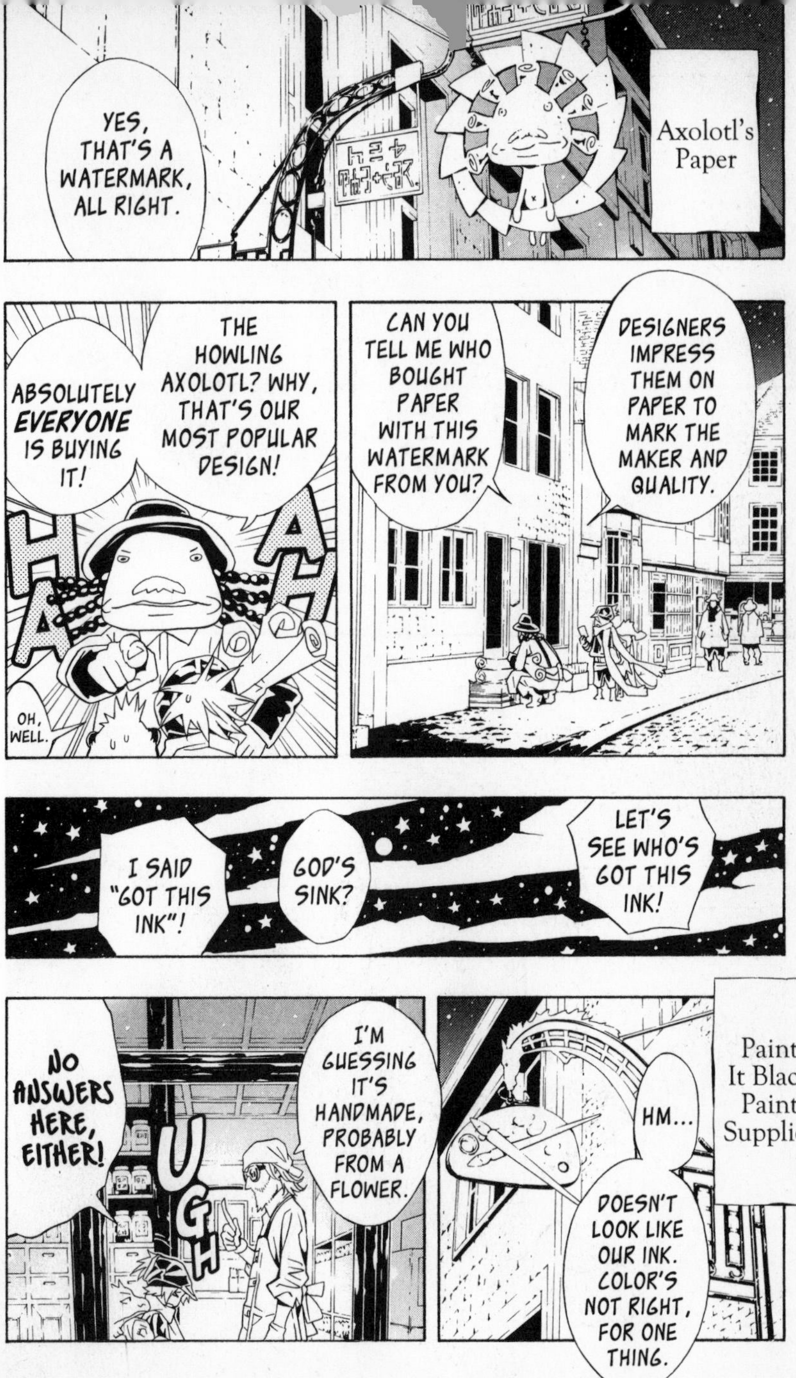
Axolotl's Paper
YES, THAT'S A WATERMARK, ALL RIGHT.
DESIGNERS IMPRESS THEM ON PAPER TO MARK THE MAKER AND QUALITY.
CAN YOU TELL ME WHO BOUGHT PAPER WITH THIS WATERMARK FROM YOU?
THE HOWLING AXOLOTL? WHY, THAT'S OUR MOST POPULAR DESIGN!
AH
ABSOLUTELY EVERYONE IS BUYING IT!
HA
OH, WELL.
LET'S SEE WHO'S GOT THIS INK!
GOD'S SINK?
I SAID "GOT THIS INK"!
Paint It Black Paint Supplies
HM...
DOESN'T LOOK LIKE OUR INK. COLOR'S NOT RIGHT, FOR ONE THING.
I'M GUESSING IT'S HANDMADE, PROBABLY FROM A FLOWER.
UGH
NO ANSWERS HERE, EITHER!

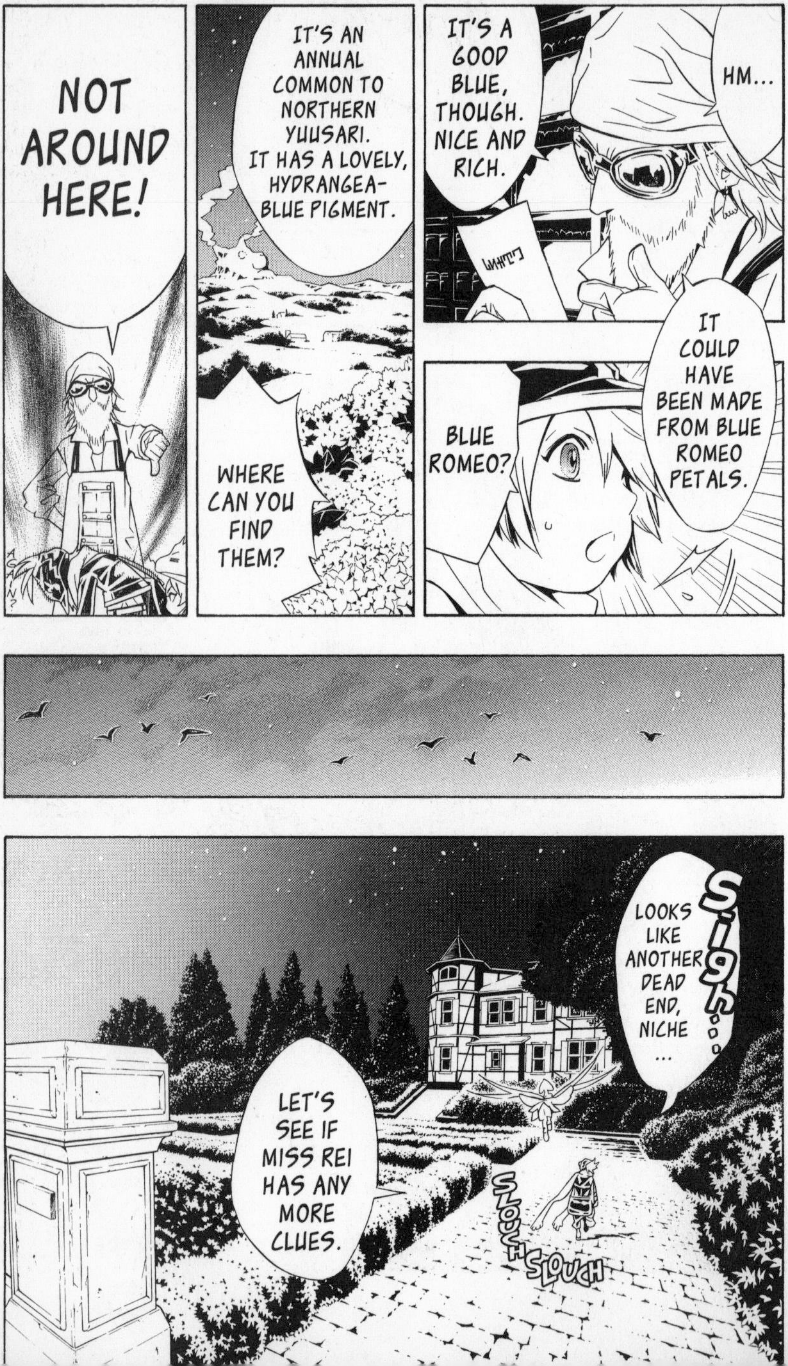
HM...
IT'S A GOOD BLUE, THOUGH. NICE AND RICH.
IT COULD HAVE BEEN MADE FROM BLUE ROMEO PETALS.
BLUE ROMEO?
IT'S AN ANNUAL COMMON TO NORTHERN YUUSARI. IT HAS A LOVELY, HYDRANGEA-BLUE PIGMENT.
WHERE CAN YOU FIND THEM?
NOT AROUND HERE!
AGAIN?
SIGH...
LOOKS LIKE ANOTHER DEAD END, NICHE...
LET'S SEE IF MISS REI HAS ANY MORE CLUES.
SLOUCH SLOUCH

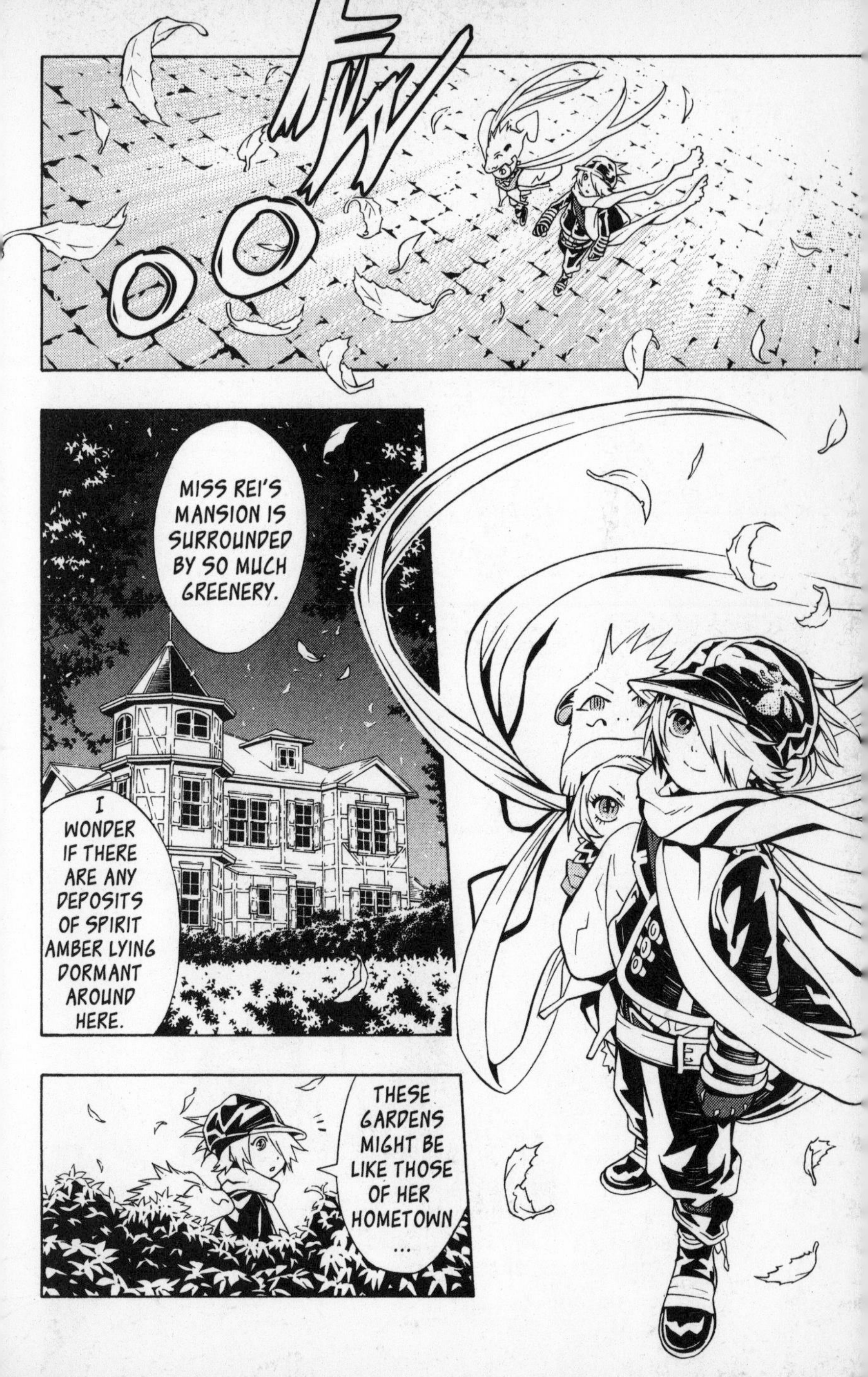
MISS REI'S MANSION IS SURROUNDED BY SO MUCH GREENERY.
I WONDER IF THERE ARE ANY DEPOSITS OF SPIRIT AMBER LYING DORMANT AROUND HERE.
THESE GARDENS MIGHT BE LIKE THOSE OF HER HOMETOWN ...

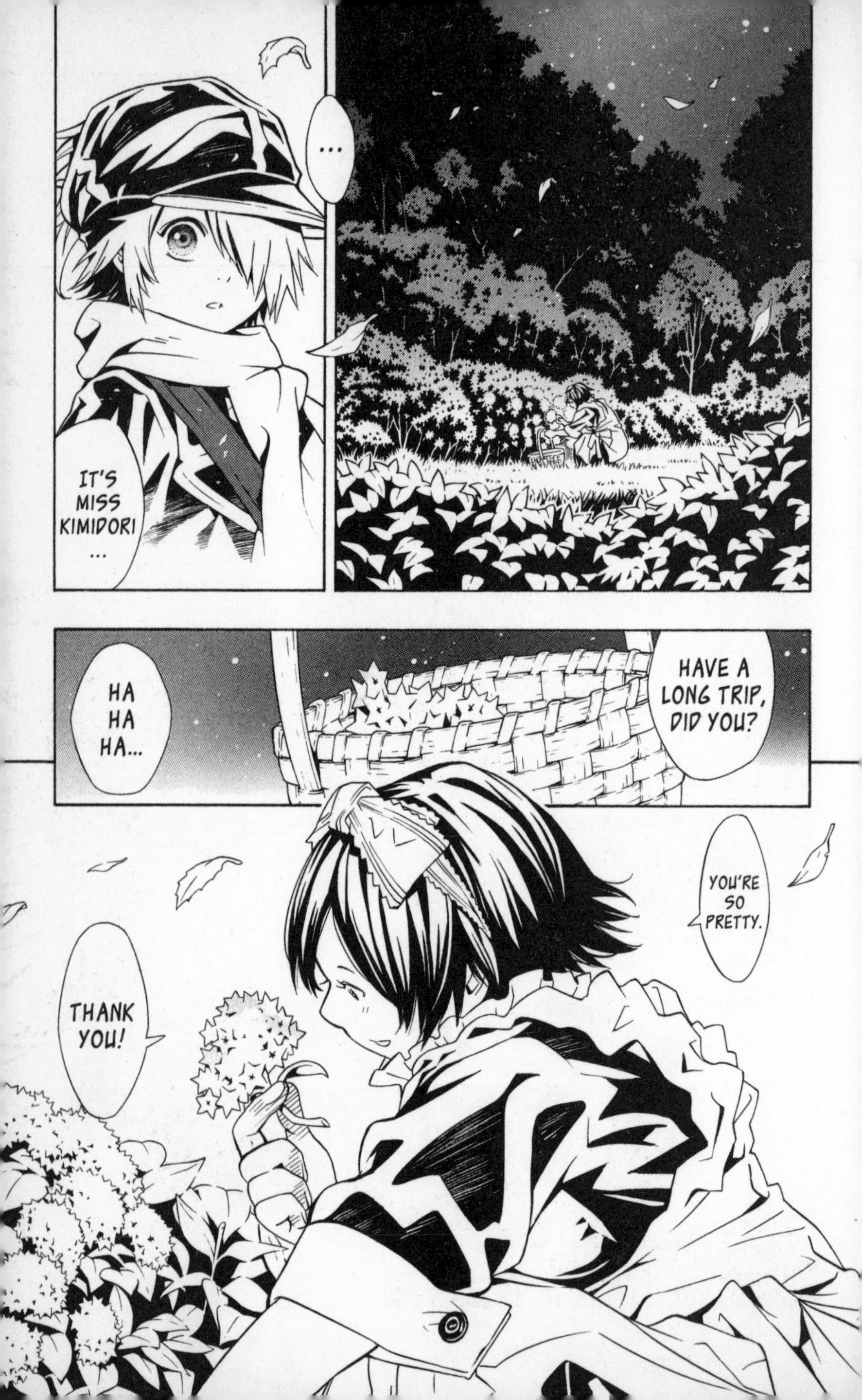
...
IT'S MISS KIMIDORI ...
HAVE A LONG TRIP, DID YOU?
HA HA HA...
YOU'RE SO PRETTY.
THANK YOU!

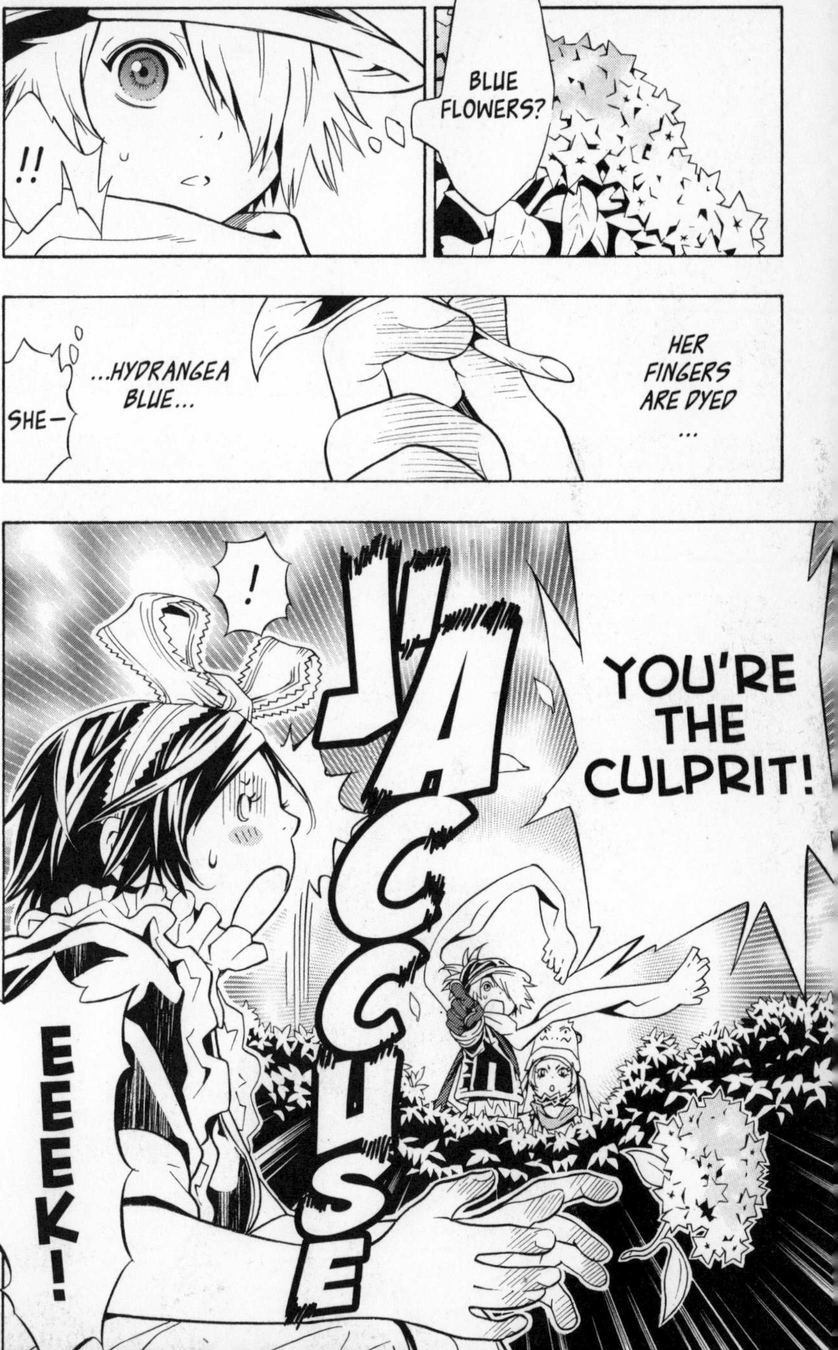
BLUE FLOWERS?
!!
HER FINGERS ARE DYED ...
...HYDRANGEA BLUE...
SHE—
YOU'RE THE CULPRIT!
J'ACCUSE
!
EEEK!

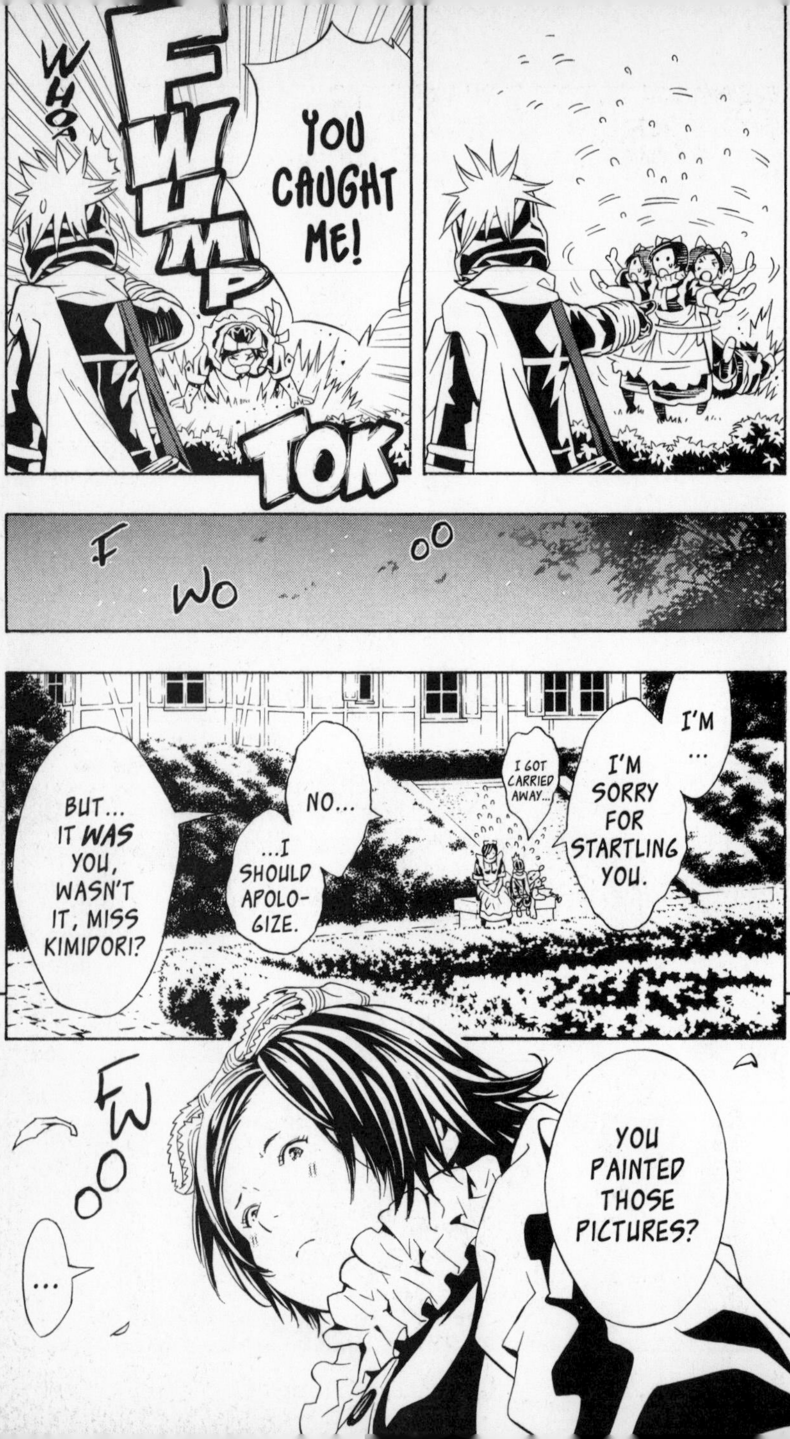
YOU CAUGHT ME!
FWUMP
WHOA
TOK
FWOO
I'M ...
I'M SORRY FOR STARTLING YOU.
I GOT CARRIED AWAY...
NO...
...I SHOULD APOLOGIZE.
BUT... IT WAS YOU, WASN'T IT, MISS KIMIDORI?
YOU PAINTED THOSE PICTURES?
FWOO
...

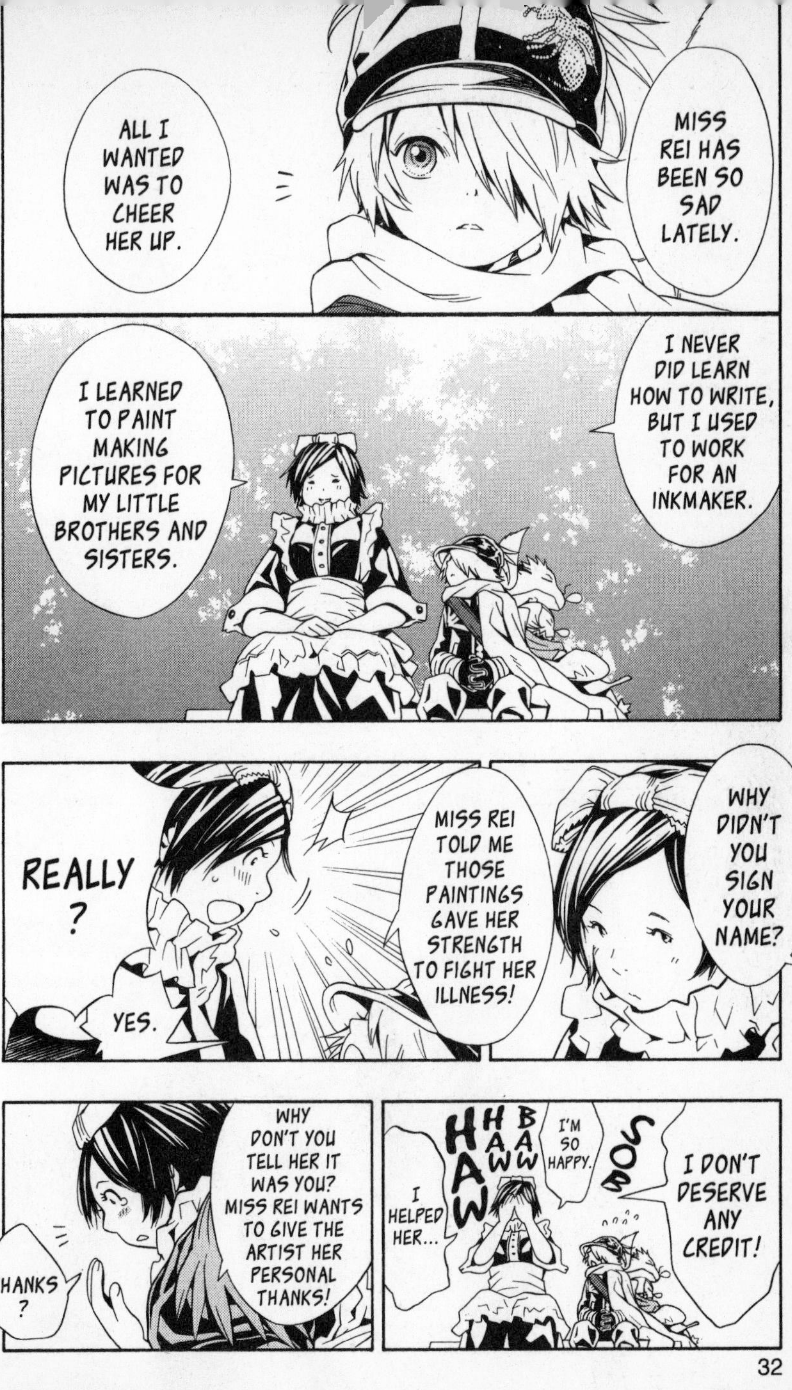
MISS REI HAS BEEN SO SAD LATELY.
ALL I WANTED WAS TO CHEER HER UP.
I NEVER DID LEARN HOW TO WRITE, BUT I USED TO WORK FOR AN INKMAKER.
I LEARNED TO PAINT MAKING PICTURES FOR MY LITTLE BROTHERS AND SISTERS.
WHY DIDN'T YOU SIGN YOUR NAME?
MISS REI TOLD ME THOSE PAINTINGS GAVE HER STRENGTH TO FIGHT HER ILLNESS!
REALLY?
YES.
I DON'T DESERVE ANY CREDIT!
SOB
I'M SO HAPPY.
BAW
HAW
HAW
I HELPED HER...
WHY DON'T YOU TELL HER IT WAS YOU? MISS REI WANTS TO GIVE THE ARTIST HER PERSONAL THANKS!
THANKS?

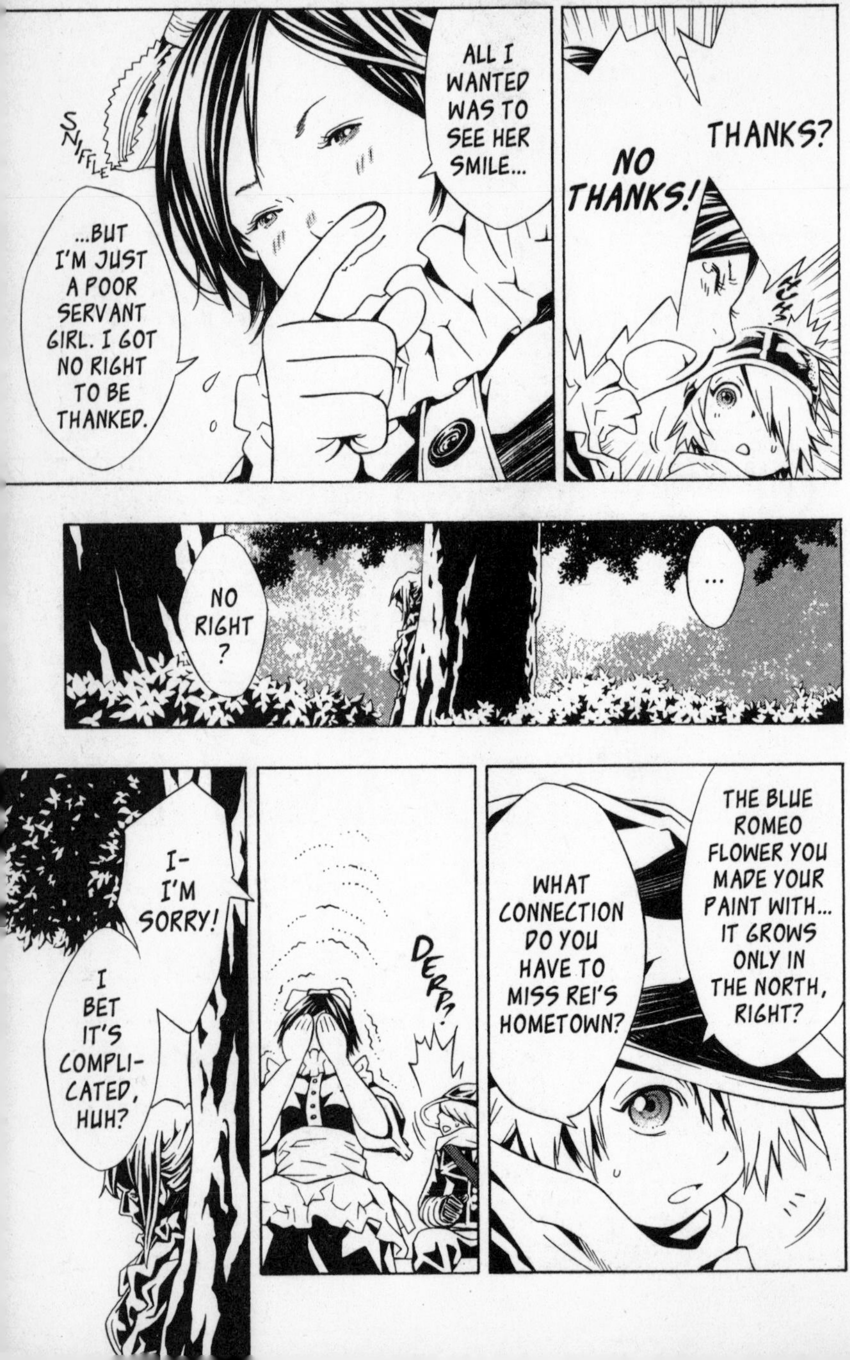
THANKS?
NO THANKS!
HUH?
ALL I WANTED WAS TO SEE HER SMILE...
SNIFFLE
...BUT I'M JUST A POOR SERVANT GIRL. I GOT NO RIGHT TO BE THANKED.
...
NO RIGHT ?
THE BLUE ROMEO FLOWER YOU MADE YOUR PAINT WITH... IT GROWS ONLY IN THE NORTH, RIGHT?
WHAT CONNECTION DO YOU HAVE TO MISS REI'S HOMETOWN?
DERP?!
I- I'M SORRY!
I BET IT'S COMPLICATED, HUH?

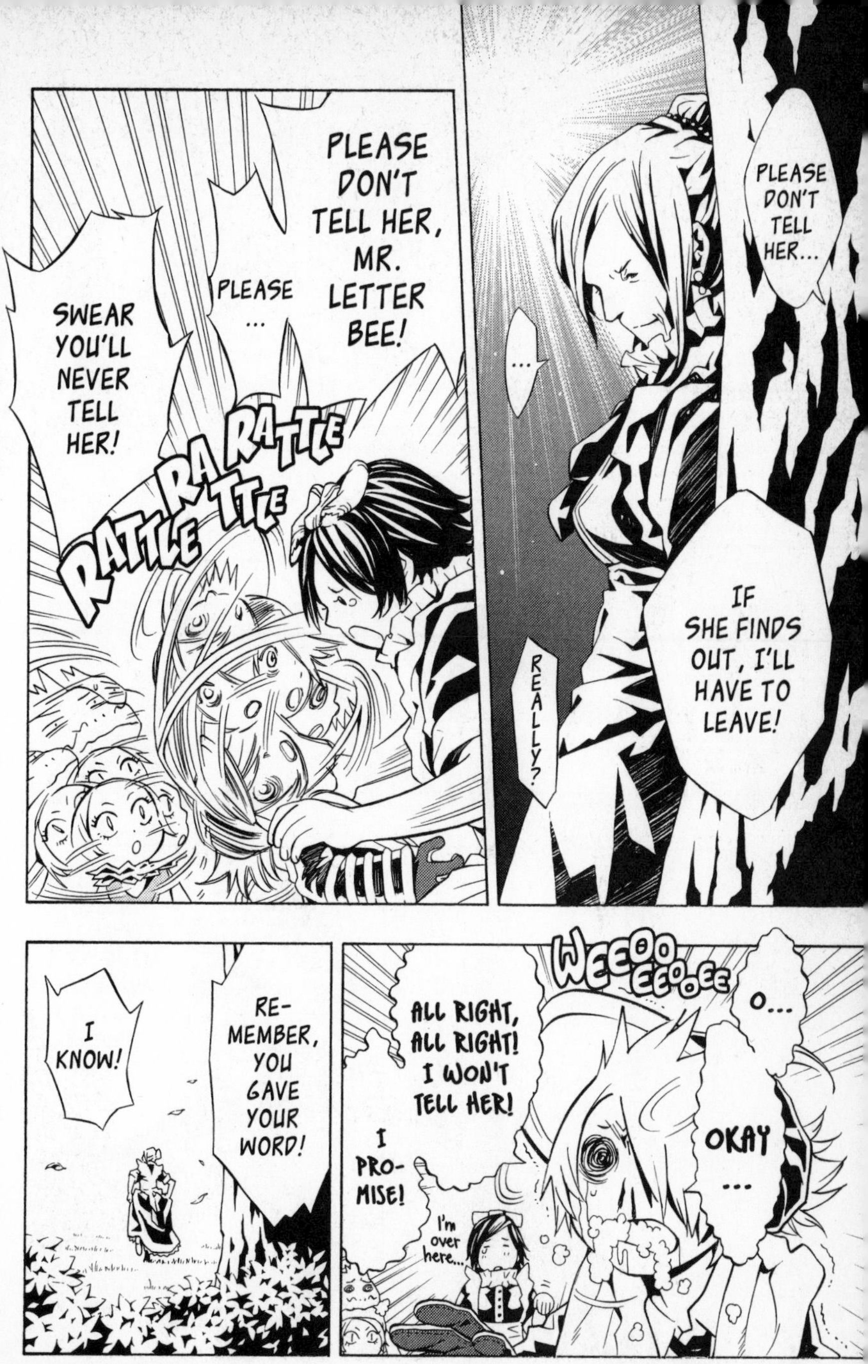
PLEASE DON'T TELL HER...
...
IF SHE FINDS OUT, I'LL HAVE TO LEAVE!
REALLY?
PLEASE DON'T TELL HER, MR. LETTER BEE!
PLEASE ...
SWEAR YOU'LL NEVER TELL HER!
RATTLE RATTLE RATTLE
O...
WEEOO EEOOEE
OKAY ...
ALL RIGHT, ALL RIGHT! I WON'T TELL HER!
I PROMISE!
I'm over here...
RE-MEMBER, YOU GAVE YOUR WORD!
I KNOW!

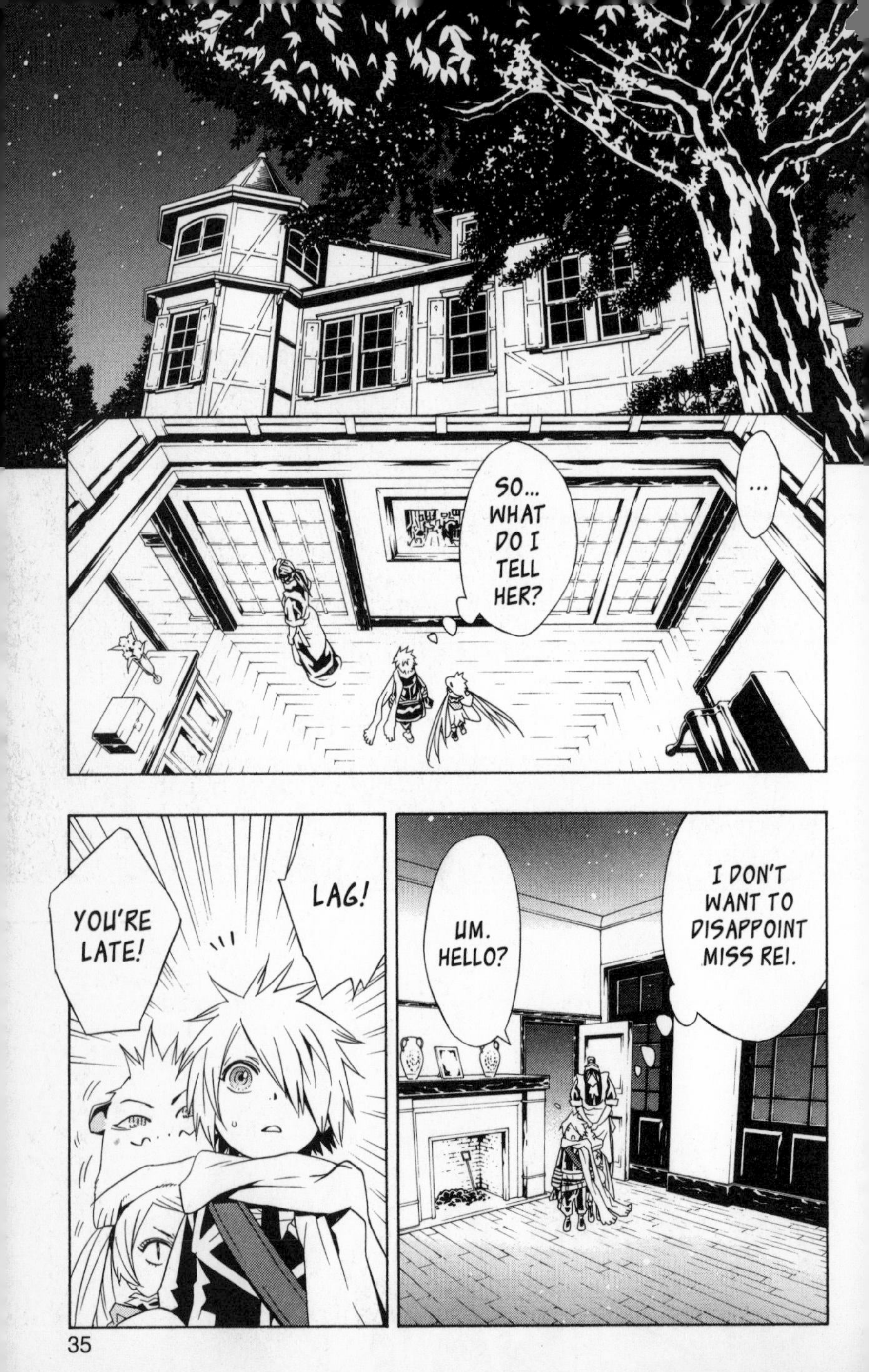
...
SO... WHAT DO I TELL HER?
I DON'T WANT TO DISAPPOINT MISS REI.
UM. HELLO?
LAG!
YOU'RE LATE!

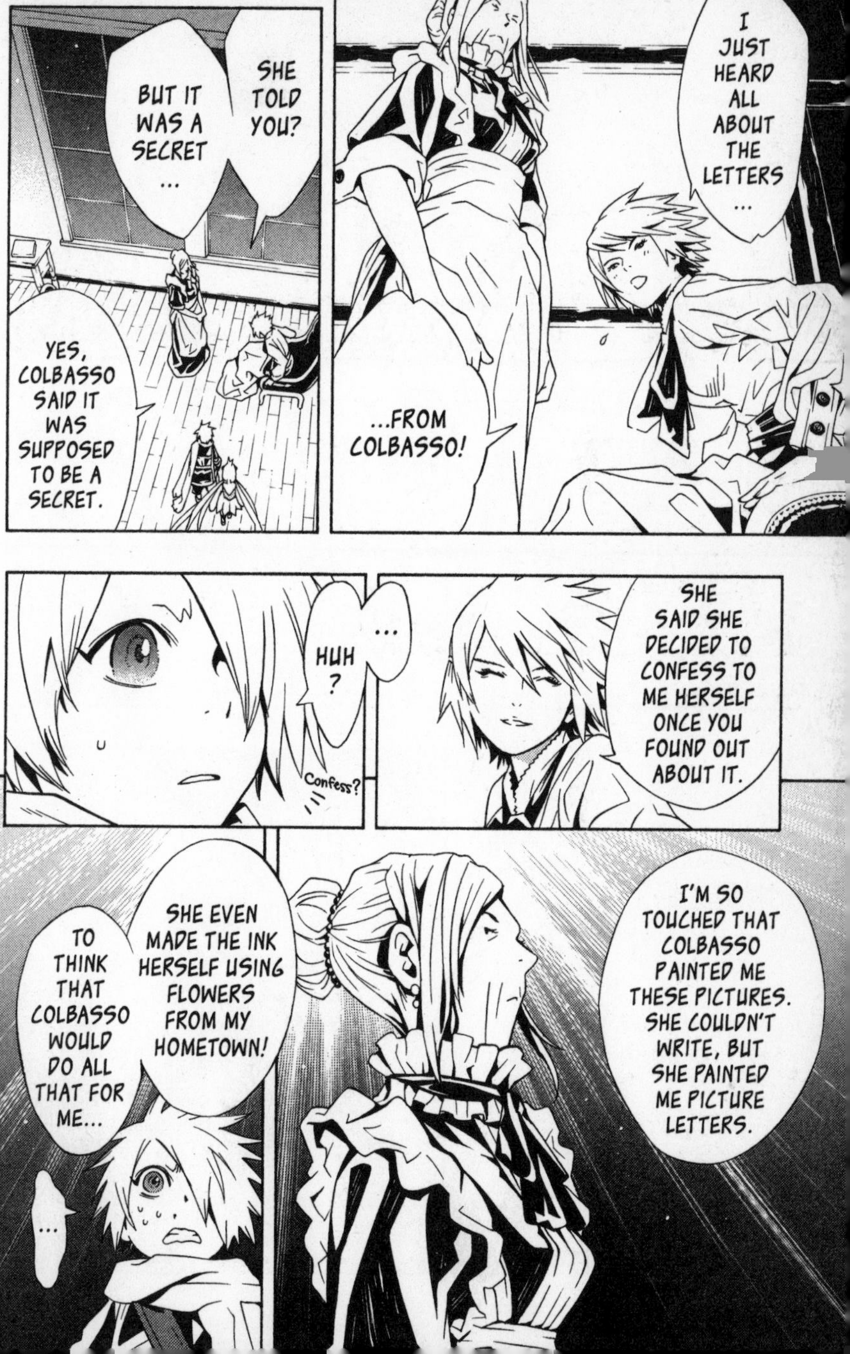
I JUST HEARD ALL ABOUT THE LETTERS ...
...FROM COLBASSO!
SHE TOLD YOU?
BUT IT WAS A SECRET ...
YES, COLBASSO SAID IT WAS SUPPOSED TO BE A SECRET.
SHE SAID SHE DECIDED TO CONFESS TO ME HERSELF ONCE YOU FOUND OUT ABOUT IT.
...
HUH ?
Confess?
I'M SO TOUCHED THAT COLBASSO PAINTED ME THESE PICTURES. SHE COULDN'T WRITE, BUT SHE PAINTED ME PICTURE LETTERS.
SHE EVEN MADE THE INK HERSELF USING FLOWERS FROM MY HOMETOWN!
TO THINK THAT COLBASSO WOULD DO ALL THAT FOR ME...
...

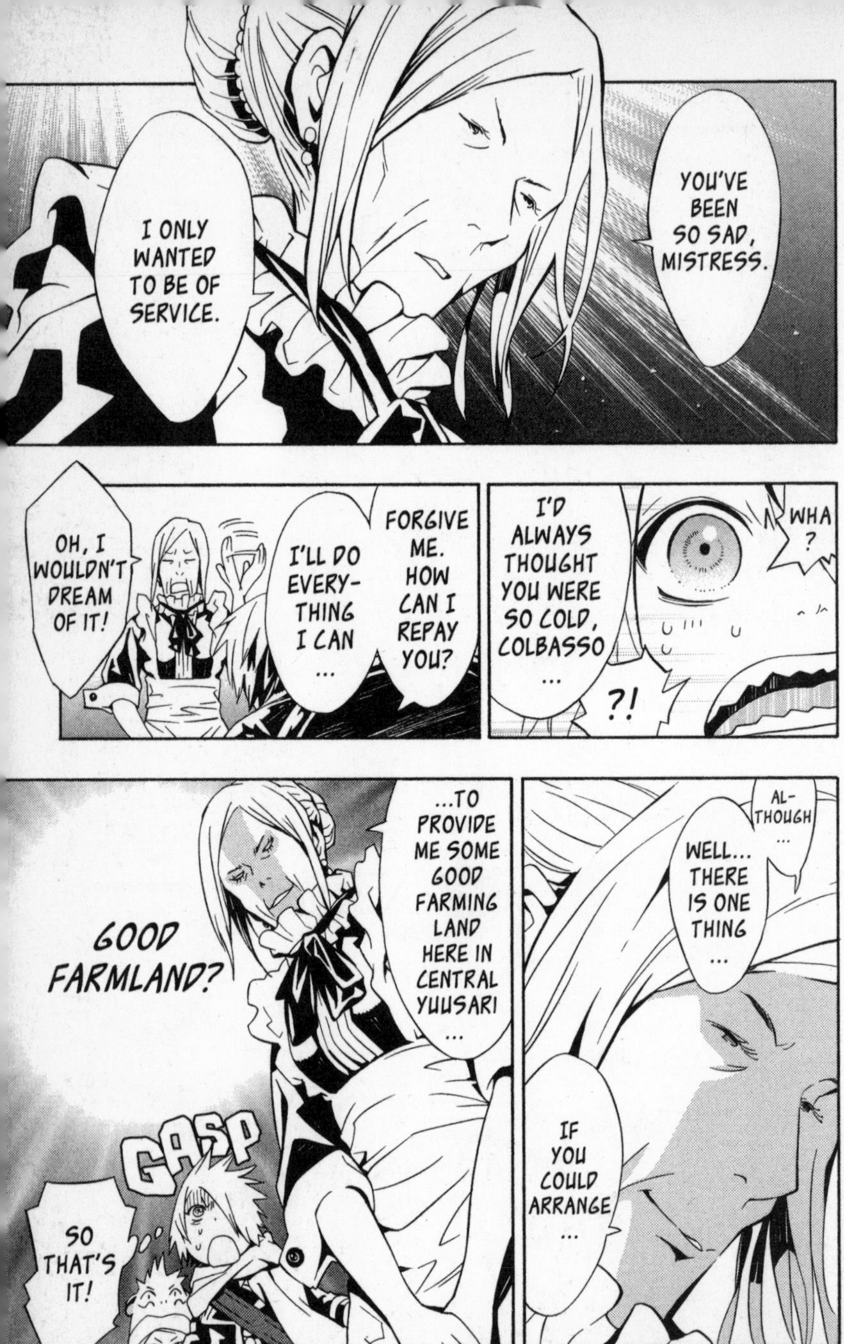
YOU'VE BEEN SO SAD, MISTRESS.
I ONLY WANTED TO BE OF SERVICE.
WHA?
I'D ALWAYS THOUGHT YOU WERE SO COLD, COLBASSO...
?!
FORGIVE ME. HOW CAN I REPAY YOU?
I'LL DO EVERY-THING I CAN...
OH, I WOULDN'T DREAM OF IT!
AL-THOUGH...
WELL... THERE IS ONE THING...
IF YOU COULD ARRANGE...
...TO PROVIDE ME SOME GOOD FARMING LAND HERE IN CENTRAL YUUSARI...
GOOD FARMLAND?
GASP
SO THAT'S IT!

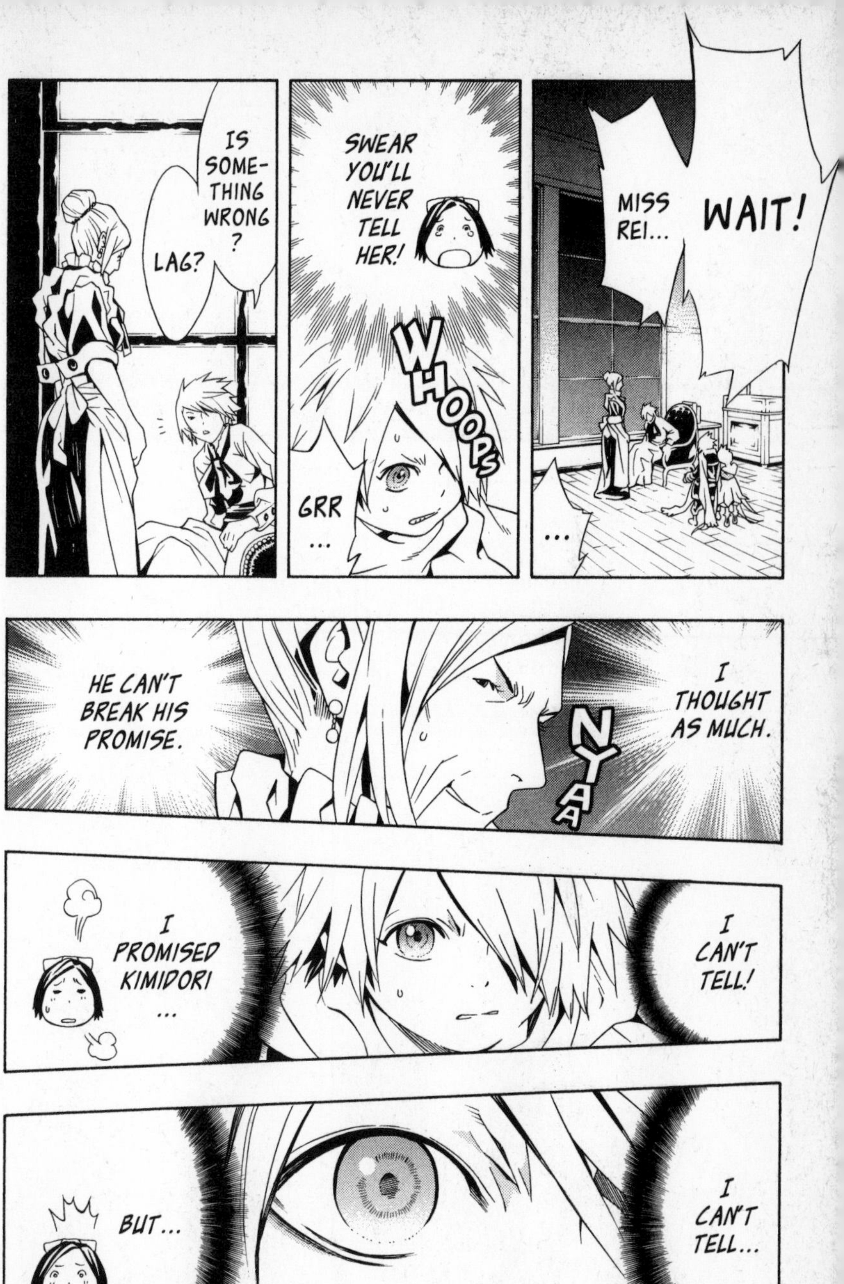
WAIT!
MISS REI...
...
SWEAR YOU'LL NEVER TELL HER!
WHOOPS
GRR...
IS SOMETHING WRONG?
LAG?
I THOUGHT AS MUCH.
NYAA
HE CAN'T BREAK HIS PROMISE.
I CAN'T TELL!
I PROMISED KIMIDORI...
I CAN'T TELL...
BUT...

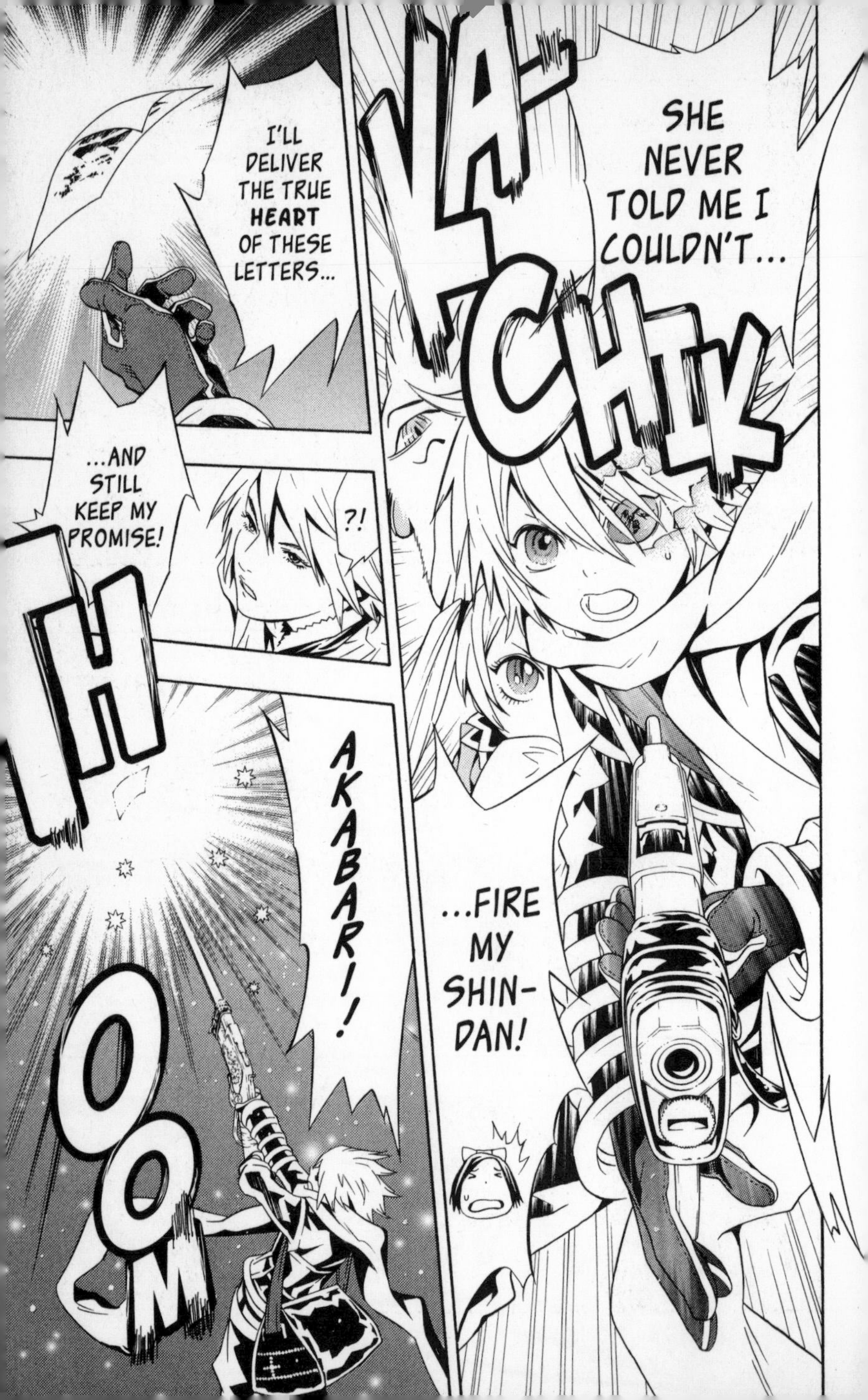
VA-CHIK
SHE NEVER TOLD ME I COULDN'T...
...FIRE MY SHIN-DAN!
I'LL DELIVER THE TRUE HEART OF THESE LETTERS...
...AND STILL KEEP MY PROMISE!
?!
AKABARI!!
HOOM

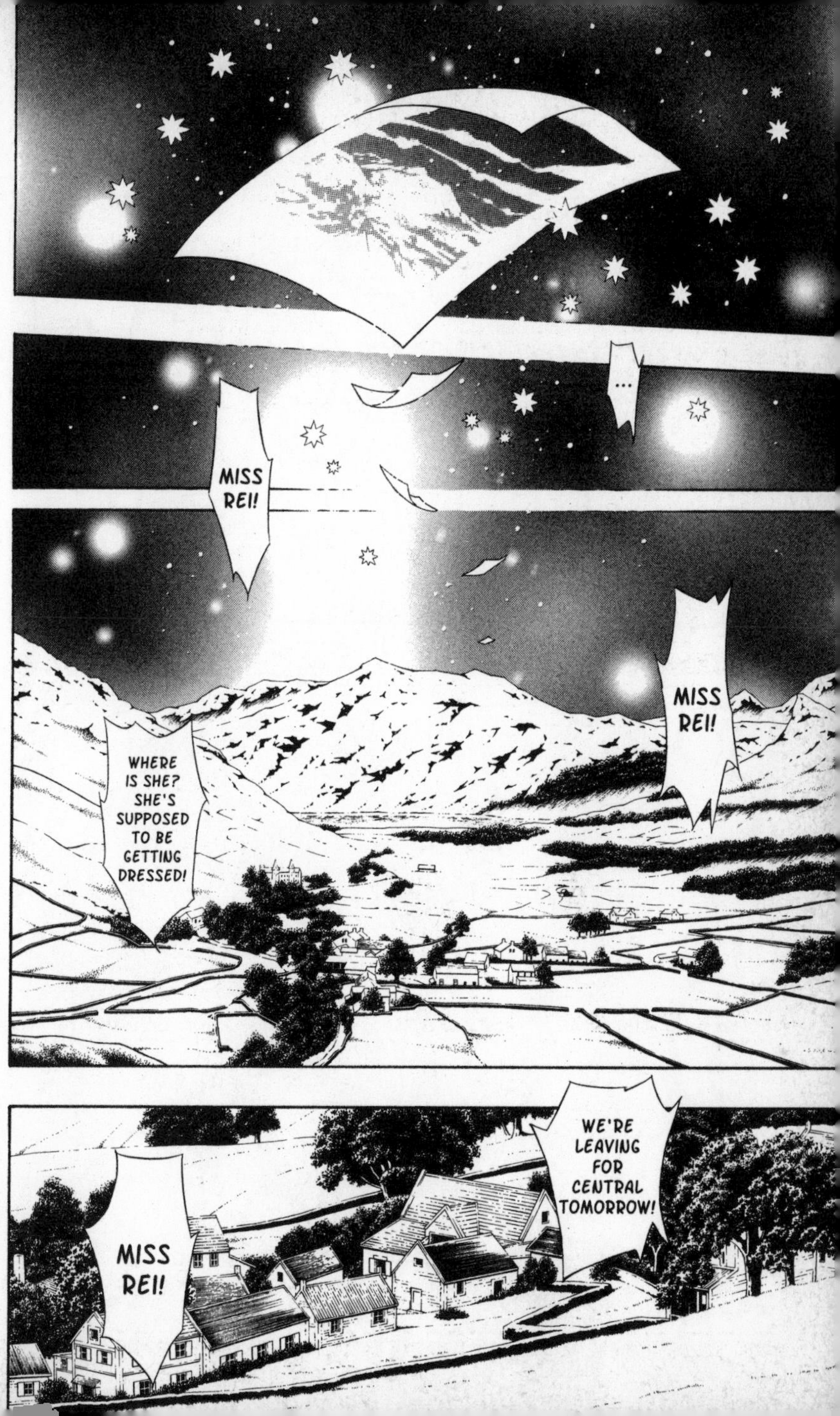
...
MISS REI!
MISS REI!
WHERE IS SHE? SHE'S SUPPOSED TO BE GETTING DRESSED!
WE'RE LEAVING FOR CENTRAL TOMORROW!
MISS REI!

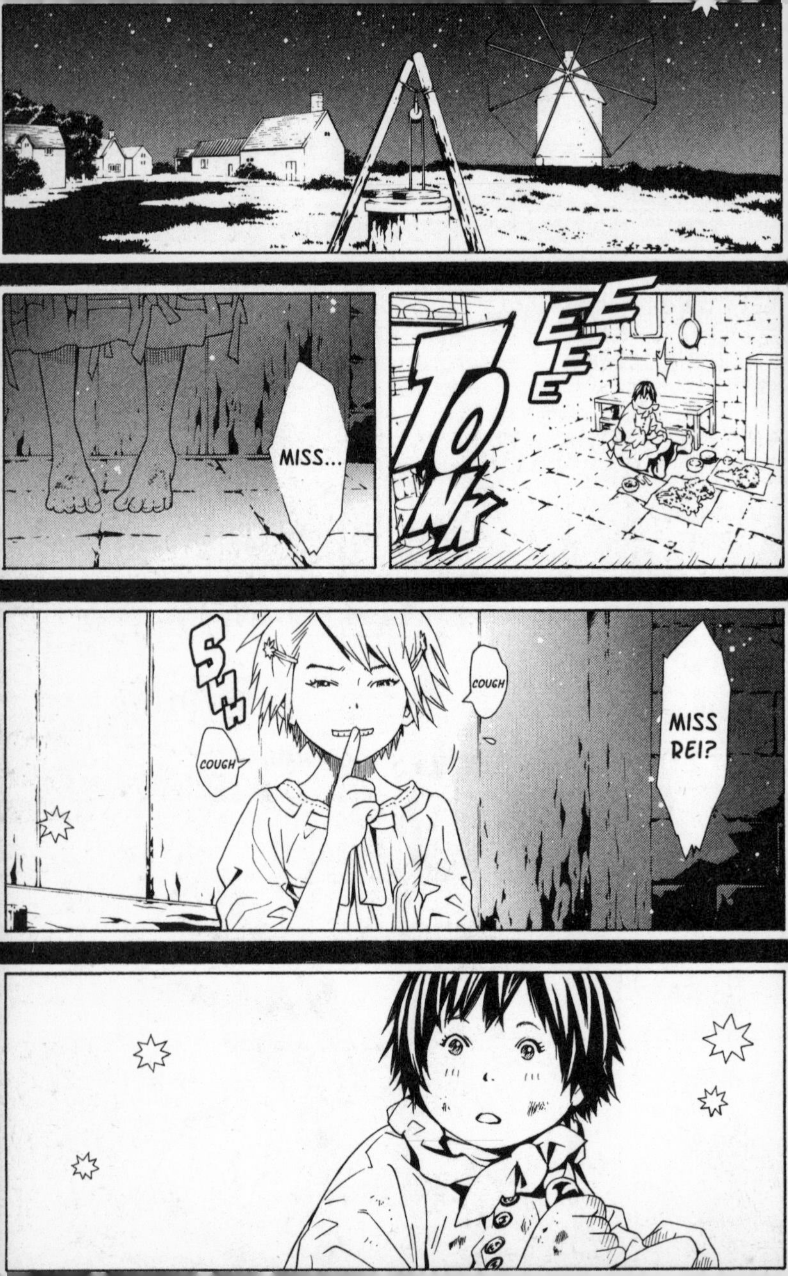
EEEE
TONK
MISS...
MISS REI?
COUGH
SHH
COUGH

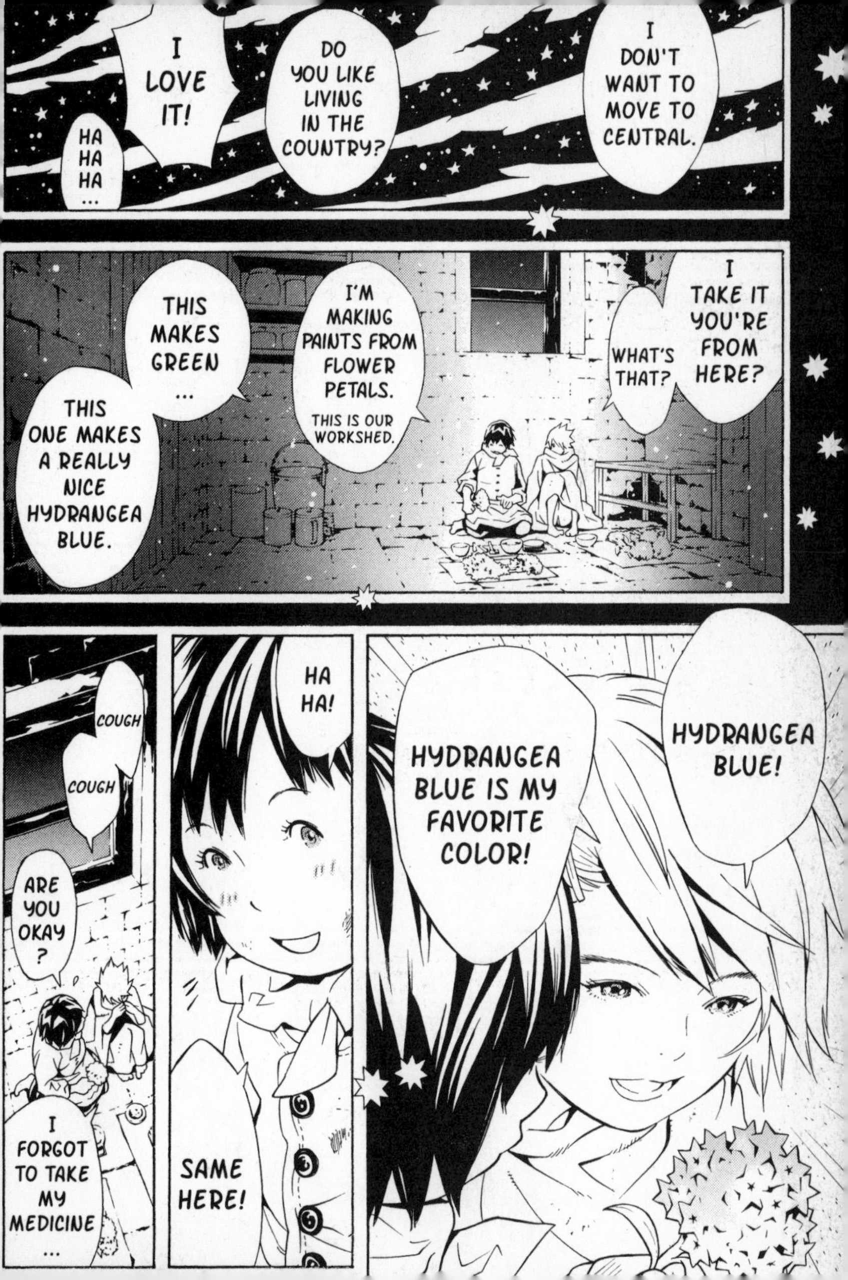
I DON'T WANT TO MOVE TO CENTRAL.
DO YOU LIKE LIVING IN THE COUNTRY?
I LOVE IT!
HA HA HA ...
I TAKE IT YOU'RE FROM HERE?
WHAT'S THAT?
I'M MAKING PAINTS FROM FLOWER PETALS.
THIS IS OUR WORKSHED.
THIS MAKES GREEN ...
THIS ONE MAKES A REALLY NICE HYDRANGEA BLUE.
HYDRANGEA BLUE!
HYDRANGEA BLUE IS MY FAVORITE COLOR!
HA HA!
SAME HERE!
COUGH
COUGH
ARE YOU OKAY?
I FORGOT TO TAKE MY MEDICINE ...

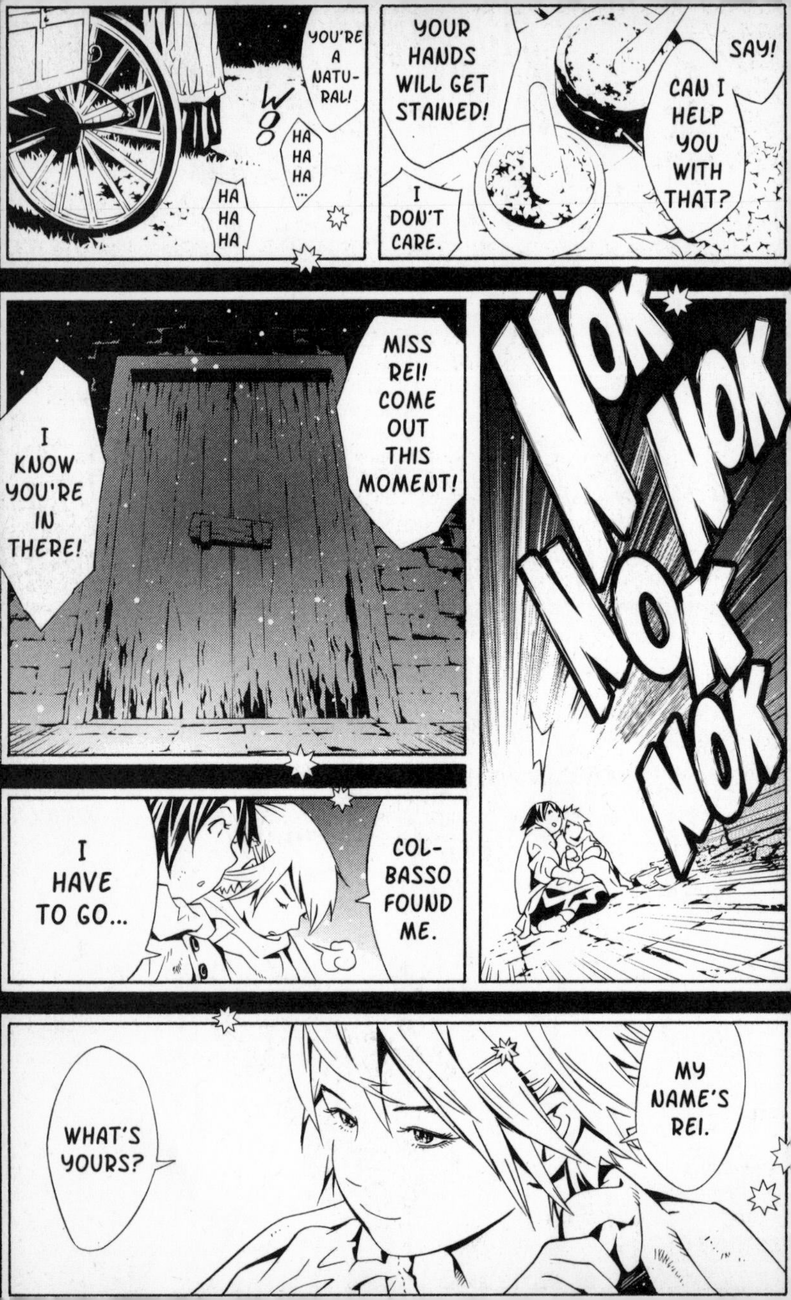
SAY!
CAN I HELP YOU WITH THAT?
YOUR HANDS WILL GET STAINED!
I DON'T CARE.
YOU'RE A NATU-RAL!
WOO
HA HA HA...
HA HA HA
NOK NOK NOK NOK NOK
MISS REI! COME OUT THIS MOMENT!
I KNOW YOU'RE IN THERE!
COL-BASSO FOUND ME.
I HAVE TO GO...
MY NAME'S REI.
WHAT'S YOURS?

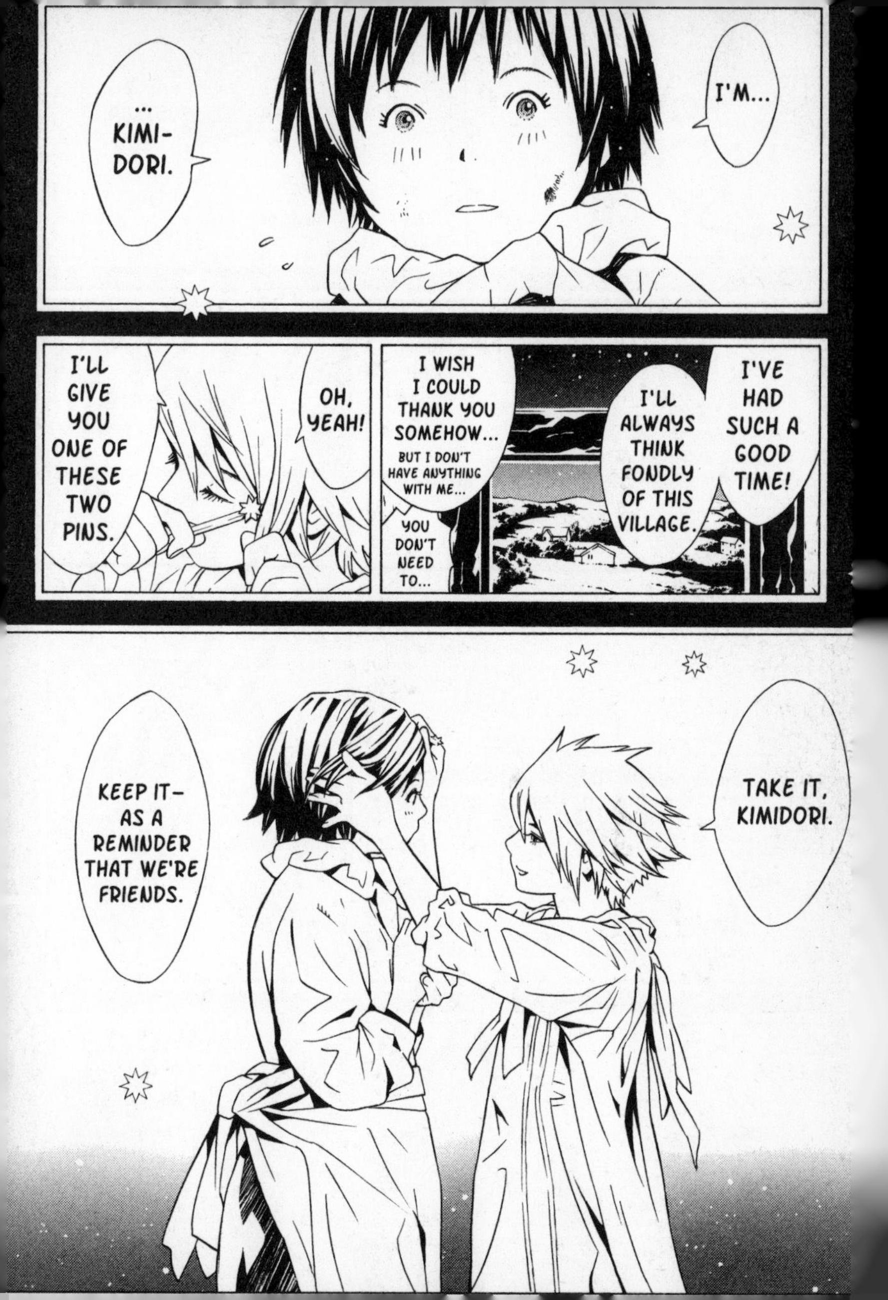
I'M...
... KIMI-DORI.
I'VE HAD SUCH A GOOD TIME!
I'LL ALWAYS THINK FONDLY OF THIS VILLAGE.
I WISH I COULD THANK YOU SOMEHOW... BUT I DON'T HAVE ANYTHING WITH ME...
YOU DON'T NEED TO...
OH, YEAH!
I'LL GIVE YOU ONE OF THESE TWO PINS.
TAKE IT, KIMIDORI.
KEEP IT—AS A REMINDER THAT WE'RE FRIENDS.

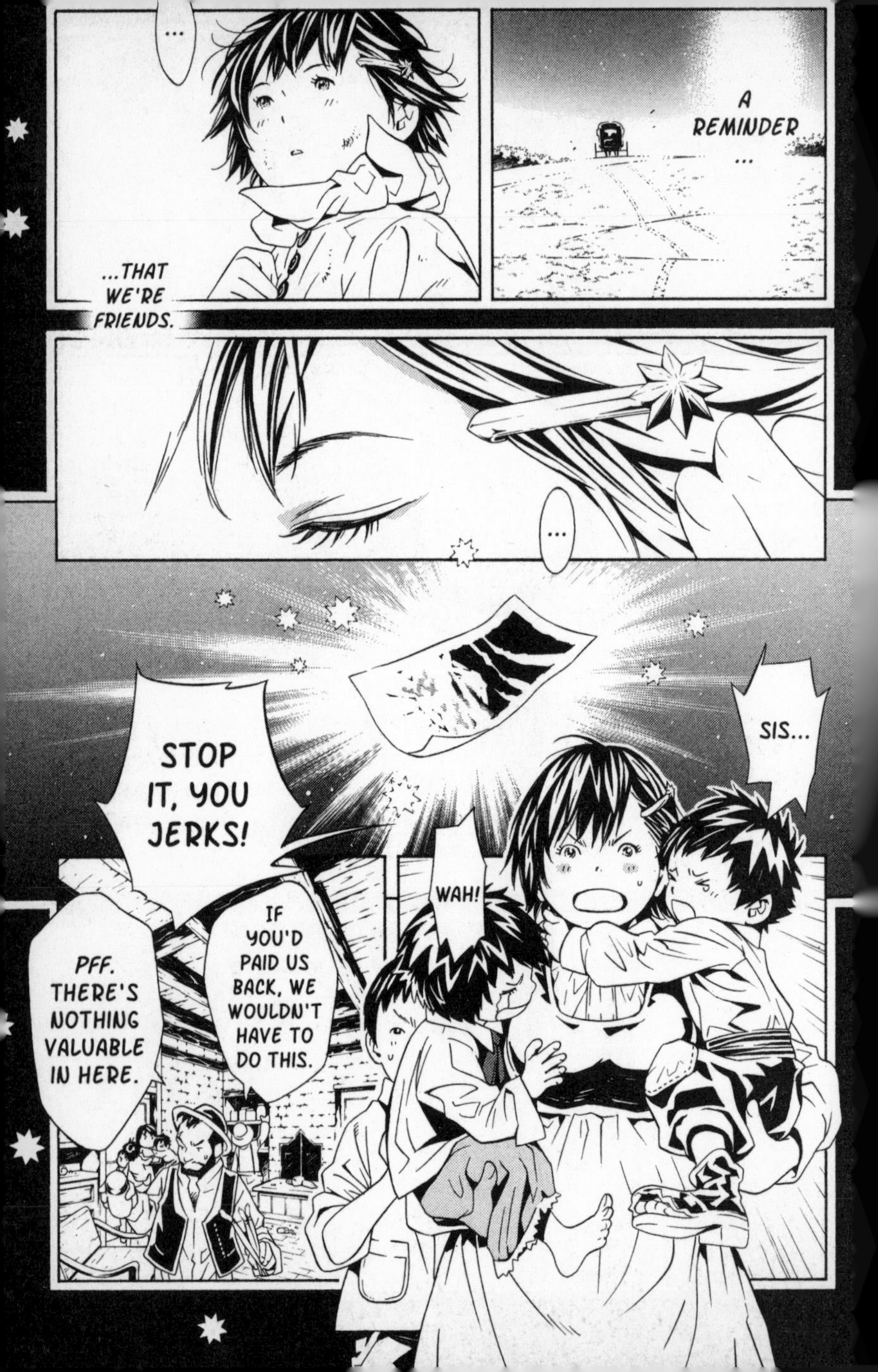
A REMINDER ...
...
...THAT WE'RE FRIENDS.
...
SIS...
STOP IT, YOU JERKS!
WAH!
IF YOU'D PAID US BACK, WE WOULDN'T HAVE TO DO THIS.
PFF. THERE'S NOTHING VALUABLE IN HERE.

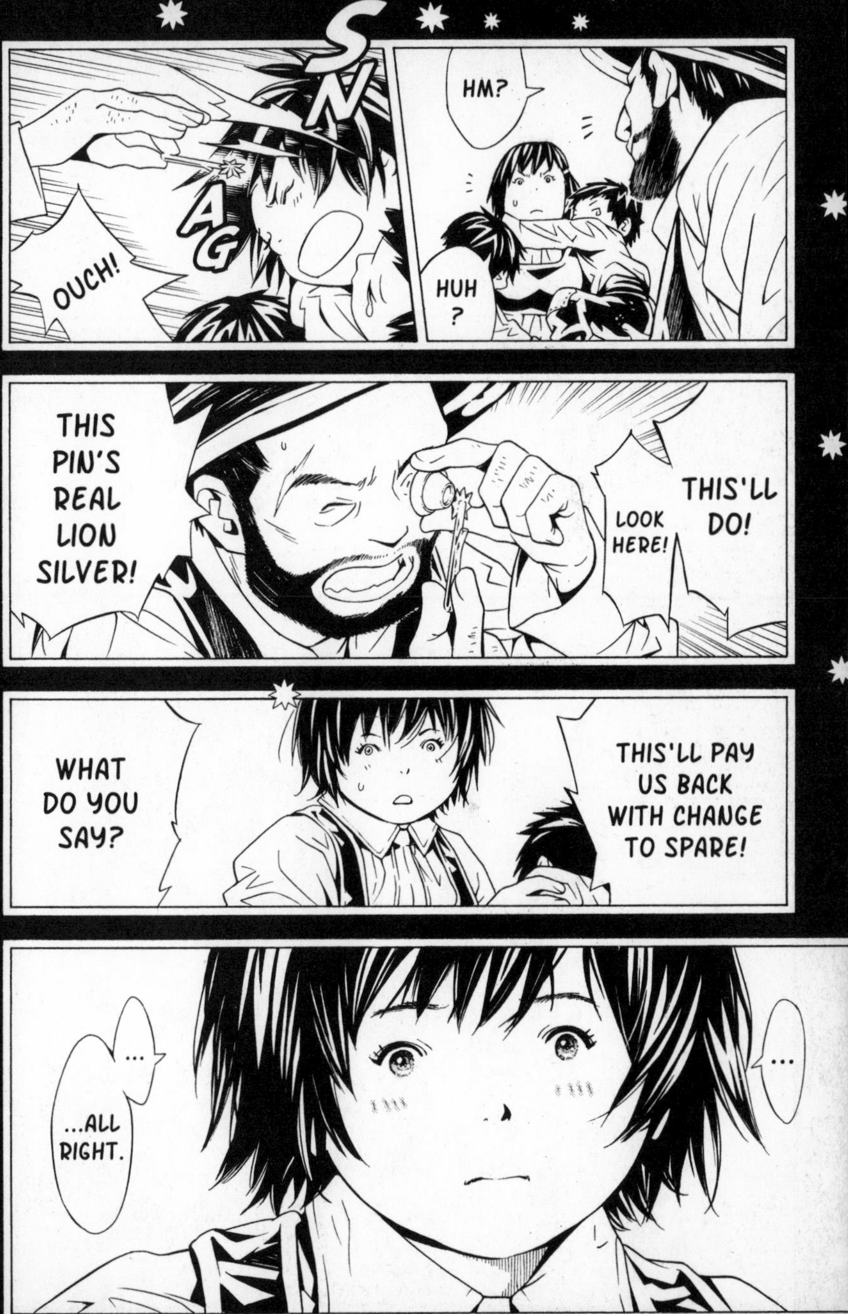
HM?
HUH ?
SNAG
OUCH!
THIS'LL DO!
LOOK HERE!
THIS PIN'S REAL LION SILVER!
THIS'LL PAY US BACK WITH CHANGE TO SPARE!
WHAT DO YOU SAY?
...
...
...ALL RIGHT.

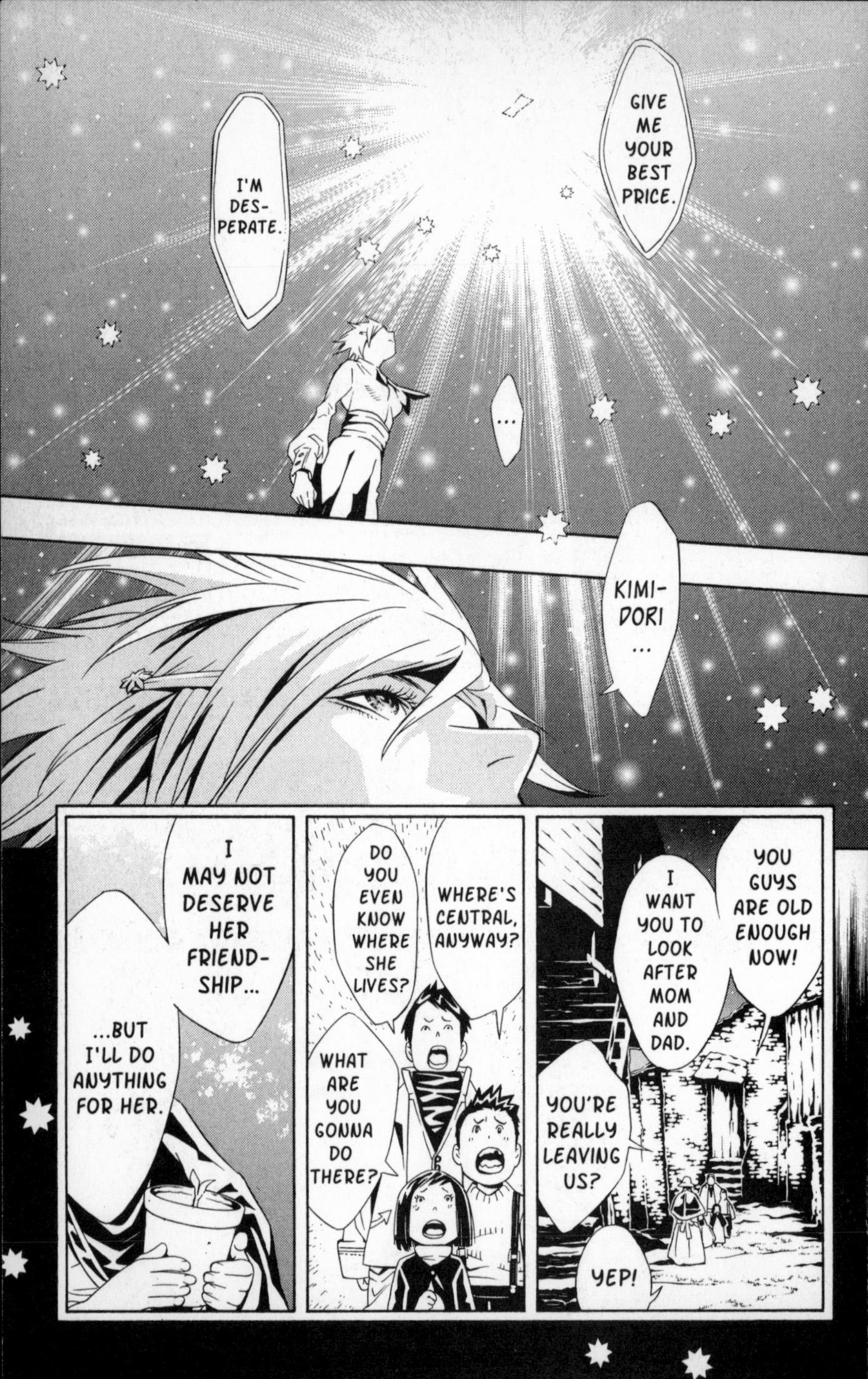
GIVE ME YOUR BEST PRICE.
I'M DES-PERATE.
...
KIMI-DORI...
YOU GUYS ARE OLD ENOUGH NOW!
I WANT YOU TO LOOK AFTER MOM AND DAD.
YOU'RE REALLY LEAVING US?
YEP!
WHERE'S CENTRAL, ANYWAY?
DO YOU EVEN KNOW WHERE SHE LIVES?
WHAT ARE YOU GONNA DO THERE?
I MAY NOT DESERVE HER FRIEND-SHIP...
...BUT I'LL DO ANYTHING FOR HER.

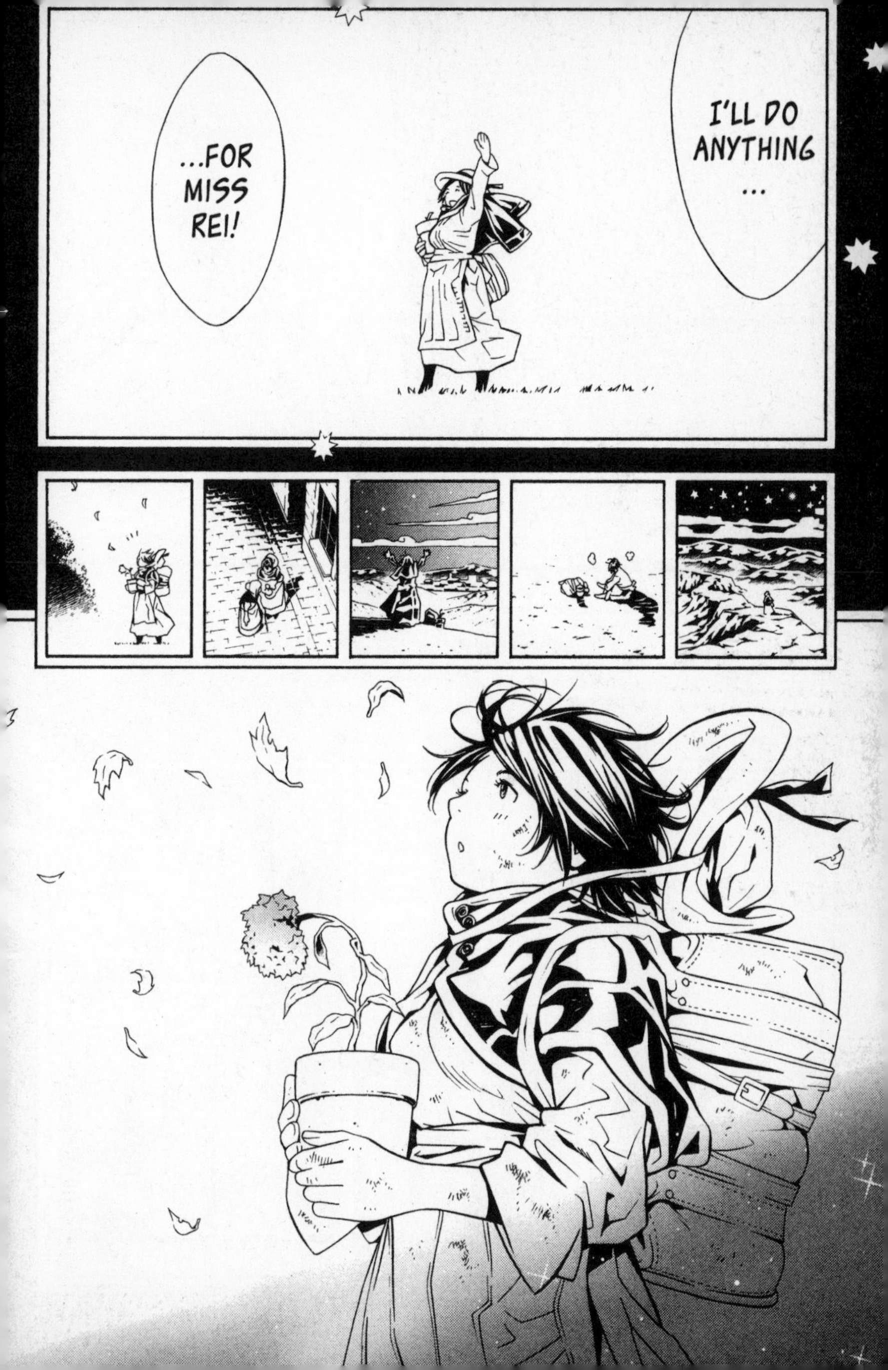
I'LL DO ANYTHING ...
...FOR MISS REI!

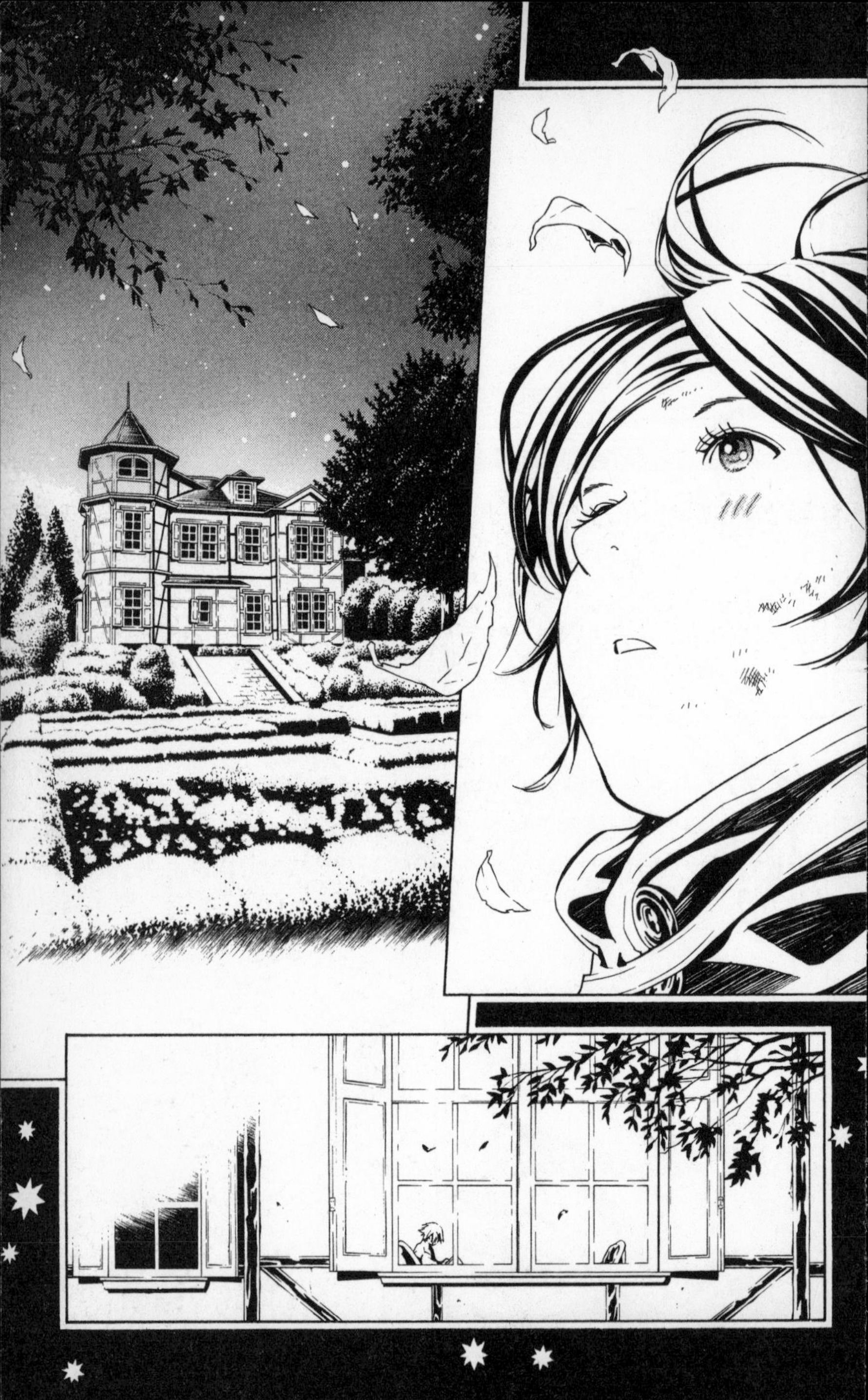

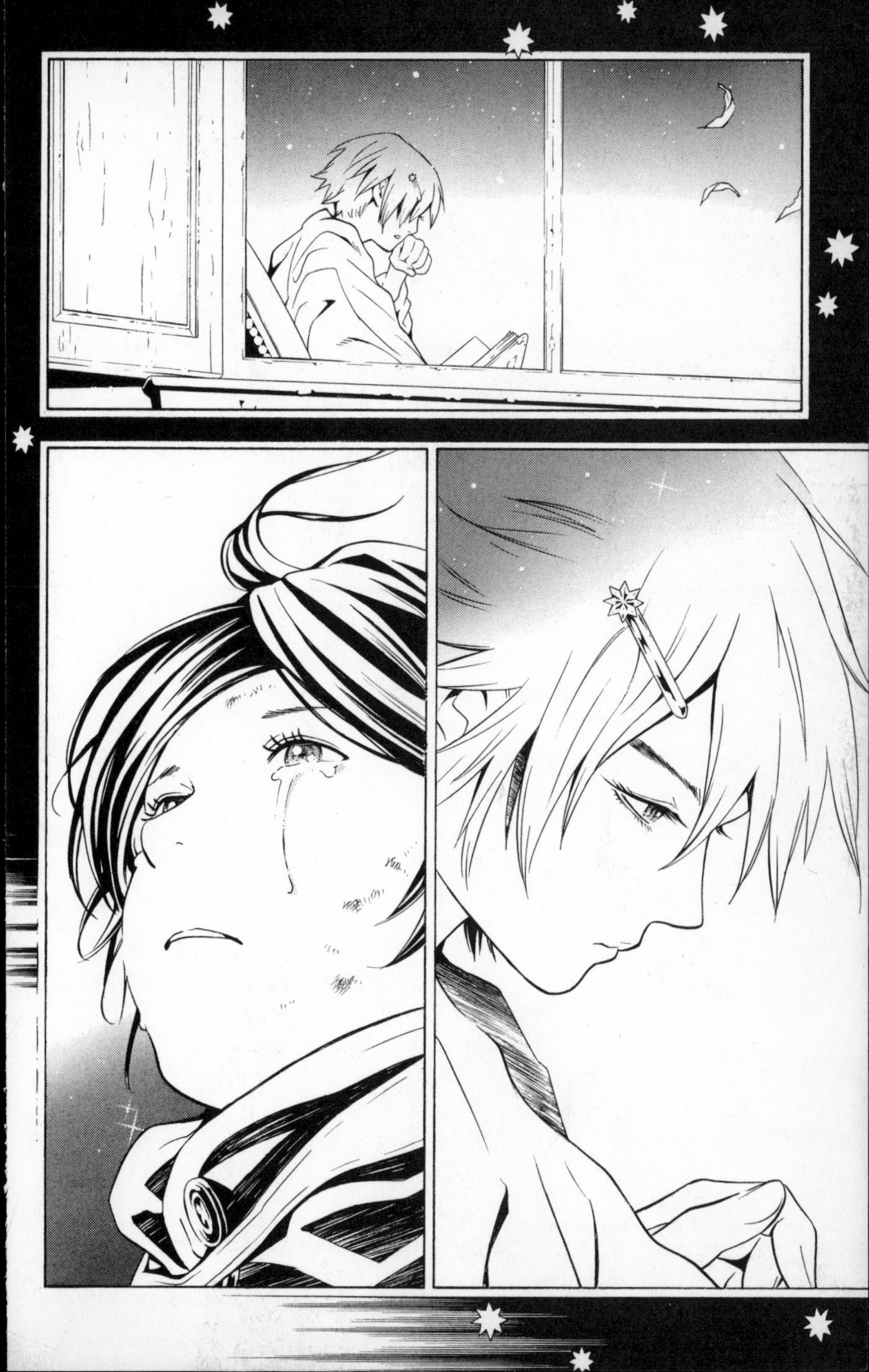

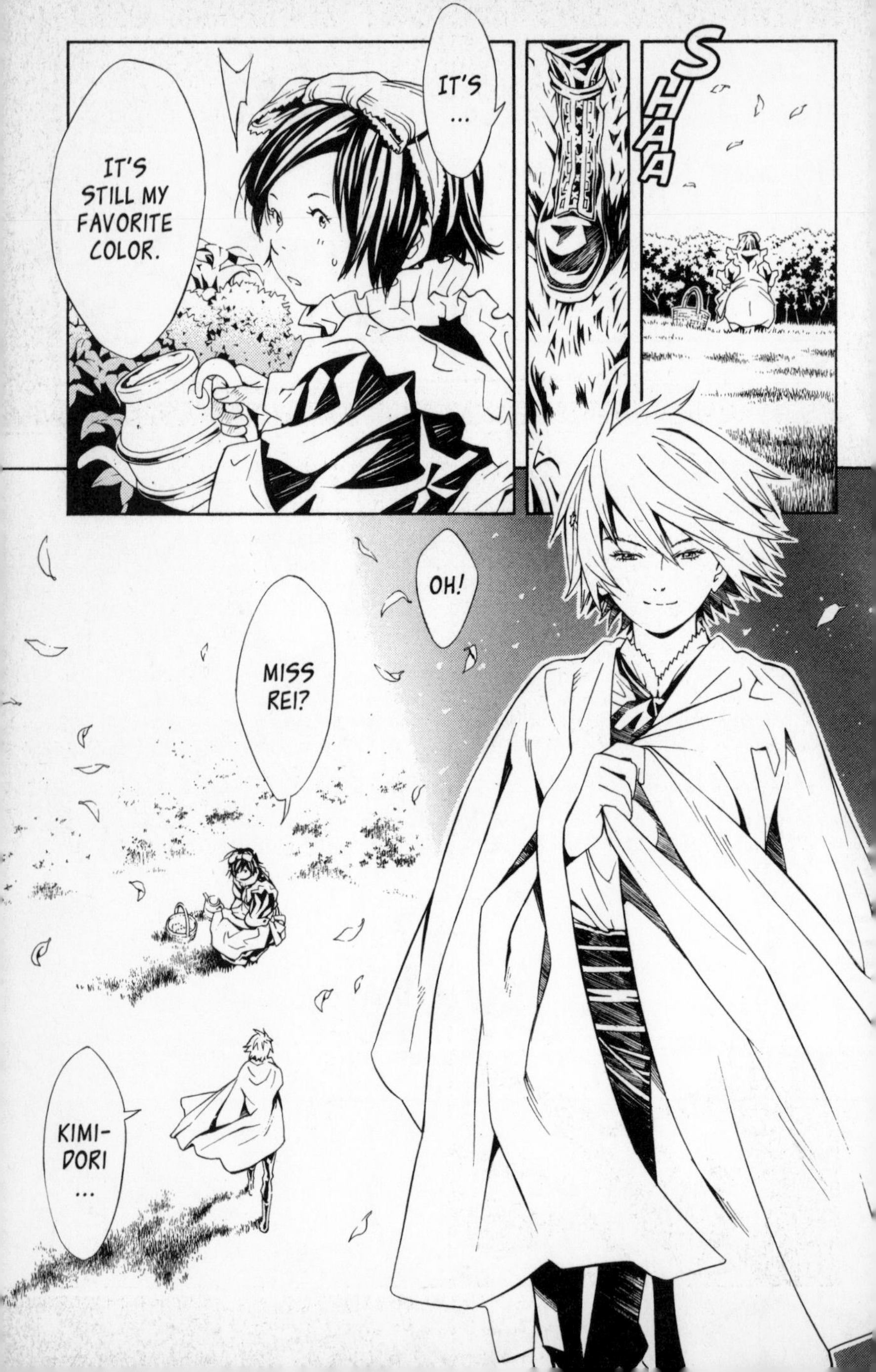
SHAAA
IT'S ...
IT'S STILL MY FAVORITE COLOR.
OH!
MISS REI?
KIMI-DORI ...

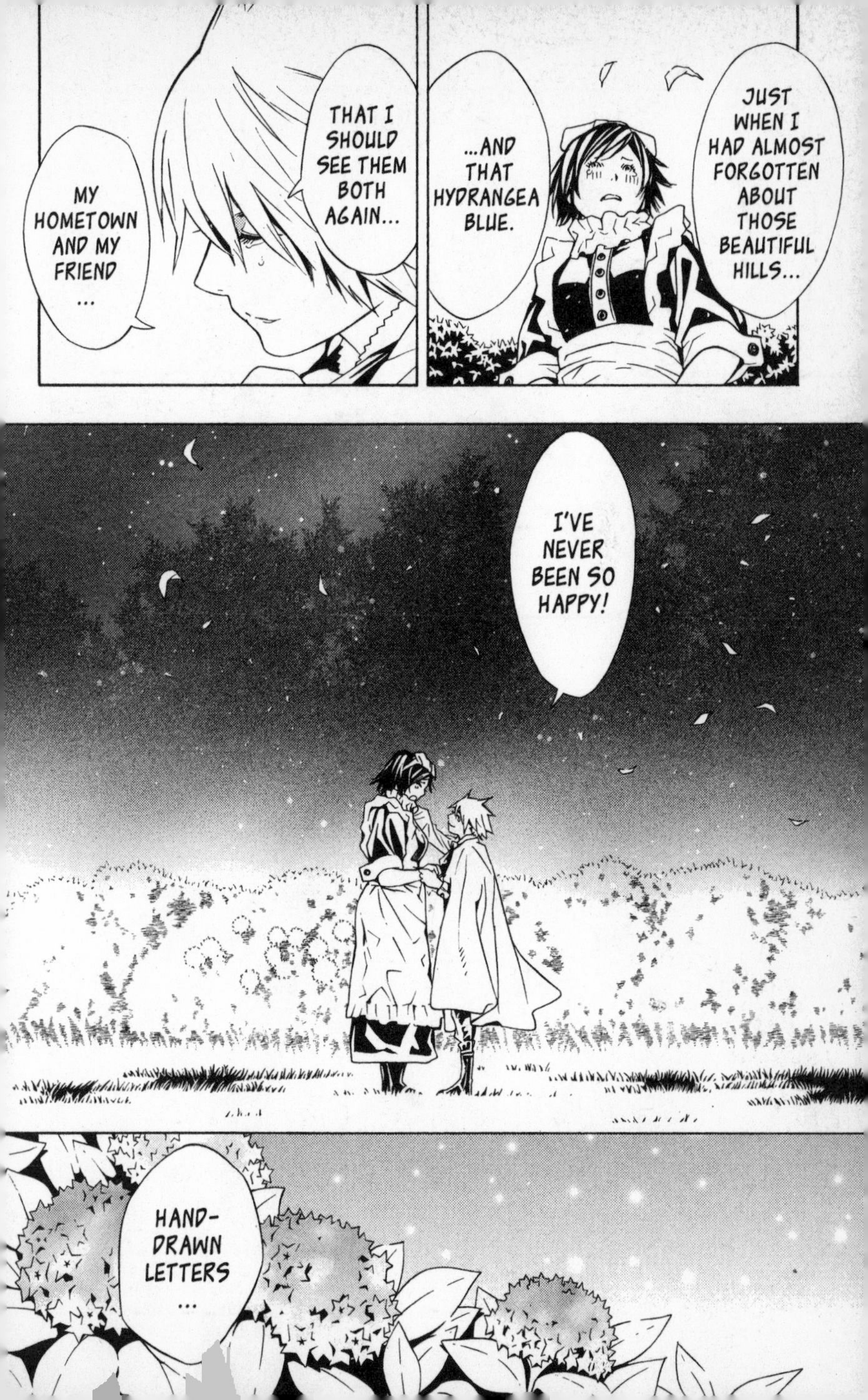
JUST WHEN I HAD ALMOST FORGOTTEN ABOUT THOSE BEAUTIFUL HILLS...
...AND THAT HYDRANGEA BLUE.
THAT I SHOULD SEE THEM BOTH AGAIN...
MY HOMETOWN AND MY FRIEND ...
I'VE NEVER BEEN SO HAPPY!
HAND-DRAWN LETTERS ...

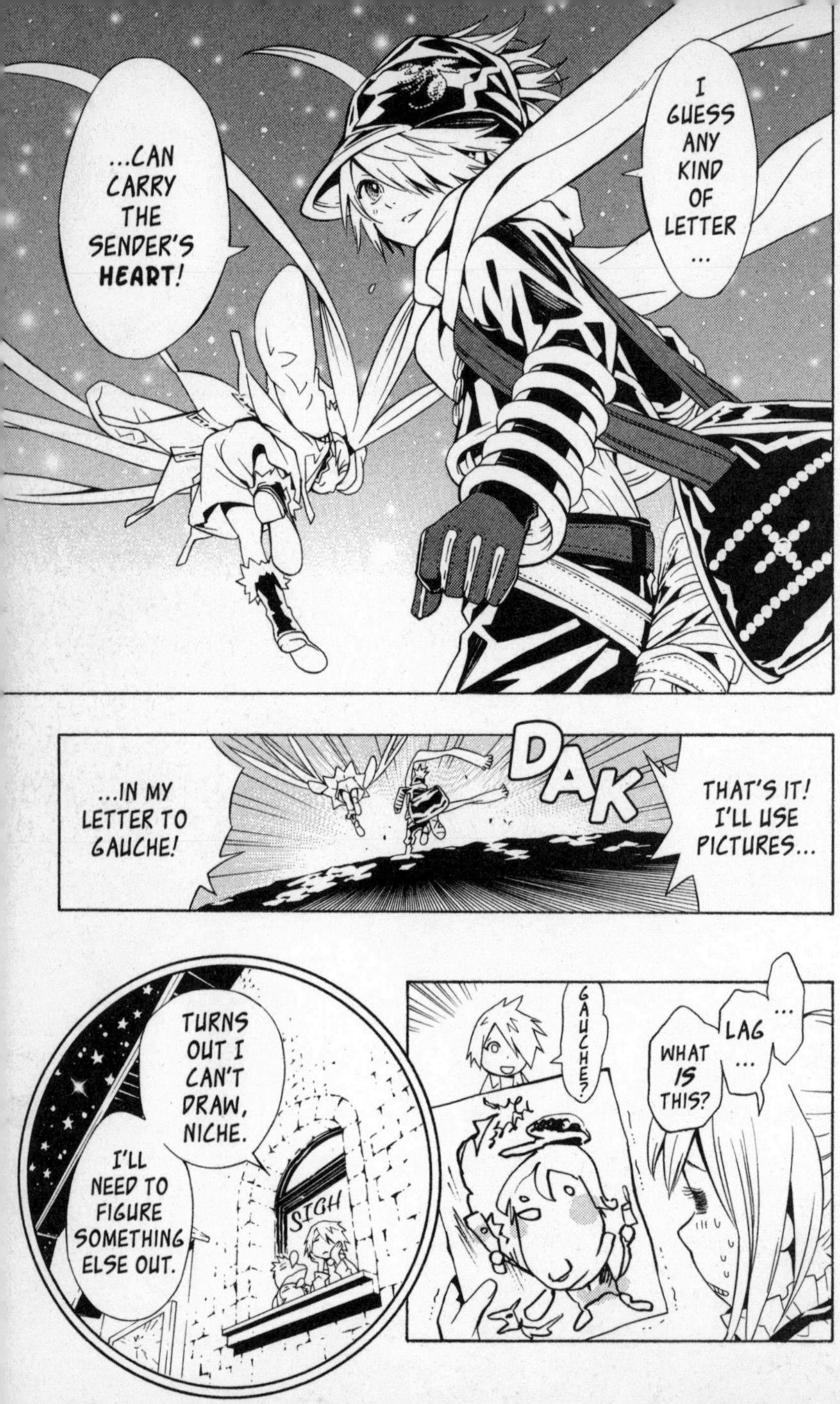
I GUESS ANY KIND OF LETTER...
...CAN CARRY THE SENDER'S HEART!
THAT'S IT! I'LL USE PICTURES...
DAK
...IN MY LETTER TO GAUCHE!
...
LAG...
WHAT IS THIS?
GAUCHE?
TURNS OUT I CAN'T DRAW, NICHE.
I'LL NEED TO FIGURE SOMETHING ELSE OUT.
SIGH

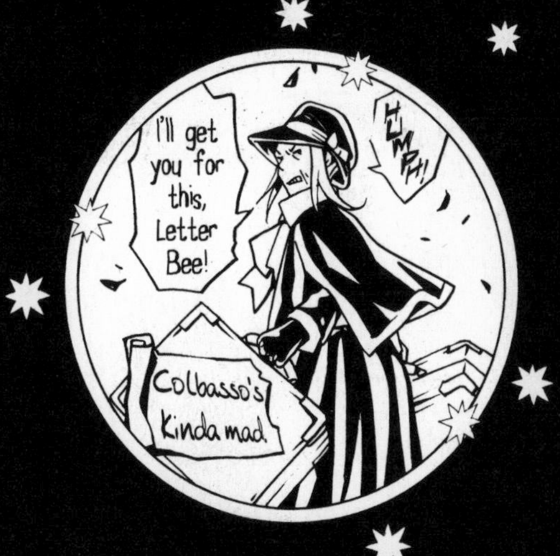
I'll get you for this, Letter Bee!
HUMPH!
Colbasso's Kinda mad.

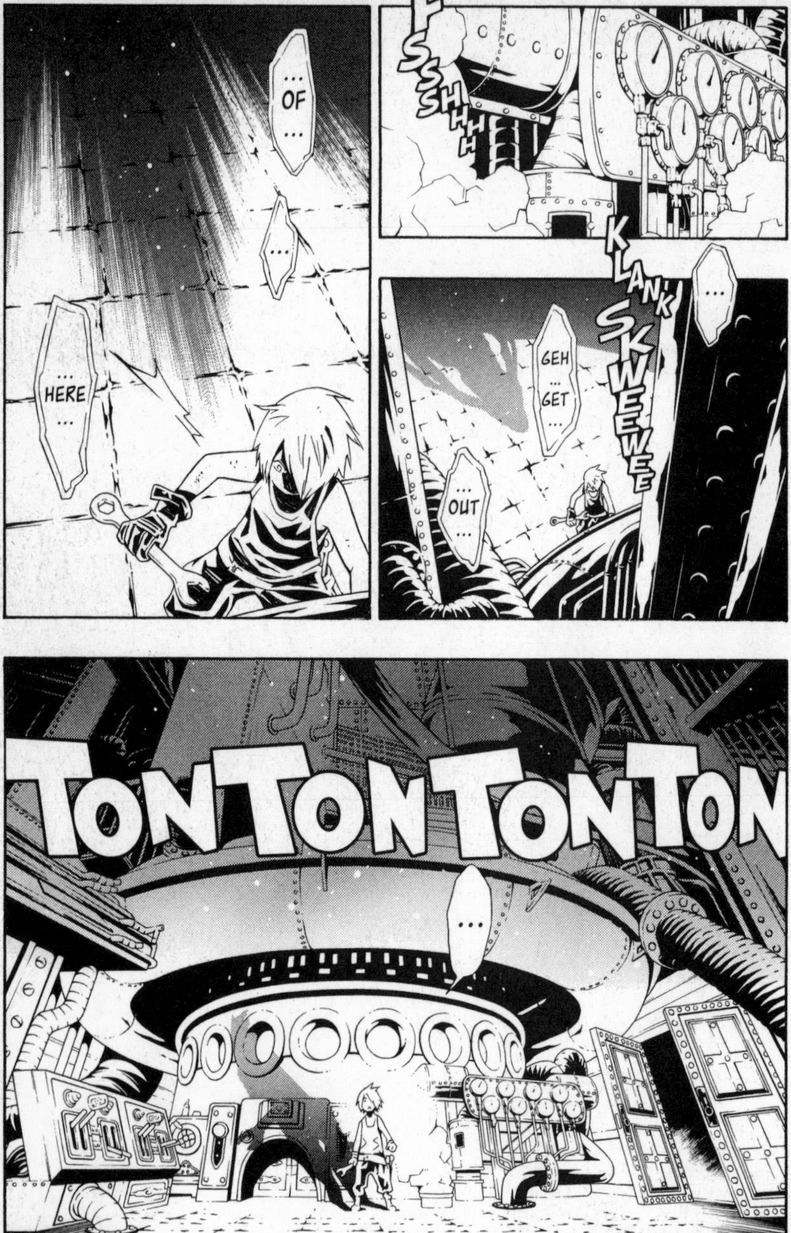
FSSHHHH
KLANK
SKWEEWEE
...
GEH ... GET ...
... OUT ...
... OF ...
...
... HERE ...
TONTONTONTON
...

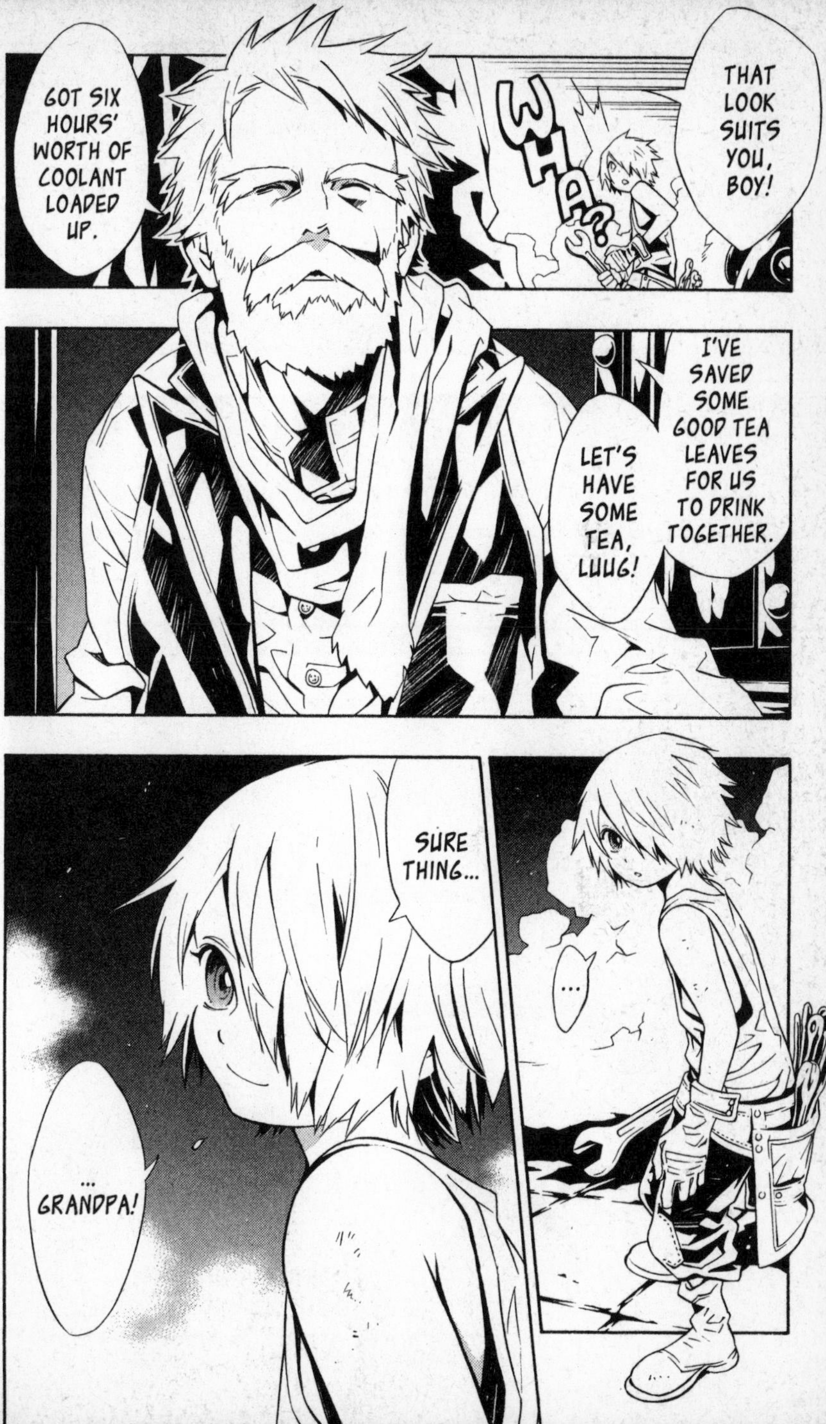
THAT LOOK SUITS YOU, BOY!
WHA?
GOT SIX HOURS' WORTH OF COOLANT LOADED UP.
I'VE SAVED SOME GOOD TEA LEAVES FOR US TO DRINK TOGETHER.
LET'S HAVE SOME TEA, LUUG!
...
SURE THING...
... GRANDPA!

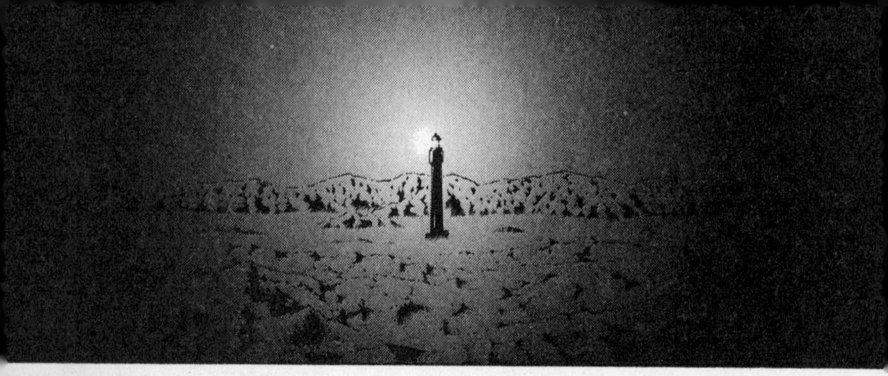

Chapter 20: The Lighthouse in the Wasteland

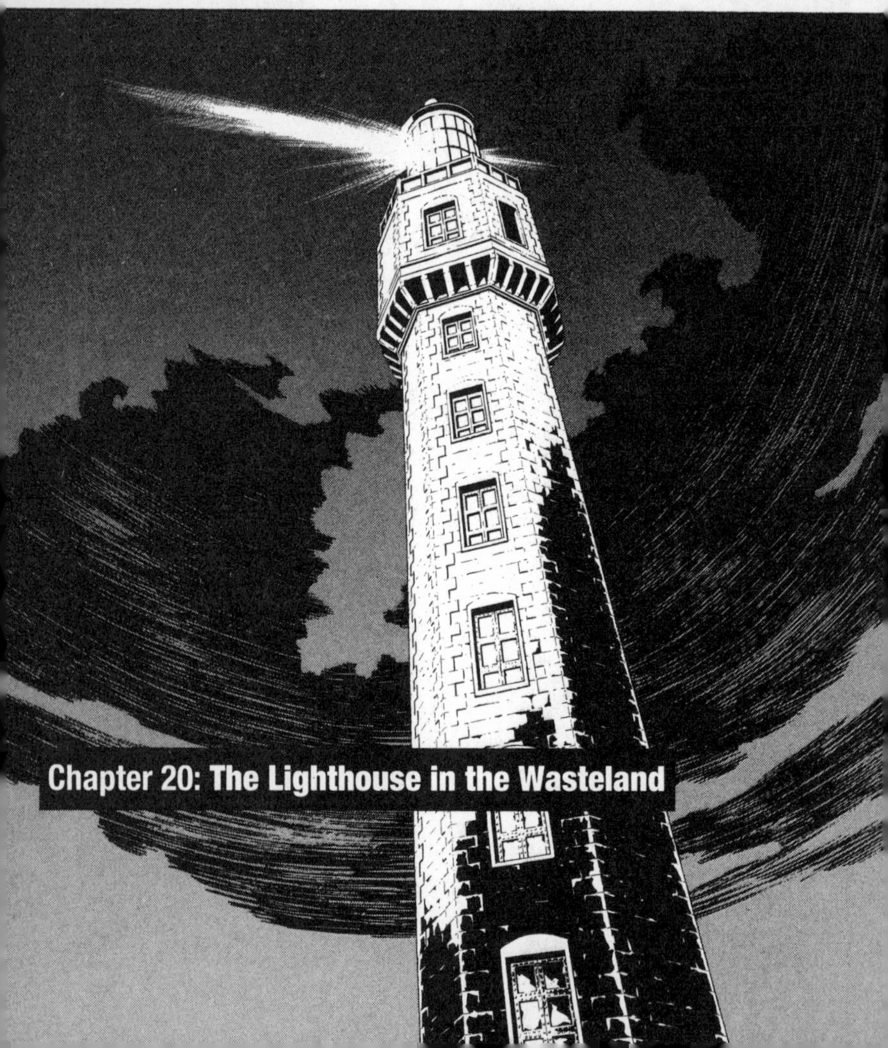

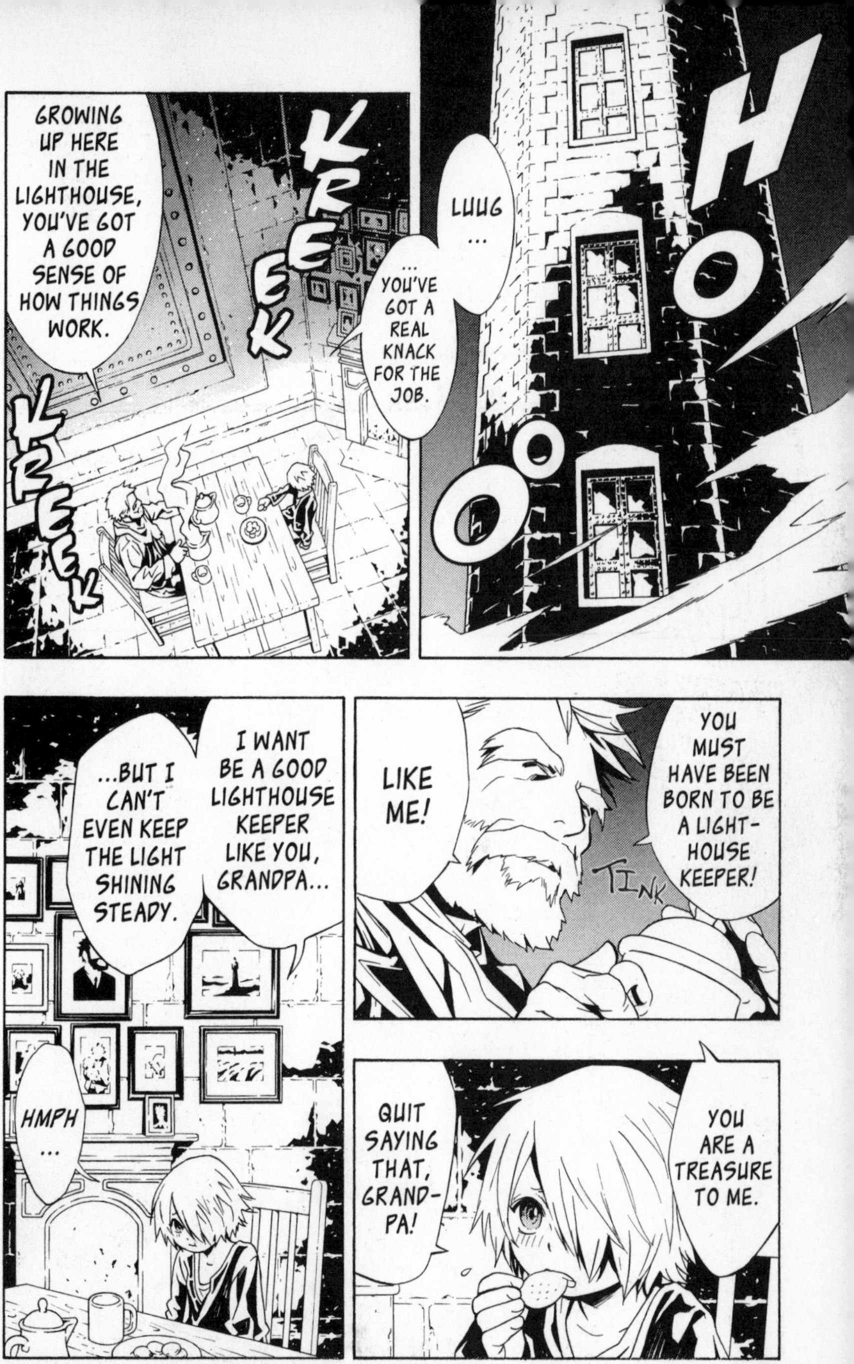
HOOOh
LUUG ...
... YOU'VE GOT A REAL KNACK FOR THE JOB.
KREEK
GROWING UP HERE IN THE LIGHTHOUSE, YOU'VE GOT A GOOD SENSE OF HOW THINGS WORK.
KREEK
YOU MUST HAVE BEEN BORN TO BE A LIGHT-HOUSE KEEPER!
TINK
LIKE ME!
YOU ARE A TREASURE TO ME.
QUIT SAYING THAT, GRAND-PA!
I WANT BE A GOOD LIGHTHOUSE KEEPER LIKE YOU, GRANDPA...
...BUT I CAN'T EVEN KEEP THE LIGHT SHINING STEADY.
HMPH ...

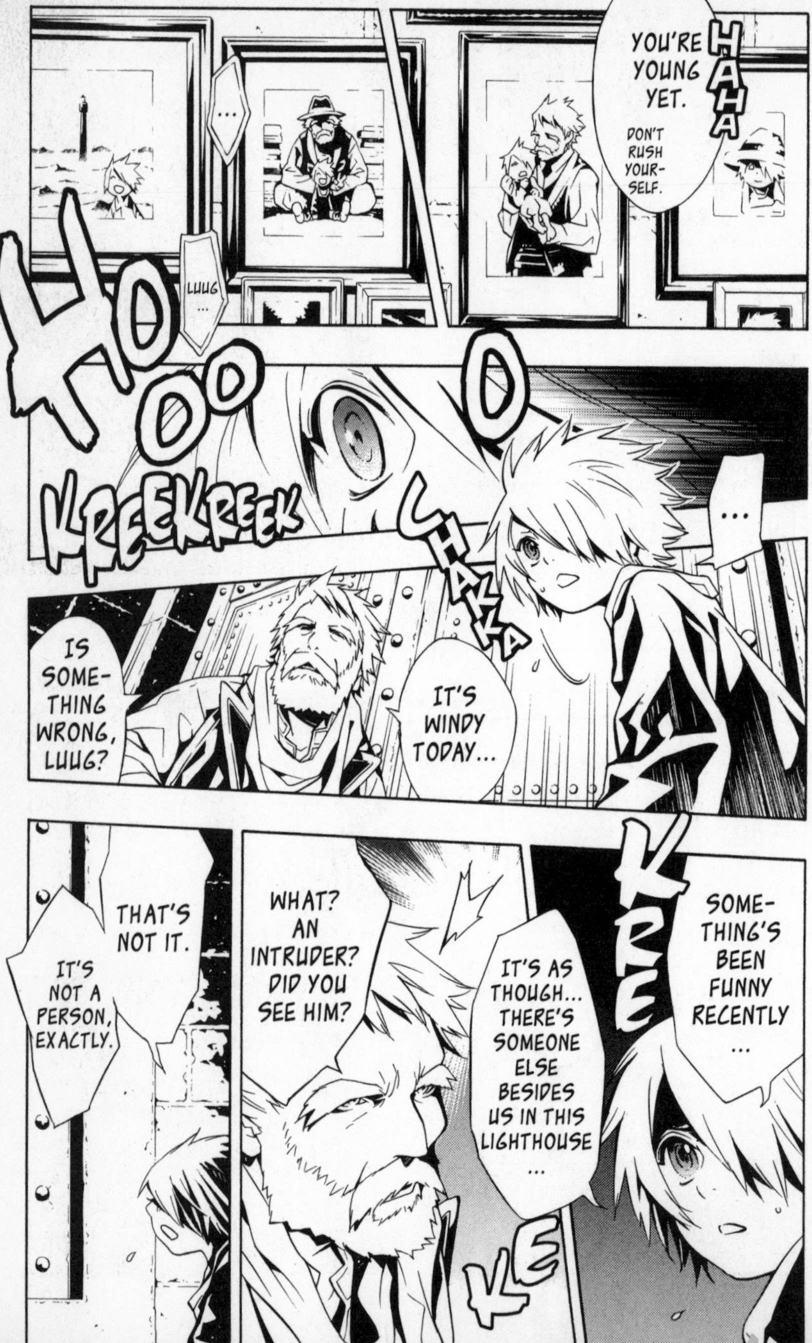
YOU'RE YOUNG YET.
DON'T RUSH YOUR-SELF.
HAHA
...
LUUG ...
HOOOO
KREEKREEK
...
CHAKKA
IT'S WINDY TODAY...
IS SOME-THING WRONG, LUUG?
SOME-THING'S BEEN FUNNY RECENTLY ...
KREKE
IT'S AS THOUGH... THERE'S SOMEONE ELSE BESIDES US IN THIS LIGHTHOUSE ...
WHAT? AN INTRUDER? DID YOU SEE HIM?
THAT'S NOT IT.
IT'S NOT A PERSON, EXACTLY.

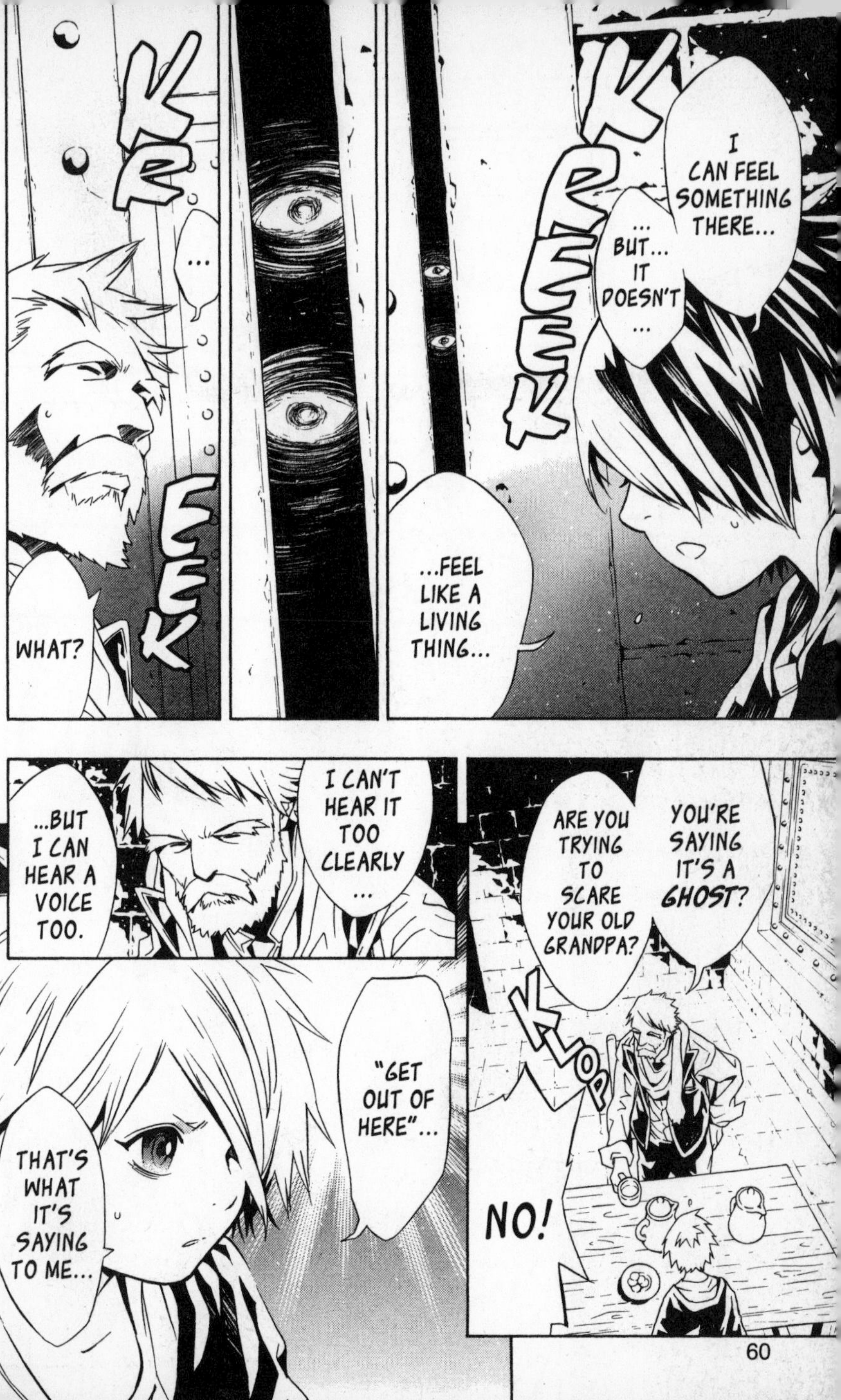

KREEEK
I CAN FEEL SOMETHING THERE...
... BUT... IT DOESN'T ...
...FEEL LIKE A LIVING THING...
KR
...
EEK
WHAT?
YOU'RE SAYING IT'S A *GHOST*?
ARE YOU TRYING TO SCARE YOUR OLD GRANDPA?
KLOP
NO!
I CAN'T HEAR IT TOO CLEARLY ...
...BUT I CAN HEAR A VOICE TOO.
"GET OUT OF HERE"...
THAT'S WHAT IT'S SAYING TO ME...

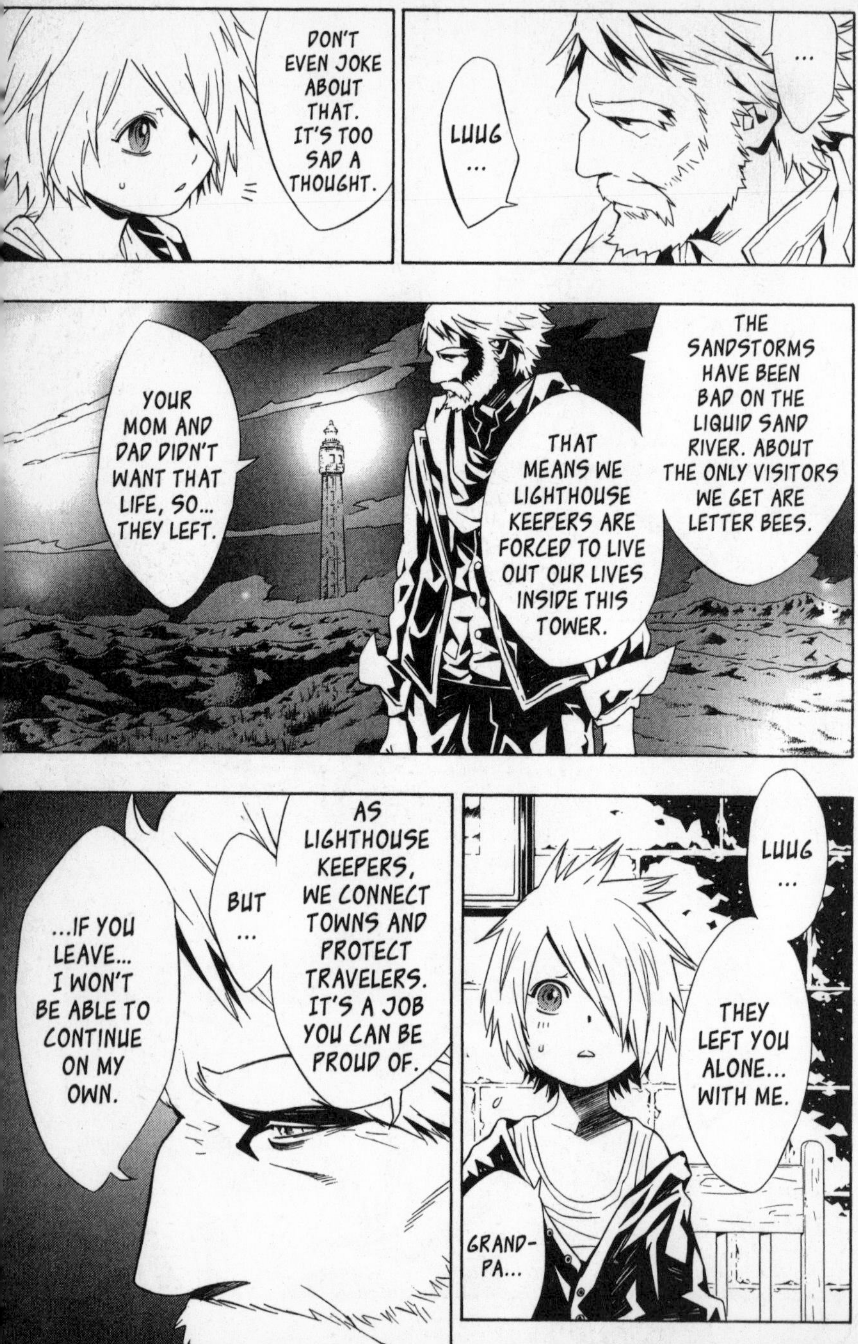
...
LUUG ...
DON'T EVEN JOKE ABOUT THAT. IT'S TOO SAD A THOUGHT.
THE SANDSTORMS HAVE BEEN BAD ON THE LIQUID SAND RIVER. ABOUT THE ONLY VISITORS WE GET ARE LETTER BEES.
THAT MEANS WE LIGHTHOUSE KEEPERS ARE FORCED TO LIVE OUT OUR LIVES INSIDE THIS TOWER.
YOUR MOM AND DAD DIDN'T WANT THAT LIFE, SO... THEY LEFT.
LUUG ...
THEY LEFT YOU ALONE... WITH ME.
GRAND-PA...
AS LIGHTHOUSE KEEPERS, WE CONNECT TOWNS AND PROTECT TRAVELERS. IT'S A JOB YOU CAN BE PROUD OF.
BUT ...
...IF YOU LEAVE... I WON'T BE ABLE TO CONTINUE ON MY OWN.

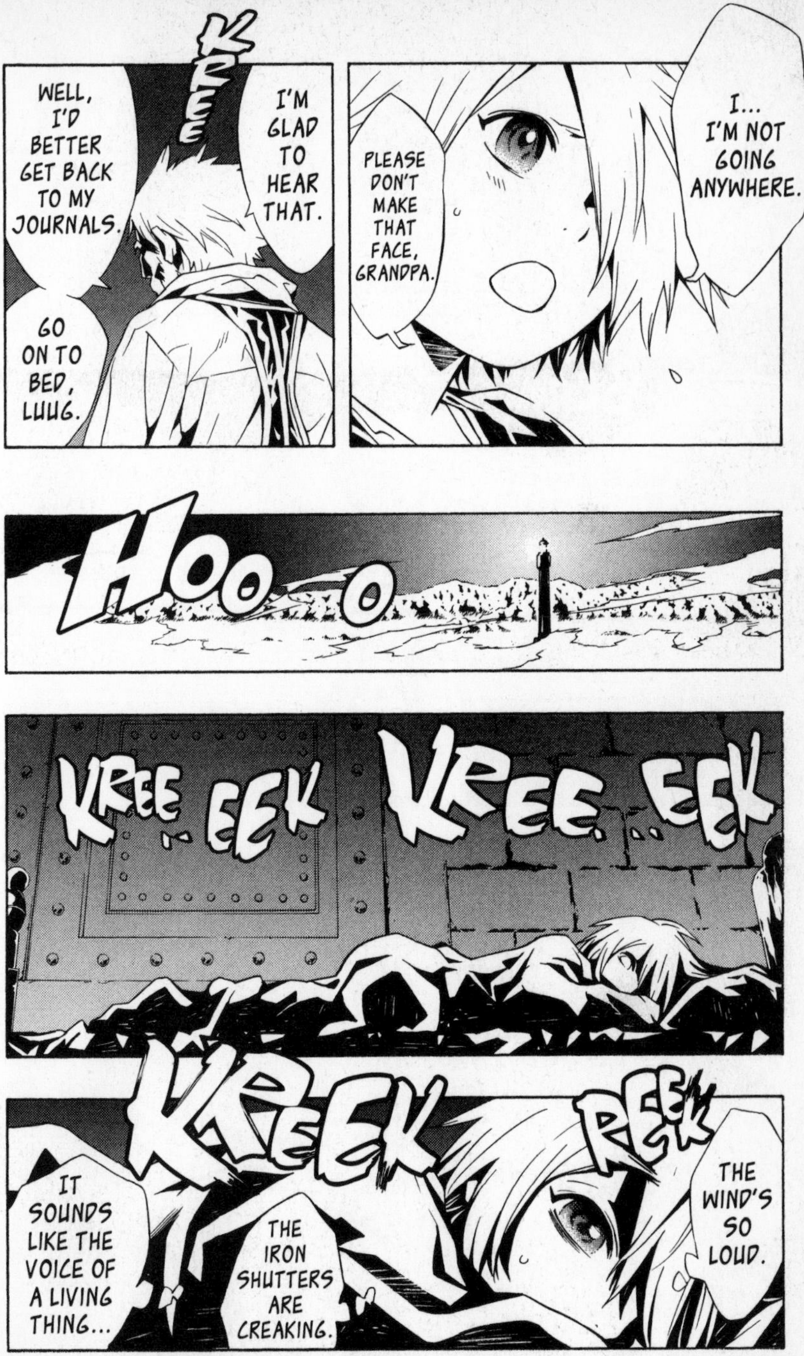
I... I'M NOT GOING ANYWHERE.
PLEASE DON'T MAKE THAT FACE, GRANDPA.
KREE
I'M GLAD TO HEAR THAT.
WELL, I'D BETTER GET BACK TO MY JOURNALS.
GO ON TO BED, LUUG.
HOO O
KREE EEK
KREE EEK
REEK
KREEK
THE WIND'S SO LOUD.
THE IRON SHUTTERS ARE CREAKING.
IT SOUNDS LIKE THE VOICE OF A LIVING THING...

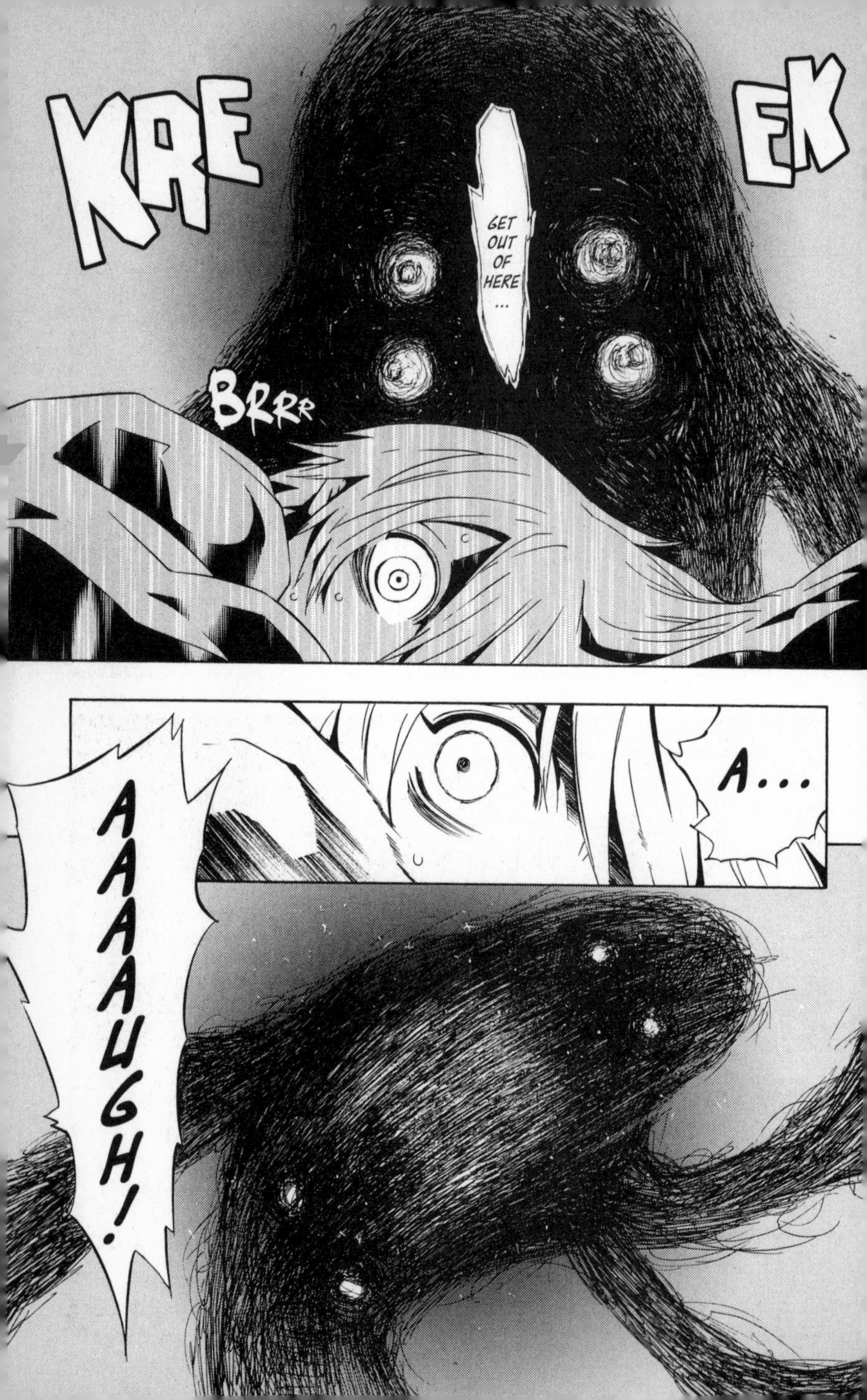
KRE EK
GET OUT OF HERE...
BRRR
A...
AAAAAUGH!

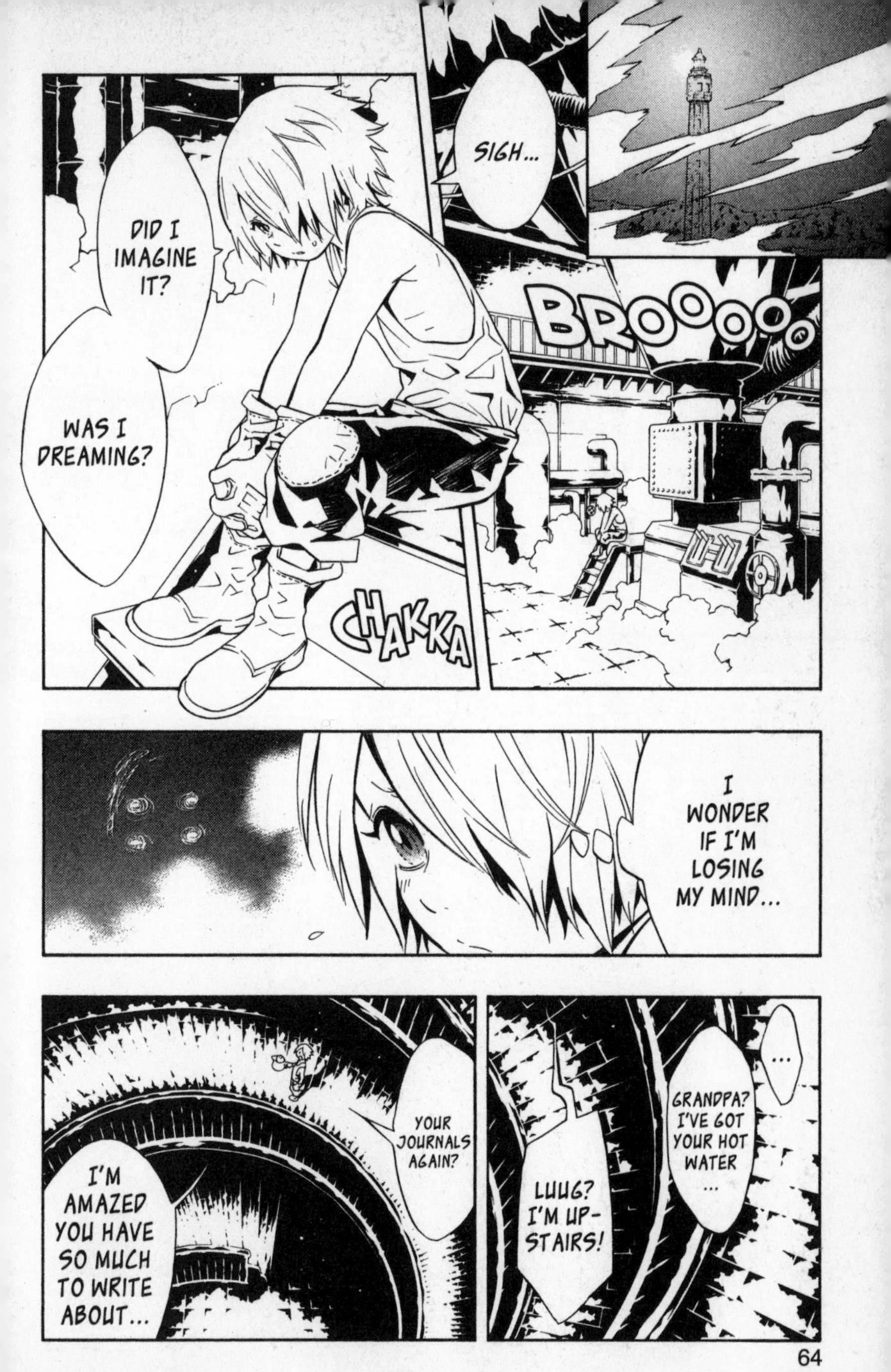
SIGH...
BROOOOOO
DID I IMAGINE IT?
WAS I DREAMING?
CHAKKA
I WONDER IF I'M LOSING MY MIND...
...
GRANDPA? I'VE GOT YOUR HOT WATER...
LUUG? I'M UP-STAIRS!
YOUR JOURNALS AGAIN?
I'M AMAZED YOU HAVE SO MUCH TO WRITE ABOUT...

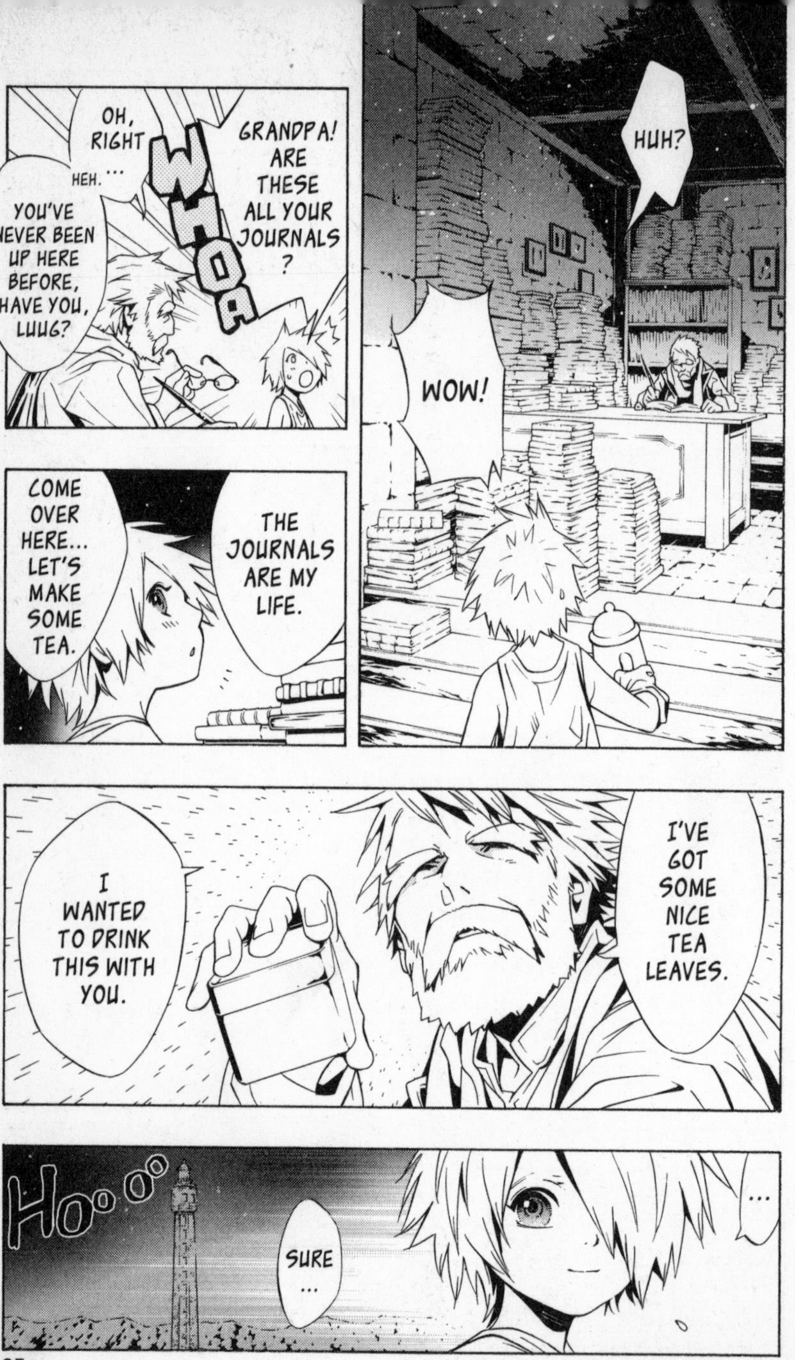
HUH?
WOW!
GRANDPA! ARE THESE ALL YOUR JOURNALS?
WHOA
OH, RIGHT...
HEH.
YOU'VE NEVER BEEN UP HERE BEFORE, HAVE YOU, LUUG?
THE JOURNALS ARE MY LIFE.
COME OVER HERE... LET'S MAKE SOME TEA.
I'VE GOT SOME NICE TEA LEAVES.
I WANTED TO DRINK THIS WITH YOU.
...
SURE...
HOOOO

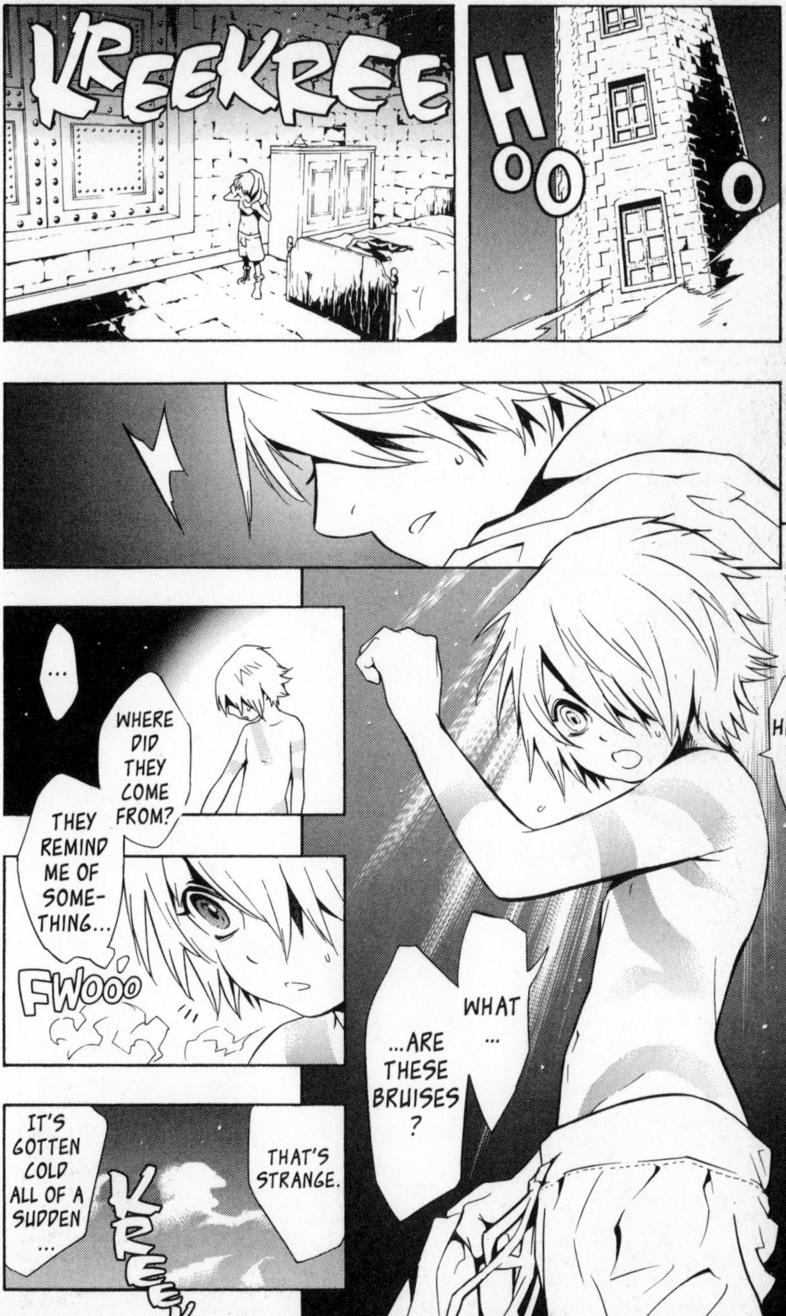
KREEKREEHOOO
HUH?
WHAT...
...ARE THESE BRUISES?
...
WHERE DID THEY COME FROM?
THEY REMIND ME OF SOMETHING...
FWOOO
IT'S GOTTEN COLD ALL OF A SUDDEN...
THAT'S STRANGE.
KREEK

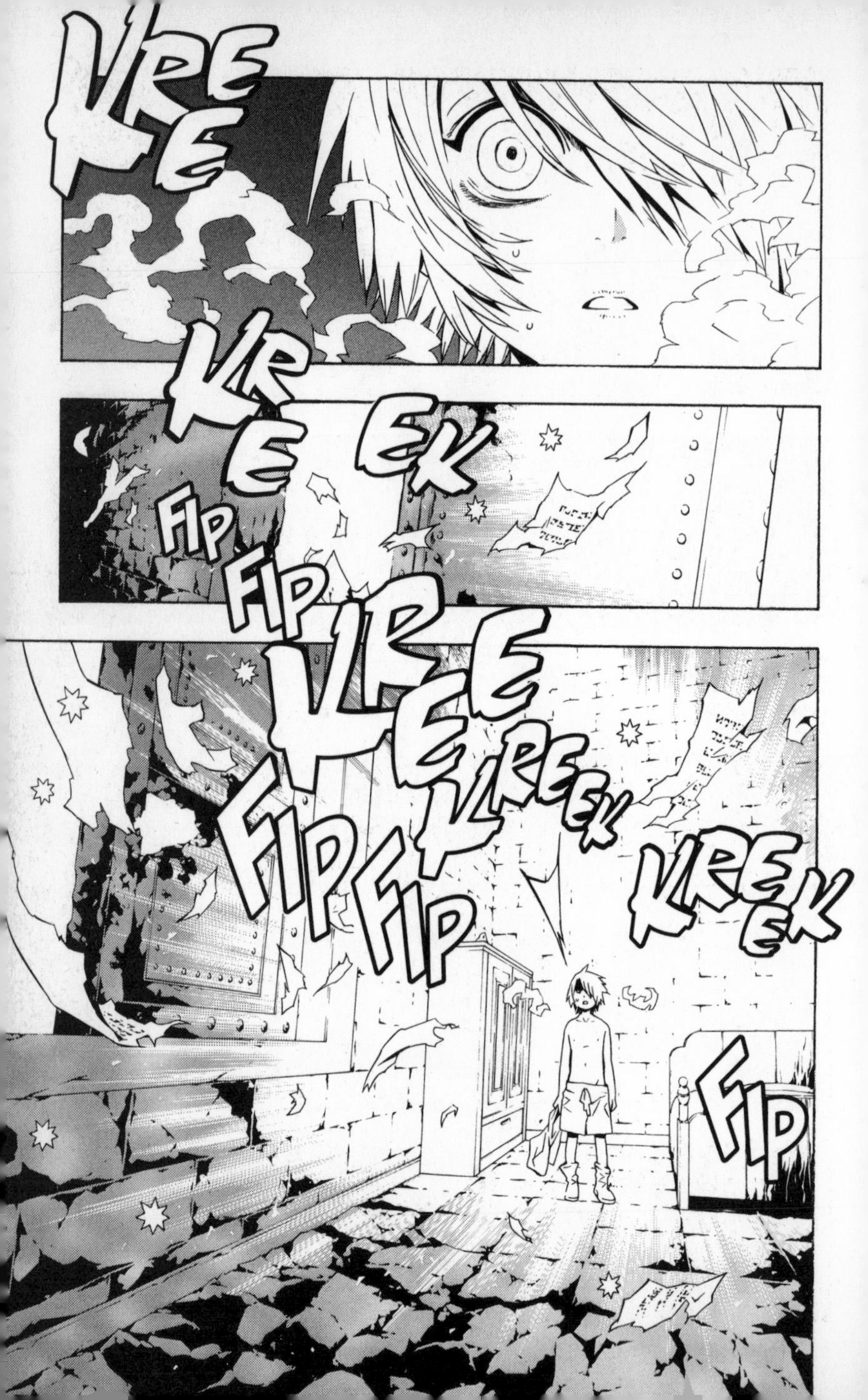

KREEE
KREEK
FLIP
FLIP
KREE
KREEK
KREEEK
FLIP
FLIP
FLIP

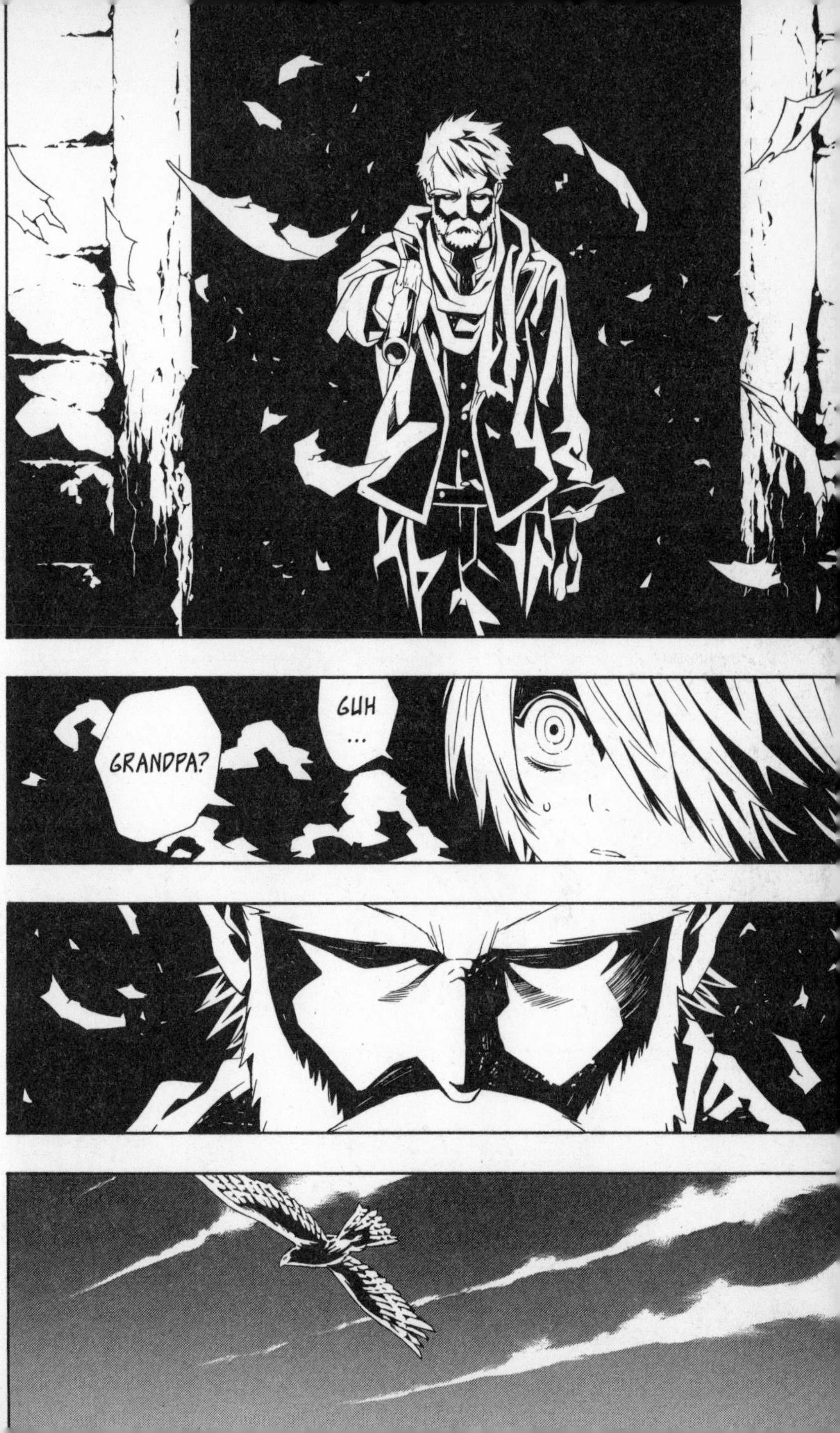
GUH ...
GRANDPA?

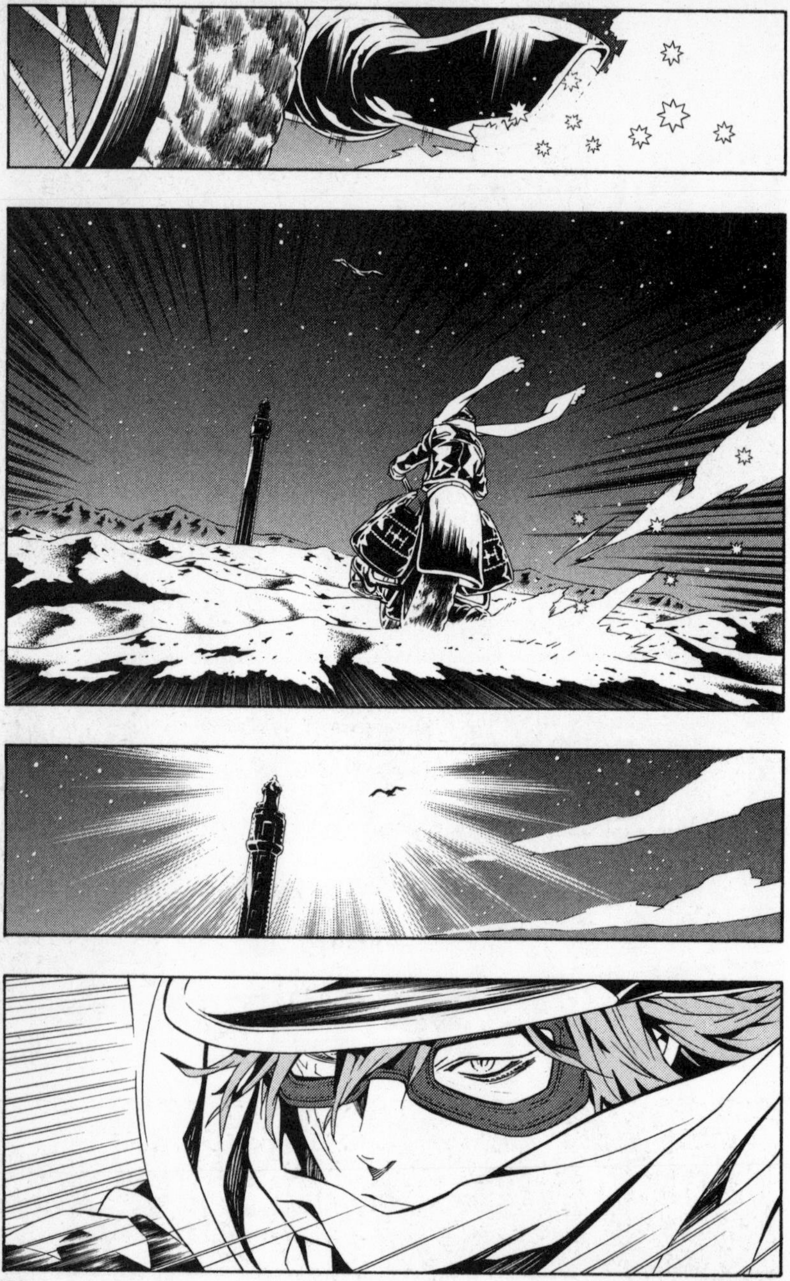

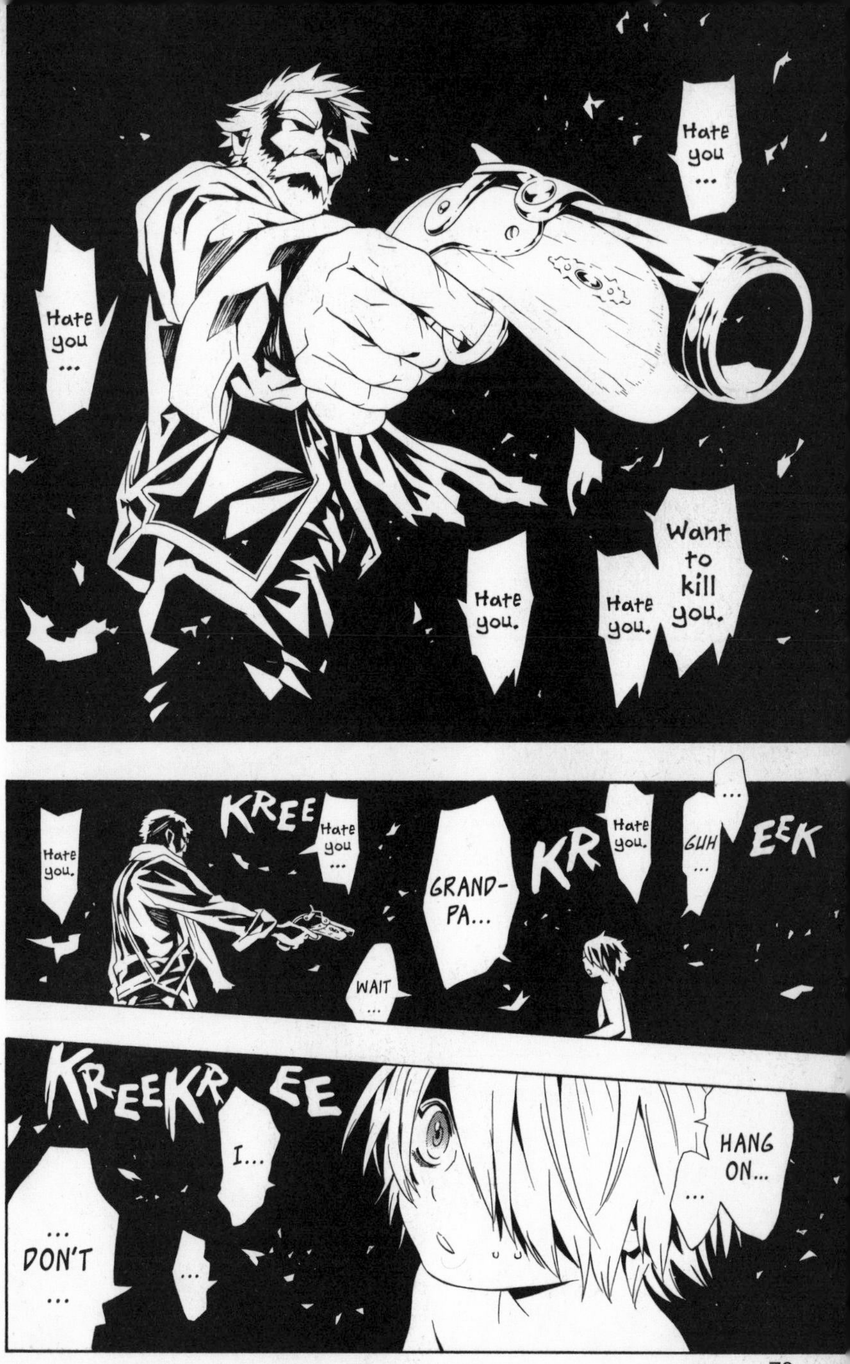
Hate you ...
Want to kill you.
Hate you.
Hate you.
Hate you ...
...
GUH ...
EEK
KR
Hate you.
GRAND-PA...
Hate you ...
KREE
WAIT ...
Hate you.
HANG ON... ...
I...
...
... DON'T ...
KREEKR EE

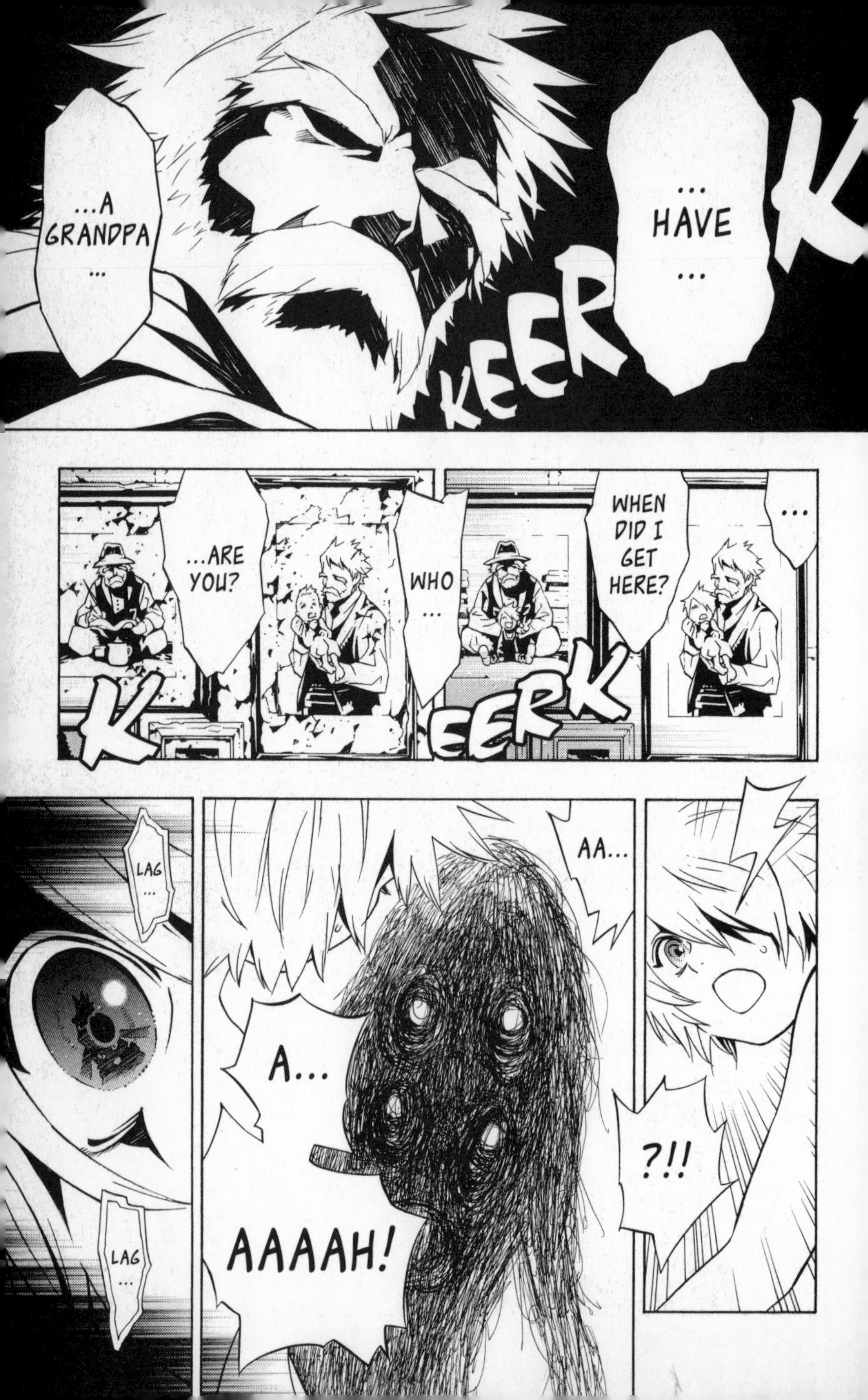

... HAVE ...
KEERK
...A GRANDPA ...
...
WHEN DID I GET HERE?
EERK
WHO ...
...ARE YOU?
K
?!!
AA...
A...
AAAAH!
LAG ...
LAG ...

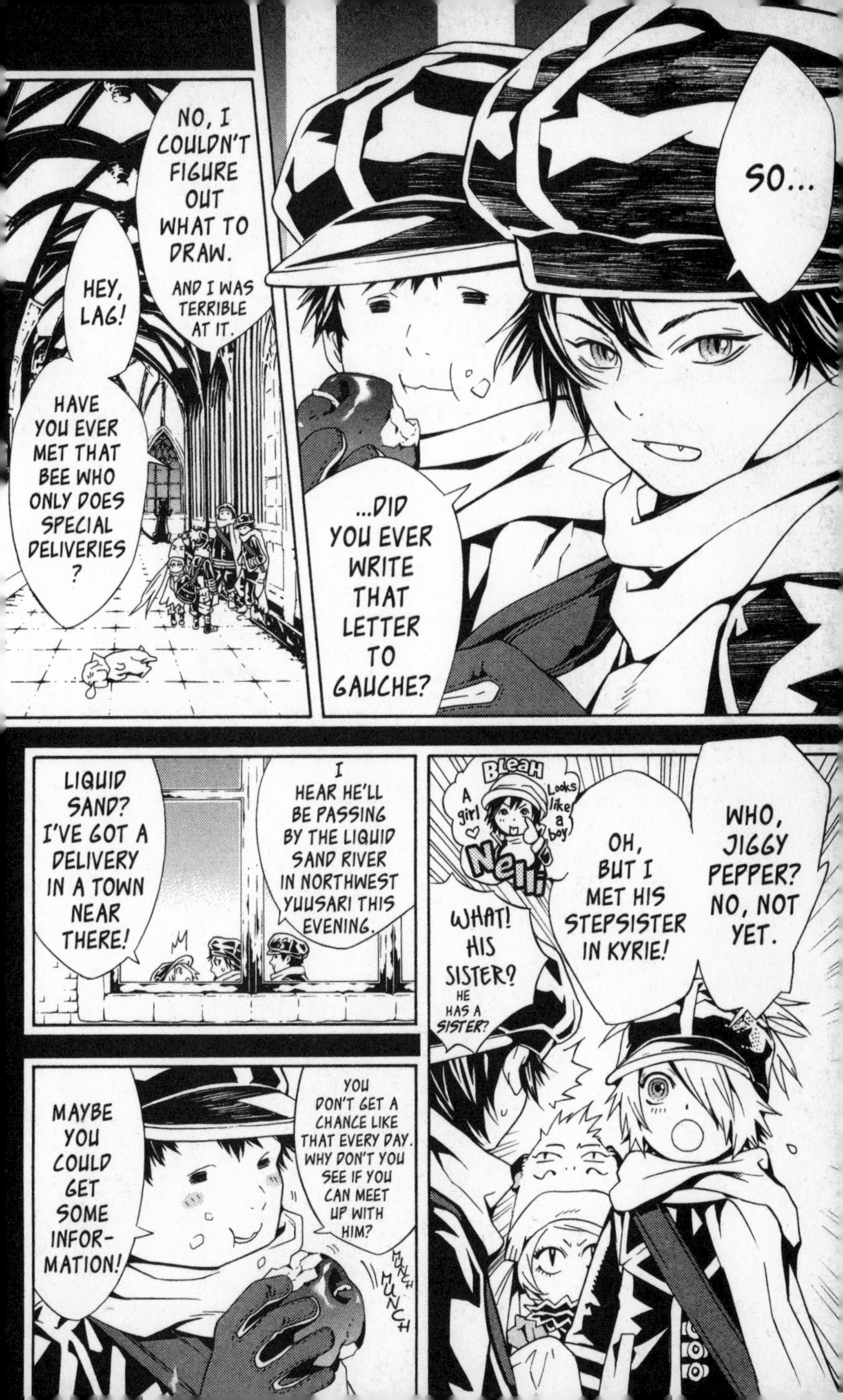
SO...
...DID YOU EVER WRITE THAT LETTER TO GAUCHE?
NO, I COULDN'T FIGURE OUT WHAT TO DRAW.
AND I WAS TERRIBLE AT IT.
HEY, LAG!
HAVE YOU EVER MET THAT BEE WHO ONLY DOES SPECIAL DELIVERIES?
WHO, JIGGY PEPPER? NO, NOT YET.
OH, BUT I MET HIS STEPSISTER IN KYRIE!
BLEAH
A girl
Looks like a boy
Nelli
WHAT! HIS SISTER?
HE HAS A SISTER?
I HEAR HE'LL BE PASSING BY THE LIQUID SAND RIVER IN NORTHWEST YUUSARI THIS EVENING.
LIQUID SAND? I'VE GOT A DELIVERY IN A TOWN NEAR THERE!
YOU DON'T GET A CHANCE LIKE THAT EVERY DAY. WHY DON'T YOU SEE IF YOU CAN MEET UP WITH HIM?
MAYBE YOU COULD GET SOME INFOR-MATION!
MUNCH MUNCH

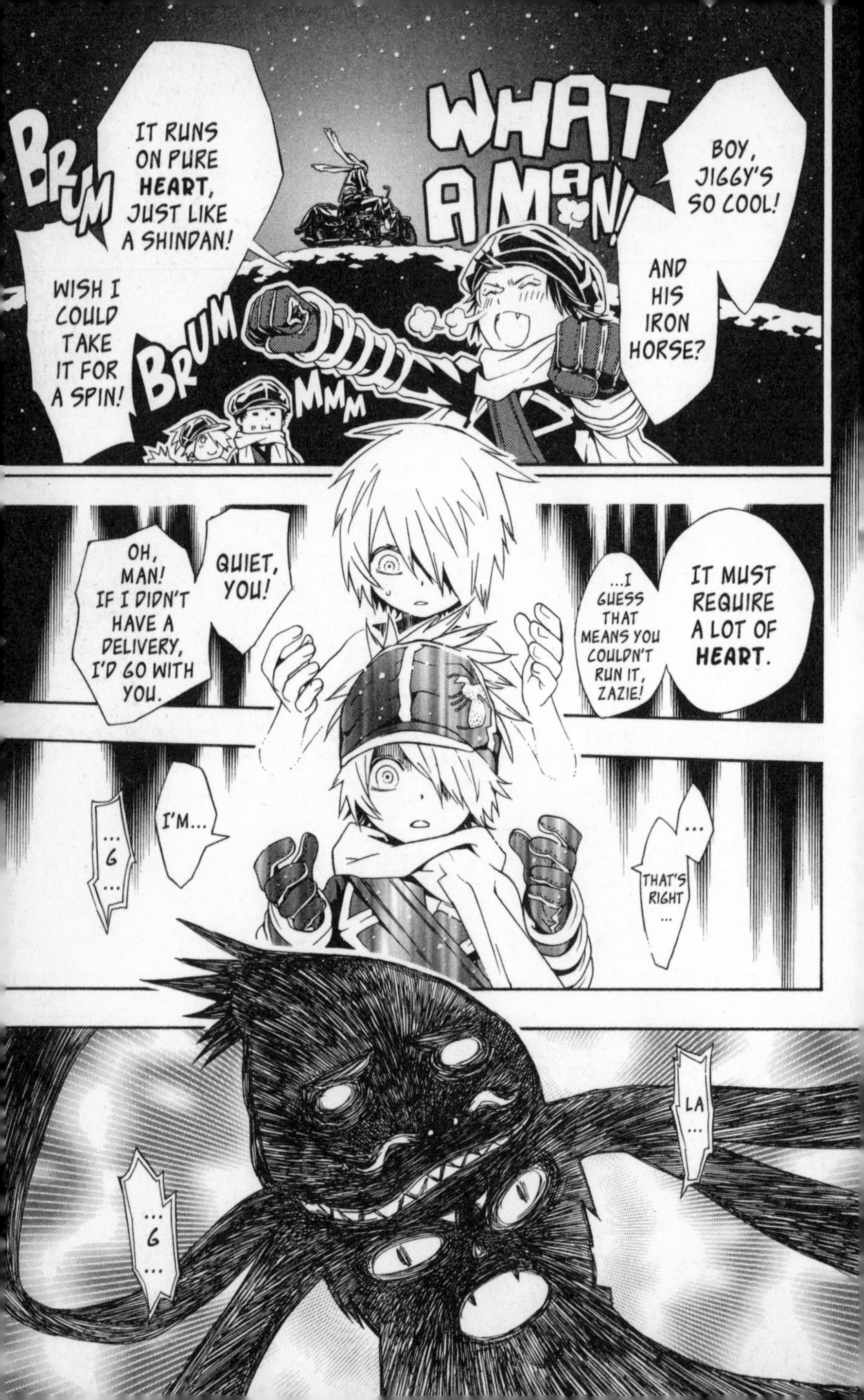
BOY, JIGGY'S SO COOL!
AND HIS IRON HORSE?
WHAT A MAN!!
IT RUNS ON PURE **HEART**, JUST LIKE A SHINDAN!
BRUM
WISH I COULD TAKE IT FOR A SPIN!
BRUM
BRUMMMM
IT MUST REQUIRE A LOT OF **HEART**.
...I GUESS THAT MEANS YOU COULDN'T RUN IT, ZAZIE!
QUIET, YOU!
OH, MAN! IF I DIDN'T HAVE A DELIVERY, I'D GO WITH YOU.
... THAT'S RIGHT ...
I'M...
...G...
LA...
...G...

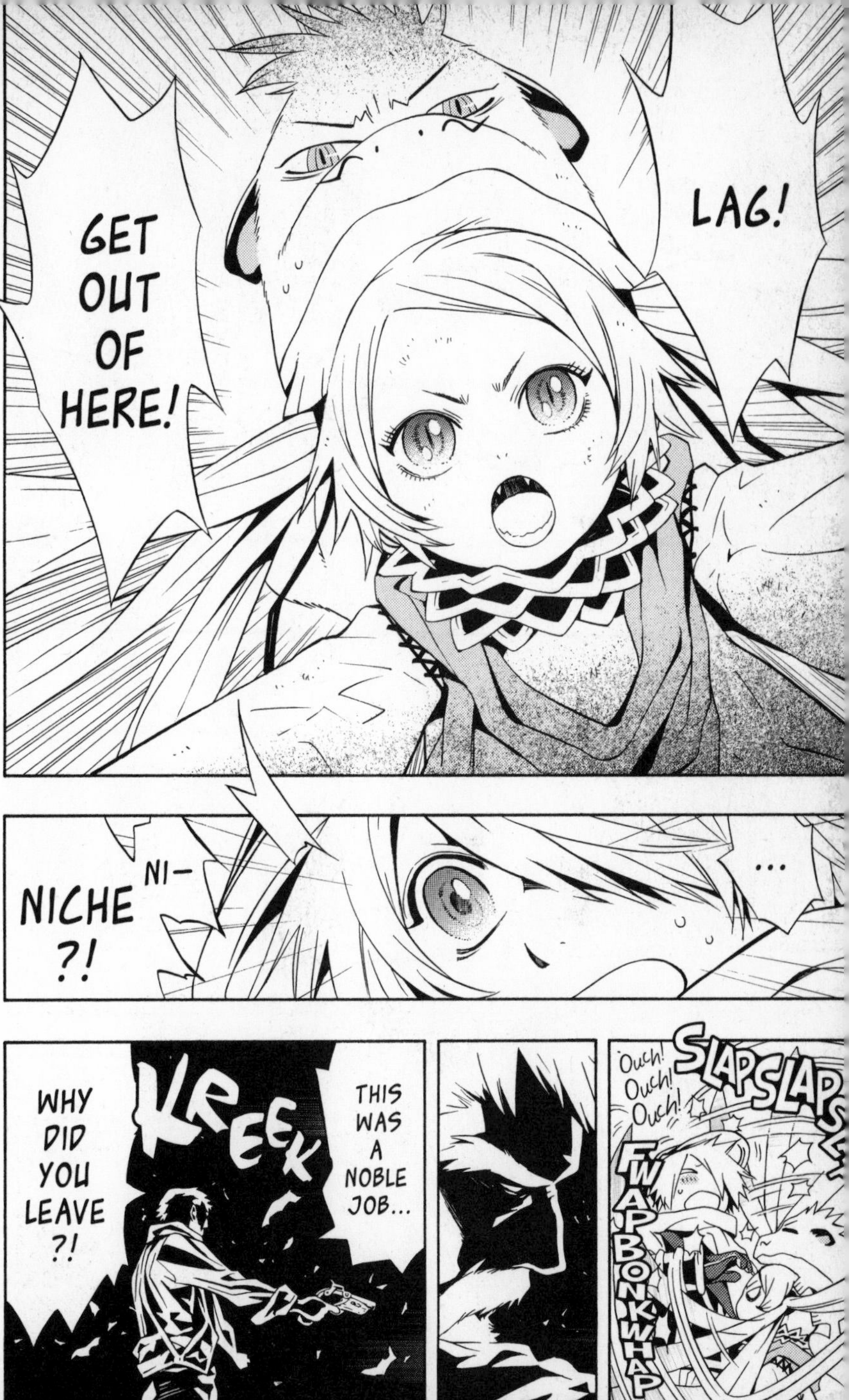
LAG!
GET OUT OF HERE!
...
NI— NICHE ?!
Ouch! Ouch! Ouch!
SLAPSLAPS
FWAPBONKWHAP
THIS WAS A NOBLE JOB...
KREEK
WHY DID YOU LEAVE ?!

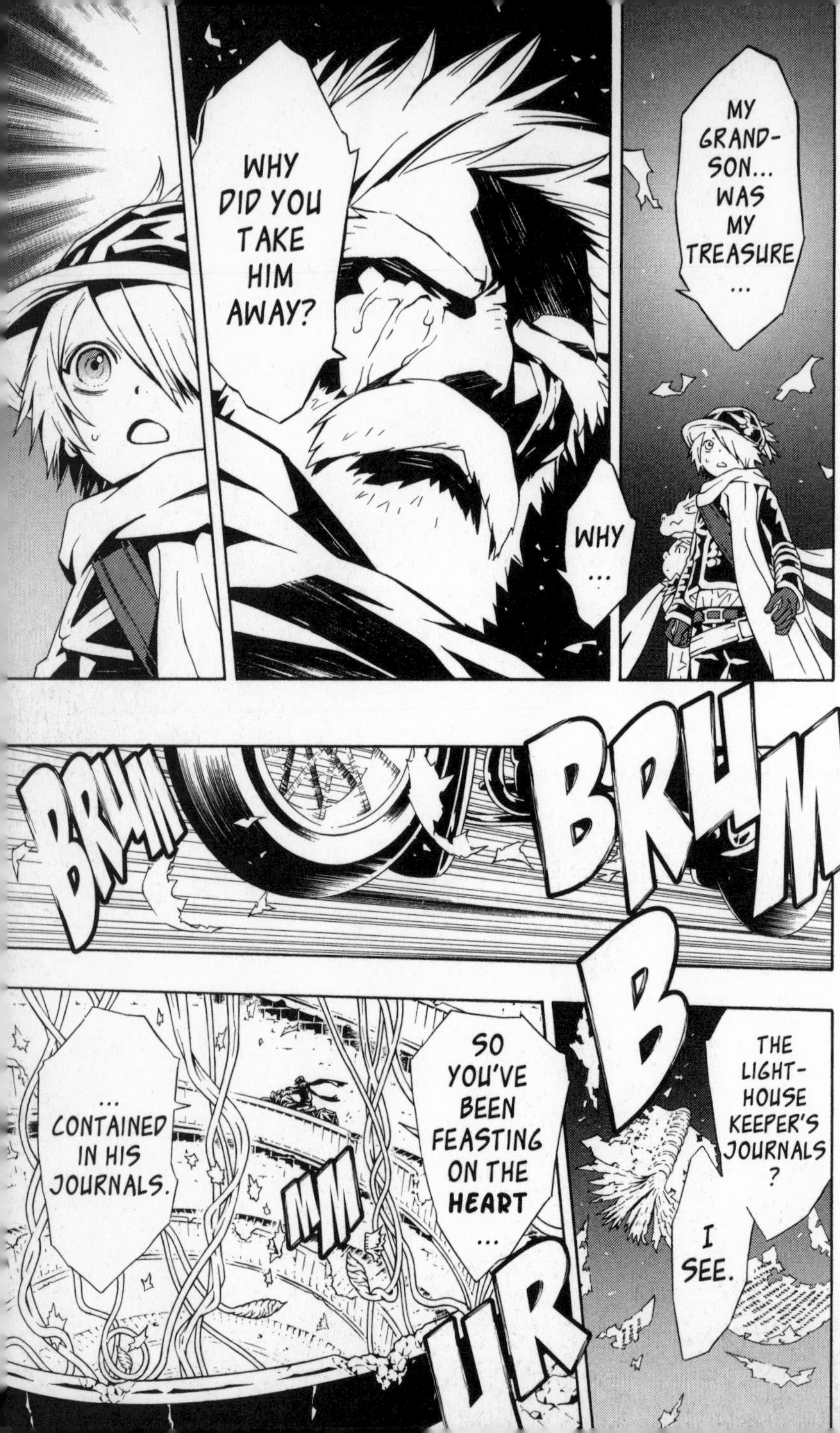
MY GRAND-SON... WAS MY TREASURE ...
WHY ...
WHY DID YOU TAKE HIM AWAY?
BRUM
BRUM
B
THE LIGHT-HOUSE KEEPER'S JOURNALS ?
I SEE.
UR
SO YOU'VE BEEN FEASTING ON THE HEART ...
MM
... CONTAINED IN HIS JOURNALS.

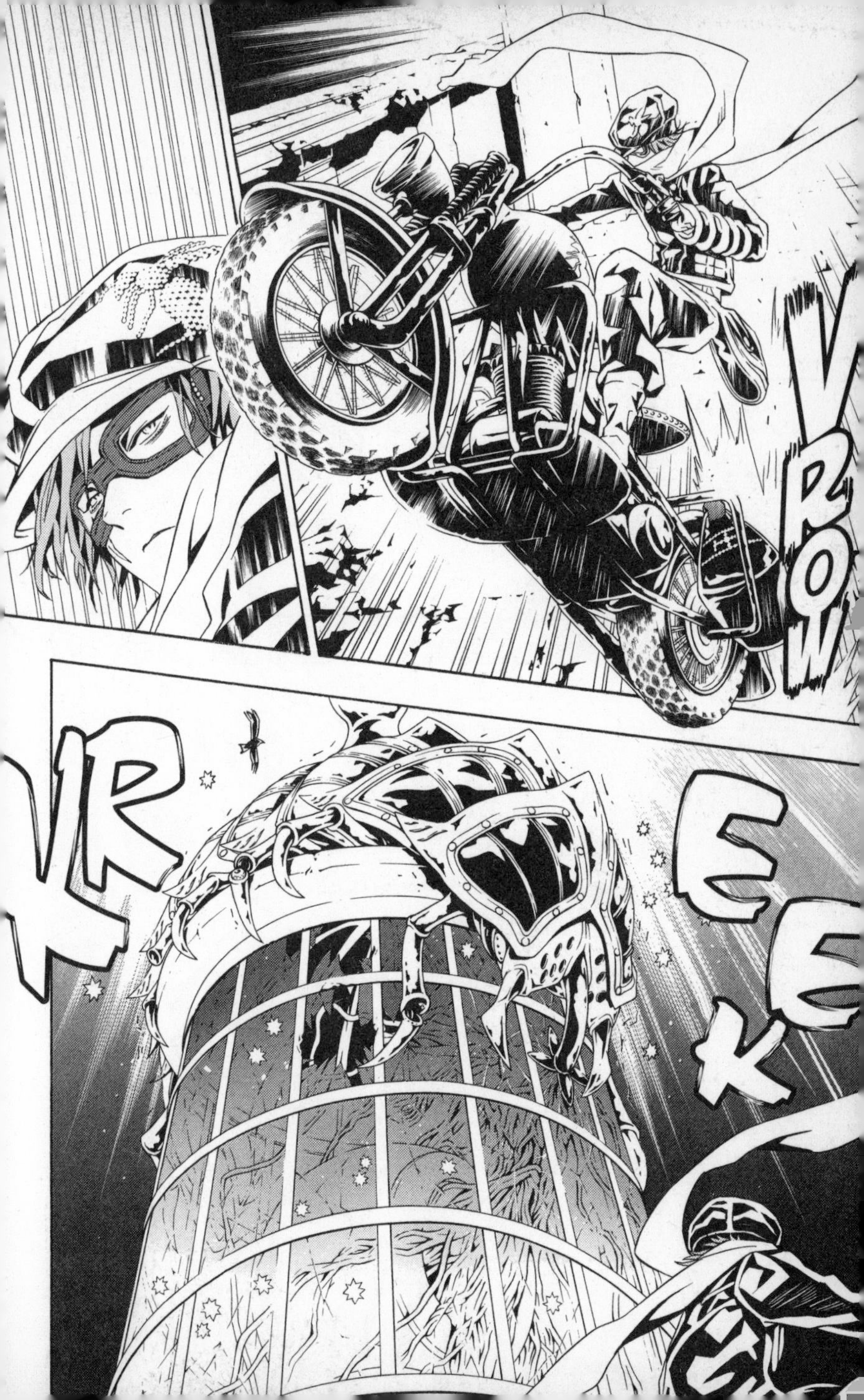
VROW
R
EEK

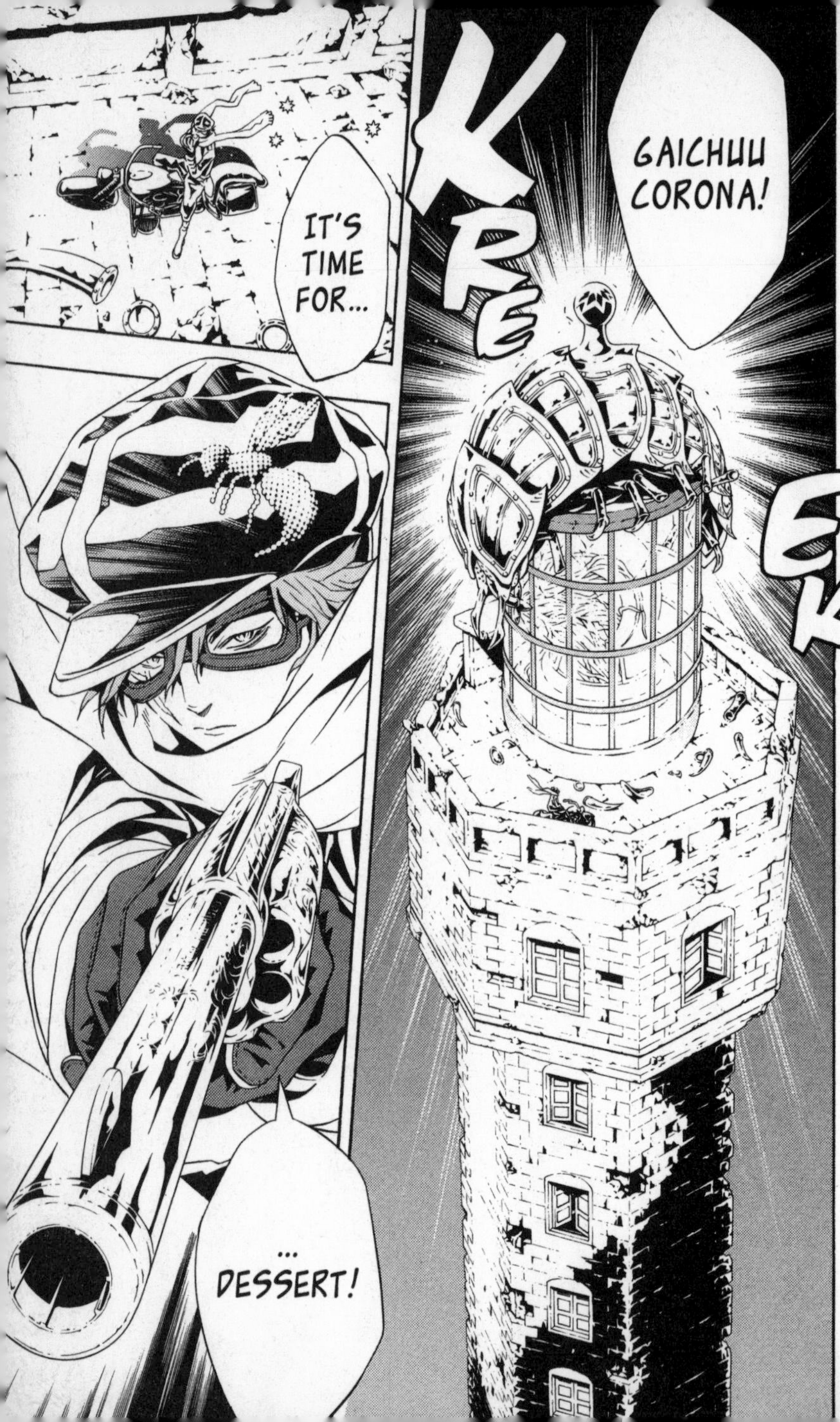
GAICHUU CORONA!
KREEK
IT'S TIME FOR...
...DESSERT!

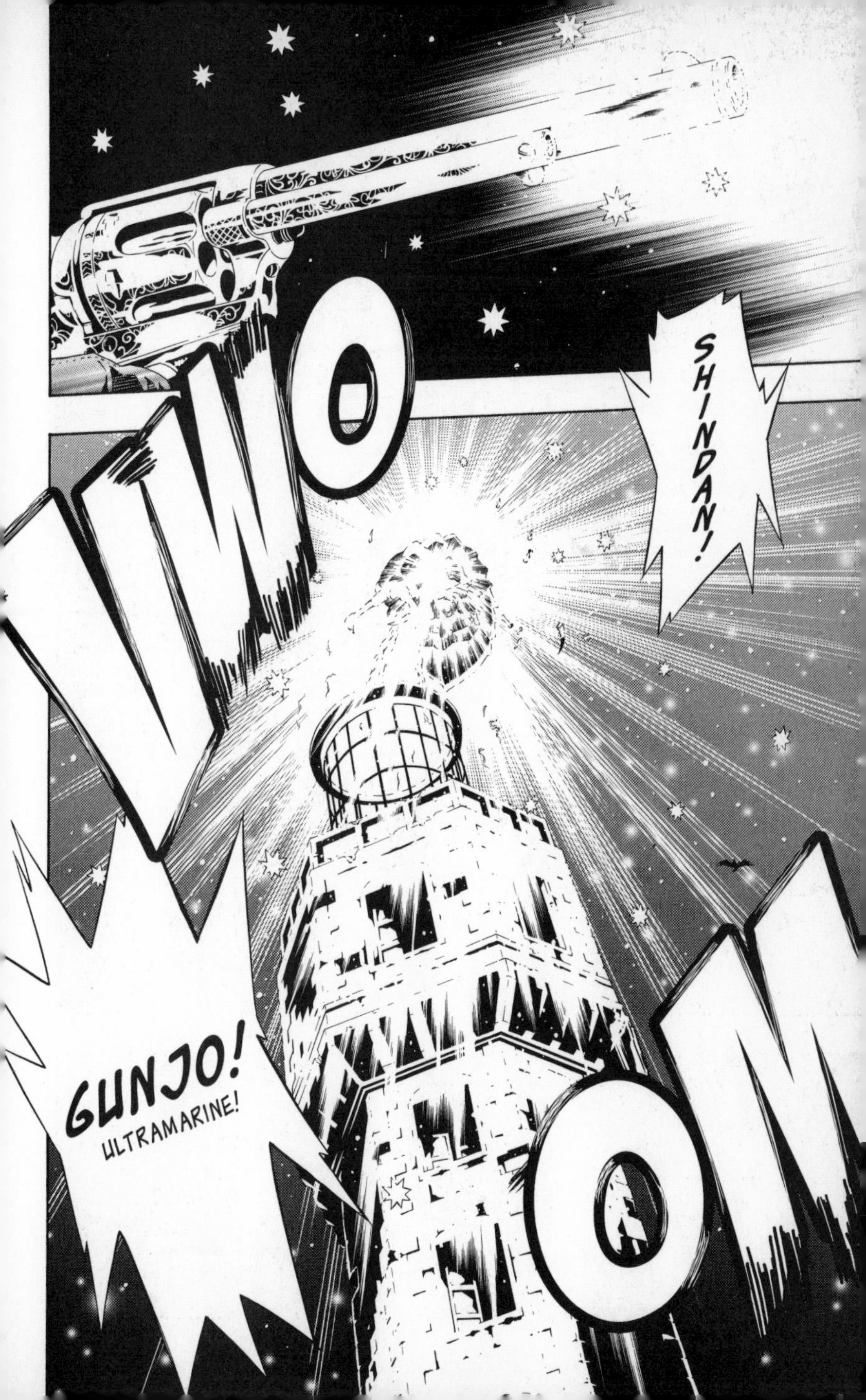
SHINDAN!
GUNJO!
ULTRAMARINE!

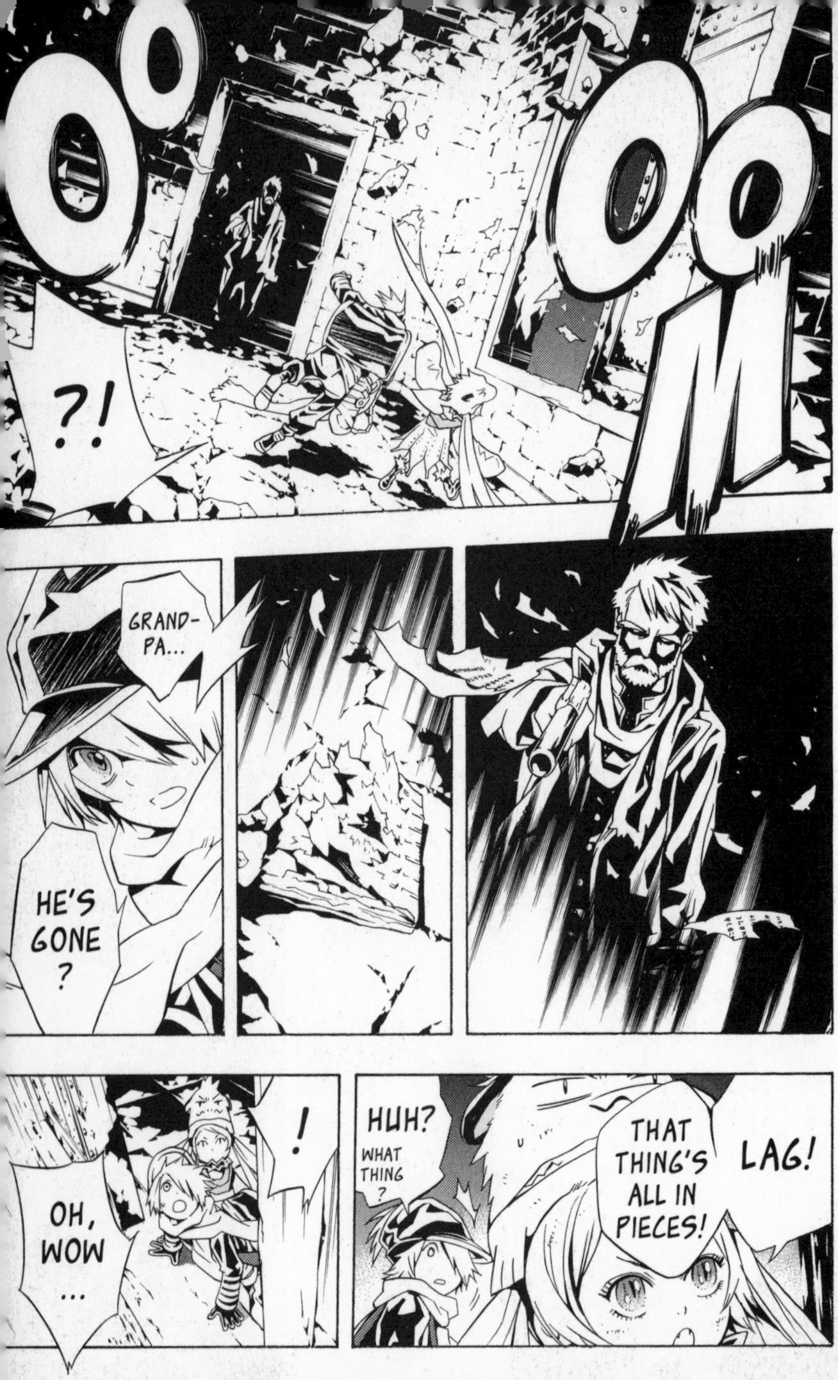
OOOOM
?!
GRAND-PA...
HE'S GONE?
LAG!
THAT THING'S ALL IN PIECES!
HUH?
WHAT THING?
!
OH, WOW ...

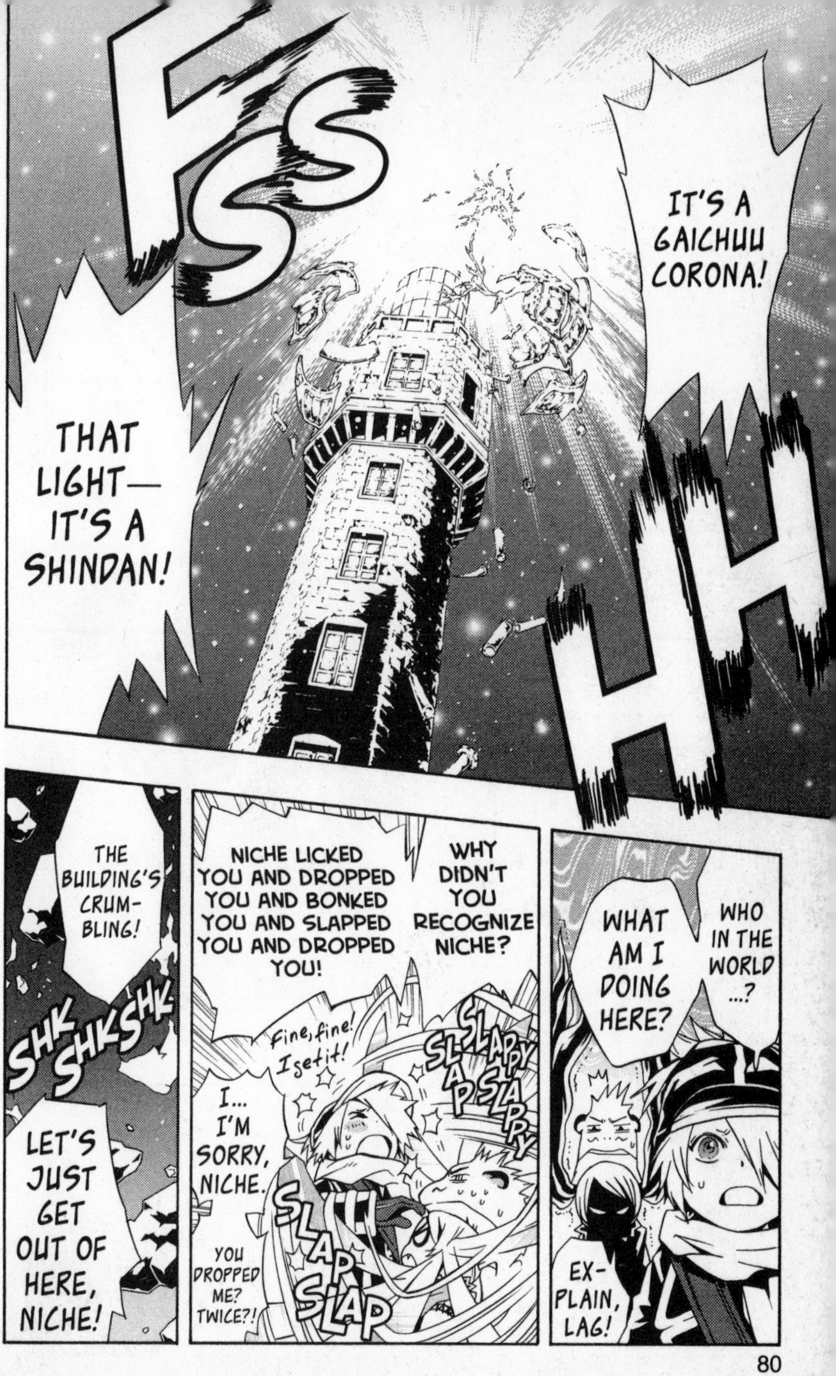
FSS
IT'S A GAICHUU CORONA!
HH
THAT LIGHT— IT'S A SHINDAN!
WHO IN THE WORLD ...?
WHAT AM I DOING HERE?
EX-PLAIN, LAG!
WHY DIDN'T YOU RECOGNIZE NICHE?
NICHE LICKED YOU AND DROPPED YOU AND BONKED YOU AND SLAPPED YOU AND DROPPED YOU!
Fine, fine! I get it!
SLAPPY SLAPPY
SLAP SLAPPY
I... I'M SORRY, NICHE.
SLAP SLAP SLAP
YOU DROPPED ME? TWICE?!
THE BUILDING'S CRUM-BLING!
SHK SHKSHK
LET'S JUST GET OUT OF HERE, NICHE!

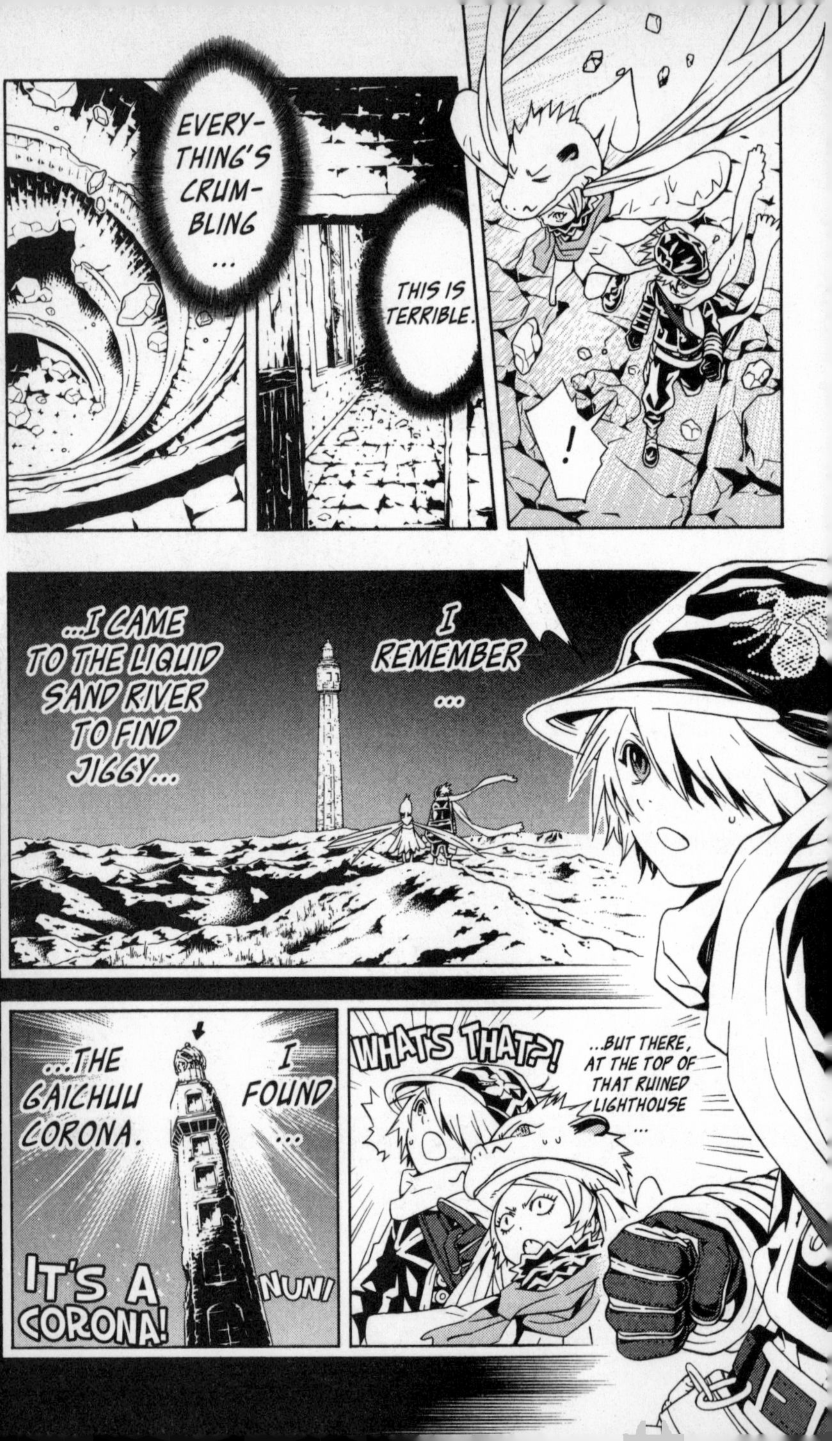
!
THIS IS TERRIBLE.
EVERY-THING'S CRUM-BLING ...
I REMEMBER ...
...I CAME TO THE LIQUID SAND RIVER TO FIND JIGGY...
...BUT THERE, AT THE TOP OF THAT RUINED LIGHTHOUSE ...
WHAT'S THAT?!
I FOUND ...
...THE GAICHUU CORONA.
NUNI
IT'S A CORONA!

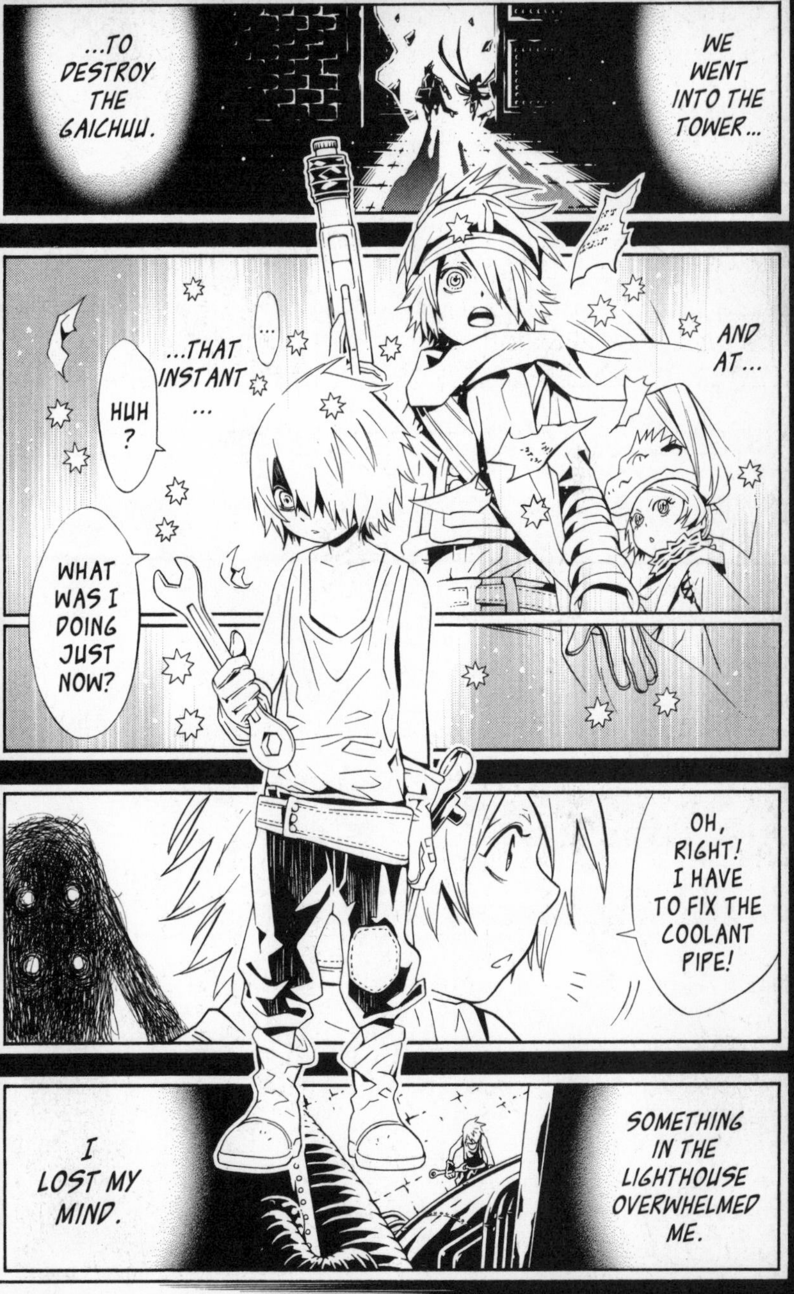
WE WENT INTO THE TOWER...
...TO DESTROY THE GAICHUU.
AND AT...
...
...THAT INSTANT ...
HUH?
WHAT WAS I DOING JUST NOW?
OH, RIGHT! I HAVE TO FIX THE COOLANT PIPE!
SOMETHING IN THE LIGHTHOUSE OVERWHELMED ME.
I LOST MY MIND.

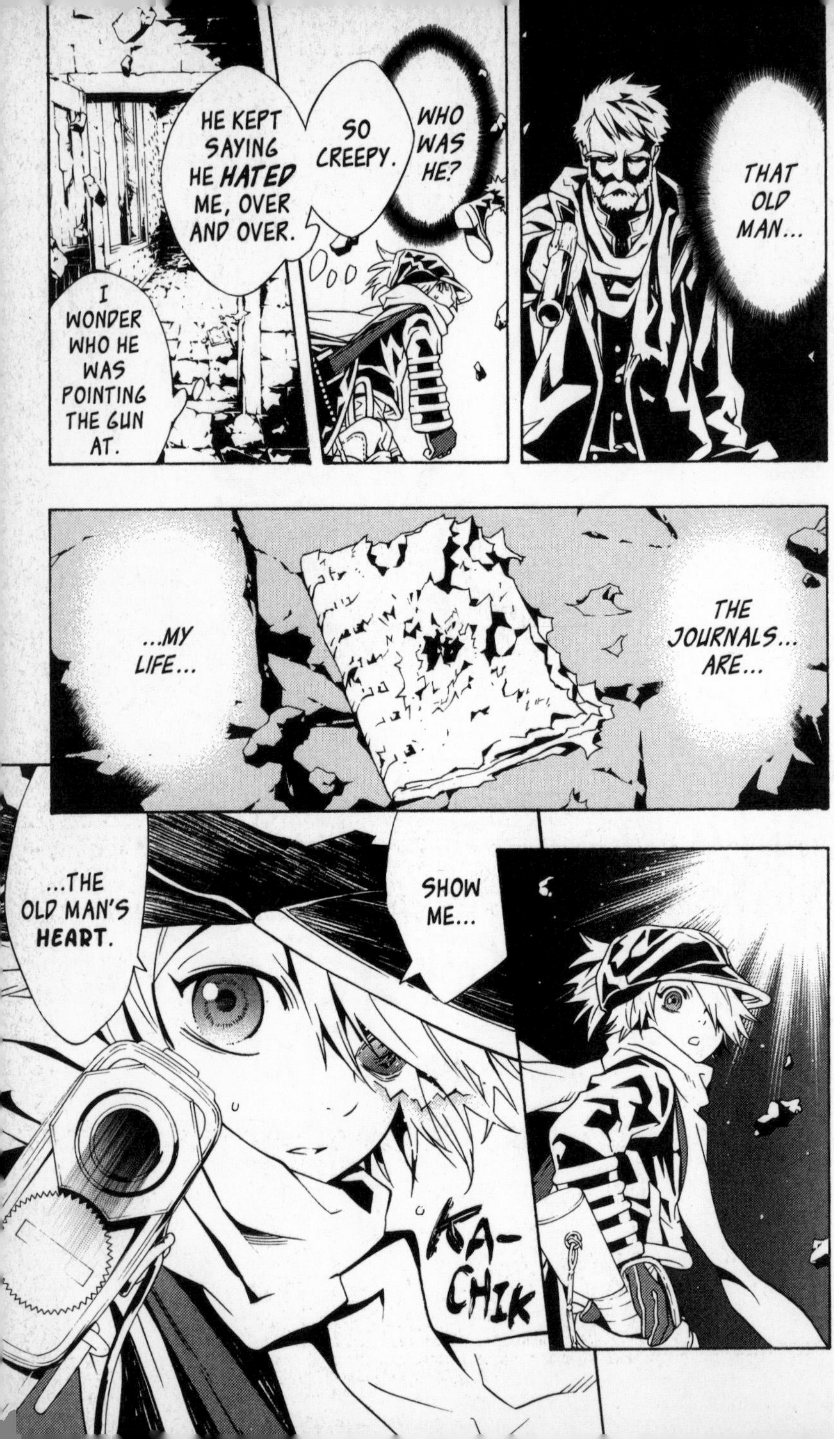
THAT OLD MAN...
WHO WAS HE?
SO CREEPY.
HE KEPT SAYING HE **HATED** ME, OVER AND OVER.
I WONDER WHO HE WAS POINTING THE GUN AT.
THE JOURNALS... ARE...
...MY LIFE...
SHOW ME...
...THE OLD MAN'S **HEART**.
KA-CHIK

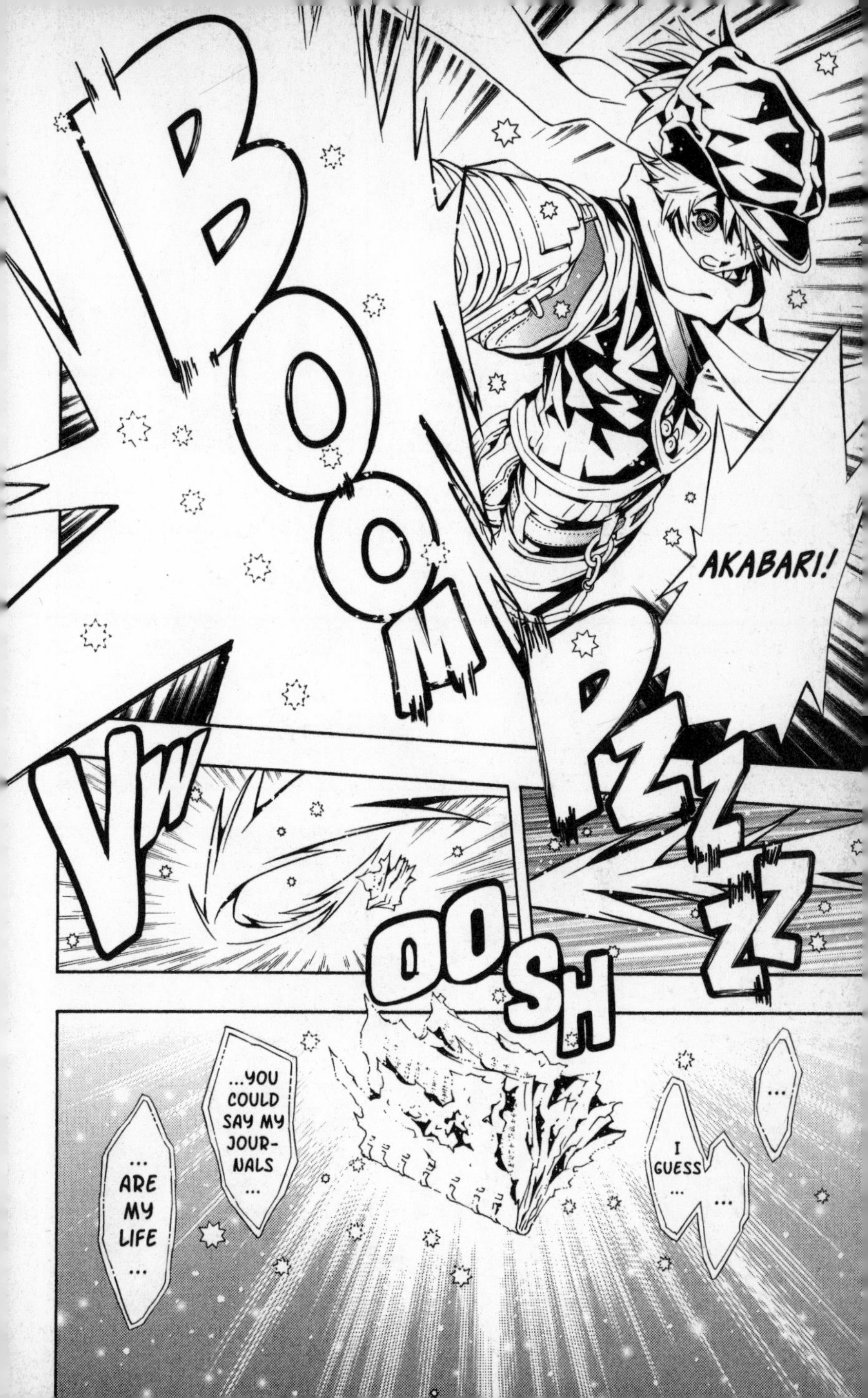
AKABARI!
BOOM
PZZZZ
VWOOSH
...
I GUESS ... ...
...YOU COULD SAY MY JOUR-NALS ...
... ARE MY LIFE ...

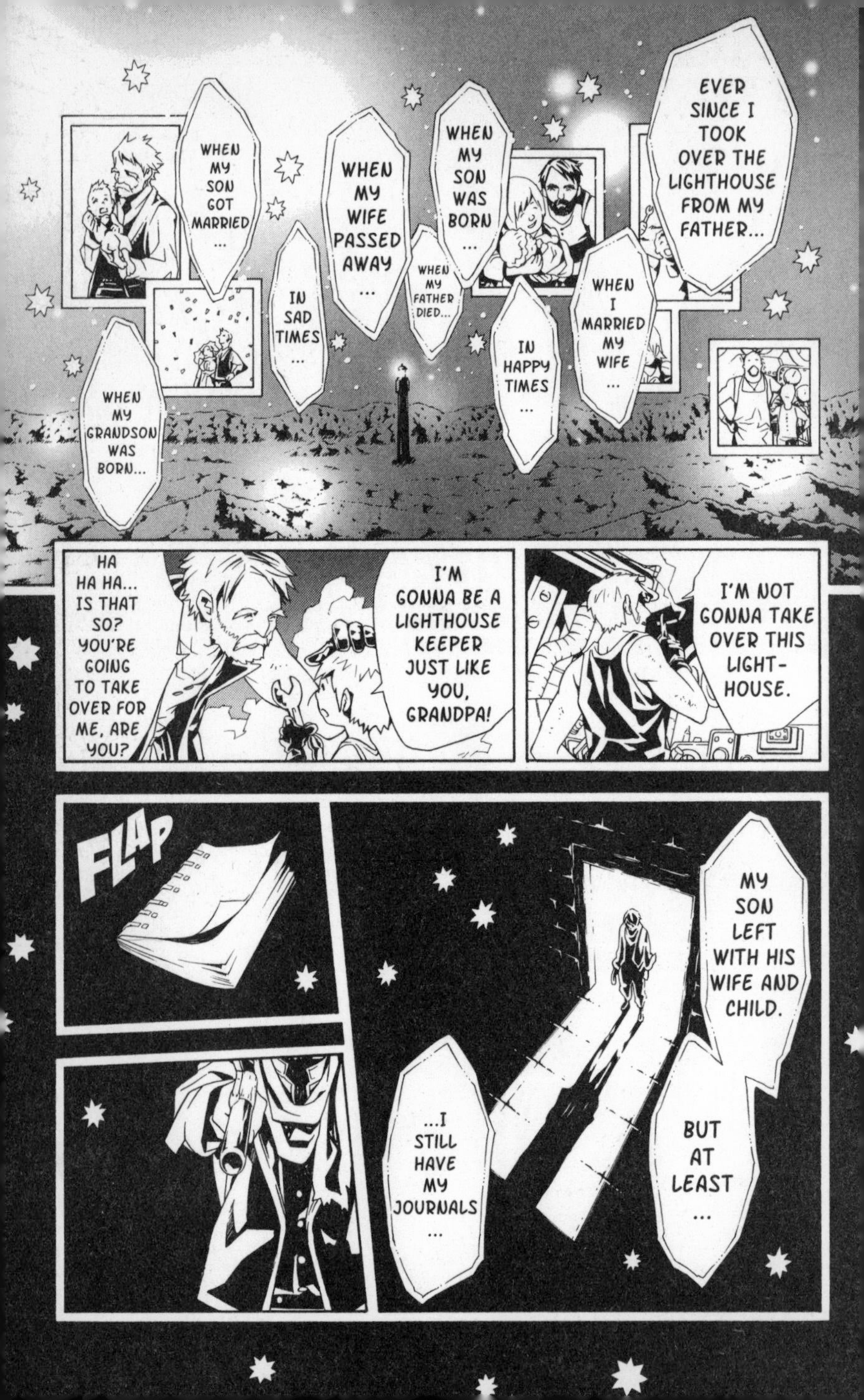
EVER SINCE I TOOK OVER THE LIGHTHOUSE FROM MY FATHER...
WHEN I MARRIED MY WIFE...
WHEN MY SON WAS BORN...
IN HAPPY TIMES...
WHEN MY FATHER DIED...
WHEN MY WIFE PASSED AWAY...
IN SAD TIMES...
WHEN MY SON GOT MARRIED...
WHEN MY GRANDSON WAS BORN...
I'M NOT GONNA TAKE OVER THIS LIGHT-HOUSE.
I'M GONNA BE A LIGHTHOUSE KEEPER JUST LIKE YOU, GRANDPA!
HA HA HA... IS THAT SO? YOU'RE GOING TO TAKE OVER FOR ME, ARE YOU?
MY SON LEFT WITH HIS WIFE AND CHILD.
BUT AT LEAST...
...I STILL HAVE MY JOURNALS...
FLAP

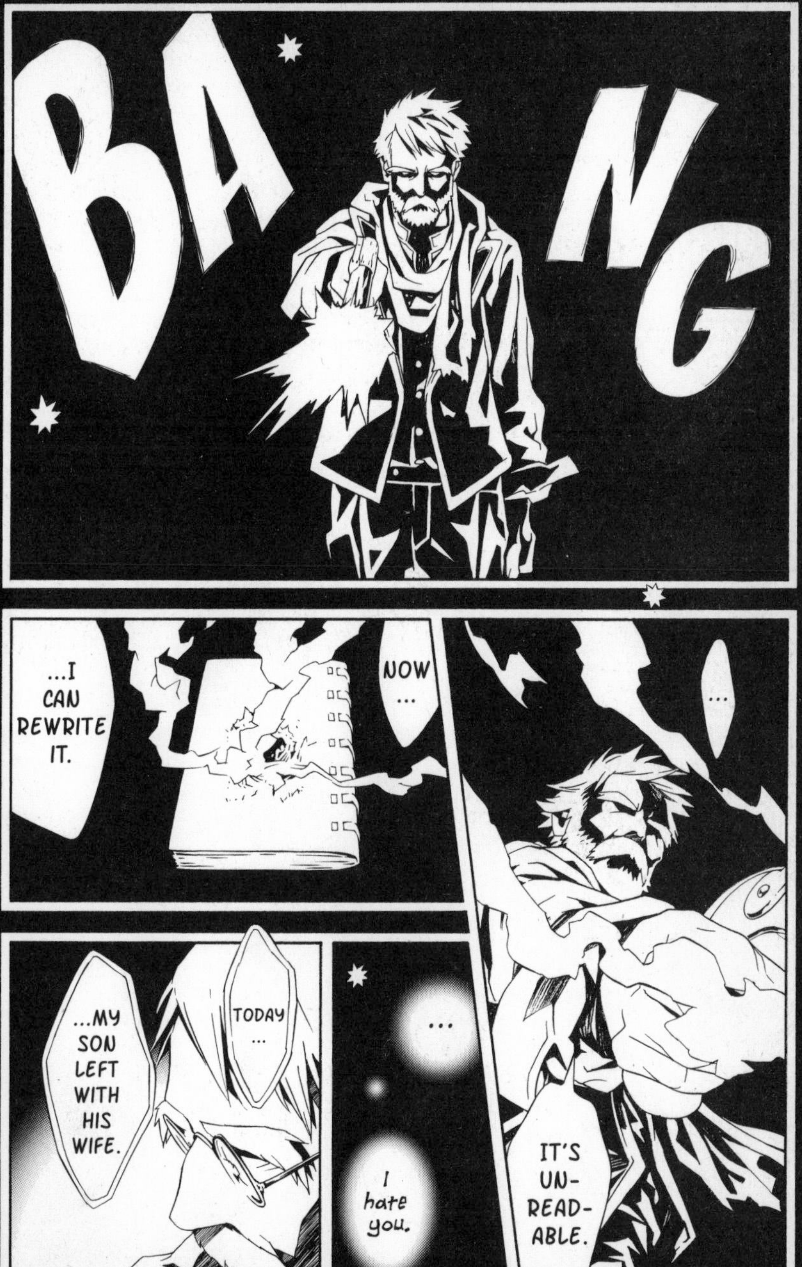
BANG
...
IT'S UN-READ-ABLE.
NOW ...
...I CAN REWRITE IT.
...
I hate you.
TODAY ...
...MY SON LEFT WITH HIS WIFE.

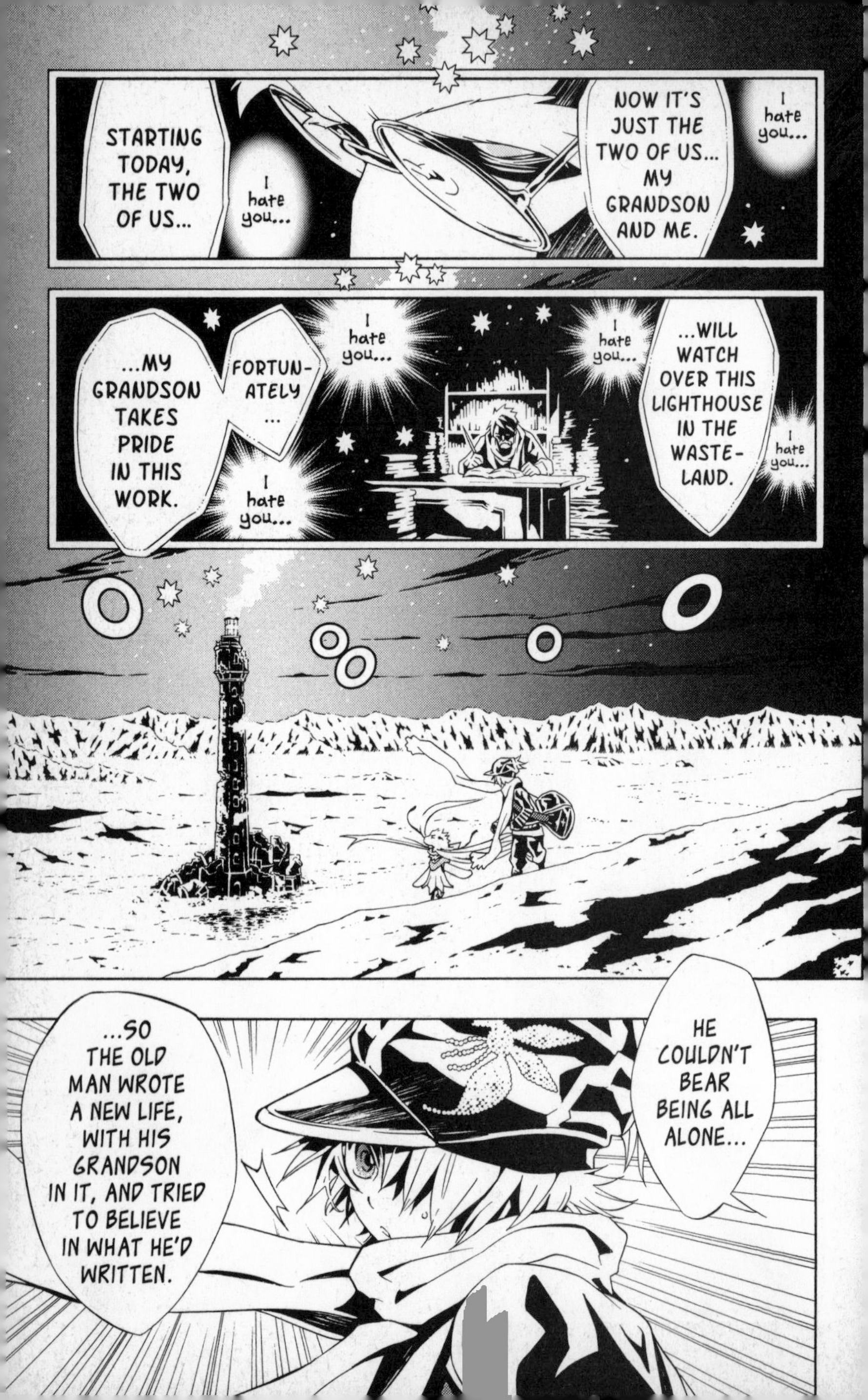
I hate you...
NOW IT'S JUST THE TWO OF US... MY GRANDSON AND ME.
I hate you...
STARTING TODAY, THE TWO OF US...
I hate you...
...WILL WATCH OVER THIS LIGHTHOUSE IN THE WASTE-LAND.
I hate you...
I hate you...
FORTUN-ATELY...
...MY GRANDSON TAKES PRIDE IN THIS WORK.
I hate you...
HE COULDN'T BEAR BEING ALL ALONE...
...SO THE OLD MAN WROTE A NEW LIFE, WITH HIS GRANDSON IN IT, AND TRIED TO BELIEVE IN WHAT HE'D WRITTEN.

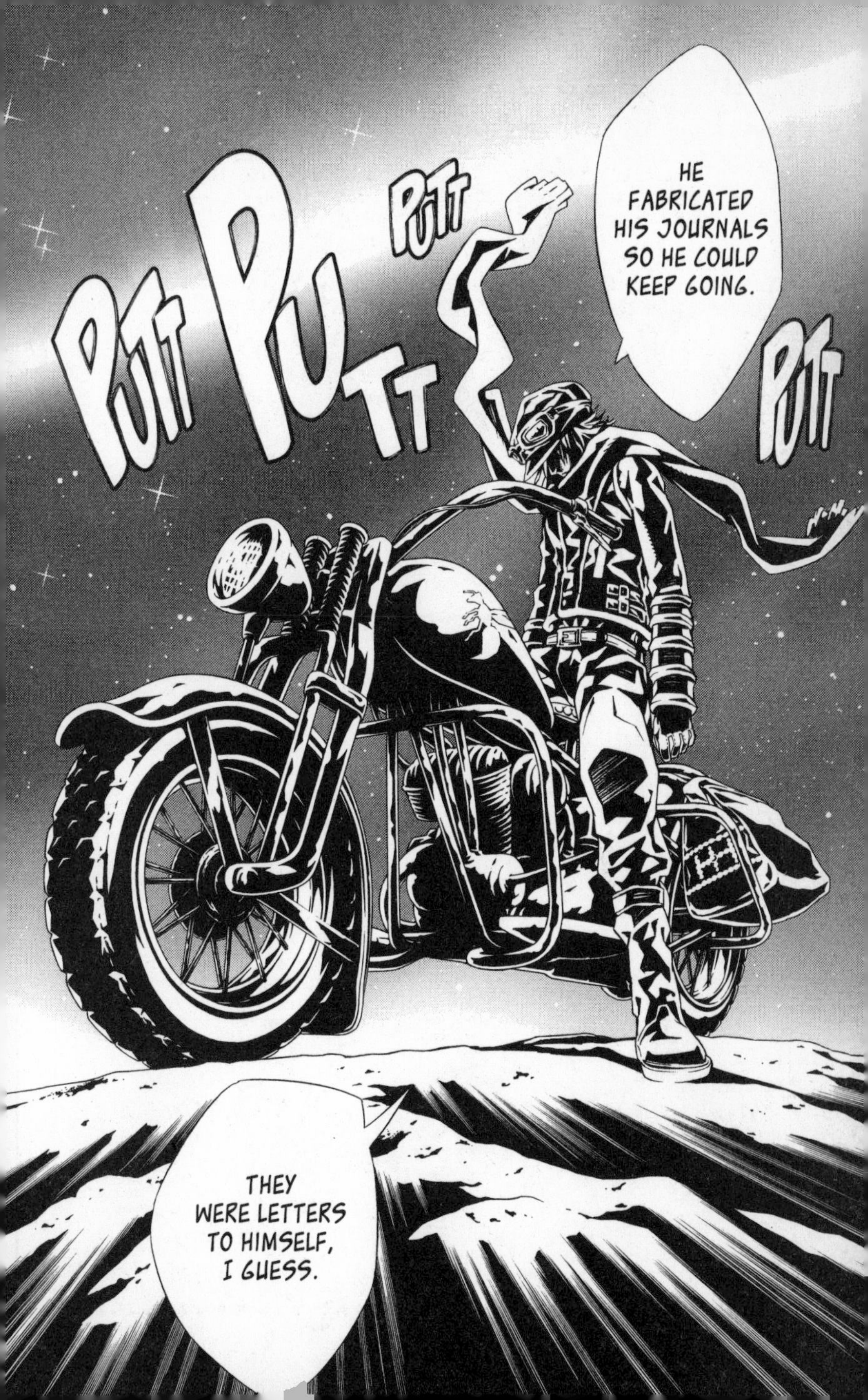
PUTT PUTT
PUTT PUTT
HE FABRICATED HIS JOURNALS SO HE COULD KEEP GOING.
PUTT
THEY WERE LETTERS TO HIMSELF, I GUESS.

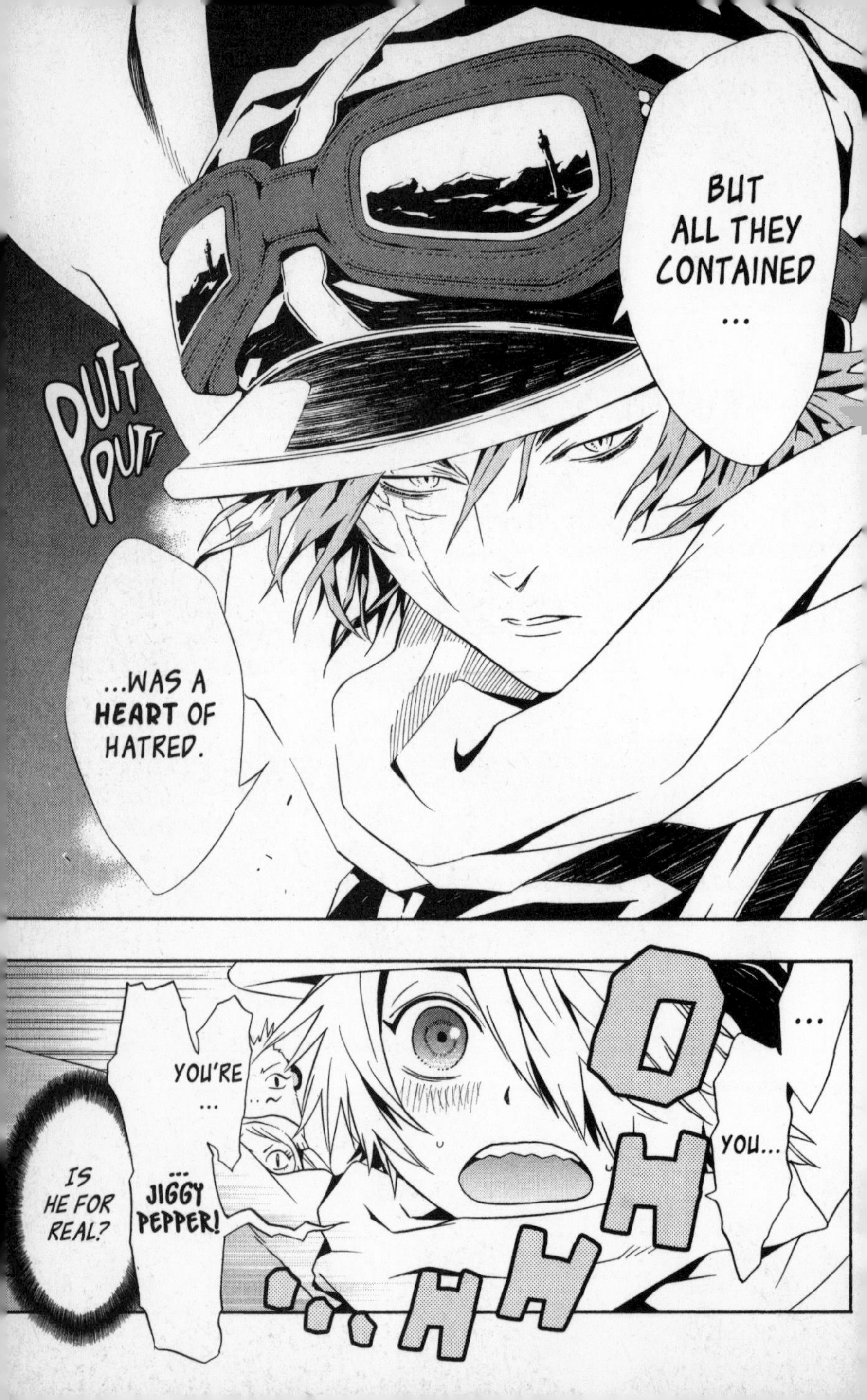
BUT ALL THEY CONTAINED ...
PUTT PUTT
...WAS A HEART OF HATRED.
...
OHHHH...
YOU...
YOU'RE ...
... JIGGY PEPPER!
IS HE FOR REAL?

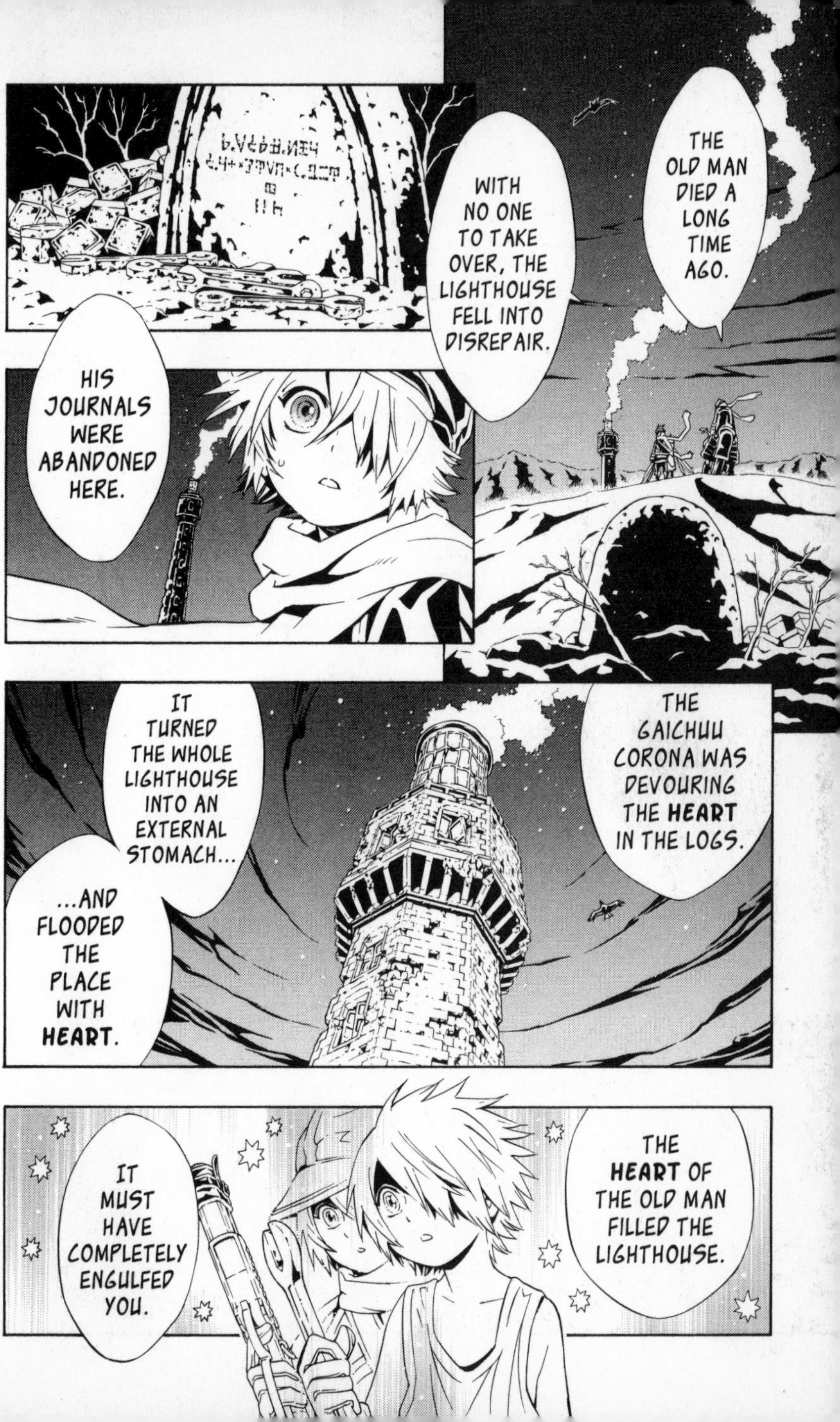
THE OLD MAN DIED A LONG TIME AGO.
WITH NO ONE TO TAKE OVER, THE LIGHTHOUSE FELL INTO DISREPAIR.
HIS JOURNALS WERE ABANDONED HERE.
THE GAICHUU CORONA WAS DEVOURING THE **HEART** IN THE LOGS.
IT TURNED THE WHOLE LIGHTHOUSE INTO AN EXTERNAL STOMACH...
...AND FLOODED THE PLACE WITH **HEART**.
THE **HEART** OF THE OLD MAN FILLED THE LIGHTHOUSE.
IT MUST HAVE COMPLETELY ENGULFED YOU.

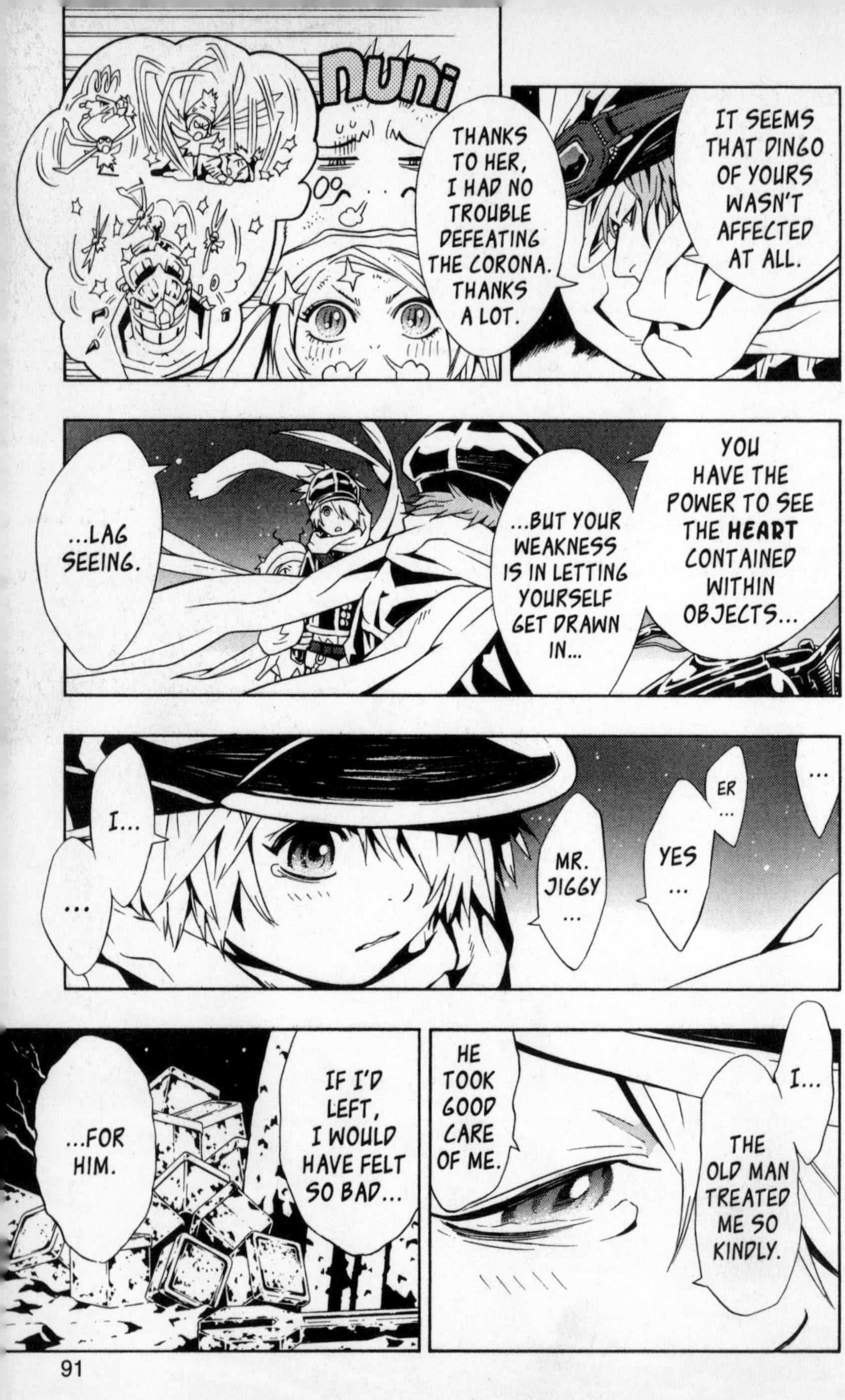
IT SEEMS THAT DINGO OF YOURS WASN'T AFFECTED AT ALL.
THANKS TO HER, I HAD NO TROUBLE DEFEATING THE CORONA. THANKS A LOT.
NUNI
YOU HAVE THE POWER TO SEE THE **HEART** CONTAINED WITHIN OBJECTS...
...BUT YOUR WEAKNESS IS IN LETTING YOURSELF GET DRAWN IN...
...LAG SEEING.
...
ER ...
YES ...
MR. JIGGY ...
I... ...
I...
THE OLD MAN TREATED ME SO KINDLY.
HE TOOK GOOD CARE OF ME.
IF I'D LEFT, I WOULD HAVE FELT SO BAD...
...FOR HIM.

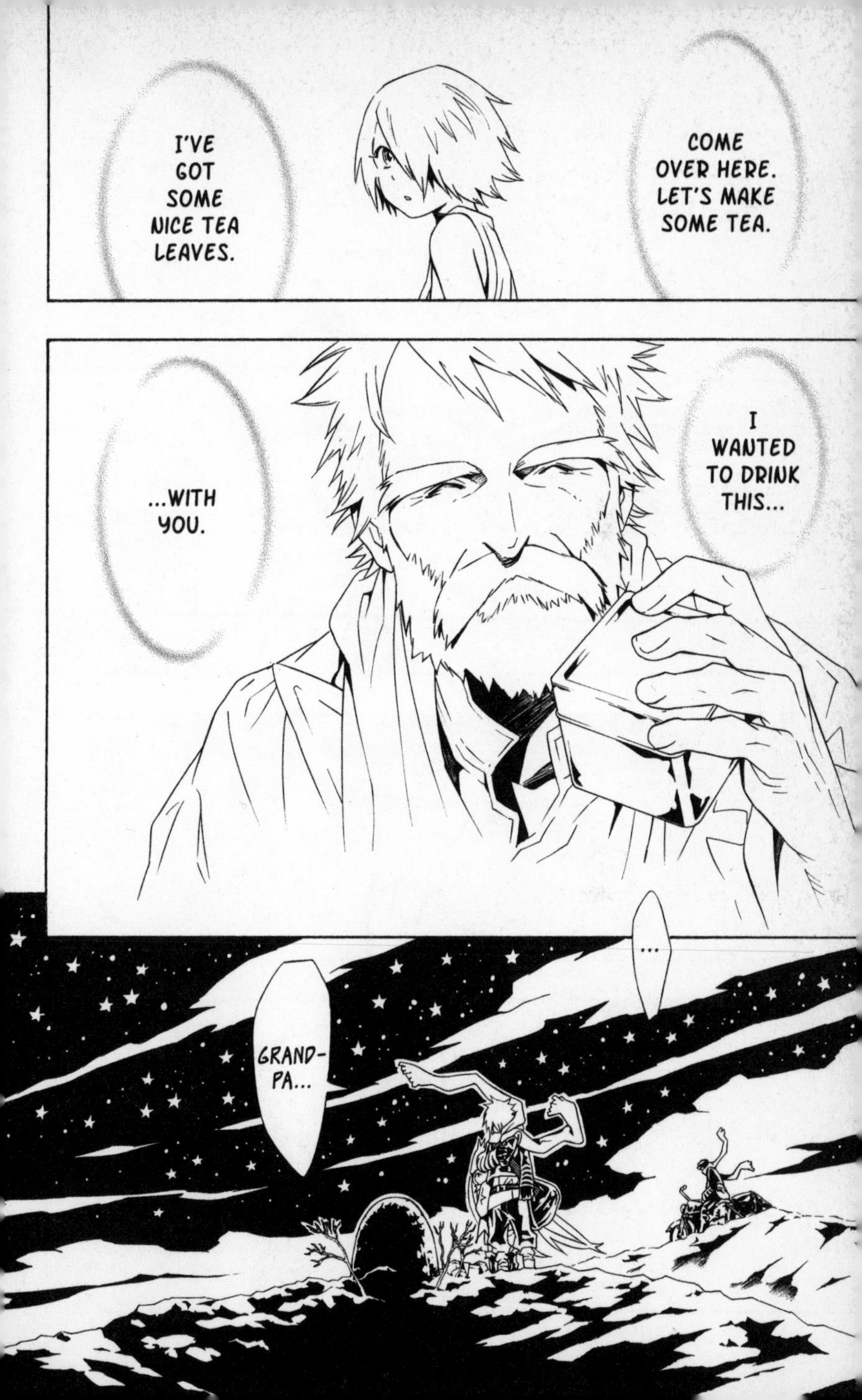
COME OVER HERE. LET'S MAKE SOME TEA.
I'VE GOT SOME NICE TEA LEAVES.
I WANTED TO DRINK THIS...
...WITH YOU.
...
GRAND-PA...

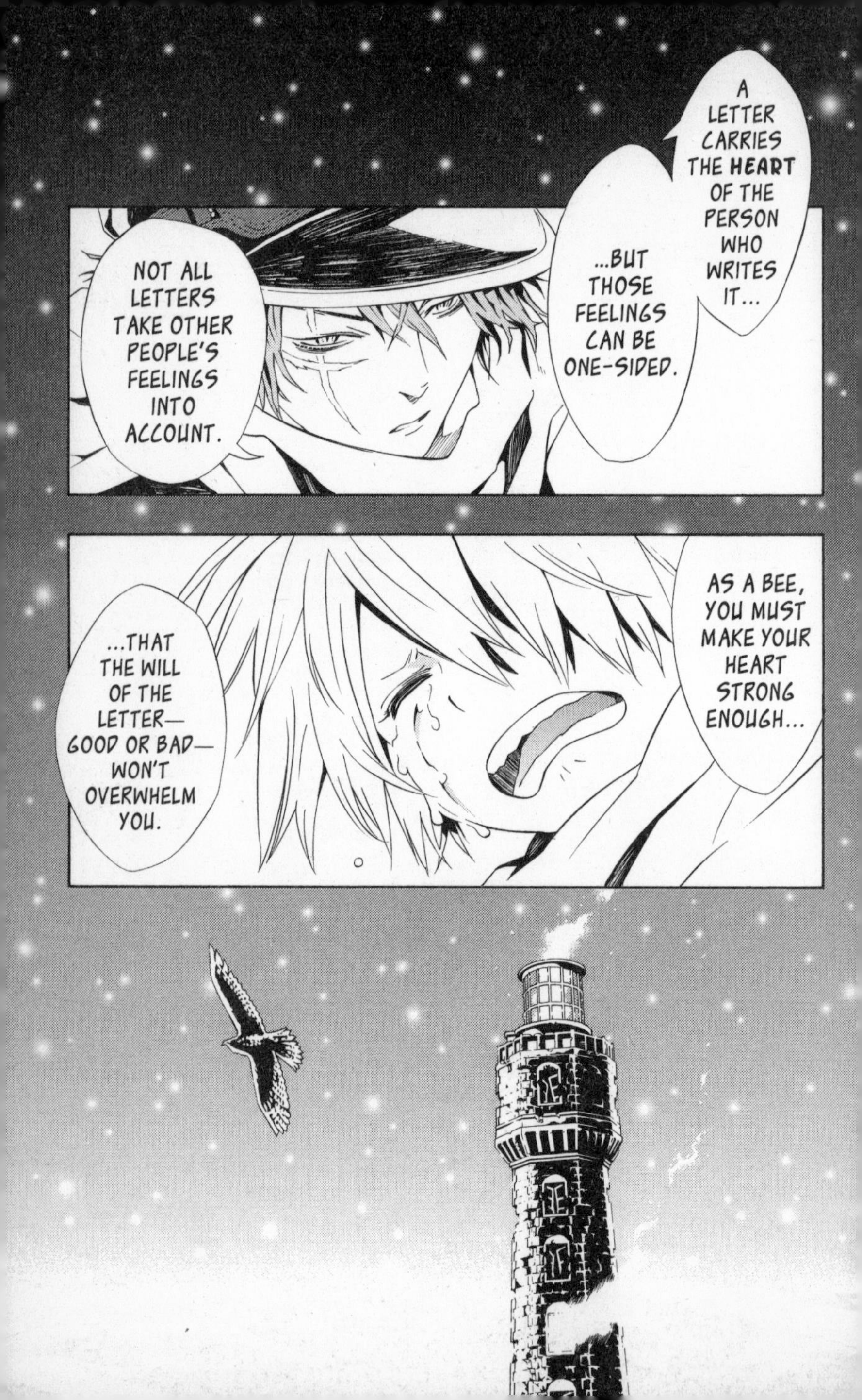
A LETTER CARRIES THE **HEART** OF THE PERSON WHO WRITES IT...
...BUT THOSE FEELINGS CAN BE ONE-SIDED.
NOT ALL LETTERS TAKE OTHER PEOPLE'S FEELINGS INTO ACCOUNT.
AS A BEE, YOU MUST MAKE YOUR HEART STRONG ENOUGH...
...THAT THE WILL OF THE LETTER—GOOD OR BAD—WON'T OVERWHELM YOU.

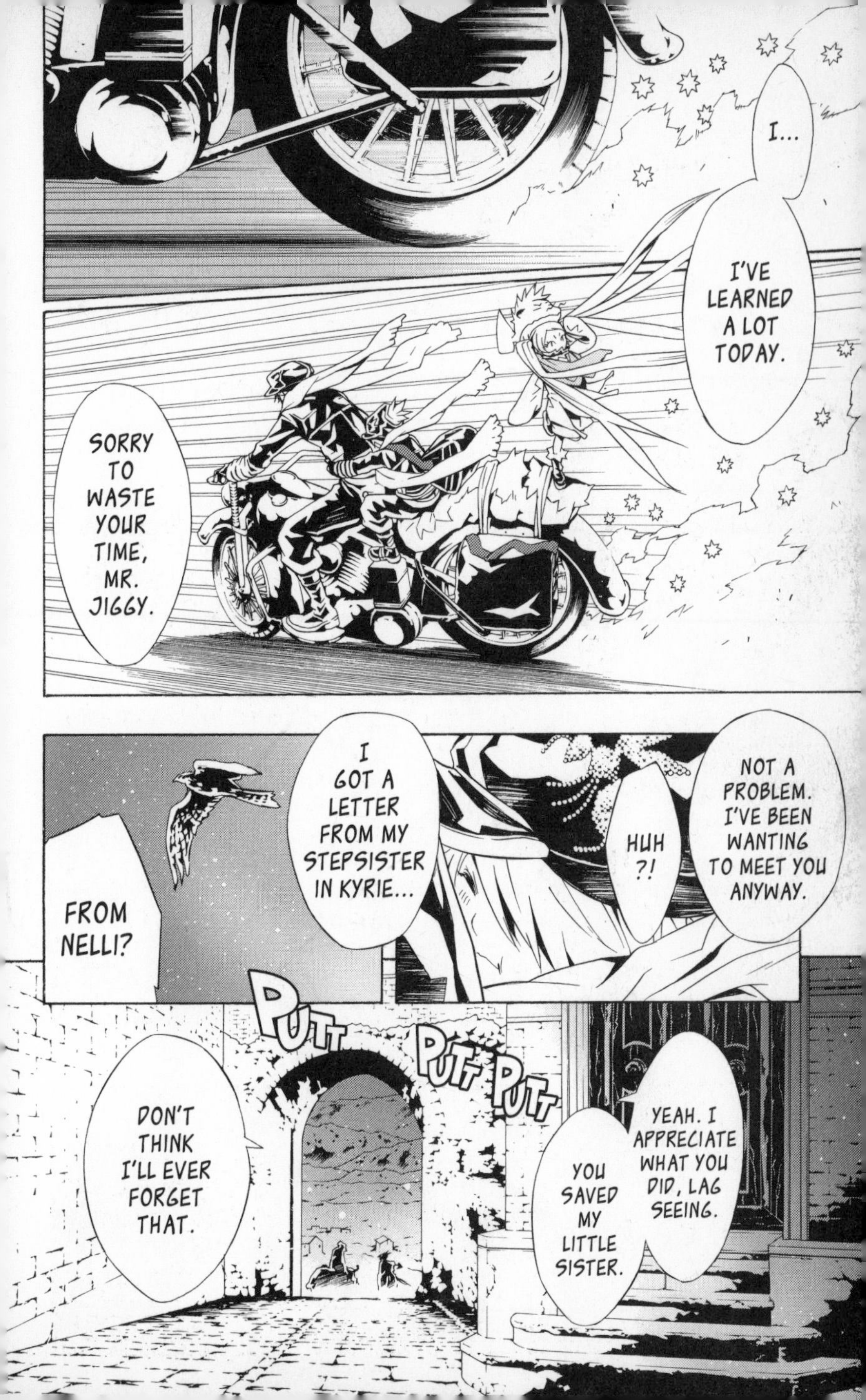
I...
I'VE LEARNED A LOT TODAY.
SORRY TO WASTE YOUR TIME, MR. JIGGY.
NOT A PROBLEM. I'VE BEEN WANTING TO MEET YOU ANYWAY.
HUH ?!
I GOT A LETTER FROM MY STEPSISTER IN KYRIE...
FROM NELLI?
PUTT
PUTT PUTT
YEAH. I APPRECIATE WHAT YOU DID, LAG SEEING.
YOU SAVED MY LITTLE SISTER.
DON'T THINK I'LL EVER FORGET THAT.

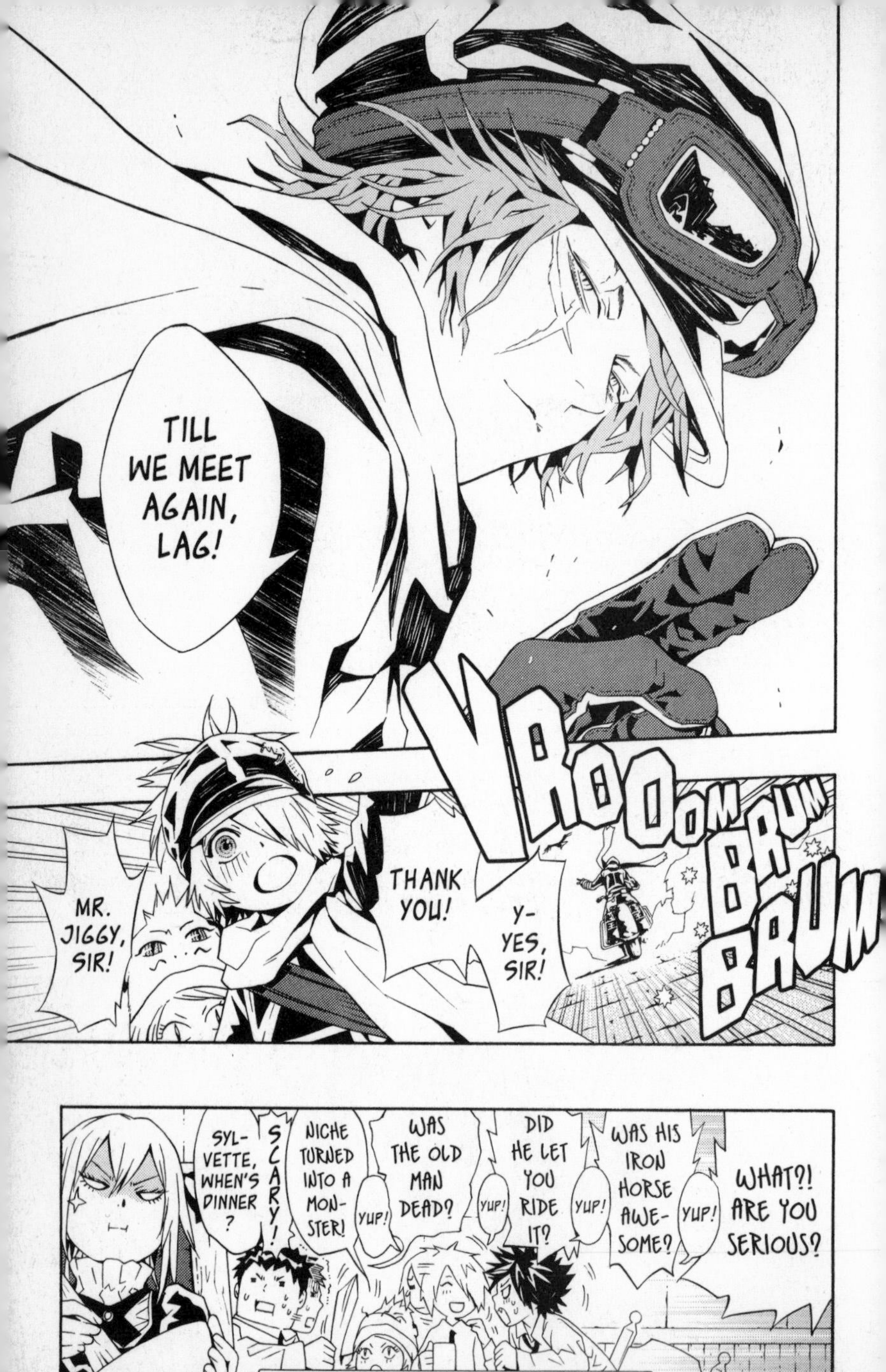
TILL WE MEET AGAIN, LAG!
VROOOOM
BRUM BRUM
Y-YES, SIR!
THANK YOU!
MR. JIGGY, SIR!
WHAT?! ARE YOU SERIOUS?
YUP!
WAS HIS IRON HORSE AWESOME?
YUP!
DID HE LET YOU RIDE IT?
YUP!
WAS THE OLD MAN DEAD?
YUP!
NICHE TURNED INTO A MONSTER!
SCARY!
SYLVETTE, WHEN'S DINNER?

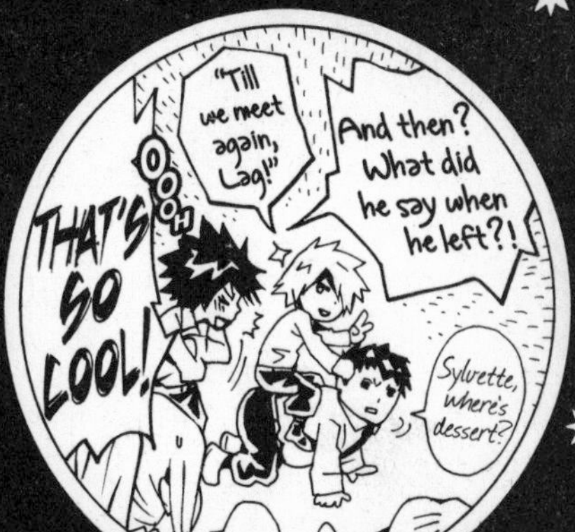
And then? What did he say when he left?!
"Till we meet again, Lag!"
OOOH
THAT'S SO COOL!
Sylvette, where's dessert?
...
Idiots!

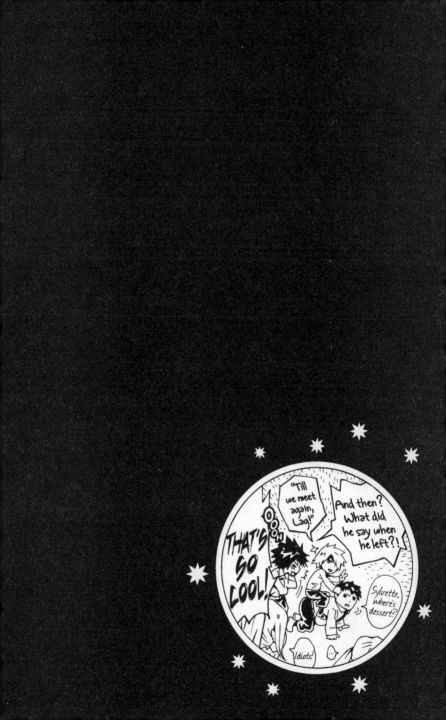

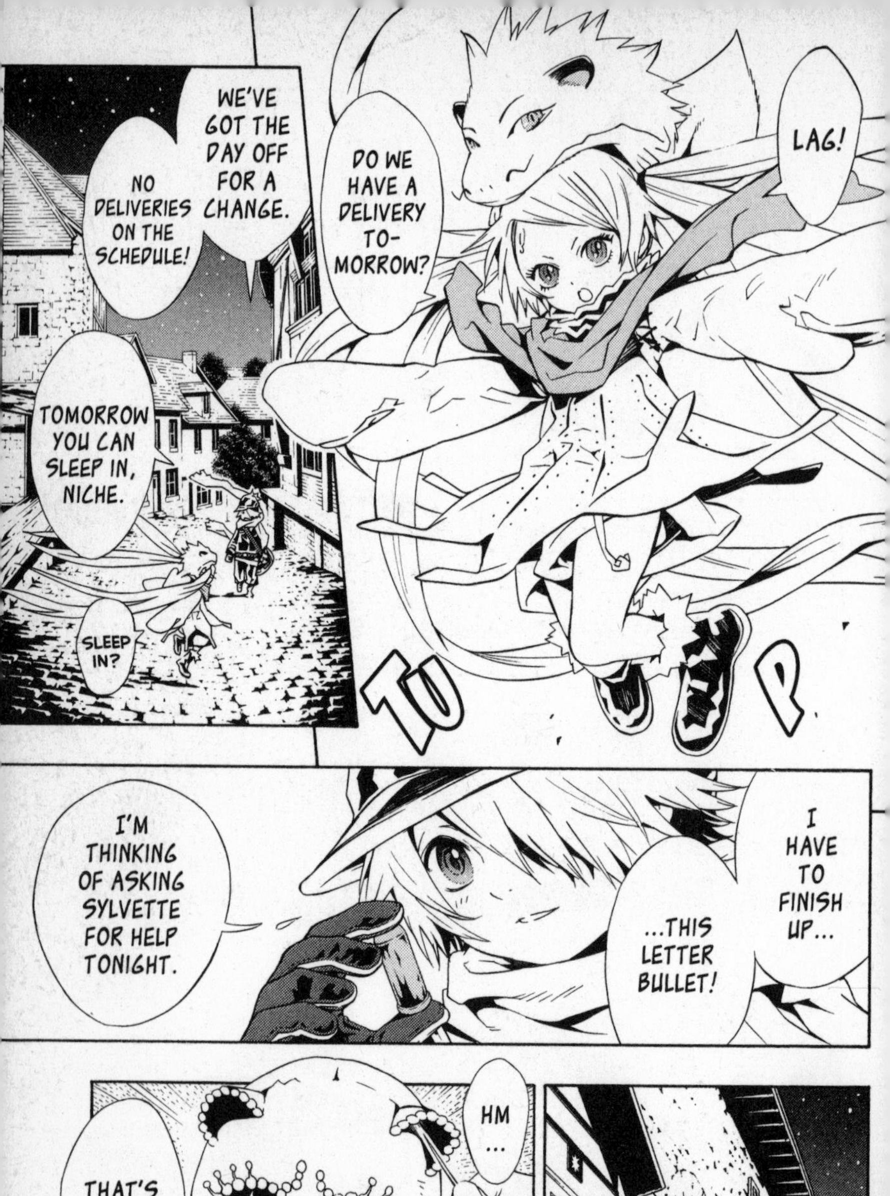
LAG!
DO WE HAVE A DELIVERY TO-MORROW?
TU P
WE'VE GOT THE DAY OFF FOR A CHANGE.
NO DELIVERIES ON THE SCHEDULE!
TOMORROW YOU CAN SLEEP IN, NICHE.
SLEEP IN?
I HAVE TO FINISH UP...
...THIS LETTER BULLET!
I'M THINKING OF ASKING SYLVETTE FOR HELP TONIGHT.
HM ...
THAT'S A GOOD FACE!
SCA -RY

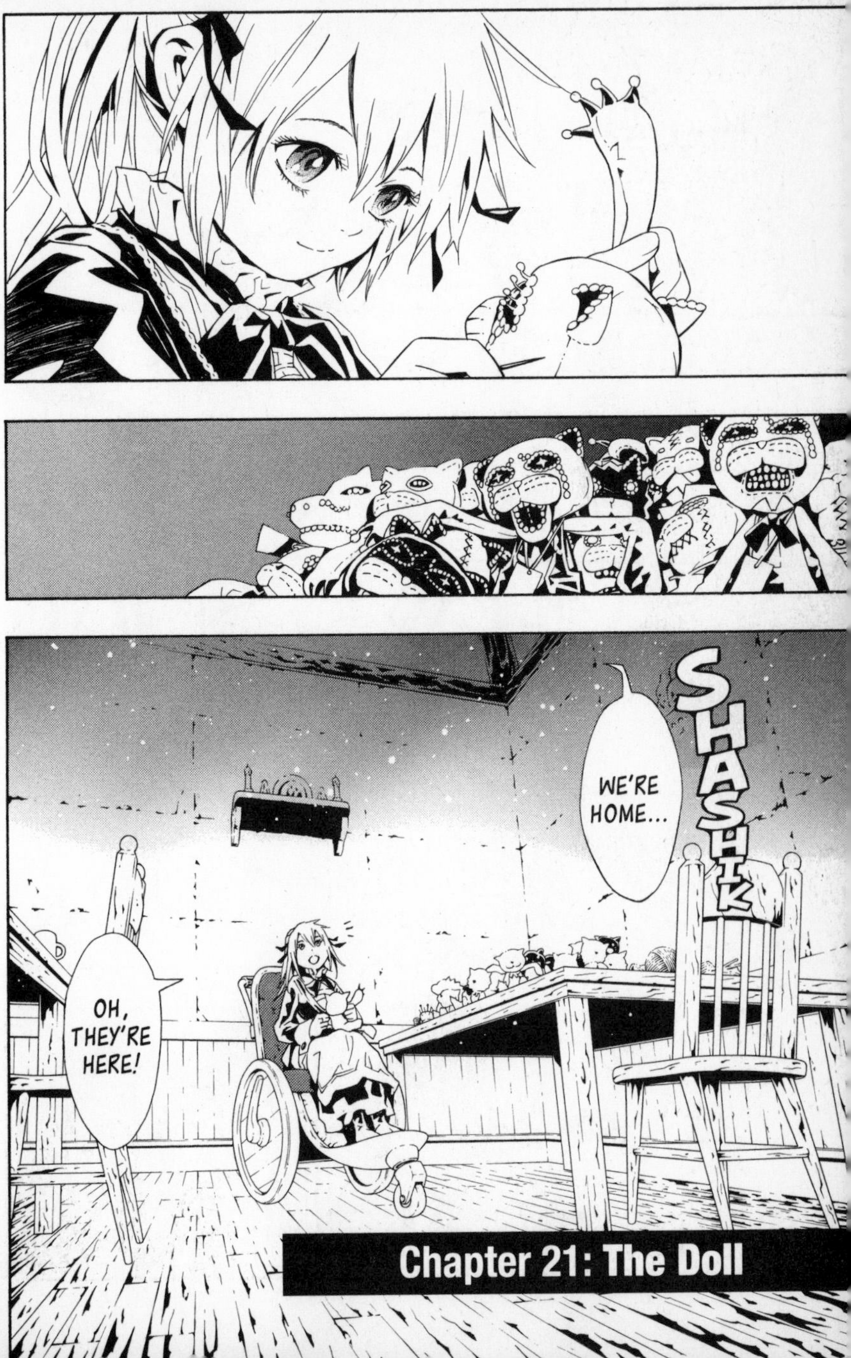
SHASHIK
WE'RE HOME...
OH, THEY'RE HERE!
Chapter 21: The Doll

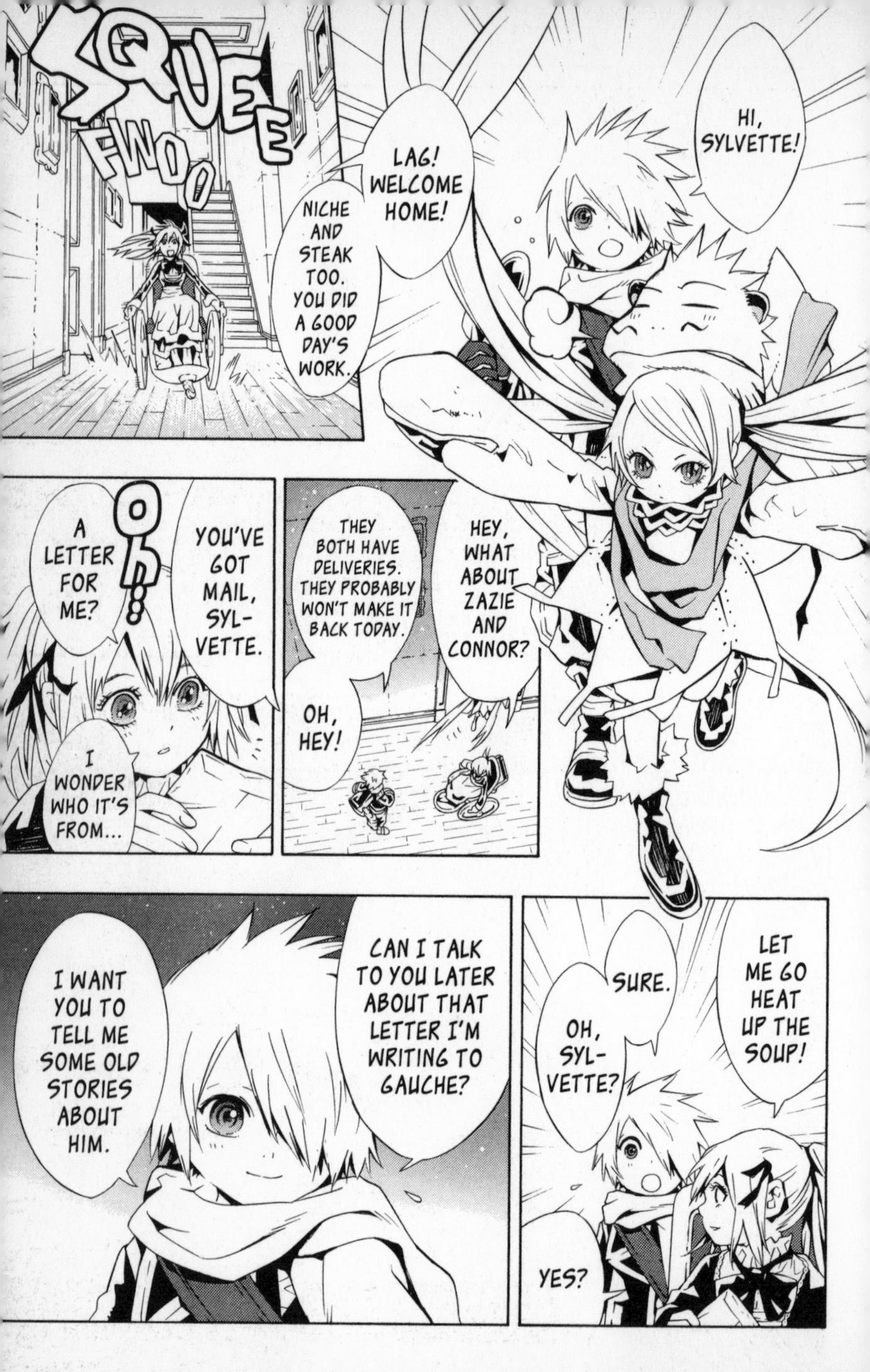
HI, SYLVETTE!
SQUEE
FWOO
LAG! WELCOME HOME!
NICHE AND STEAK TOO. YOU DID A GOOD DAY'S WORK.
HEY, WHAT ABOUT ZAZIE AND CONNOR?
THEY BOTH HAVE DELIVERIES. THEY PROBABLY WON'T MAKE IT BACK TODAY.
OH, HEY!
YOU'VE GOT MAIL, SYL-VETTE.
Oh...
A LETTER FOR ME?
I WONDER WHO IT'S FROM...
LET ME GO HEAT UP THE SOUP!
SURE.
OH, SYL-VETTE?
YES?
CAN I TALK TO YOU LATER ABOUT THAT LETTER I'M WRITING TO GAUCHE?
I WANT YOU TO TELL ME SOME OLD STORIES ABOUT HIM.

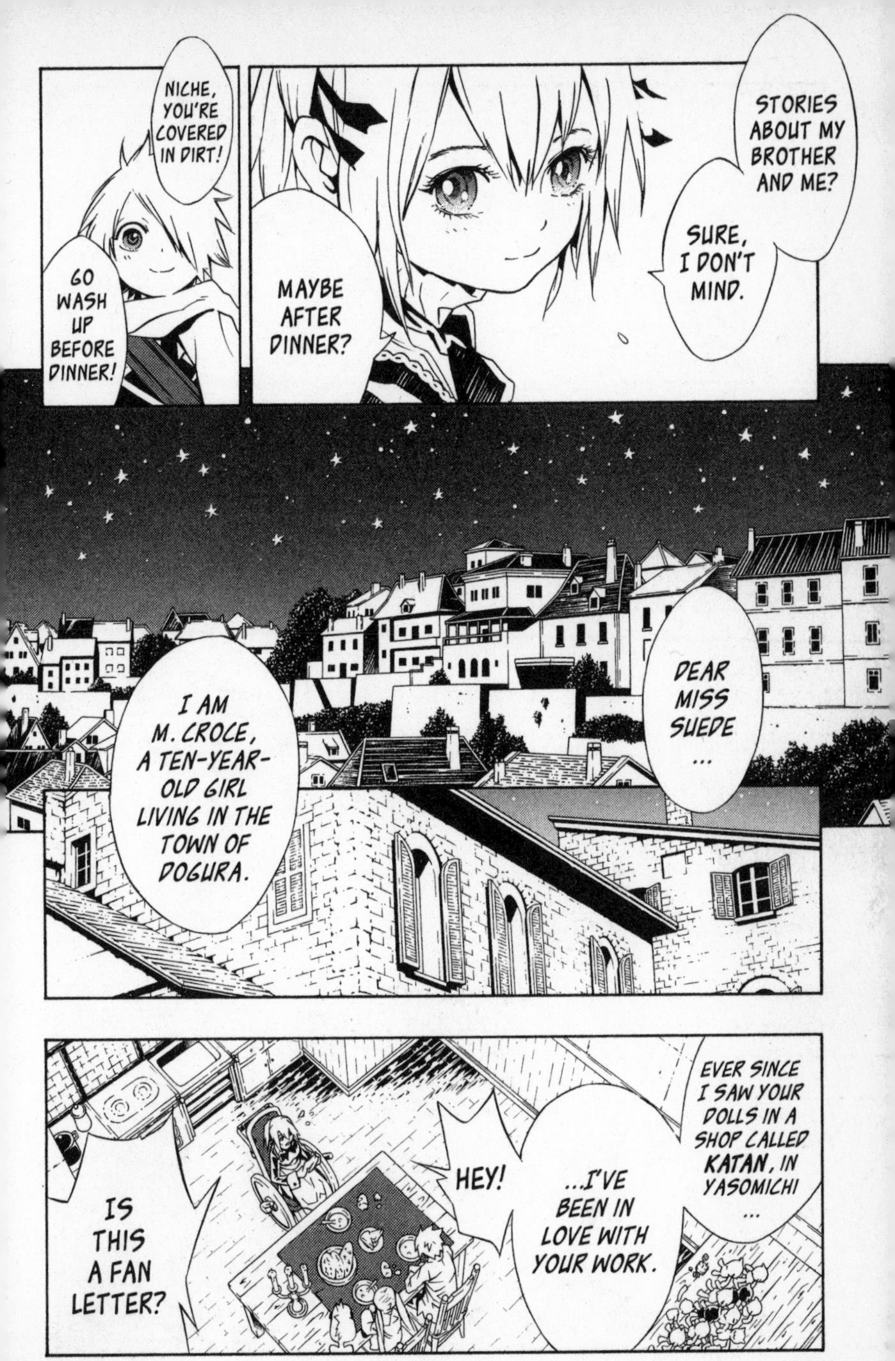
STORIES ABOUT MY BROTHER AND ME?
SURE, I DON'T MIND.
MAYBE AFTER DINNER?
NICHE, YOU'RE COVERED IN DIRT!
GO WASH UP BEFORE DINNER!
DEAR MISS SUEDE ...
I AM M. CROCE, A TEN-YEAR-OLD GIRL LIVING IN THE TOWN OF DOGURA.
EVER SINCE I SAW YOUR DOLLS IN A SHOP CALLED KATAN, IN YASOMICHI ...
...I'VE BEEN IN LOVE WITH YOUR WORK.
HEY!
IS THIS A FAN LETTER?

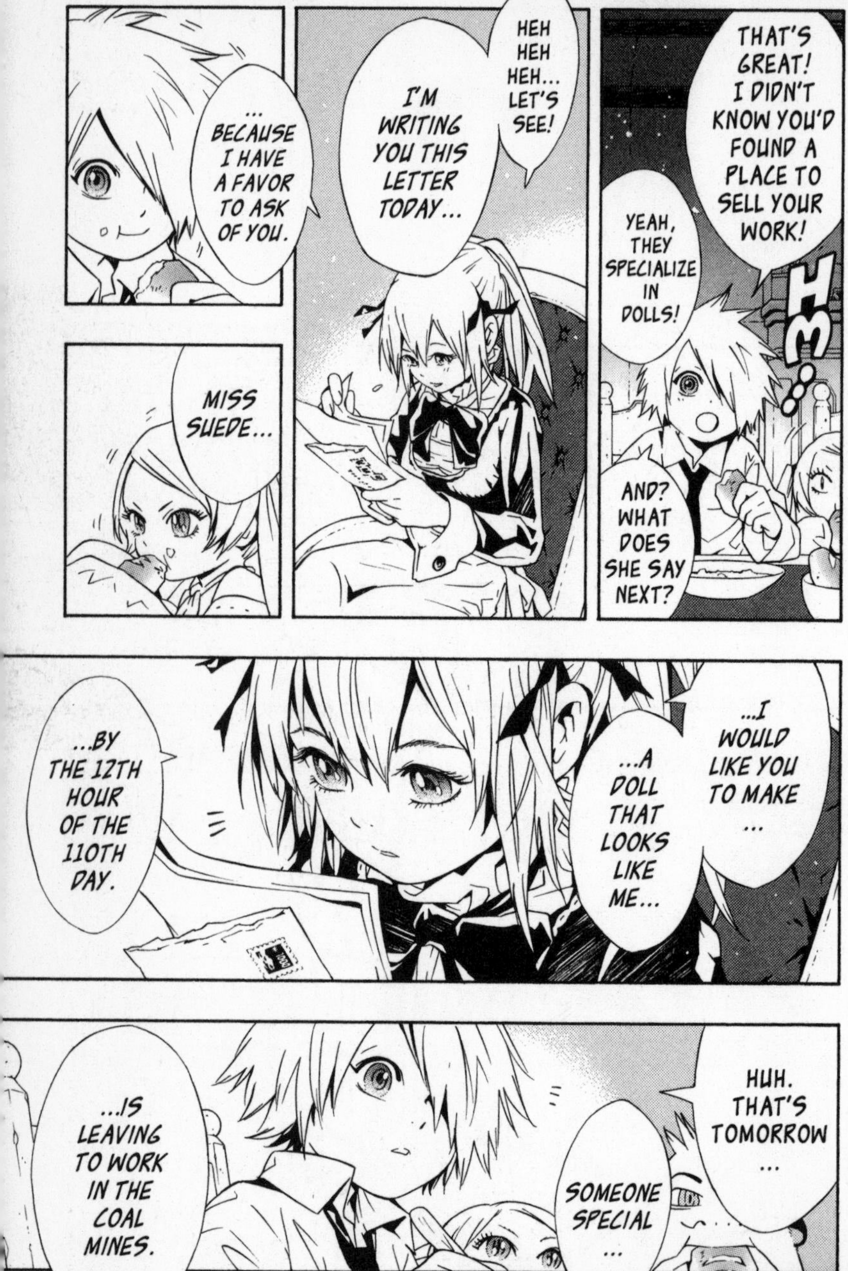
THAT'S GREAT! I DIDN'T KNOW YOU'D FOUND A PLACE TO SELL YOUR WORK!
HM...
YEAH, THEY SPECIALIZE IN DOLLS!
AND? WHAT DOES SHE SAY NEXT?
HEH HEH HEH... LET'S SEE!
I'M WRITING YOU THIS LETTER TODAY...
...BECAUSE I HAVE A FAVOR TO ASK OF YOU.
MISS SUEDE...
...I WOULD LIKE YOU TO MAKE...
...A DOLL THAT LOOKS LIKE ME...
...BY THE 12TH HOUR OF THE 110TH DAY.
HUH. THAT'S TOMORROW...
SOMEONE SPECIAL...
...IS LEAVING TO WORK IN THE COAL MINES.

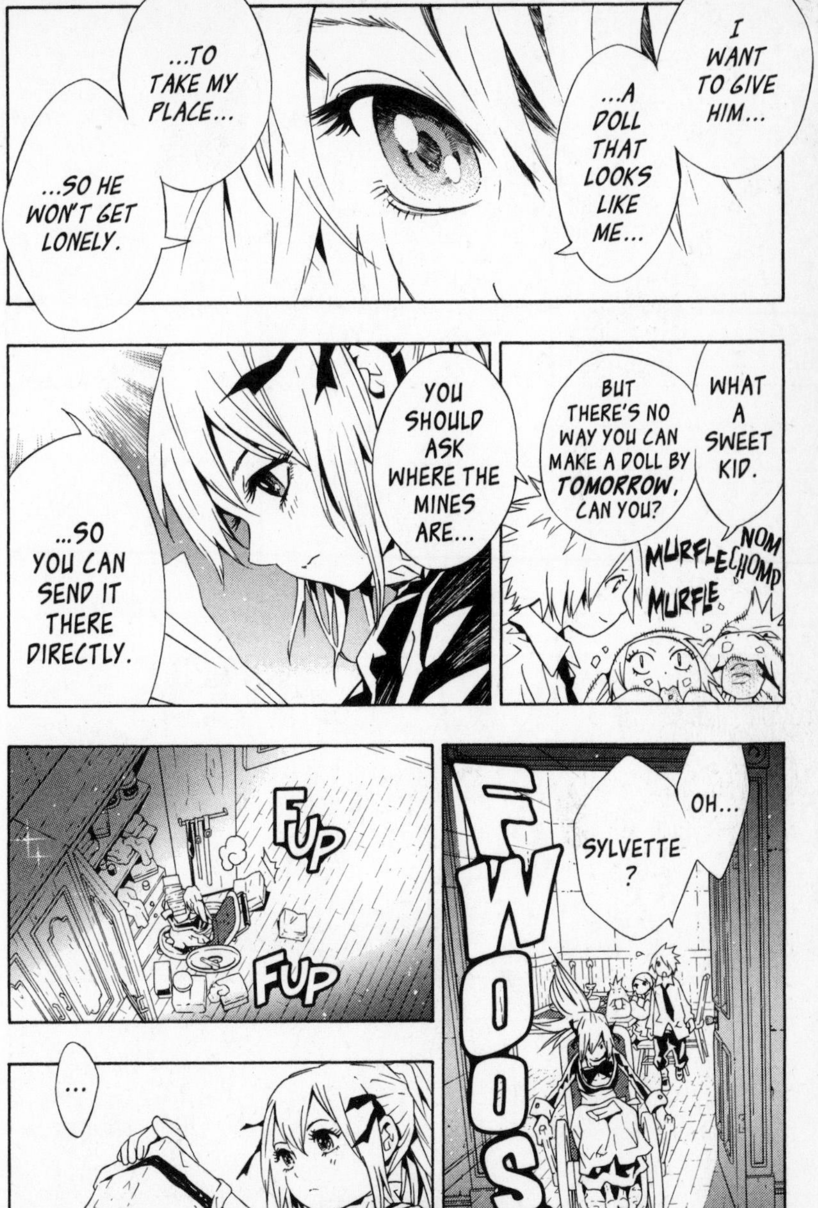
I WANT TO GIVE HIM...
...A DOLL THAT LOOKS LIKE ME...
...TO TAKE MY PLACE...
...SO HE WON'T GET LONELY.
WHAT A SWEET KID.
BUT THERE'S NO WAY YOU CAN MAKE A DOLL BY **TOMORROW**, CAN YOU?
NOM
CHOMP
MURFLE
MURFLE
YOU SHOULD ASK WHERE THE MINES ARE...
...SO YOU CAN SEND IT THERE DIRECTLY.
OH...
SYLVETTE?
FWOOSH
FUP
FUP
...

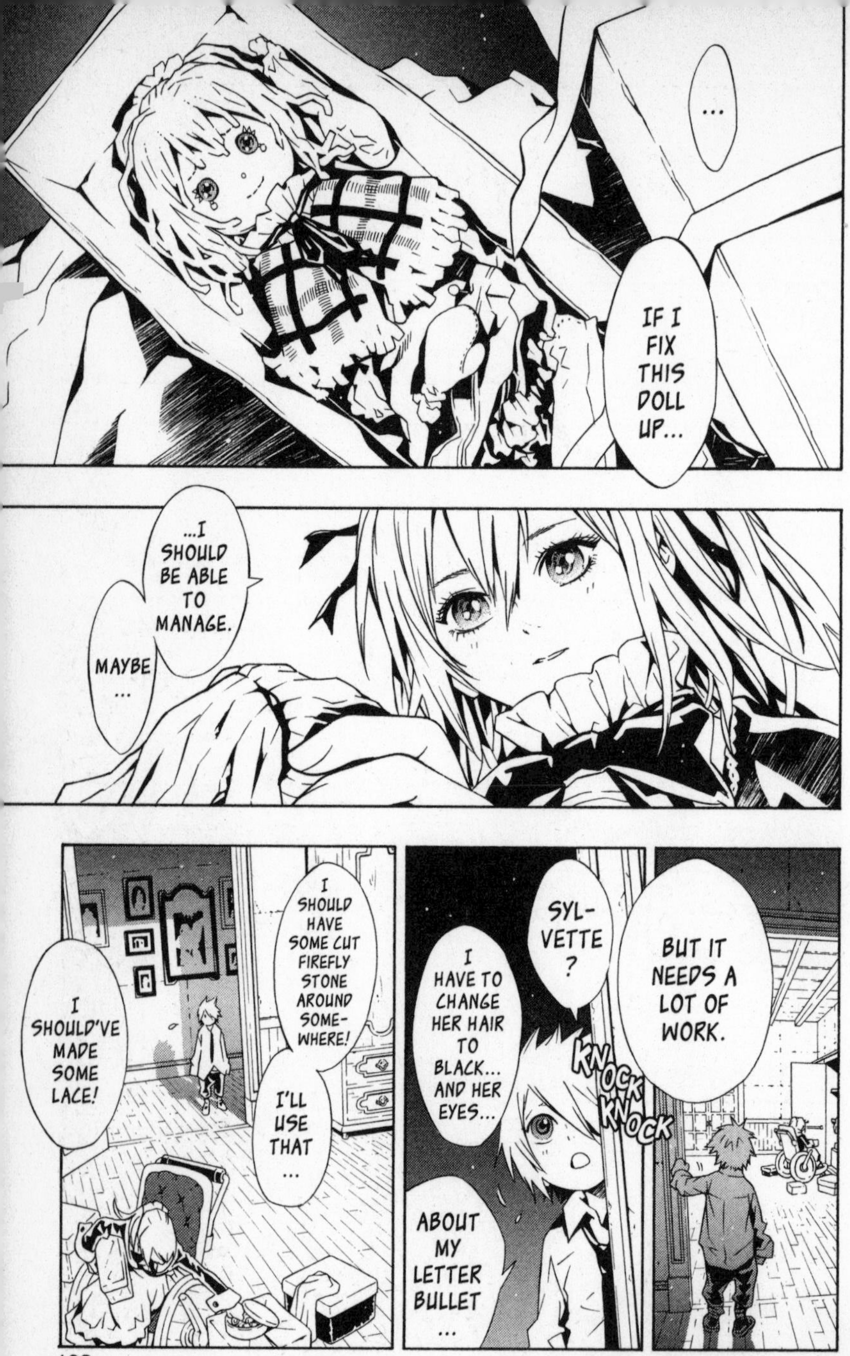
...
IF I FIX THIS DOLL UP...
...I SHOULD BE ABLE TO MANAGE.
MAYBE ...
BUT IT NEEDS A LOT OF WORK.
KNOCK KNOCK
SYL-VETTE?
I HAVE TO CHANGE HER HAIR TO BLACK... AND HER EYES...
ABOUT MY LETTER BULLET ...
I SHOULD HAVE SOME CUT FIREFLY STONE AROUND SOME-WHERE!
I'LL USE THAT ...
I SHOULD'VE MADE SOME LACE!

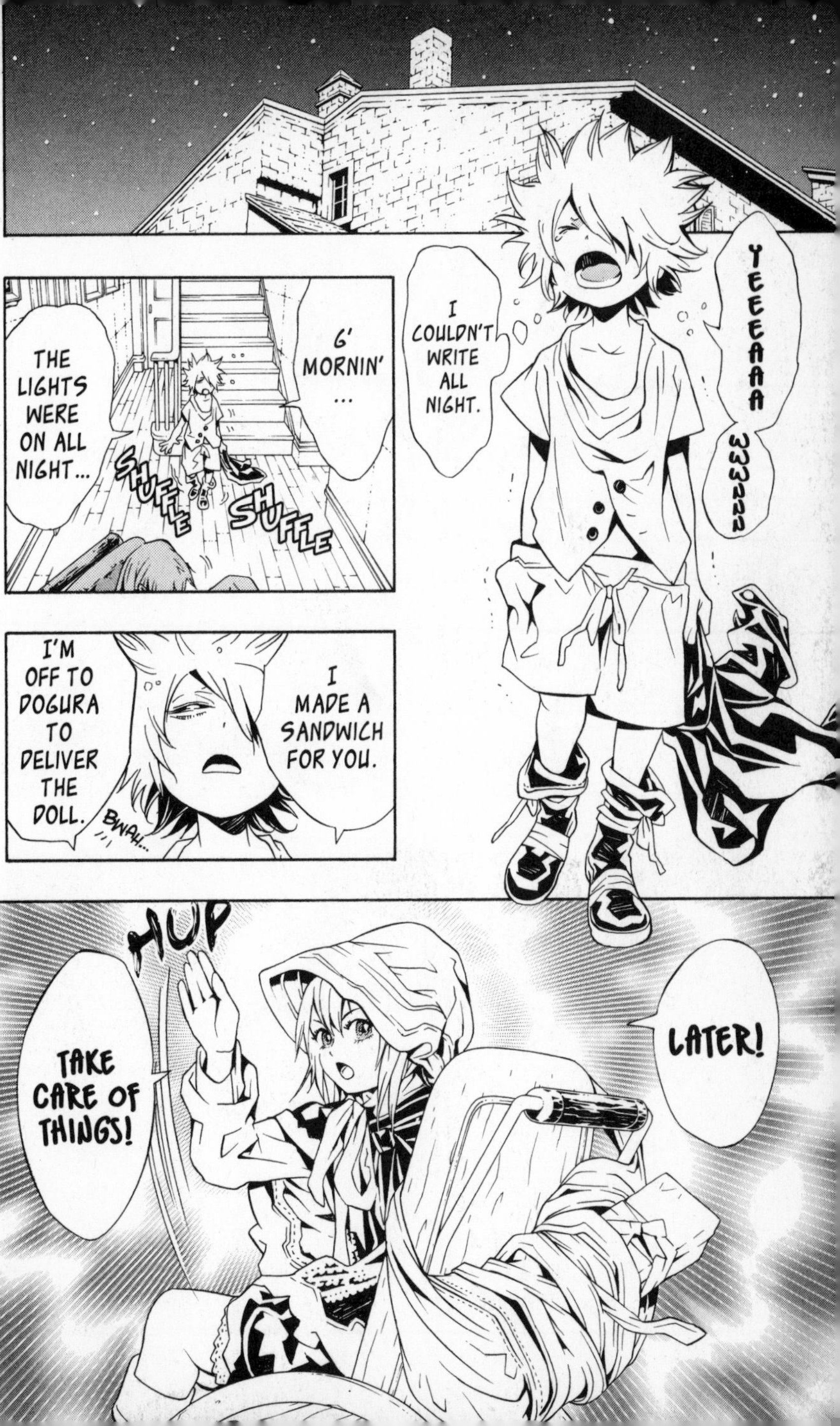
YEEEAAAA WWWNNN
I COULDN'T WRITE ALL NIGHT.
G' MORNIN' ...
THE LIGHTS WERE ON ALL NIGHT...
SHUFFLE
SHUFFLE
I MADE A SANDWICH FOR YOU.
I'M OFF TO DOGURA TO DELIVER THE DOLL.
BWAH...
LATER!
HUP
TAKE CARE OF THINGS!

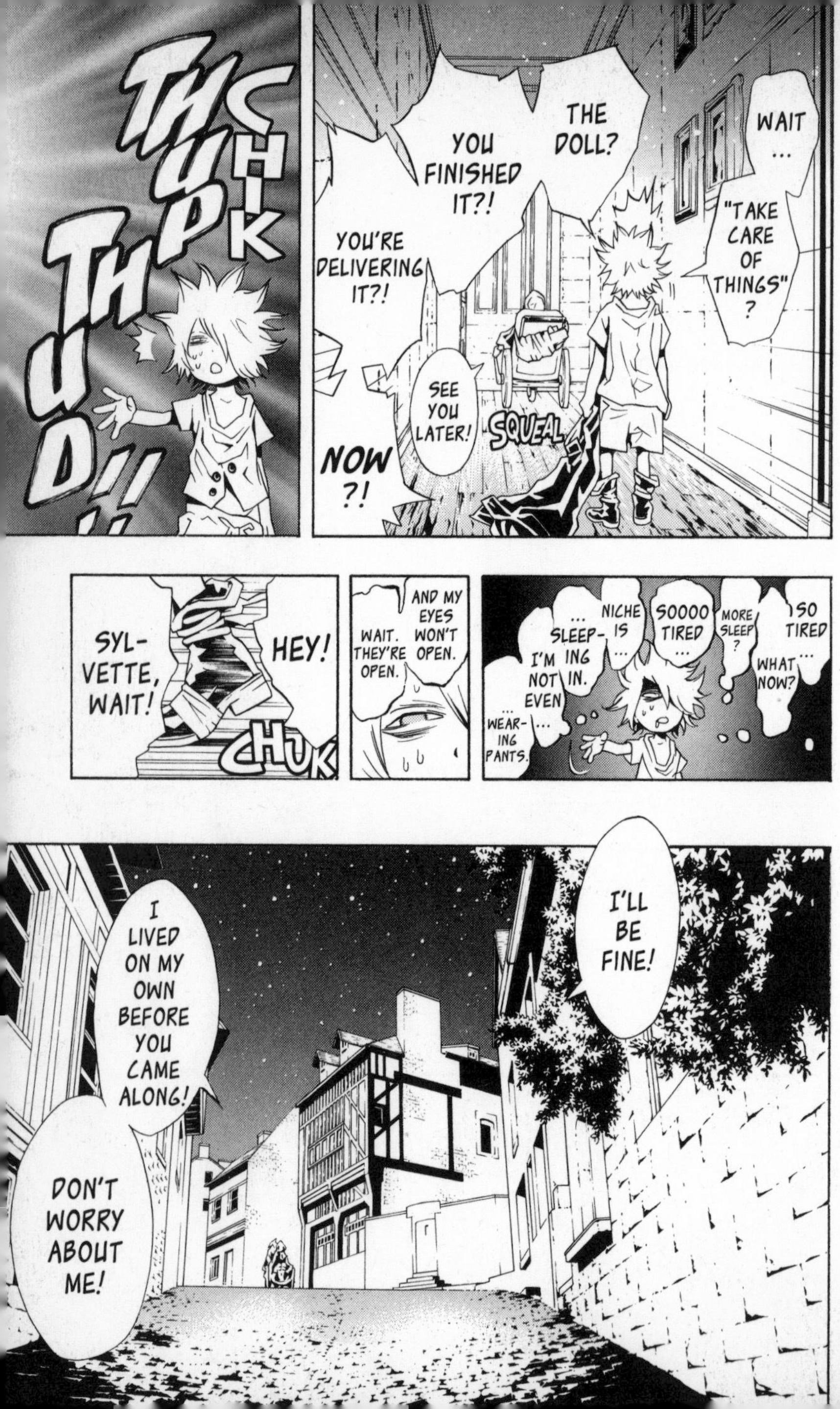
WAIT ... "TAKE CARE OF THINGS" ?
THE DOLL?
YOU FINISHED IT?!
YOU'RE DELIVERING IT?!
SEE YOU LATER!
SQUEAL
NOW ?!
THUP
CHIK
THUD!!
SO TIRED ...
MORE SLEEP ?
WHAT NOW?
SOOOO TIRED ...
NICHE IS ...
... SLEEP-ING IN.
I'M NOT EVEN ...
... WEAR-ING PANTS.
AND MY EYES WON'T OPEN.
WAIT. THEY'RE OPEN.
HEY!
SYL-VETTE, WAIT!
CHUK
I'LL BE FINE!
I LIVED ON MY OWN BEFORE YOU CAME ALONG!
DON'T WORRY ABOUT ME!

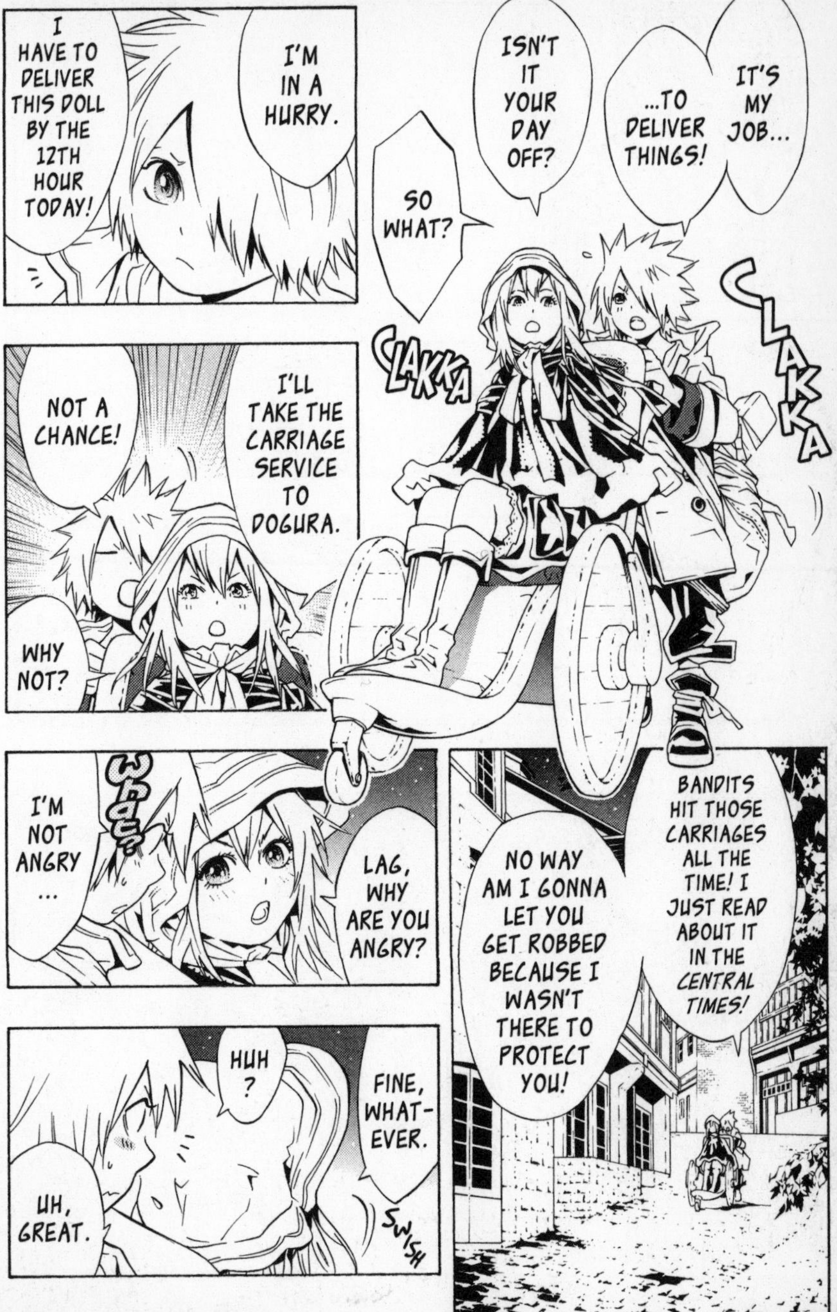
IT'S MY JOB...
...TO DELIVER THINGS!
ISN'T IT YOUR DAY OFF?
SO WHAT?
CLAKKA
CLAKKA
I'M IN A HURRY.
I HAVE TO DELIVER THIS DOLL BY THE 12TH HOUR TODAY!
I'LL TAKE THE CARRIAGE SERVICE TO DOGURA.
NOT A CHANCE!
WHY NOT?
BANDITS HIT THOSE CARRIAGES ALL THE TIME! I JUST READ ABOUT IT IN THE CENTRAL TIMES!
NO WAY AM I GONNA LET YOU GET ROBBED BECAUSE I WASN'T THERE TO PROTECT YOU!
LAG, WHY ARE YOU ANGRY?
WHAT?
I'M NOT ANGRY...
FINE, WHAT-EVER.
HUH?
SWISH
UH, GREAT.

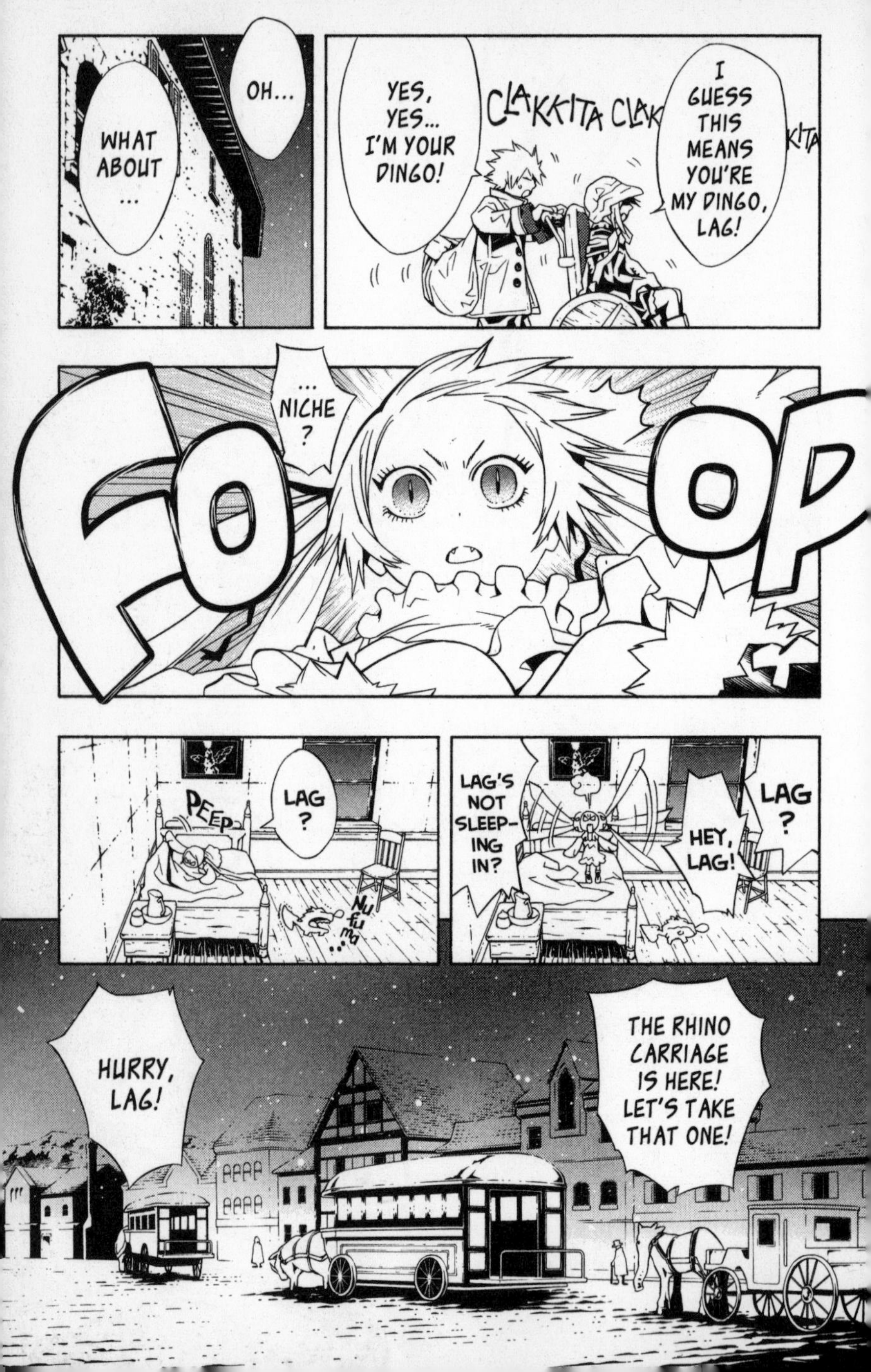
I GUESS THIS MEANS YOU'RE MY DINGO, LAG!
CLAKKITA CLAKKITA
YES, YES... I'M YOUR DINGO!
OH...
WHAT ABOUT ...
... NICHE ?
FOOP
LAG ?
HEY, LAG!
LAG'S NOT SLEEP-ING IN?
LAG ?
PEEP
NU FU MA...
THE RHINO CARRIAGE IS HERE! LET'S TAKE THAT ONE!
HURRY, LAG!

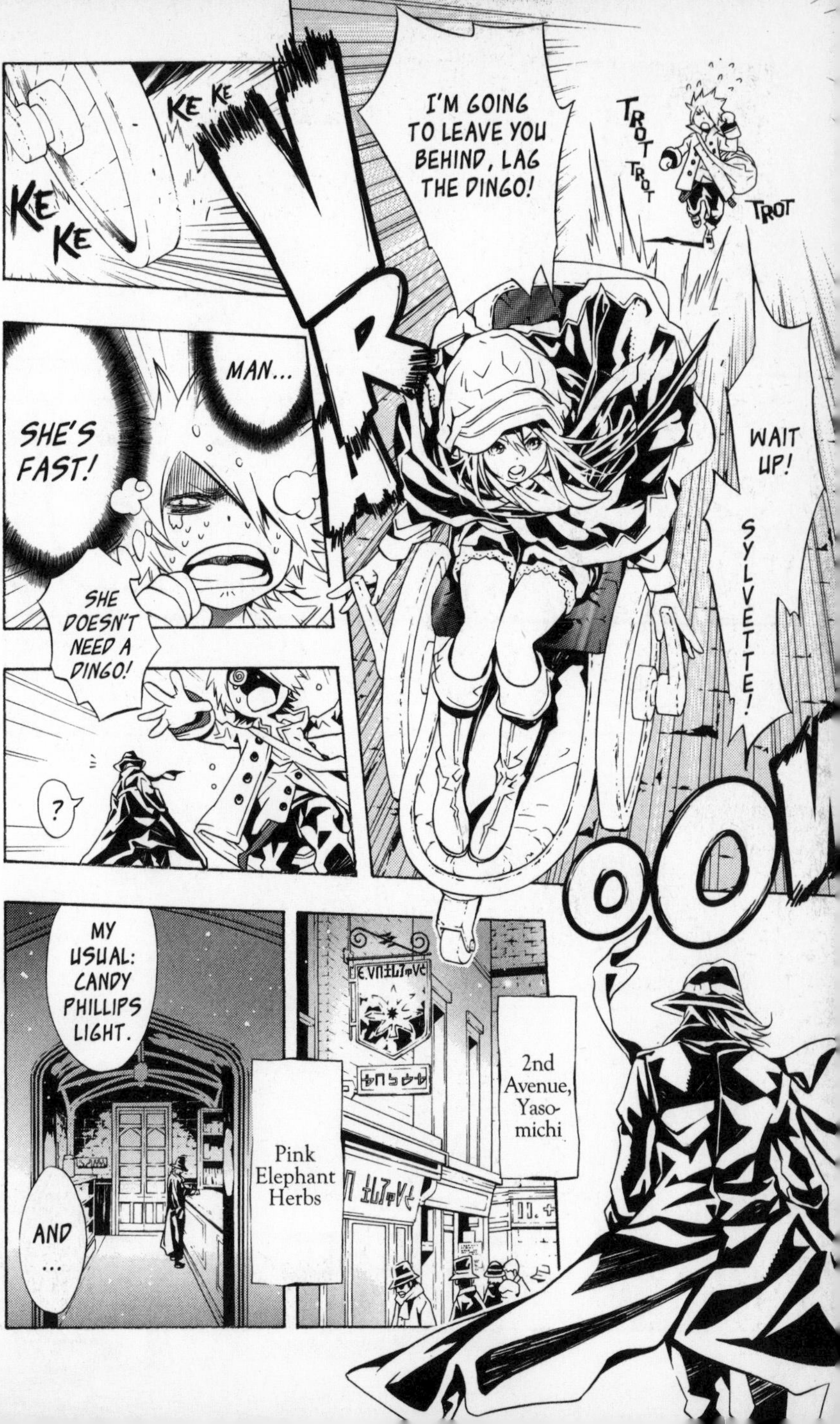

I'M GOING TO LEAVE YOU BEHIND, LAG THE DINGO!
TROT TROT TROT
TROT
WAIT UP!
SYLVETTE!
VROOM
KE KE
KE KE
MAN...
SHE'S FAST!
SHE DOESN'T NEED A DINGO!
?
2nd Avenue, Yaso-michi
Pink Elephant Herbs
MY USUAL: CANDY PHILLIPS LIGHT.
AND ...

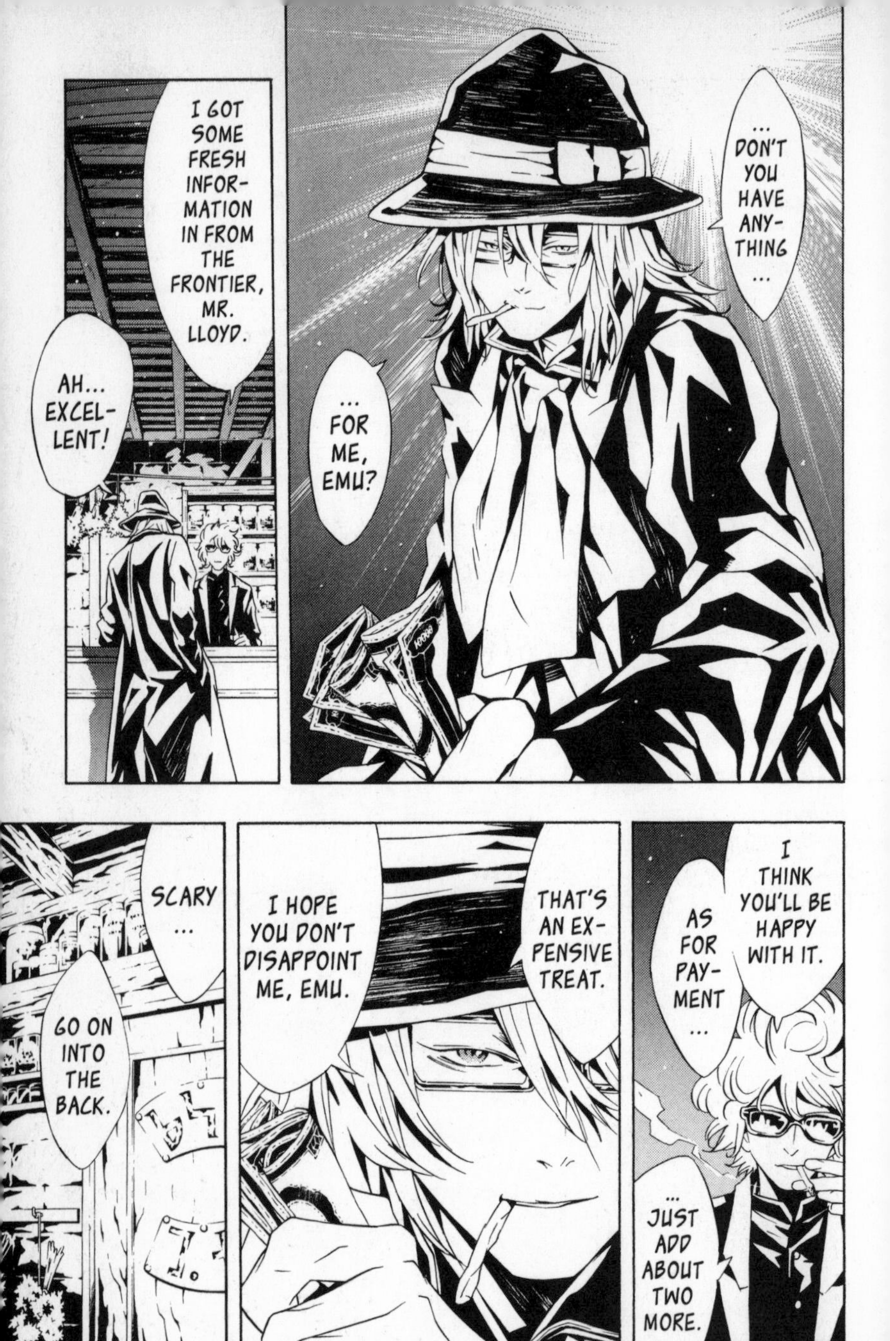

... DON'T YOU HAVE ANYTHING ...
... FOR ME, EMU?
I GOT SOME FRESH INFORMATION IN FROM THE FRONTIER, MR. LLOYD.
AH... EXCELLENT!
I THINK YOU'LL BE HAPPY WITH IT.
AS FOR PAYMENT ...
... JUST ADD ABOUT TWO MORE.
THAT'S AN EXPENSIVE TREAT.
I HOPE YOU DON'T DISAPPOINT ME, EMU.
SCARY ...
GO ON INTO THE BACK.

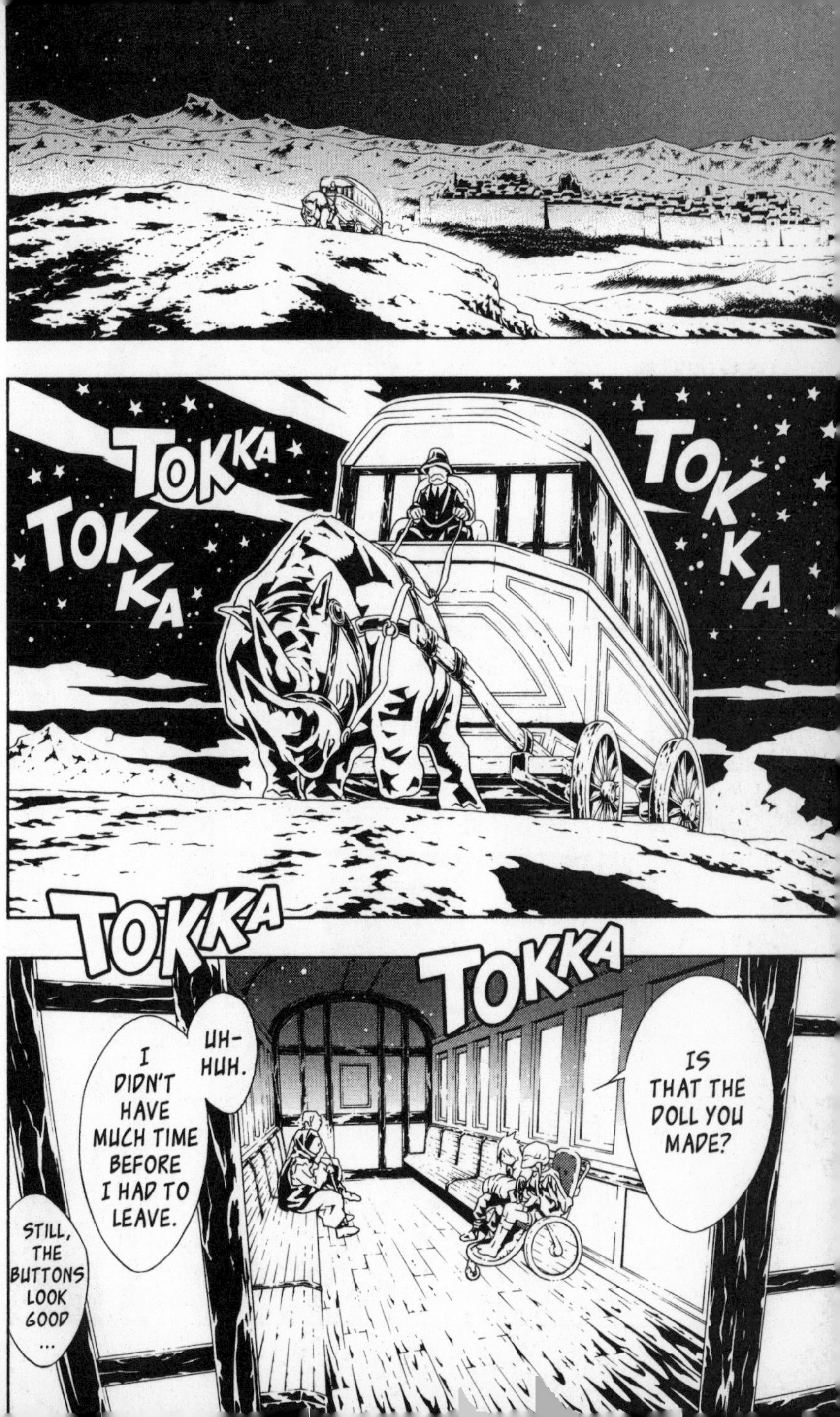
TOKKA
TOKKA
TOKKA
TOKKA
TOKKA
IS THAT THE DOLL YOU MADE?
UH-HUH.
I DIDN'T HAVE MUCH TIME BEFORE I HAD TO LEAVE.
STILL, THE BUTTONS LOOK GOOD ...

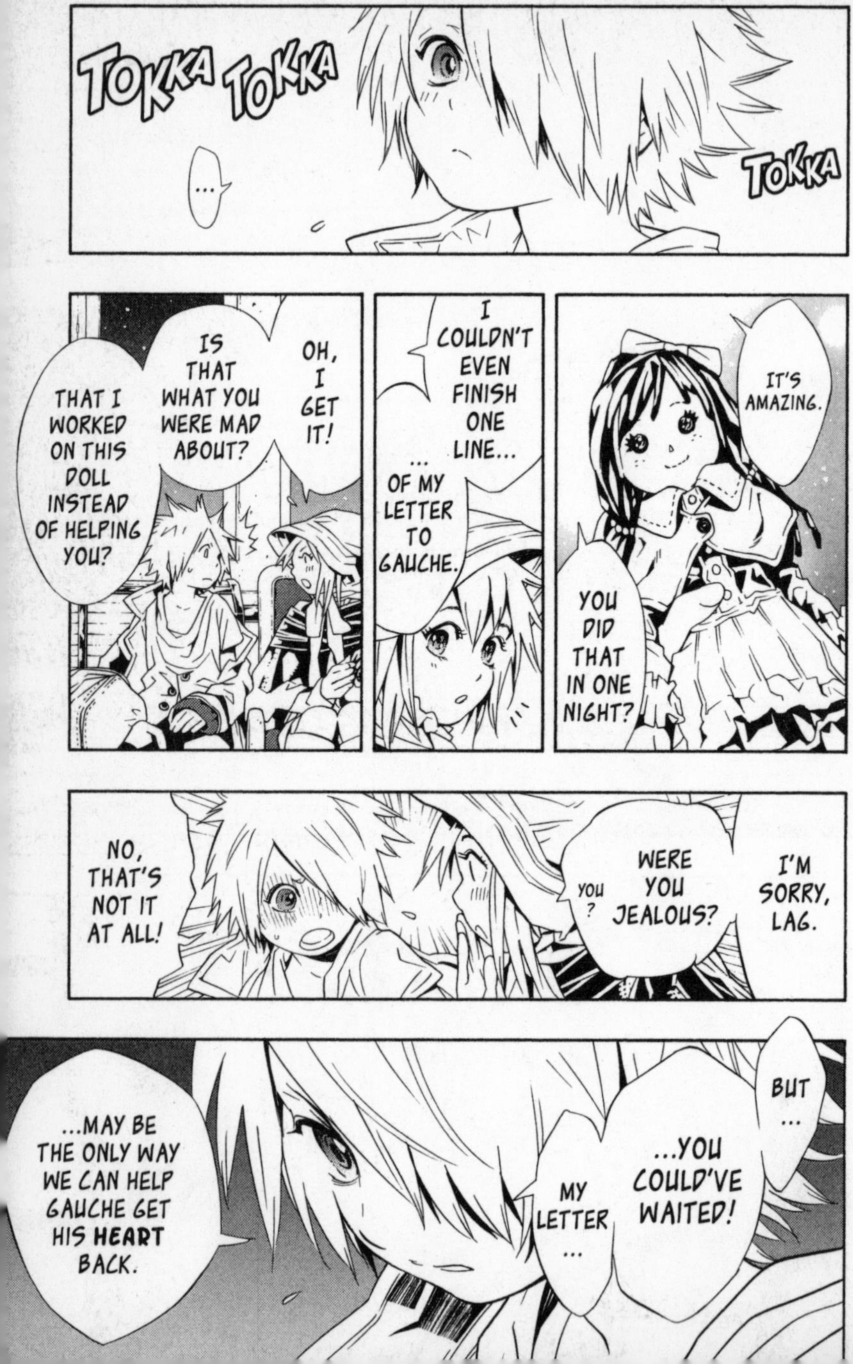
TOKKA
TOKKA TOKKA
...
IT'S AMAZING.
YOU DID THAT IN ONE NIGHT?
I COULDN'T EVEN FINISH ONE LINE...
... OF MY LETTER TO GAUCHE.
OH, I GET IT!
IS THAT WHAT YOU WERE MAD ABOUT?
THAT I WORKED ON THIS DOLL INSTEAD OF HELPING YOU?
I'M SORRY, LAG.
WERE YOU JEALOUS?
YOU ?
NO, THAT'S NOT IT AT ALL!
BUT ...
...YOU COULD'VE WAITED!
MY LETTER ...
...MAY BE THE ONLY WAY WE CAN HELP GAUCHE GET HIS **HEART** BACK.

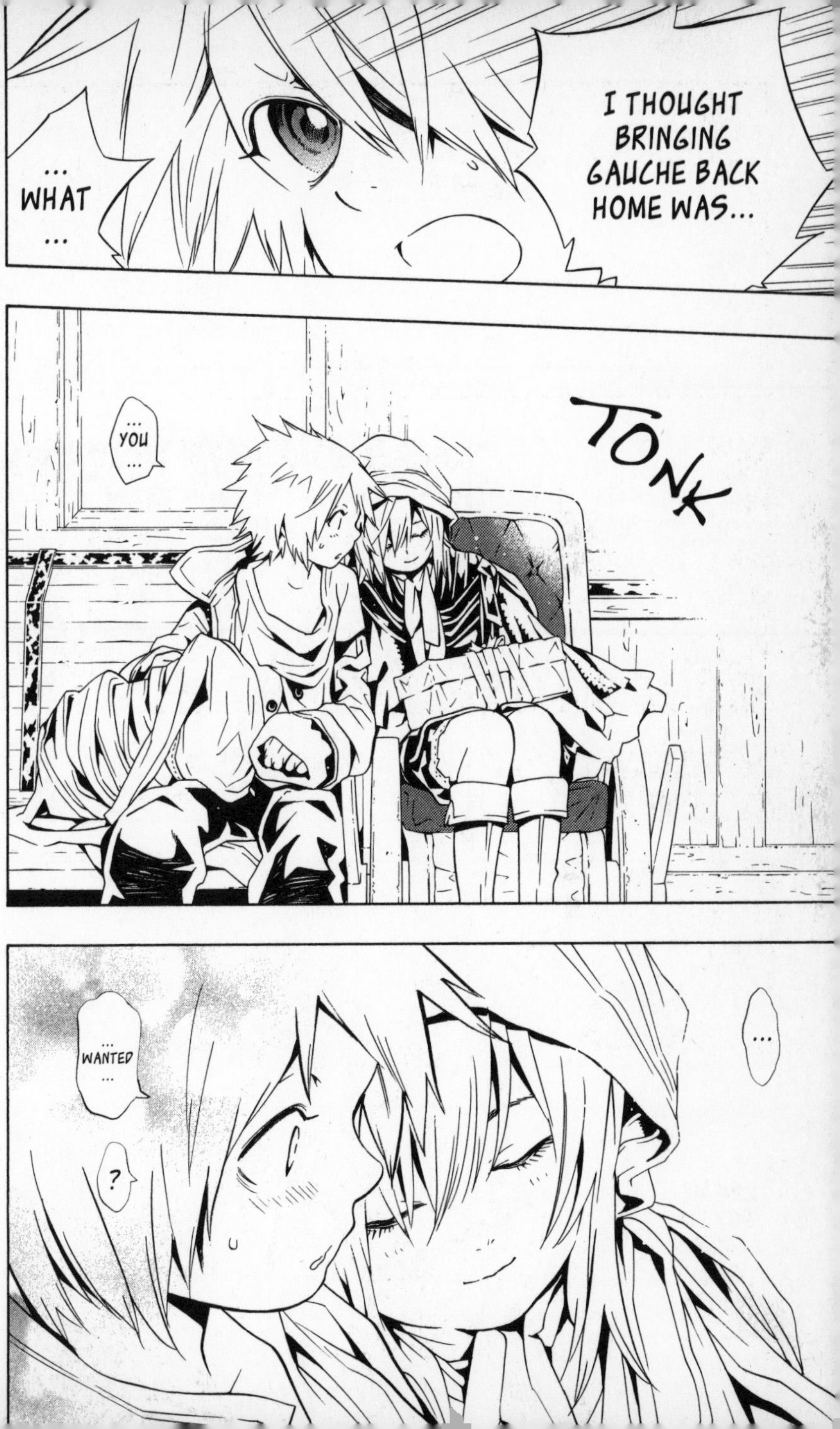
I THOUGHT BRINGING GAUCHE BACK HOME WAS...
... WHAT ...
TONK
... YOU ...
...
... WANTED ...
?

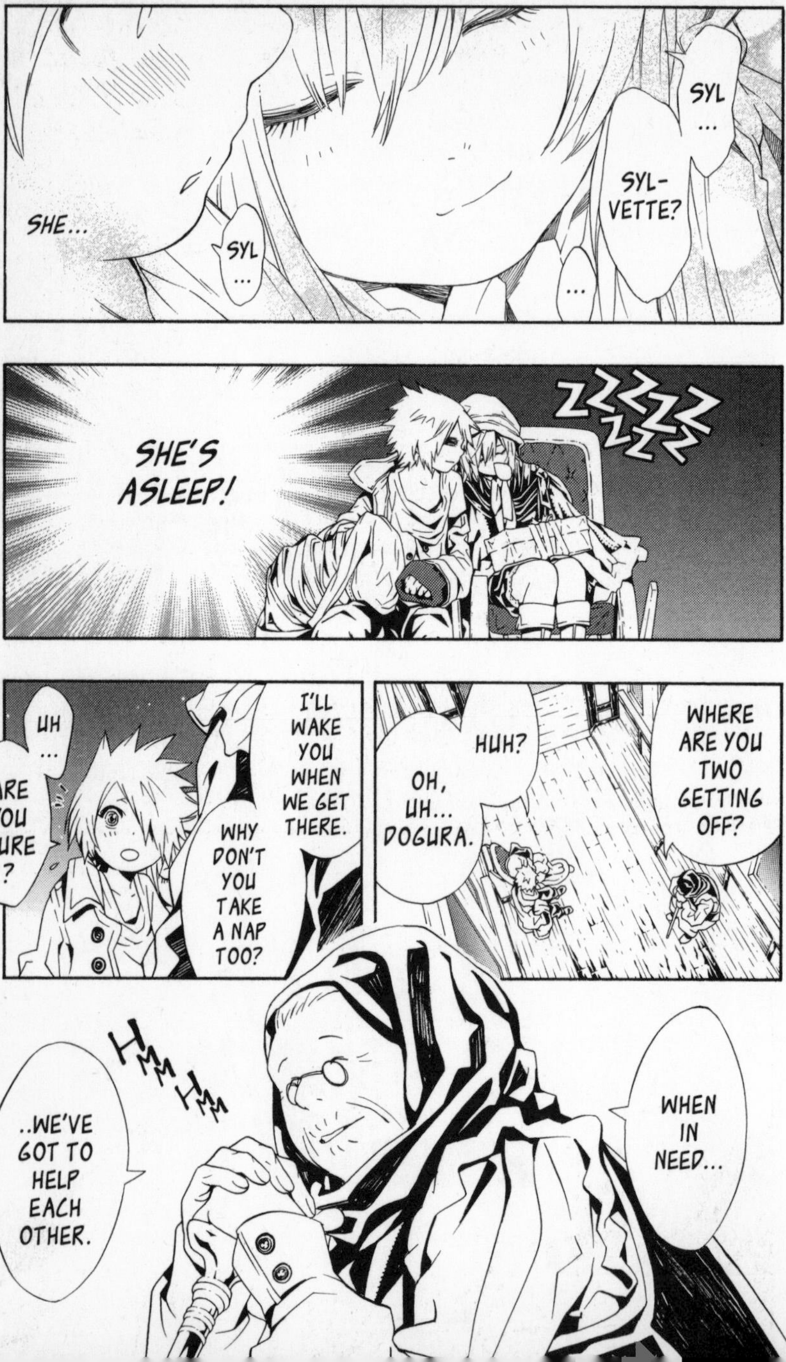
SYL...
SYL-VETTE?
...
SYL...
SHE...
ZZZZZZZ
SHE'S ASLEEP!
WHERE ARE YOU TWO GETTING OFF?
HUH?
OH, UH... DOGURA.
I'LL WAKE YOU WHEN WE GET THERE.
WHY DON'T YOU TAKE A NAP TOO?
UH ...
ARE YOU SURE ?
WHEN IN NEED...
HMM HMM
..WE'VE GOT TO HELP EACH OTHER.

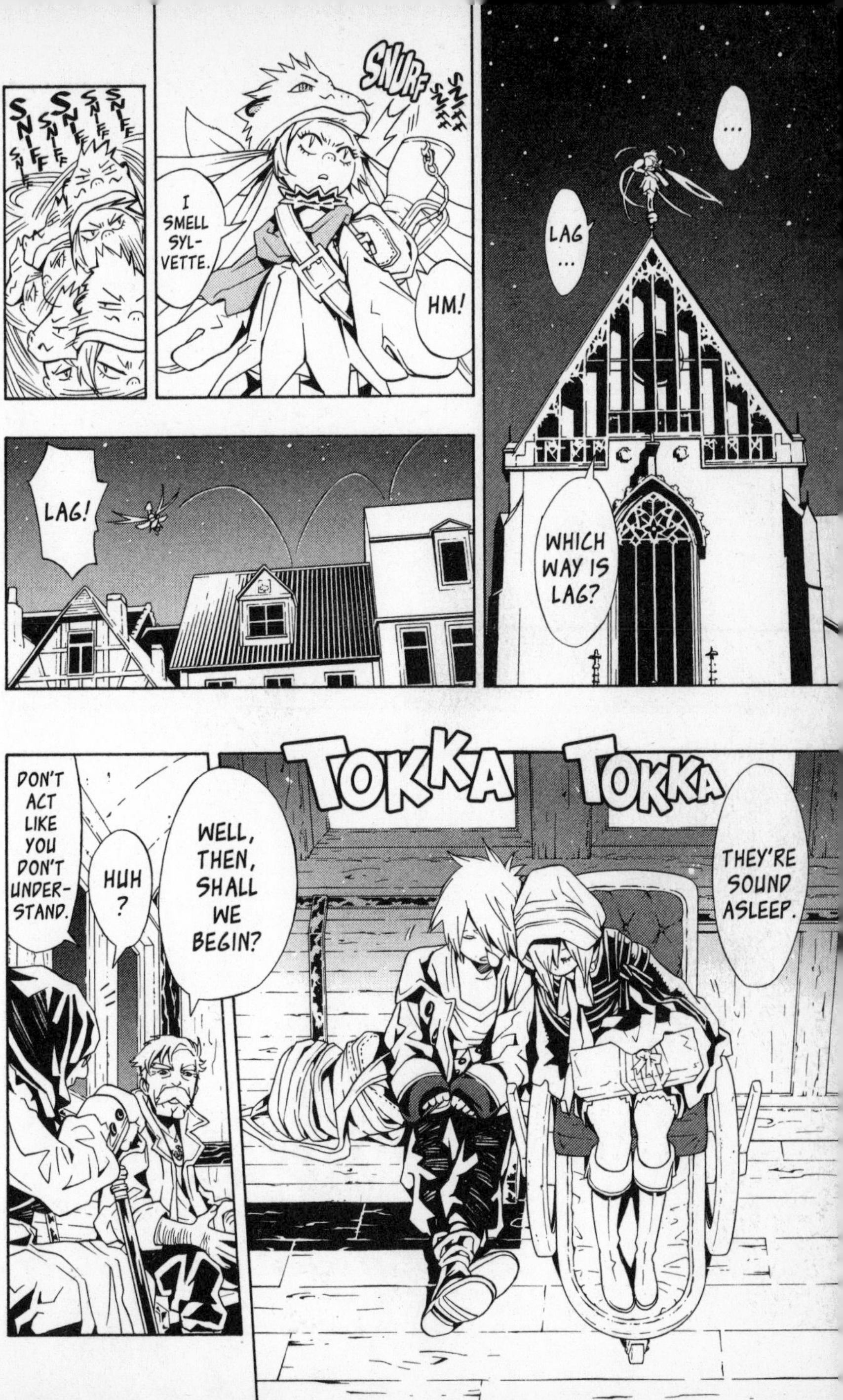
...
LAG ...
WHICH WAY IS LAG?
SNURF
SNIFF SNIFF
HM!
I SMELL SYLVETTE.
SNIFF SNIFF SNIFF SNIFF SNIFF
LAG!
TOKKA TOKKA
THEY'RE SOUND ASLEEP.
WELL, THEN, SHALL WE BEGIN?
HUH?
DON'T ACT LIKE YOU DON'T UNDERSTAND.

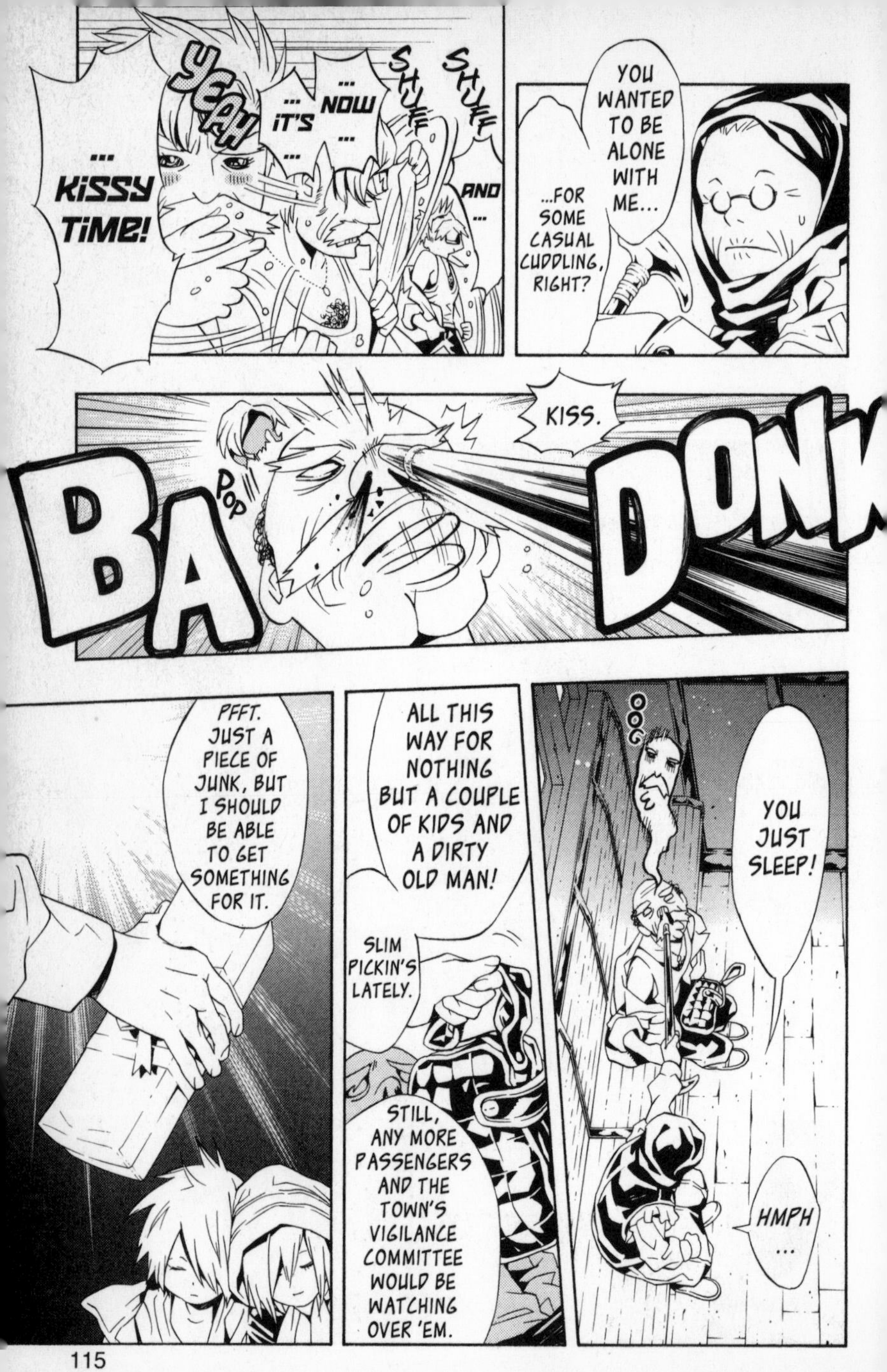
YOU WANTED TO BE ALONE WITH ME...
...FOR SOME CASUAL CUDDLING, RIGHT?
SHUFF SHUFF
AND ...
... NOW ...
... IT'S ...
... KISSY TIME!
YEAH
KISS.
BA DONK
POP
OOG
YOU JUST SLEEP!
HMPH ...
ALL THIS WAY FOR NOTHING BUT A COUPLE OF KIDS AND A DIRTY OLD MAN!
SLIM PICKIN'S LATELY.
STILL, ANY MORE PASSENGERS AND THE TOWN'S VIGILANCE COMMITTEE WOULD BE WATCHING OVER 'EM.
PFFT. JUST A PIECE OF JUNK, BUT I SHOULD BE ABLE TO GET SOMETHING FOR IT.

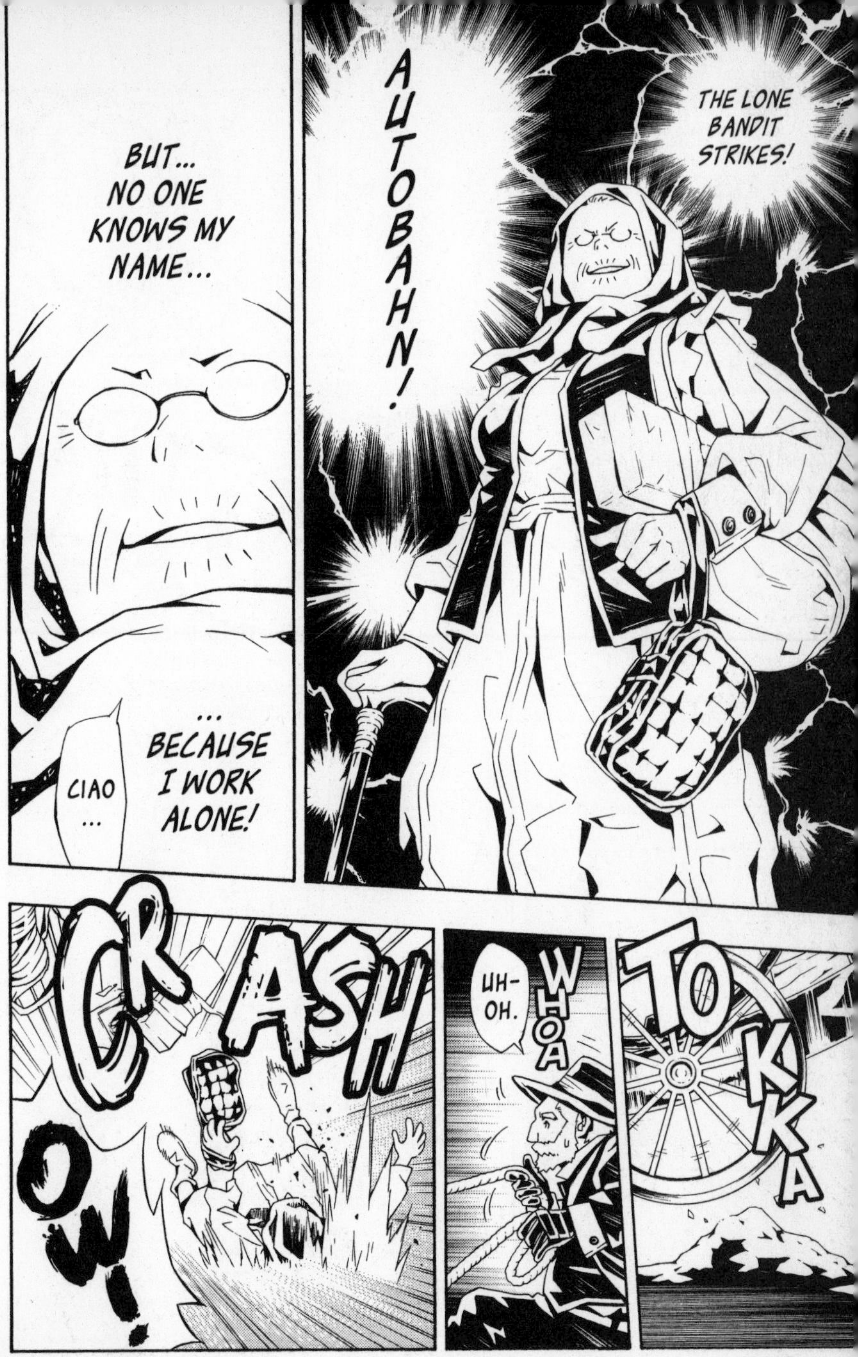
THE LONE BANDIT STRIKES!
AUTOBAHN!
BUT... NO ONE KNOWS MY NAME...
... BECAUSE I WORK ALONE!
CIAO ...
TOKKA
UH-OH.
WHOA
CRASH
OW!

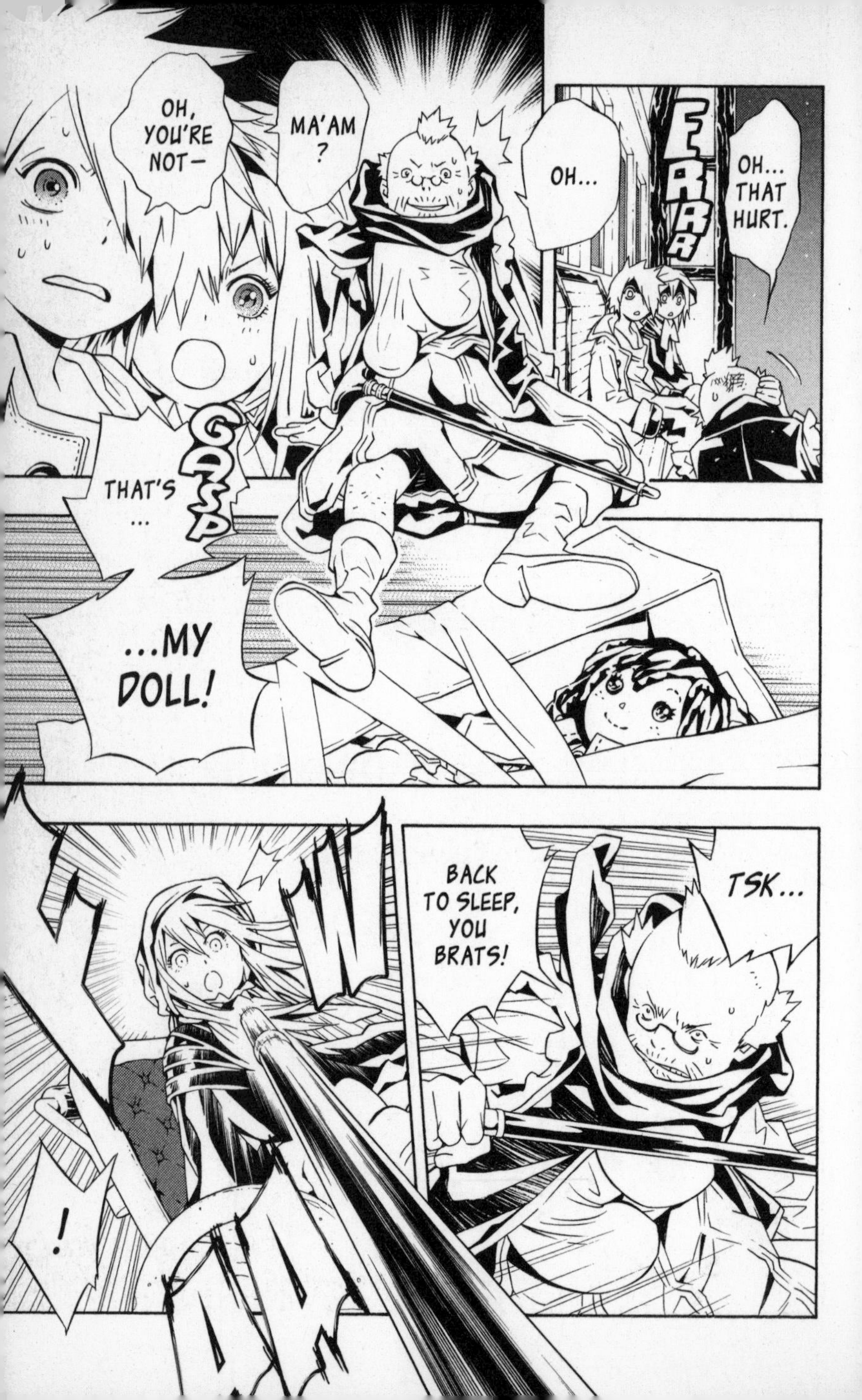
OH... THAT HURT.
ERRR
OH...
MA'AM ?
OH, YOU'RE NOT—
GASP
THAT'S ...
...MY DOLL!
TSK...
BACK TO SLEEP, YOU BRATS!
!

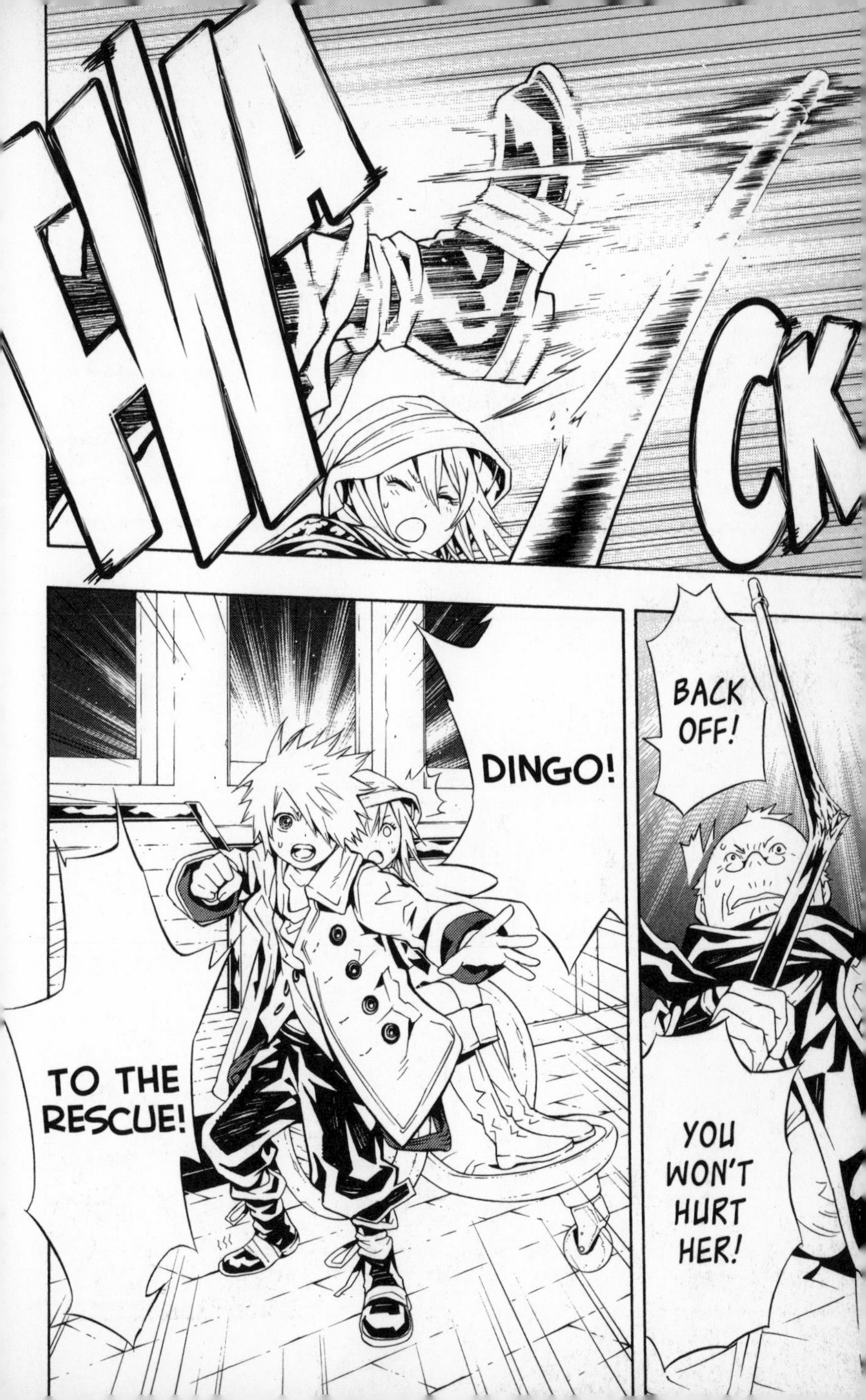
WHACK
BACK OFF!
YOU WON'T HURT HER!
DINGO!
TO THE RESCUE!

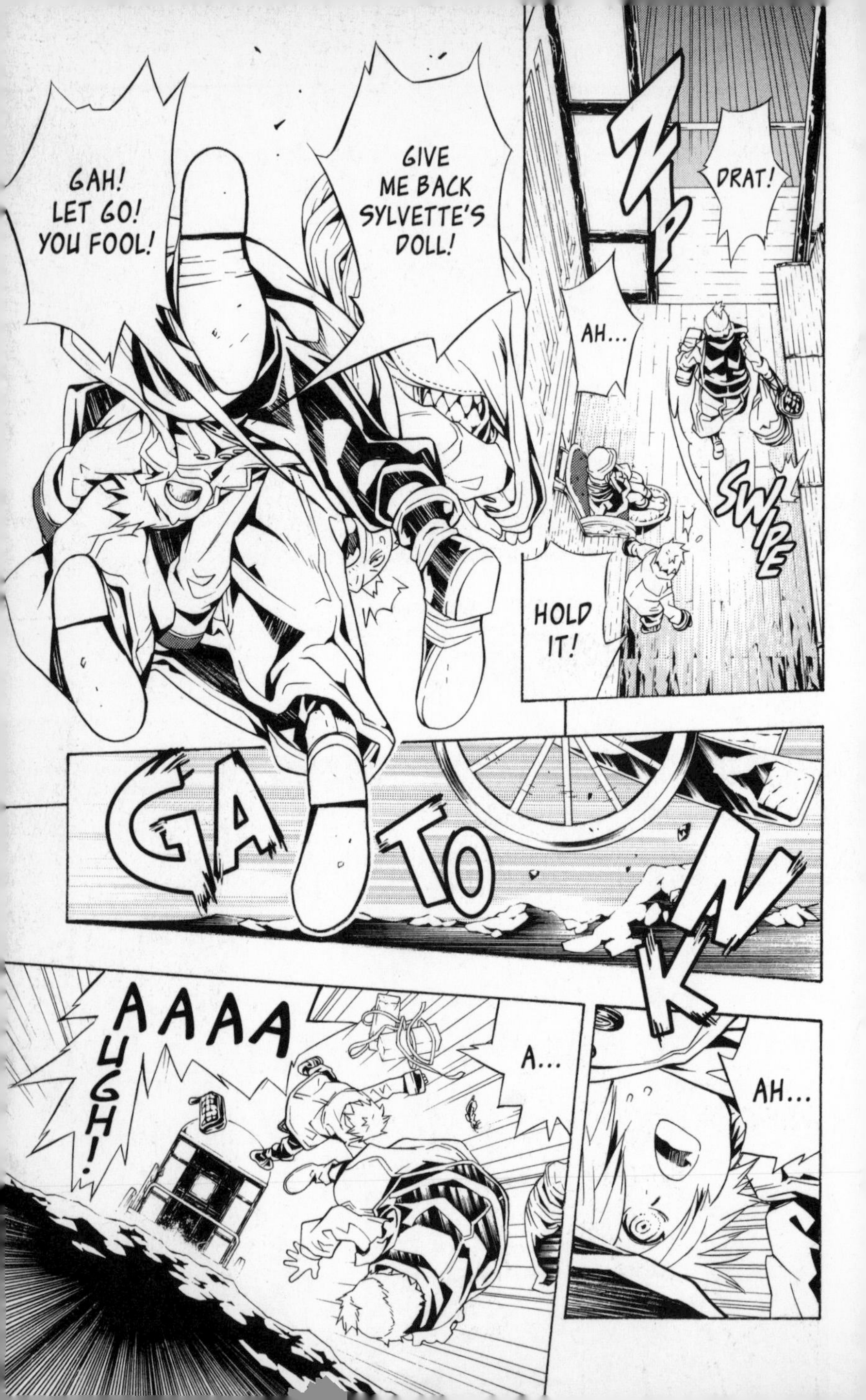
DRAT!
ZIP
AH...
SWIPE
HOLD IT!
GIVE ME BACK SYLVETTE'S DOLL!
GAH! LET GO! YOU FOOL!
GATONK
AH...
A...
AAAA
AUGH!!

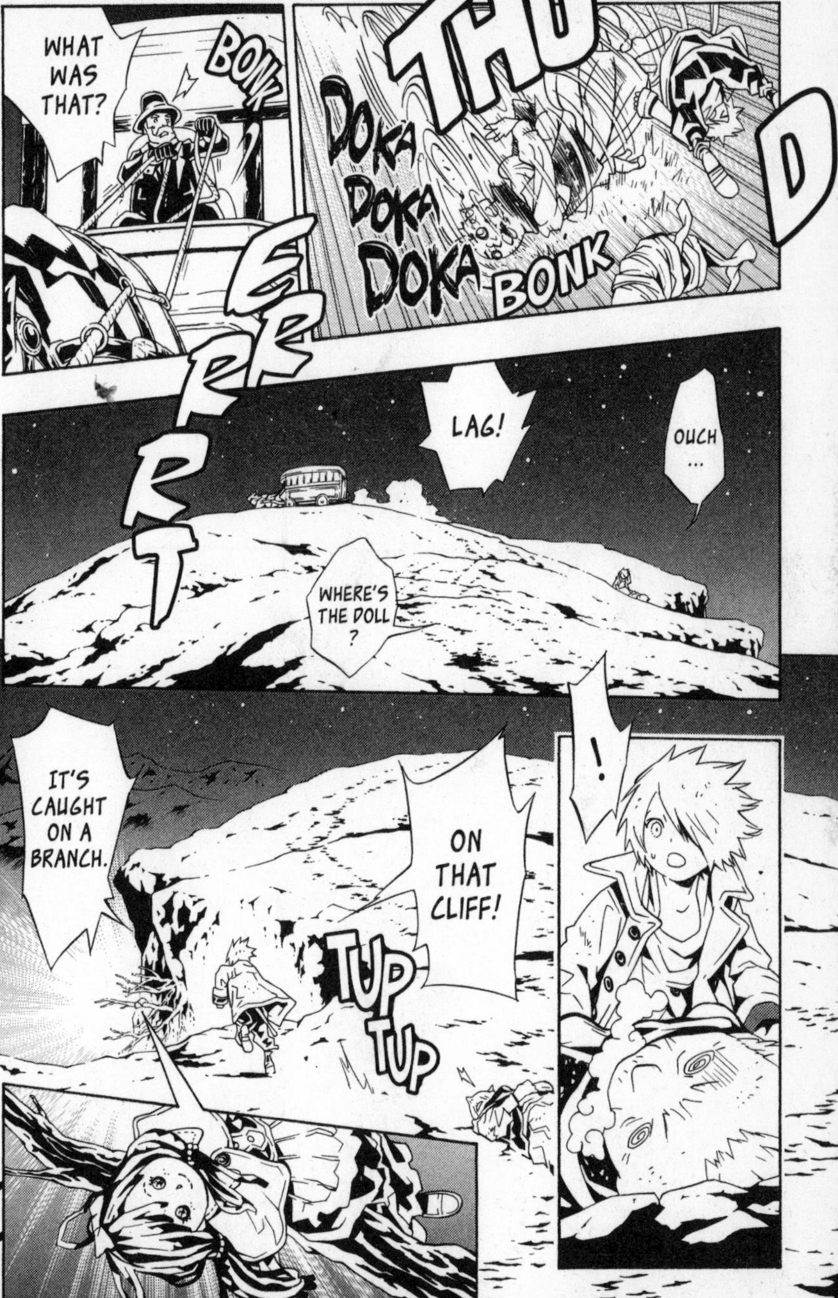
THUD
DOKA DOKA DOKA
BONK
BONK
WHAT WAS THAT?
EERRRT
OUCH ...
LAG!
WHERE'S THE DOLL ?
!
ON THAT CLIFF!
IT'S CAUGHT ON A BRANCH.
TUP TUP

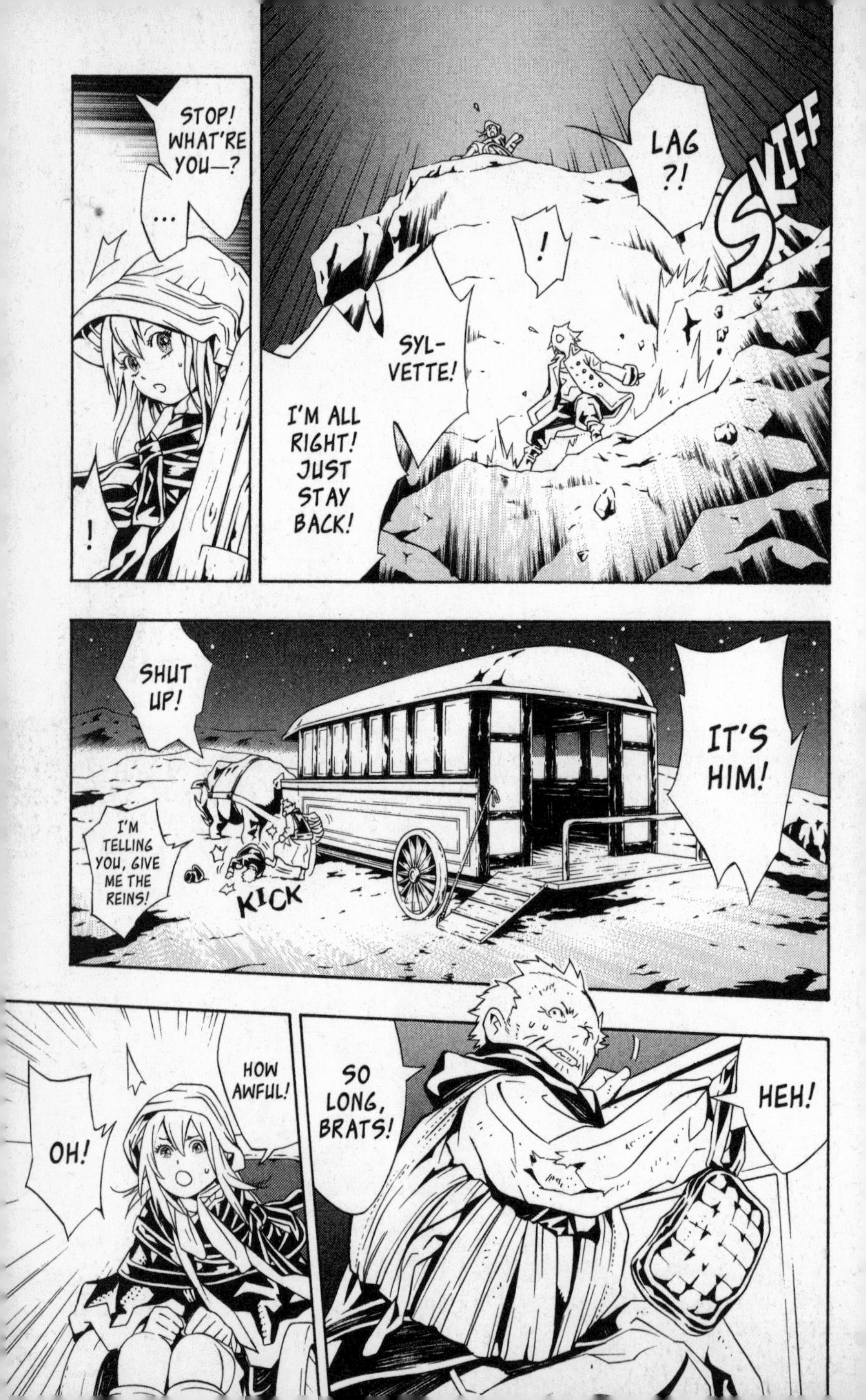
LAG ?!
SKIFF
!
SYL-VETTE!
I'M ALL RIGHT! JUST STAY BACK!
STOP! WHAT'RE YOU—?
...
!
IT'S HIM!
I'M TELLING YOU, GIVE ME THE REINS!
KICK
SHUT UP!
HEH!
SO LONG, BRATS!
HOW AWFUL!
OH!

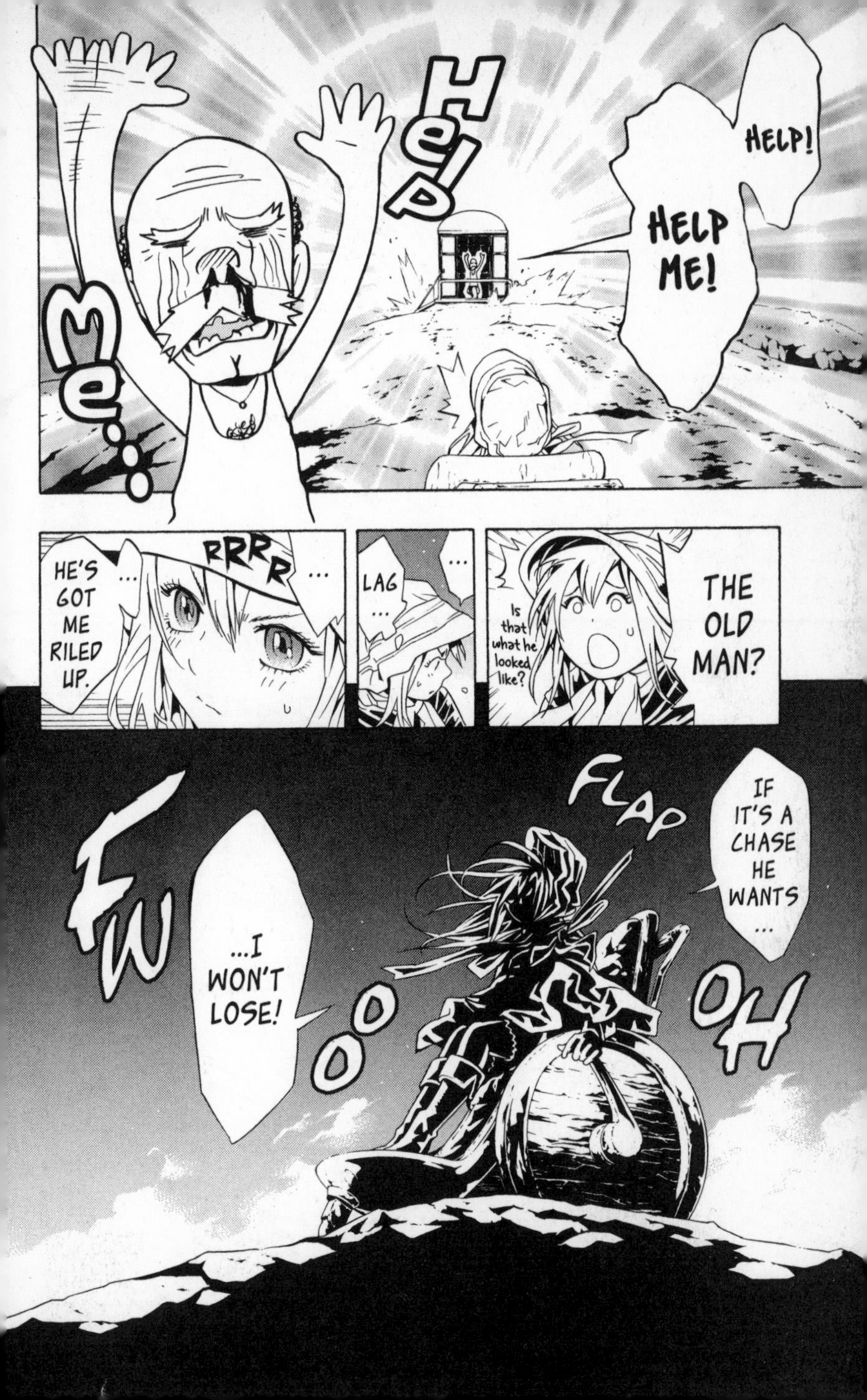
HELP!
HELP ME!
Help
Me...
THE OLD MAN?
Is that what he looked like?
...
LAG ...
...
RRRR
HE'S GOT ME RILED UP.
...
IF IT'S A CHASE HE WANTS ...
FLAP
...I WON'T LOSE!
FWOOOH

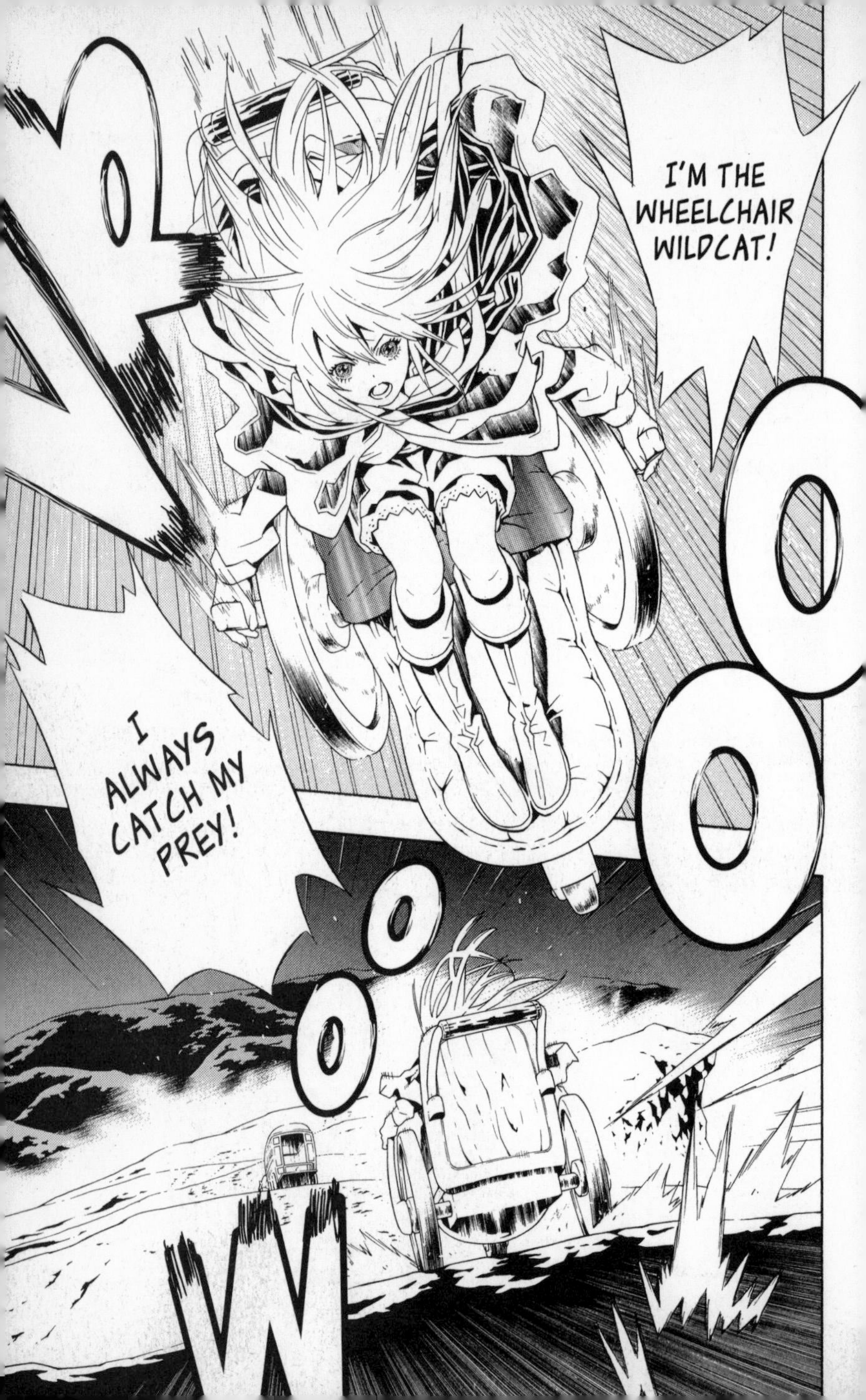
I'M THE WHEELCHAIR WILDCAT!
I ALWAYS CATCH MY PREY!

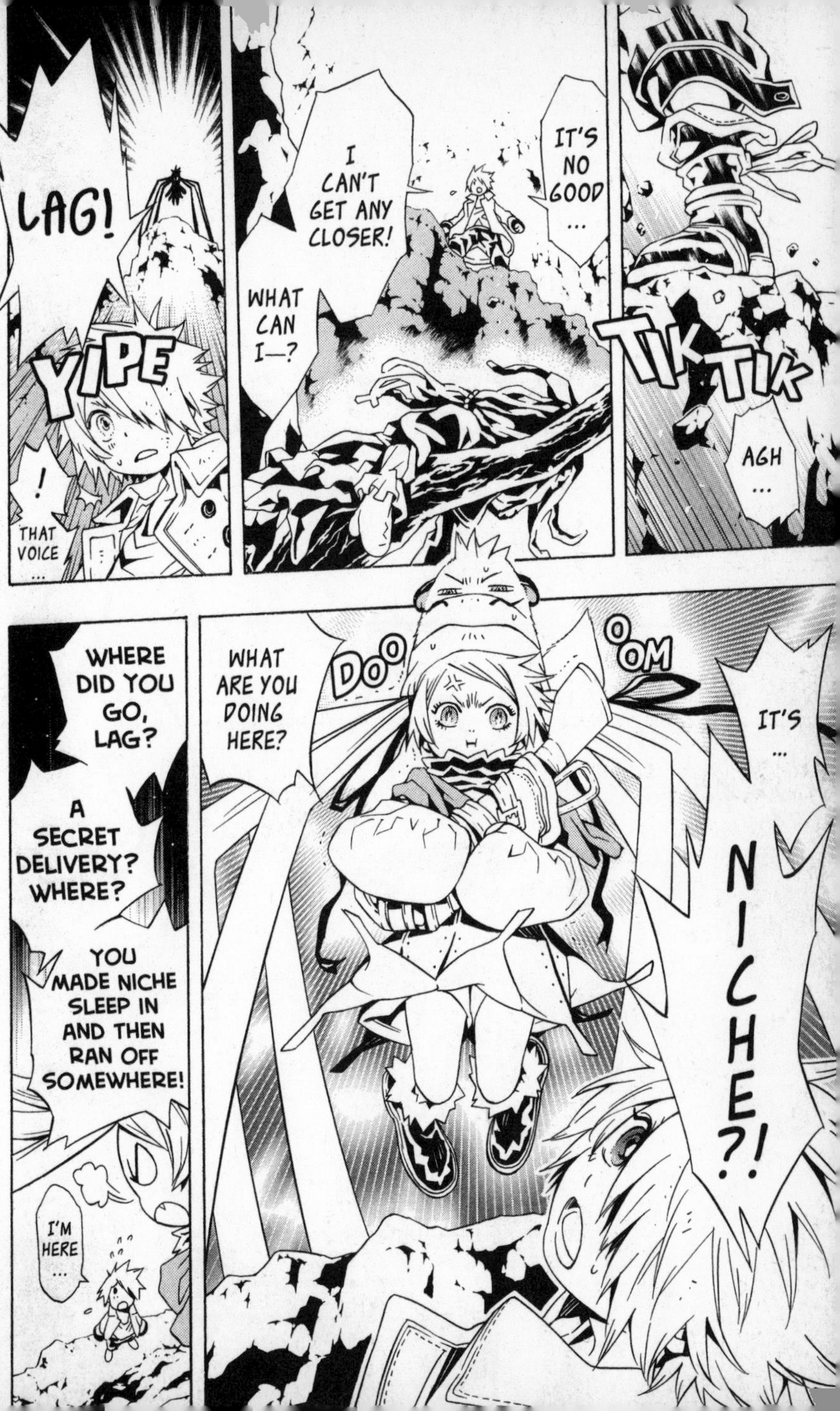
TIK TIK
AGH ...
IT'S NO GOOD ...
I CAN'T GET ANY CLOSER!
WHAT CAN I—?
LAG!
YIPE
!
THAT VOICE ...
IT'S ...
NICHE?!
DOOOOM
WHAT ARE YOU DOING HERE?
WHERE DID YOU GO, LAG?
A SECRET DELIVERY? WHERE?
YOU MADE NICHE SLEEP IN AND THEN RAN OFF SOMEWHERE!
I'M HERE ...

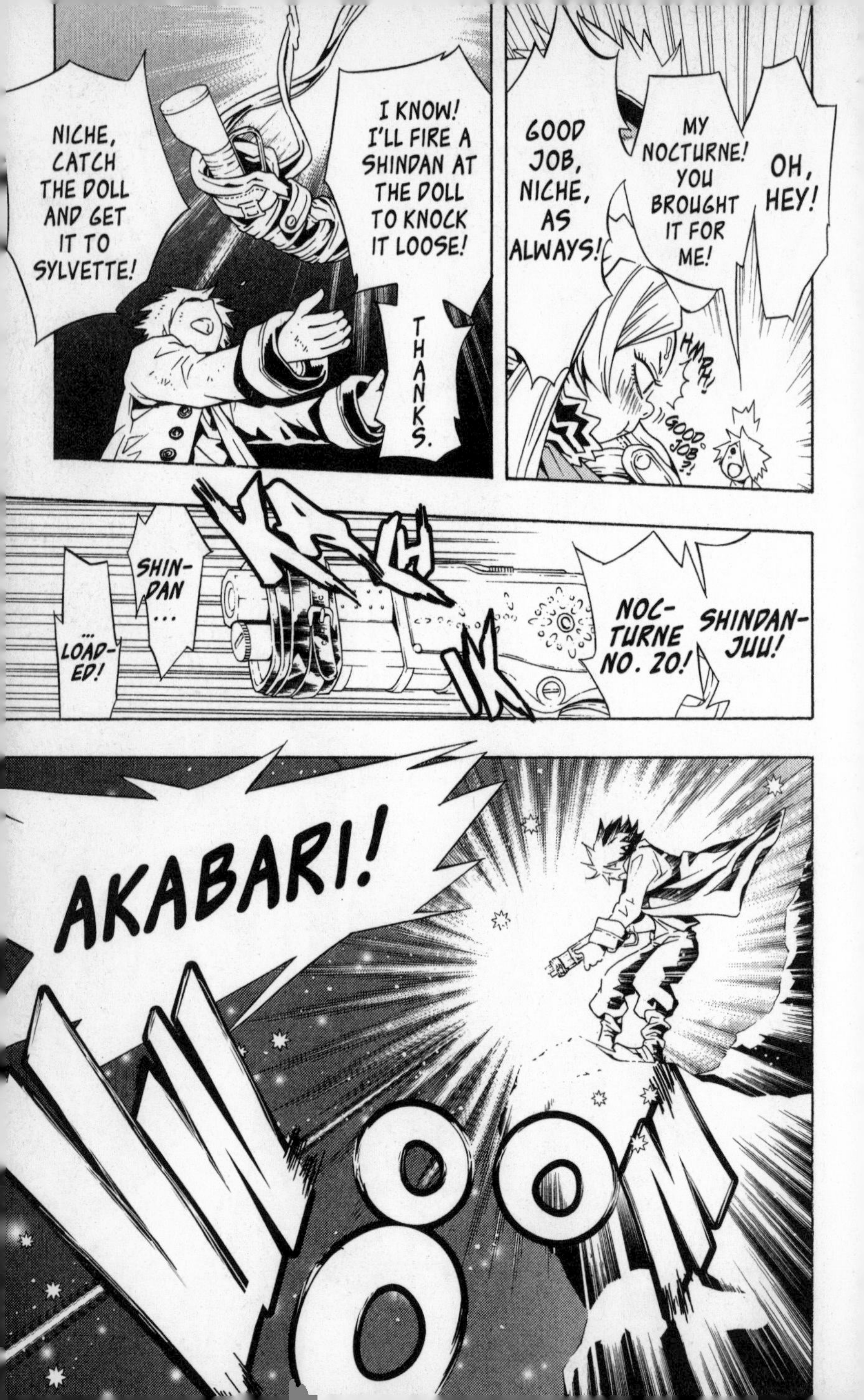
OH, HEY!
MY NOCTURNE! YOU BROUGHT IT FOR ME!
GOOD JOB, NICHE, AS ALWAYS!
HMPH!
GOOD JOB?!
I KNOW! I'LL FIRE A SHINDAN AT THE DOLL TO KNOCK IT LOOSE!
NICHE, CATCH THE DOLL AND GET IT TO SYLVETTE!
THANKS.
SHINDAN-JUU!
NOC-TURNE NO. 20!
SHIN-DAN...
...LOAD-ED!
AKABARI!

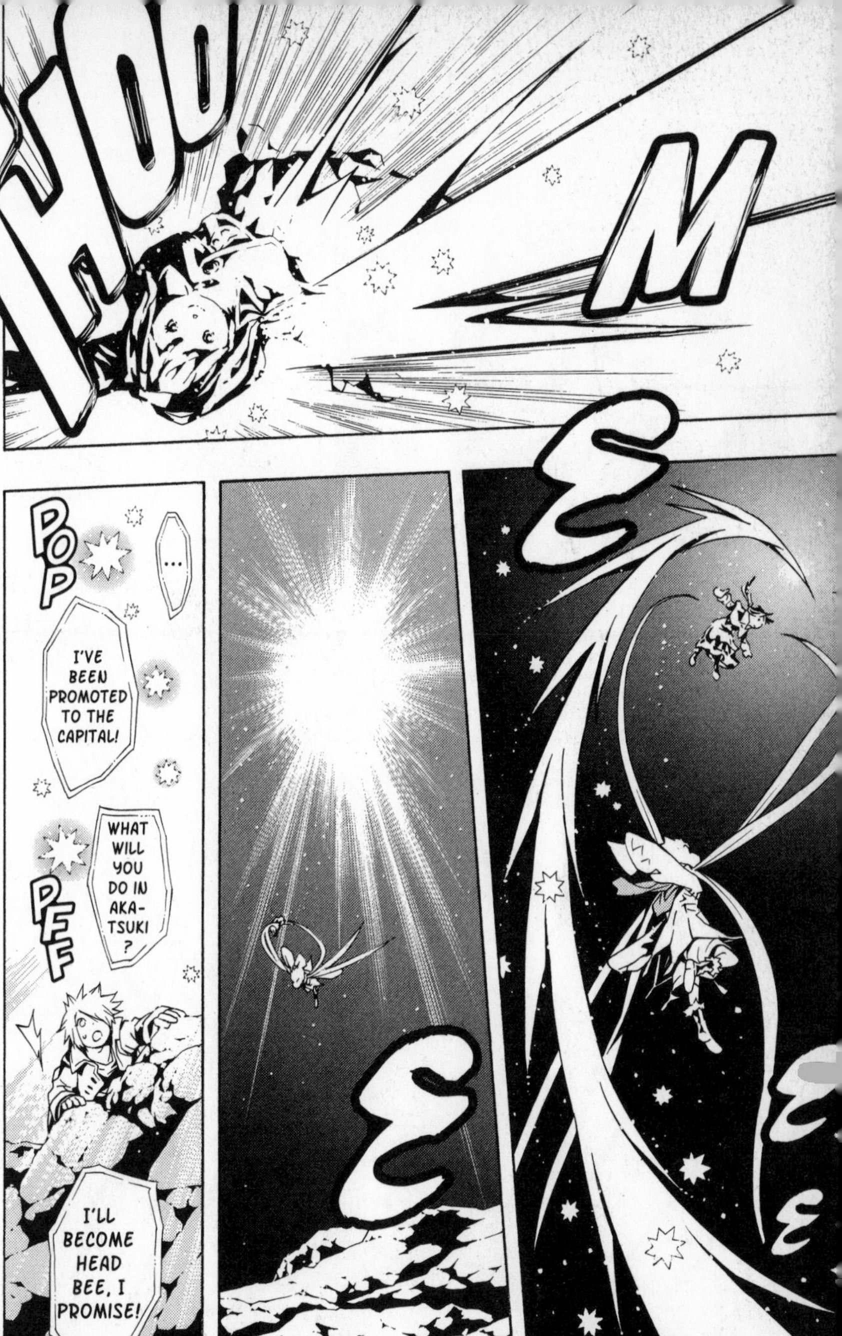
HOOM
E
EE
E
POP
...
I'VE BEEN PROMOTED TO THE CAPITAL!
PFF
WHAT WILL YOU DO IN AKATSUKI?
I'LL BECOME HEAD BEE, I PROMISE!

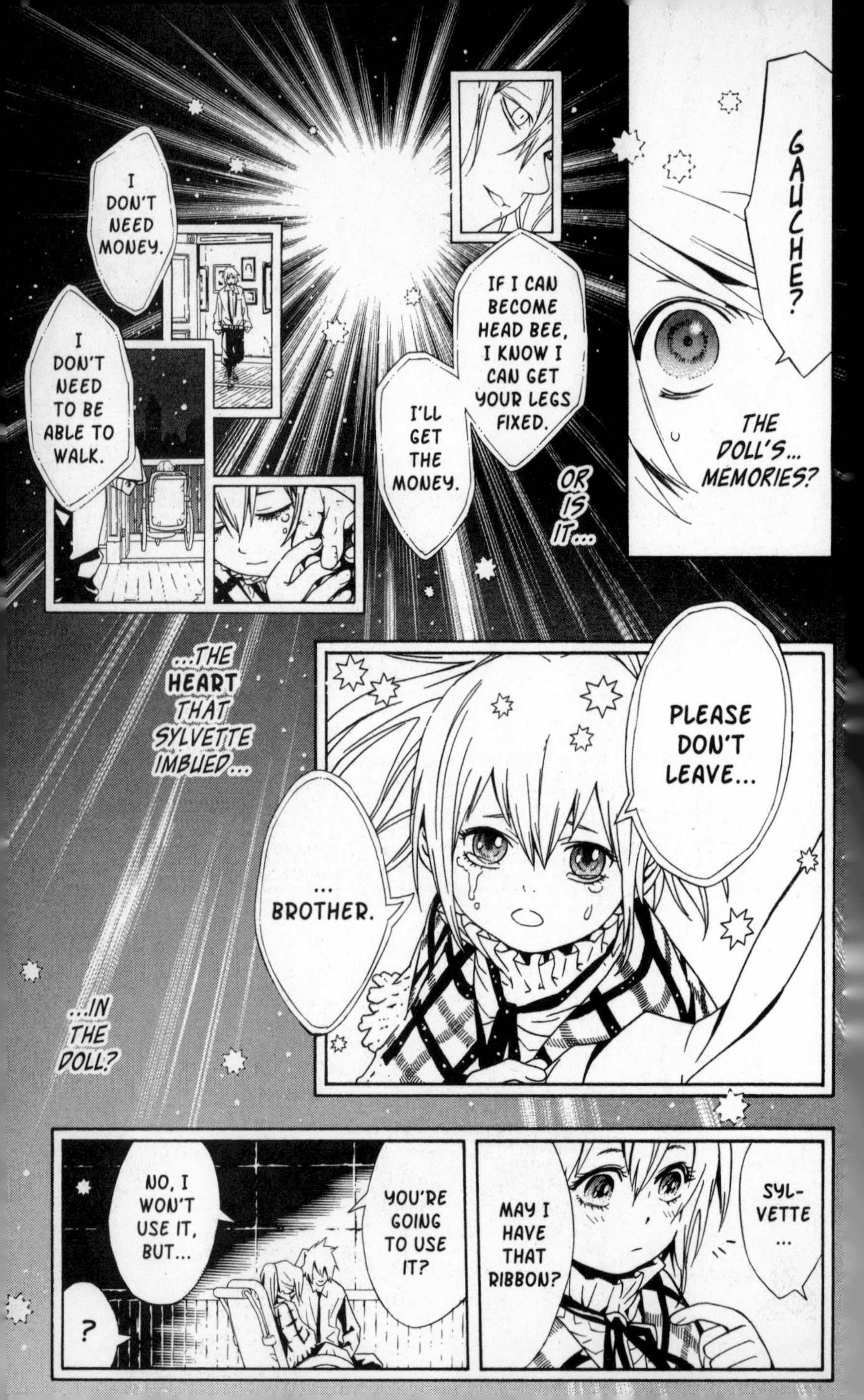
GAUCHE?
THE DOLL'S... MEMORIES?
OR IS IT...
IF I CAN BECOME HEAD BEE, I KNOW I CAN GET YOUR LEGS FIXED.
I'LL GET THE MONEY.
I DON'T NEED MONEY.
I DON'T NEED TO BE ABLE TO WALK.
...THE HEART THAT SYLVETTE IMBUED...
...IN THE DOLL?
PLEASE DON'T LEAVE...
...BROTHER.
SYL-VETTE...
MAY I HAVE THAT RIBBON?
YOU'RE GOING TO USE IT?
NO, I WON'T USE IT, BUT...
?

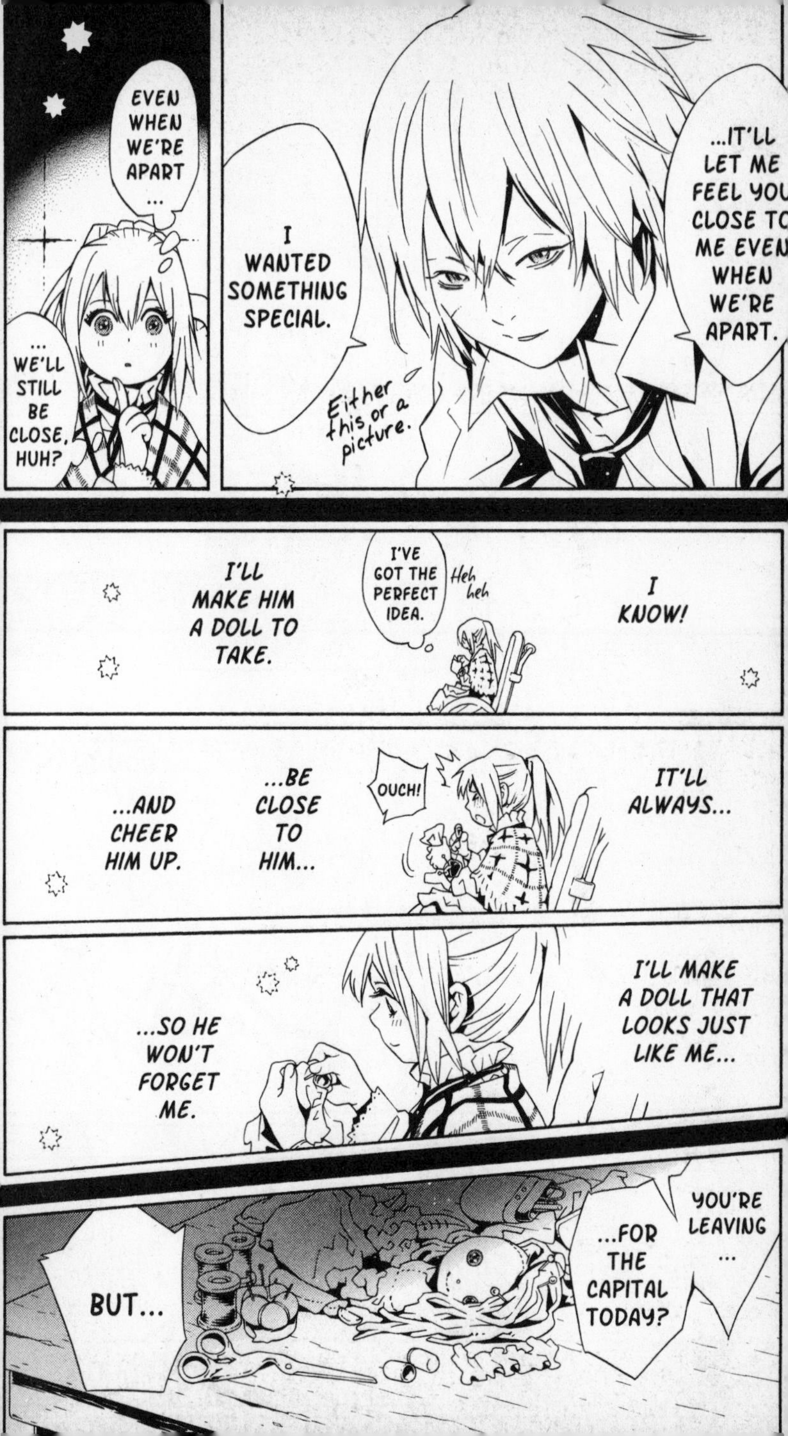
...IT'LL LET ME FEEL YOU CLOSE TO ME EVEN WHEN WE'RE APART.
I WANTED SOMETHING SPECIAL.
Either this or a picture.
EVEN WHEN WE'RE APART...
...WE'LL STILL BE CLOSE, HUH?
I KNOW!
I'VE GOT THE PERFECT IDEA.
Heh heh
I'LL MAKE HIM A DOLL TO TAKE.
IT'LL ALWAYS...
OUCH!
...BE CLOSE TO HIM...
...AND CHEER HIM UP.
I'LL MAKE A DOLL THAT LOOKS JUST LIKE ME...
...SO HE WON'T FORGET ME.
YOU'RE LEAVING...
...FOR THE CAPITAL TODAY?
BUT...

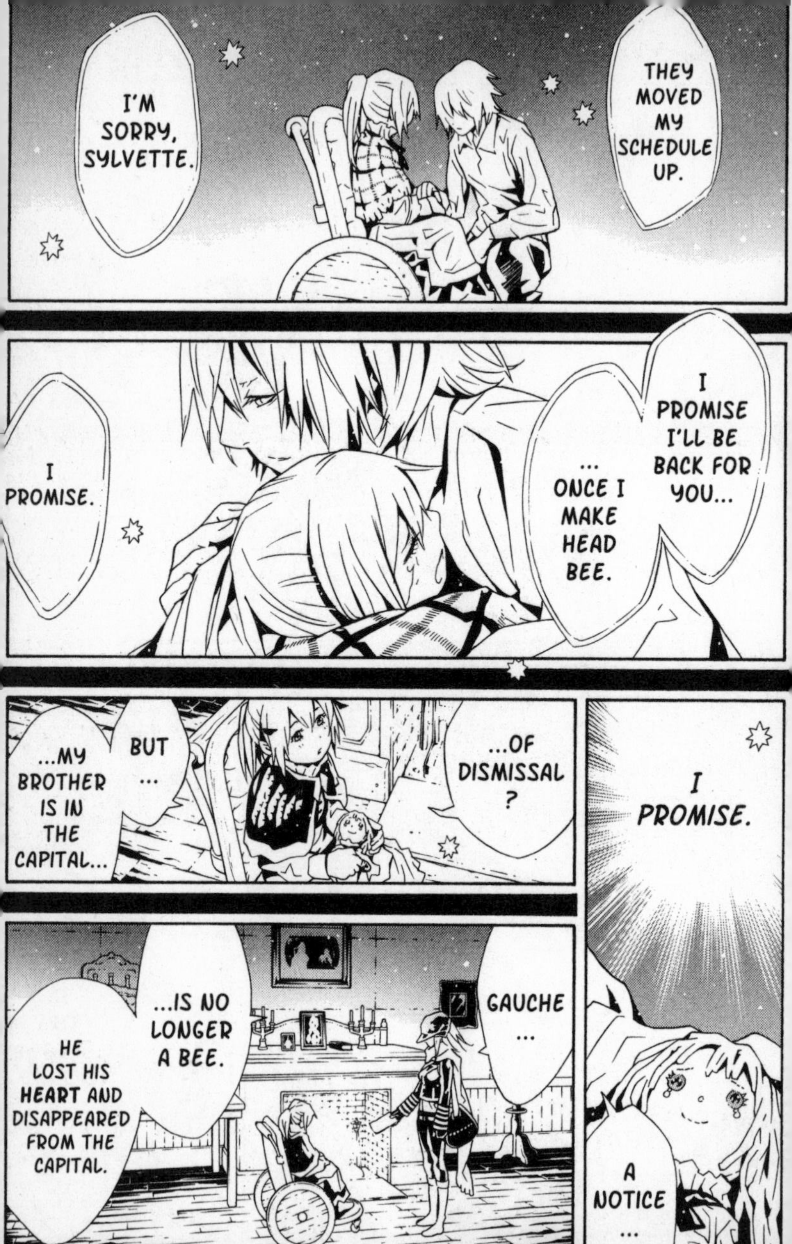
THEY MOVED MY SCHEDULE UP.
I'M SORRY, SYLVETTE.
I PROMISE I'LL BE BACK FOR YOU...
...ONCE I MAKE HEAD BEE.
I PROMISE.
I PROMISE.
A NOTICE...
...OF DISMISSAL?
BUT...
...MY BROTHER IS IN THE CAPITAL...
GAUCHE...
...IS NO LONGER A BEE.
HE LOST HIS HEART AND DISAPPEARED FROM THE CAPITAL.

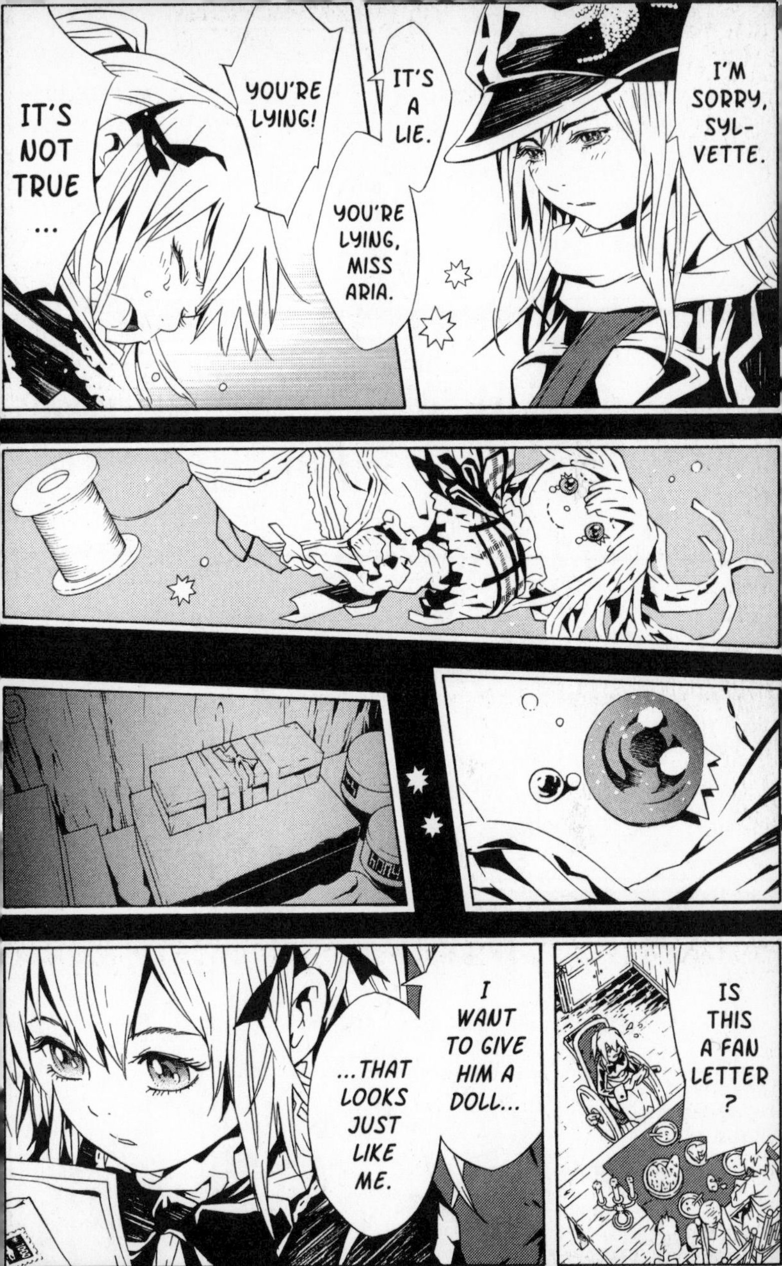
I'M SORRY, SYLVETTE.
IT'S A LIE.
YOU'RE LYING!
YOU'RE LYING, MISS ARIA.
IT'S NOT TRUE ...
IS THIS A FAN LETTER?
I WANT TO GIVE HIM A DOLL...
...THAT LOOKS JUST LIKE ME.

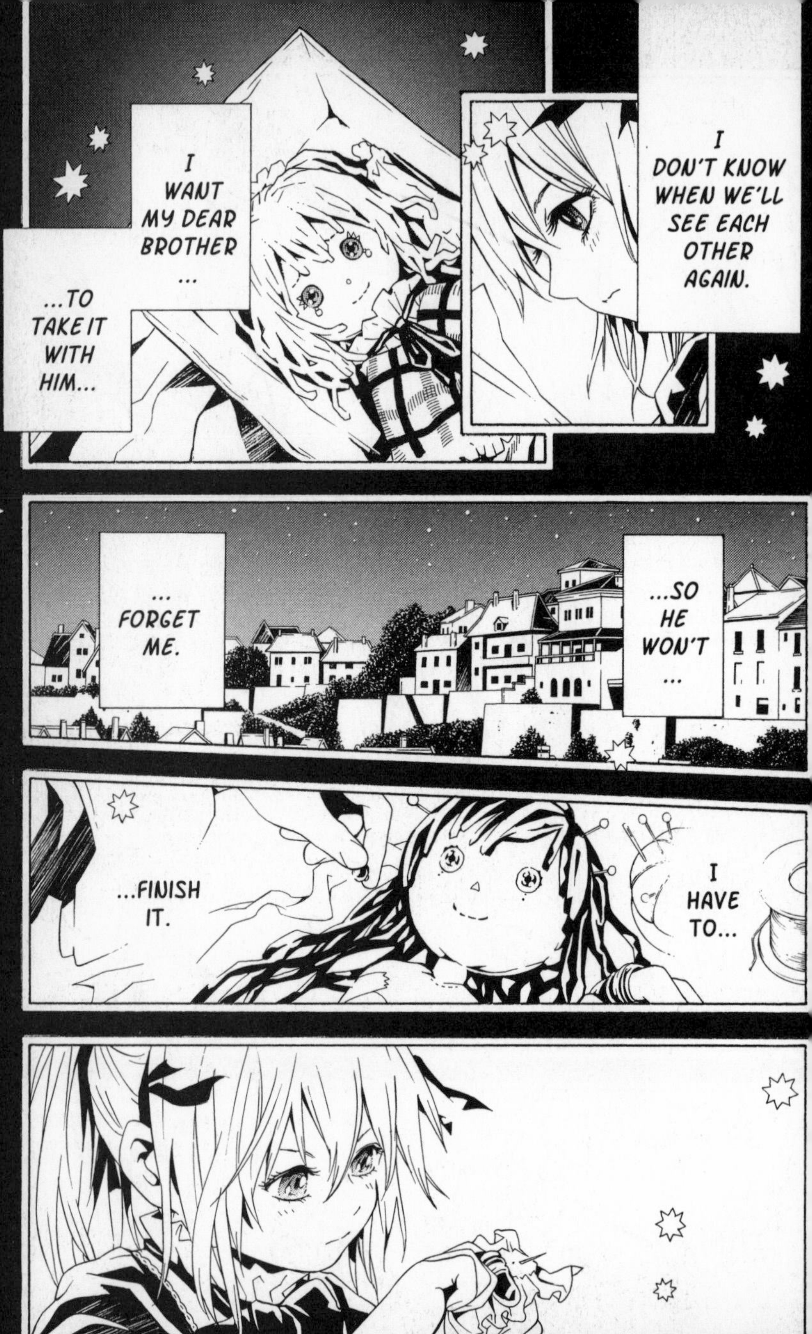
I DON'T KNOW WHEN WE'LL SEE EACH OTHER AGAIN.
I WANT MY DEAR BROTHER ...
...TO TAKE IT WITH HIM...
...SO HE WON'T ...
... FORGET ME.
I HAVE TO...
...FINISH IT.

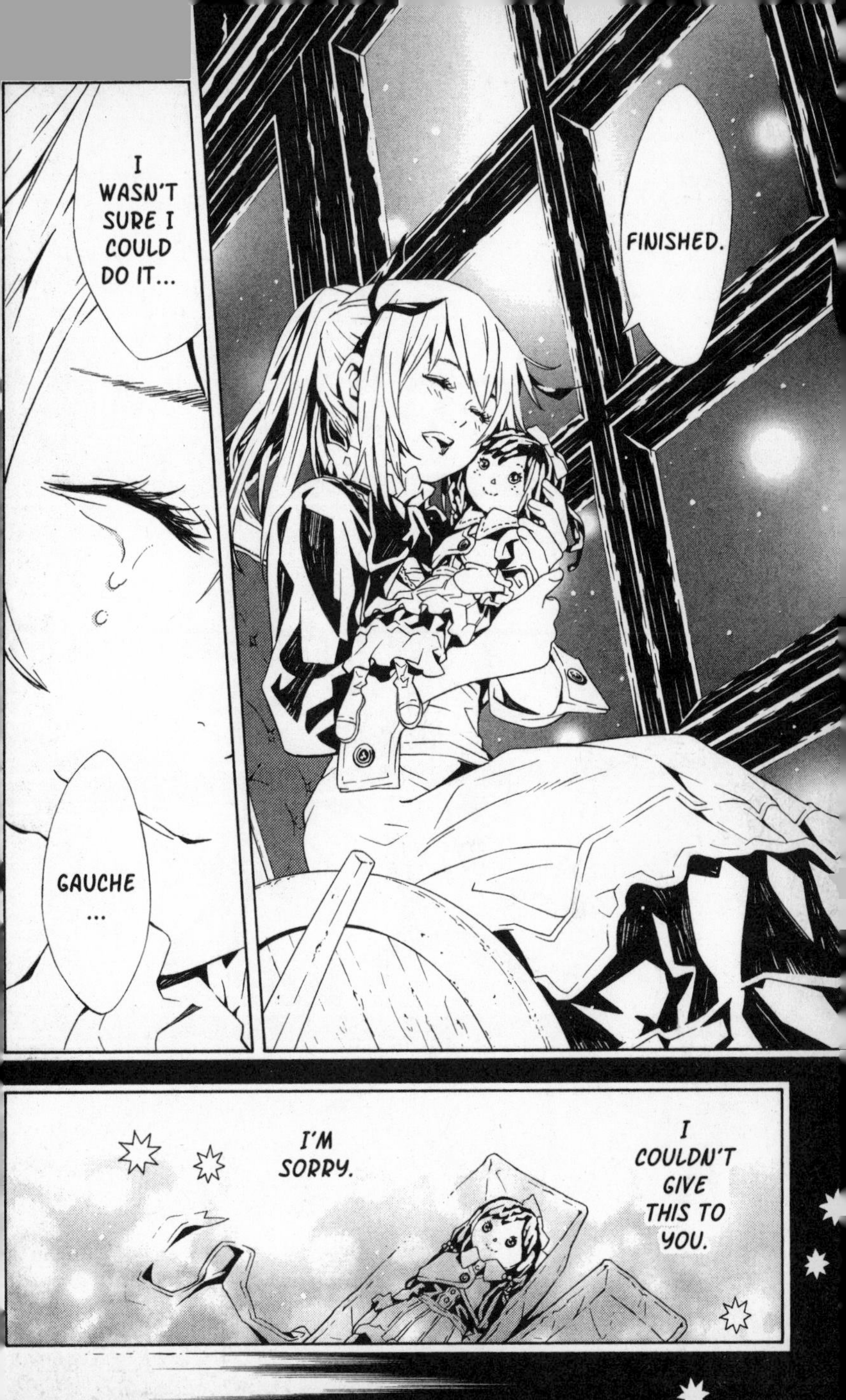
FINISHED.
I WASN'T SURE I COULD DO IT...
GAUCHE ...
I COULDN'T GIVE THIS TO YOU.
I'M SORRY.

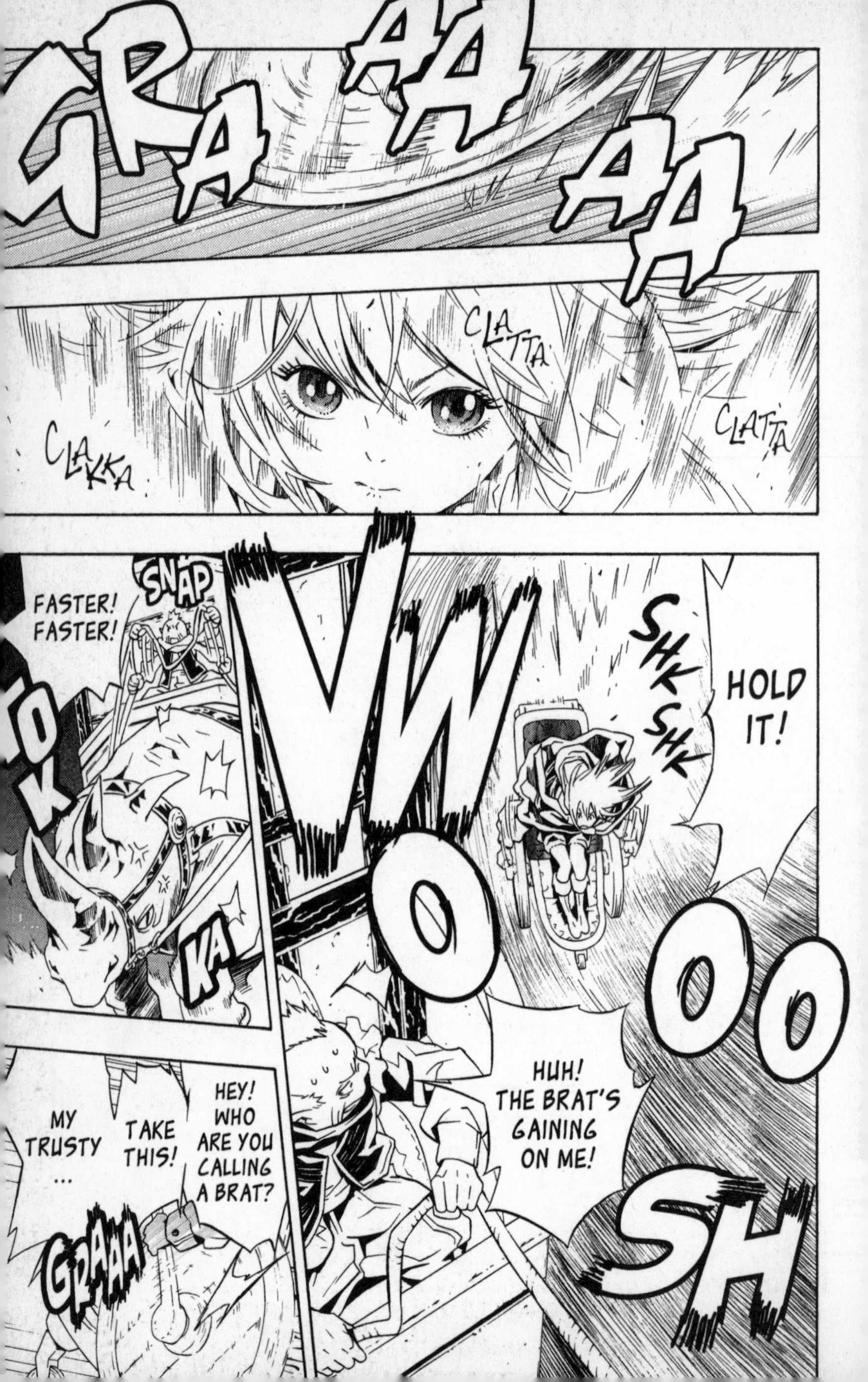
GRAAAAAA
CLATTA
CLATTA
CLAKKA
HOLD IT!
SHK SHK
VWOOOSH
SNAP
FASTER! FASTER!
KA
HUH! THE BRAT'S GAINING ON ME!
HEY! WHO ARE YOU CALLING A BRAT?
TAKE THIS!
MY TRUSTY ...
GRAAA

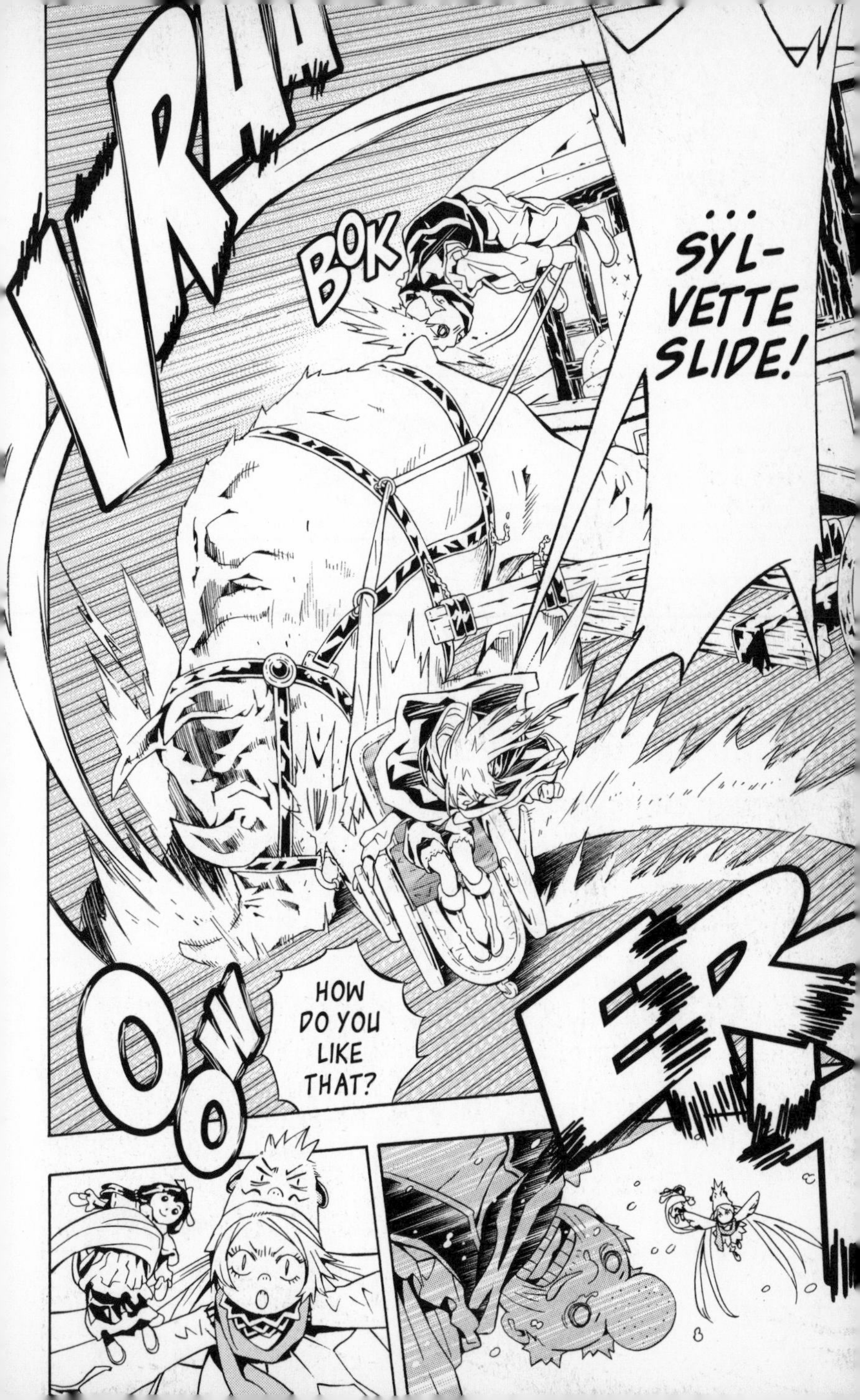
... SYL-VETTE SLIDE!
BOK
HOW DO YOU LIKE THAT?

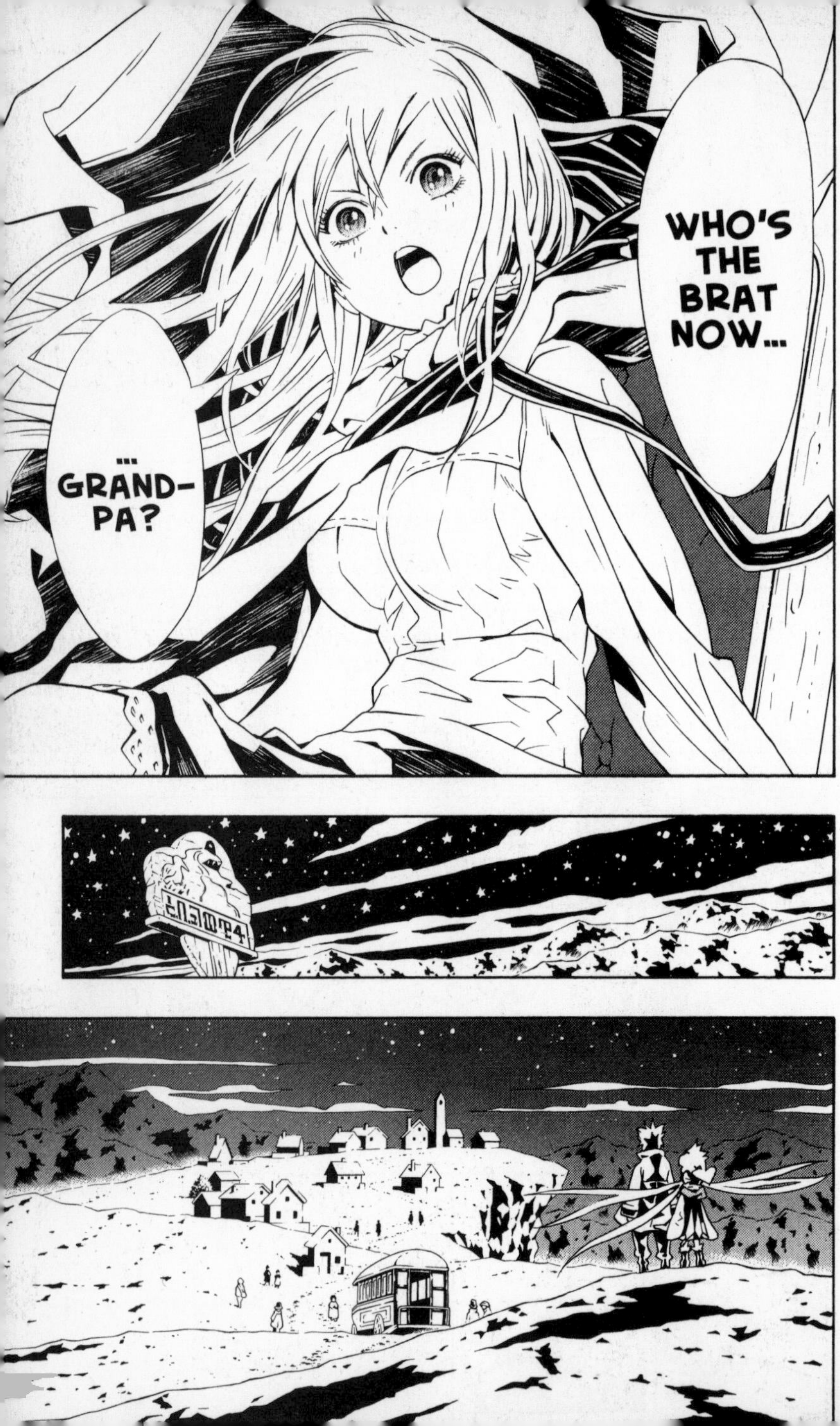
WHO'S THE BRAT NOW...
... GRAND-PA?

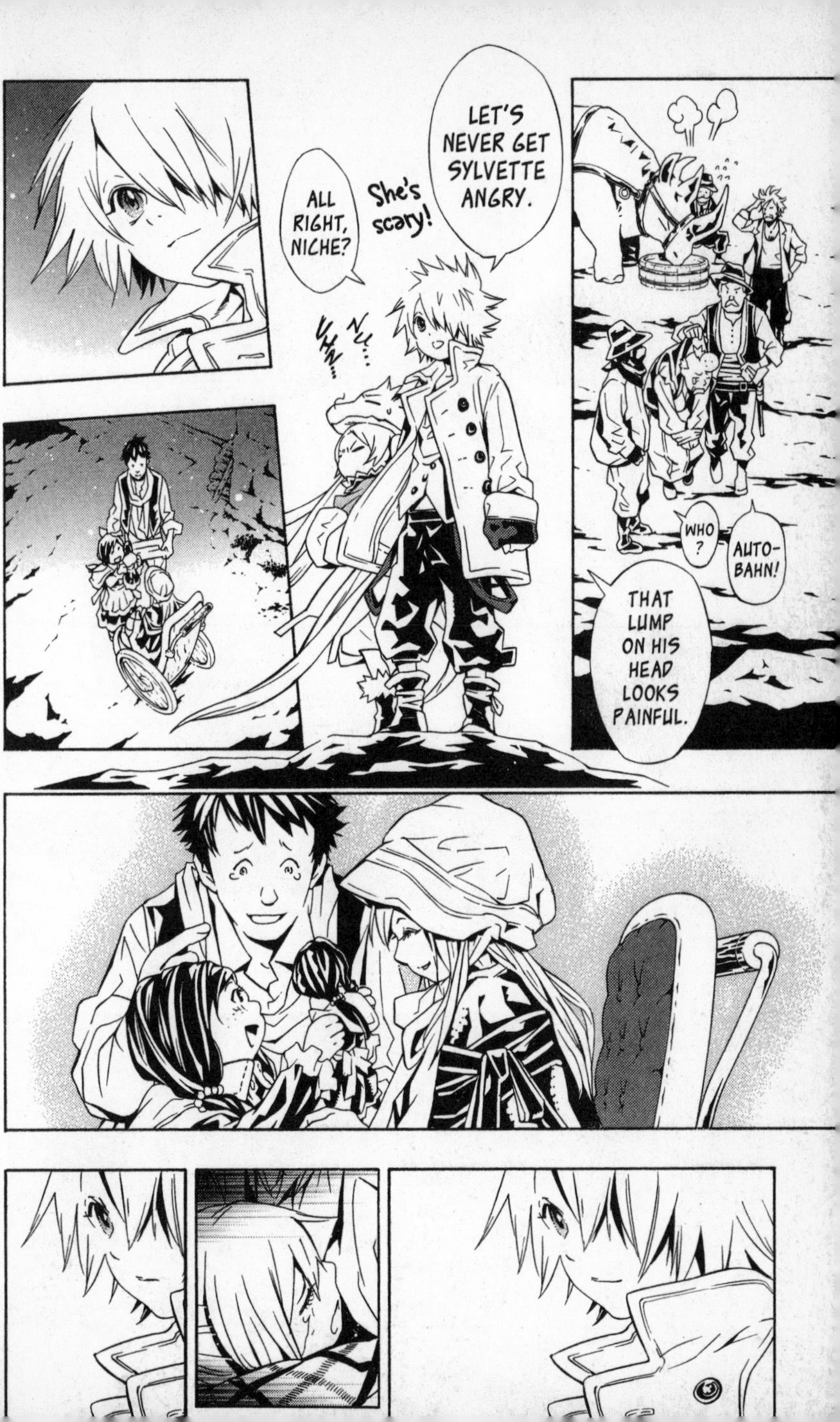
WHO?
AUTO-BAHN!
THAT LUMP ON HIS HEAD LOOKS PAINFUL.
LET'S NEVER GET SYLVETTE ANGRY.
She's scary!
ALL RIGHT, NICHE?
NU UHN...

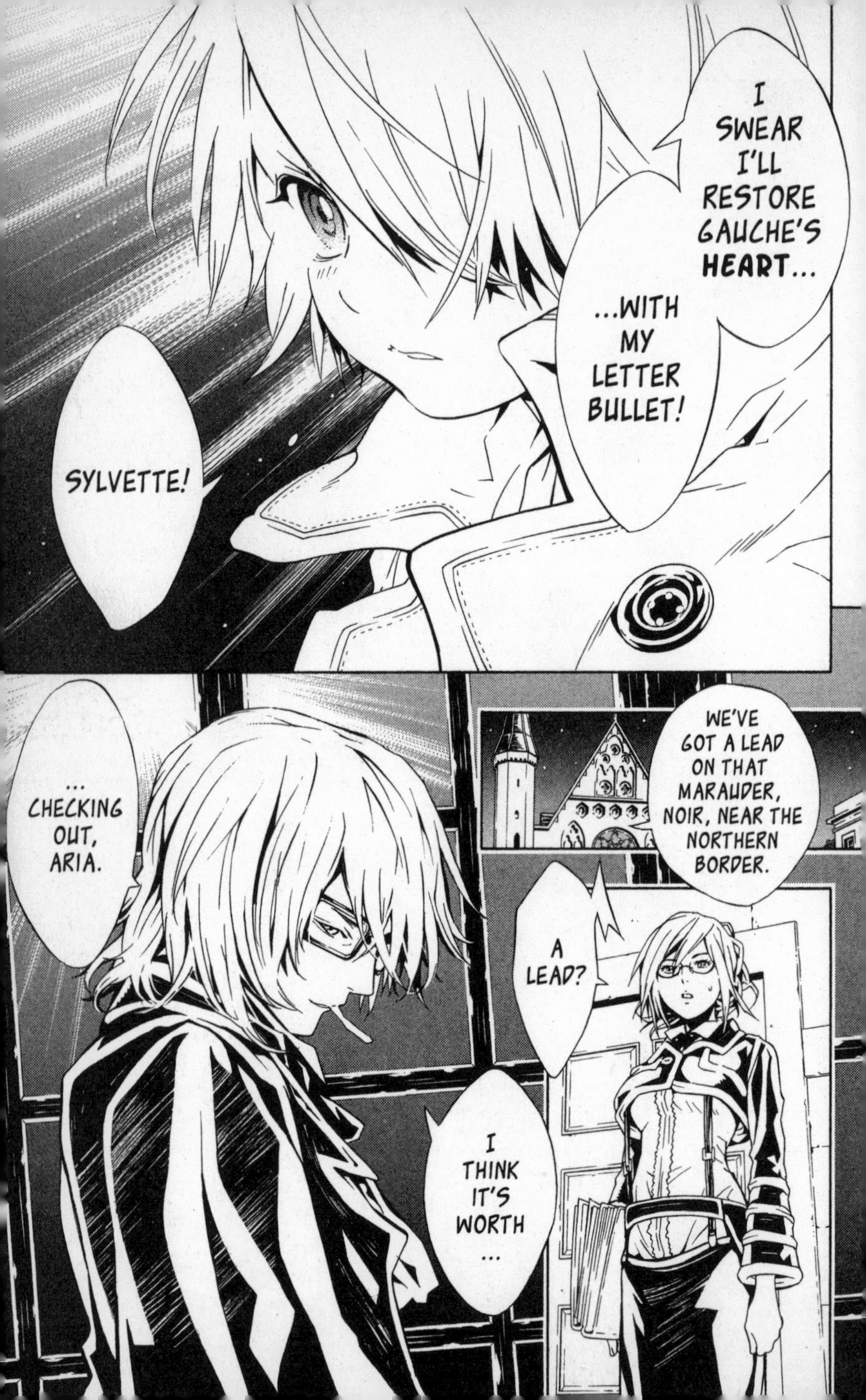
I SWEAR I'LL RESTORE GAUCHE'S HEART...
...WITH MY LETTER BULLET!
SYLVETTE!
WE'VE GOT A LEAD ON THAT MARAUDER, NOIR, NEAR THE NORTHERN BORDER.
A LEAD?
I THINK IT'S WORTH ...
... CHECKING OUT, ARIA.

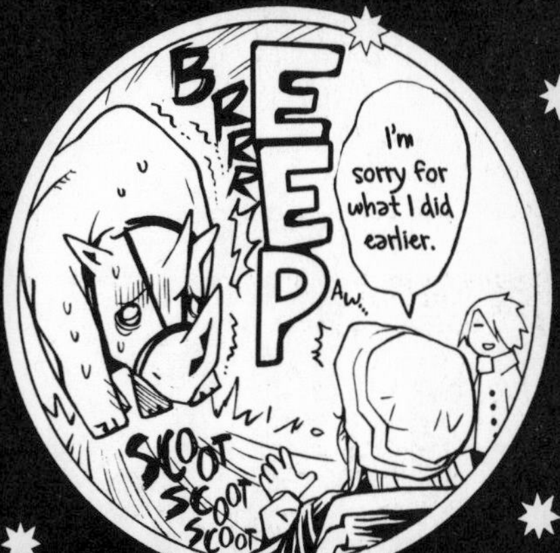
I'm sorry for what I did earlier.
BRRRREEEP
AW...
SCOOT
SCOOT
SCOOT

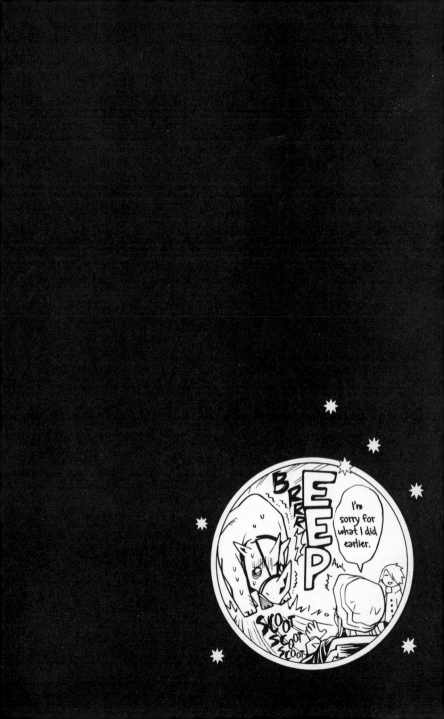

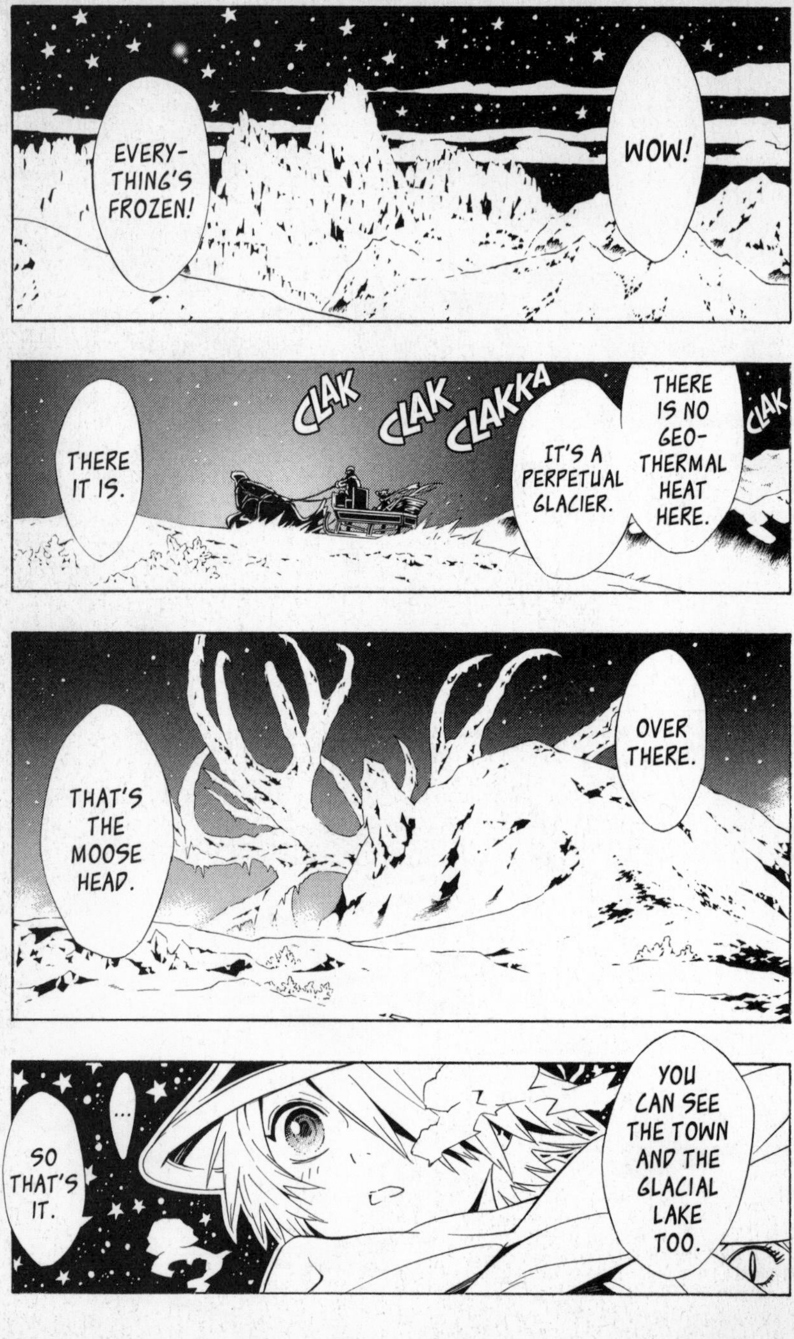
WOW!
EVERY-THING'S FROZEN!
CLAK
THERE IS NO GEO-THERMAL HEAT HERE.
IT'S A PERPETUAL GLACIER.
CLAKKA
CLAK
CLAK
THERE IT IS.
OVER THERE.
THAT'S THE MOOSE HEAD.
YOU CAN SEE THE TOWN AND THE GLACIAL LAKE TOO.
...
SO THAT'S IT.

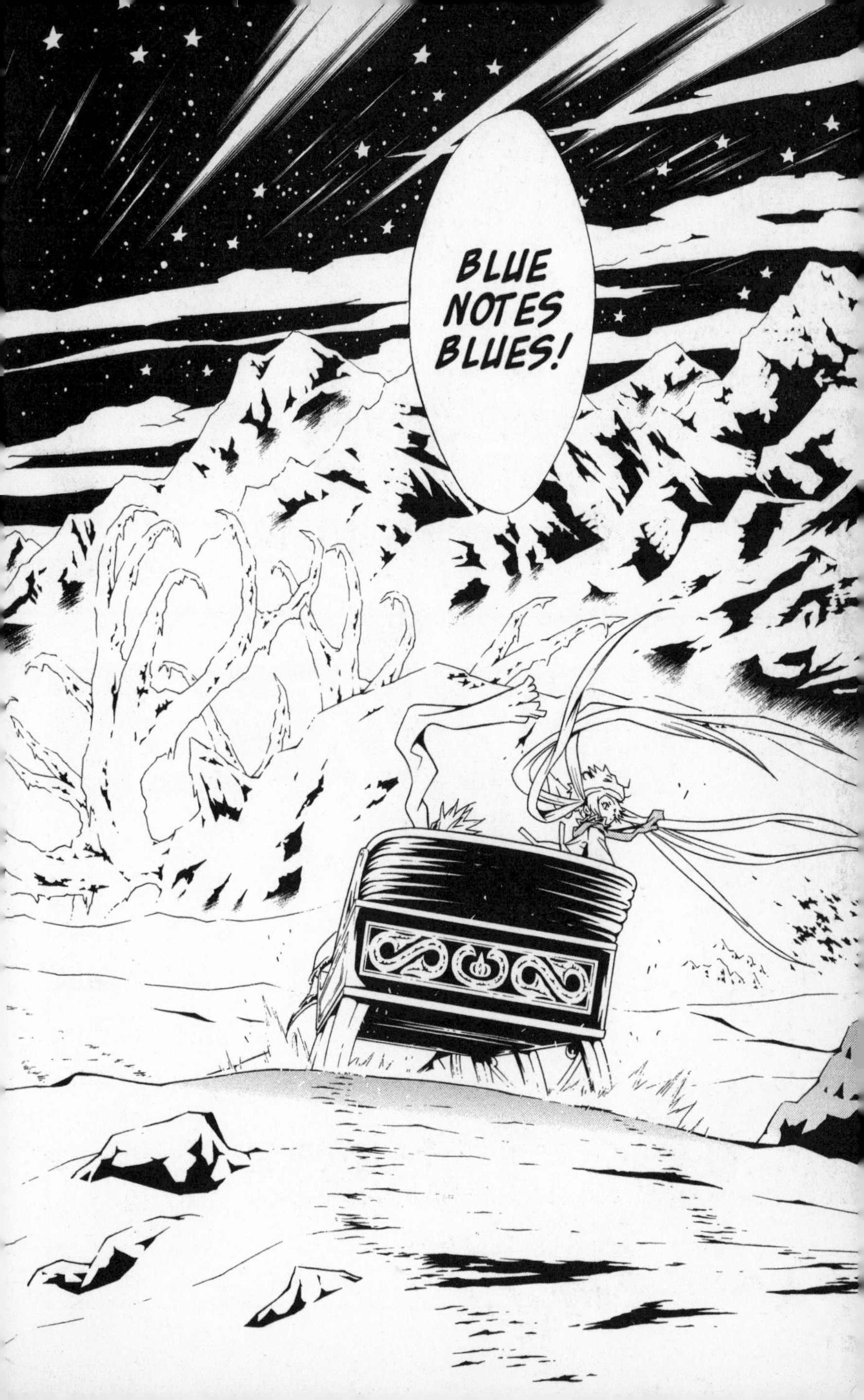
BLUE NOTES BLUES!

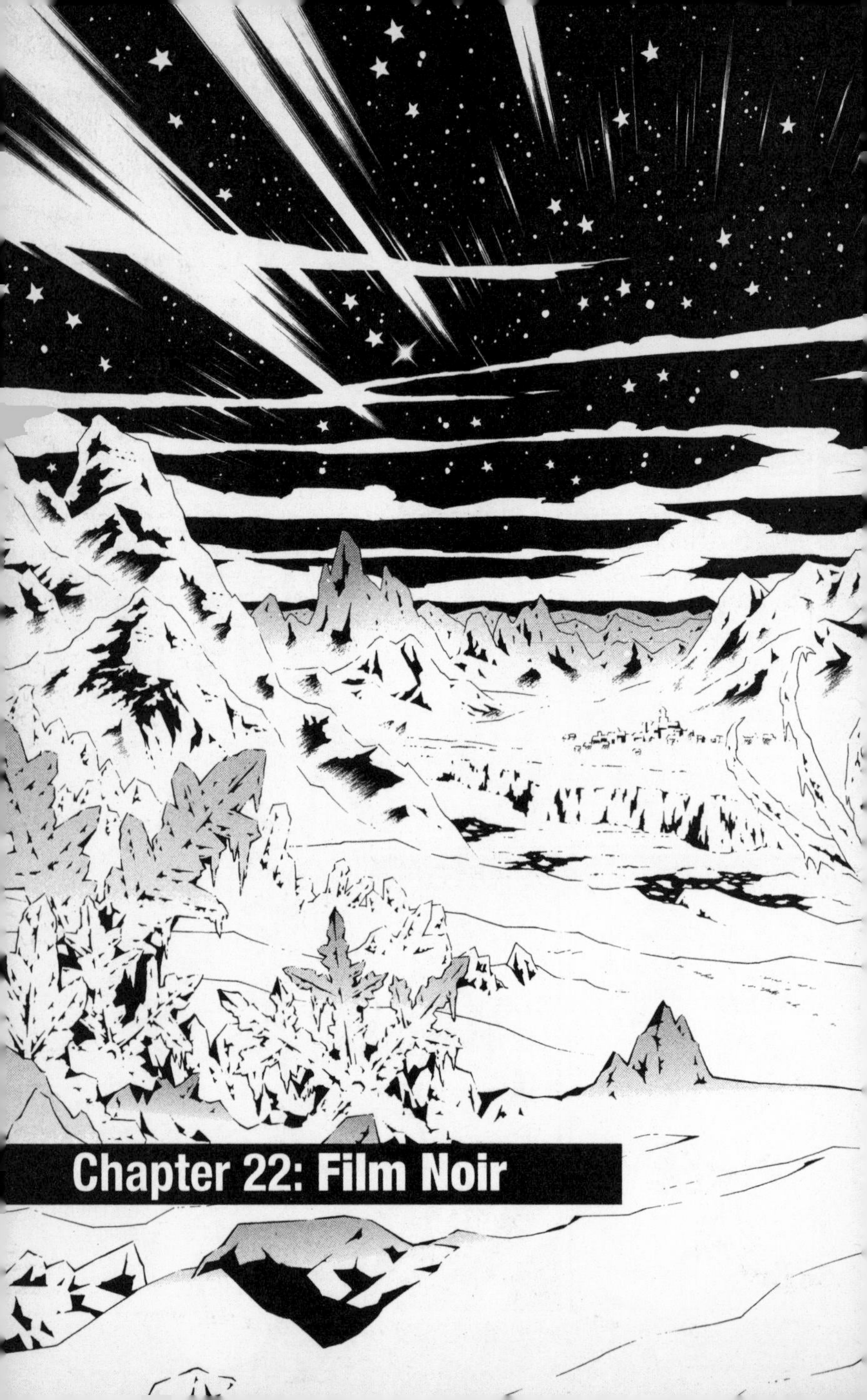

Chapter 22: Film Noir

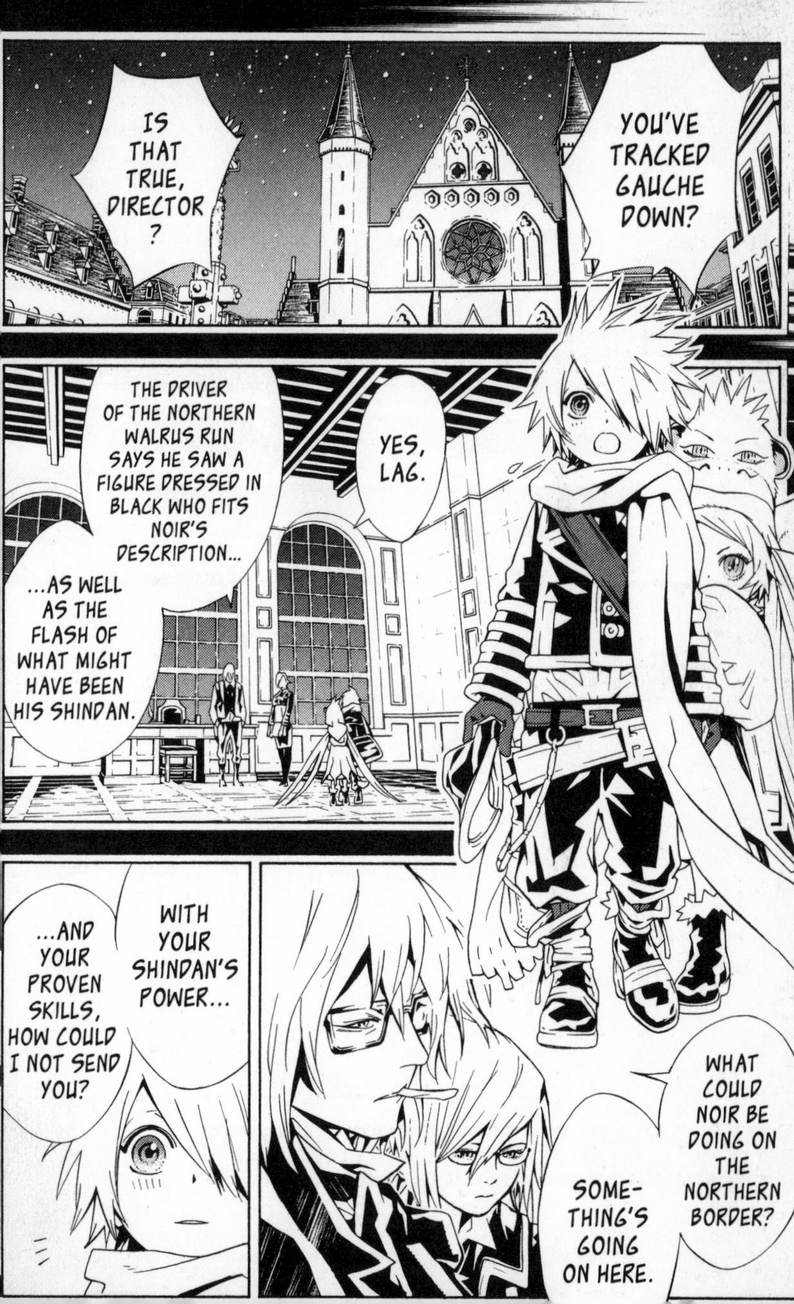
YOU'VE TRACKED GAUCHE DOWN?
IS THAT TRUE, DIRECTOR?
YES, LAG.
THE DRIVER OF THE NORTHERN WALRUS RUN SAYS HE SAW A FIGURE DRESSED IN BLACK WHO FITS NOIR'S DESCRIPTION...
...AS WELL AS THE FLASH OF WHAT MIGHT HAVE BEEN HIS SHINDAN.
WHAT COULD NOIR BE DOING ON THE NORTHERN BORDER?
SOME-THING'S GOING ON HERE.
WITH YOUR SHINDAN'S POWER...
...AND YOUR PROVEN SKILLS, HOW COULD I NOT SEND YOU?

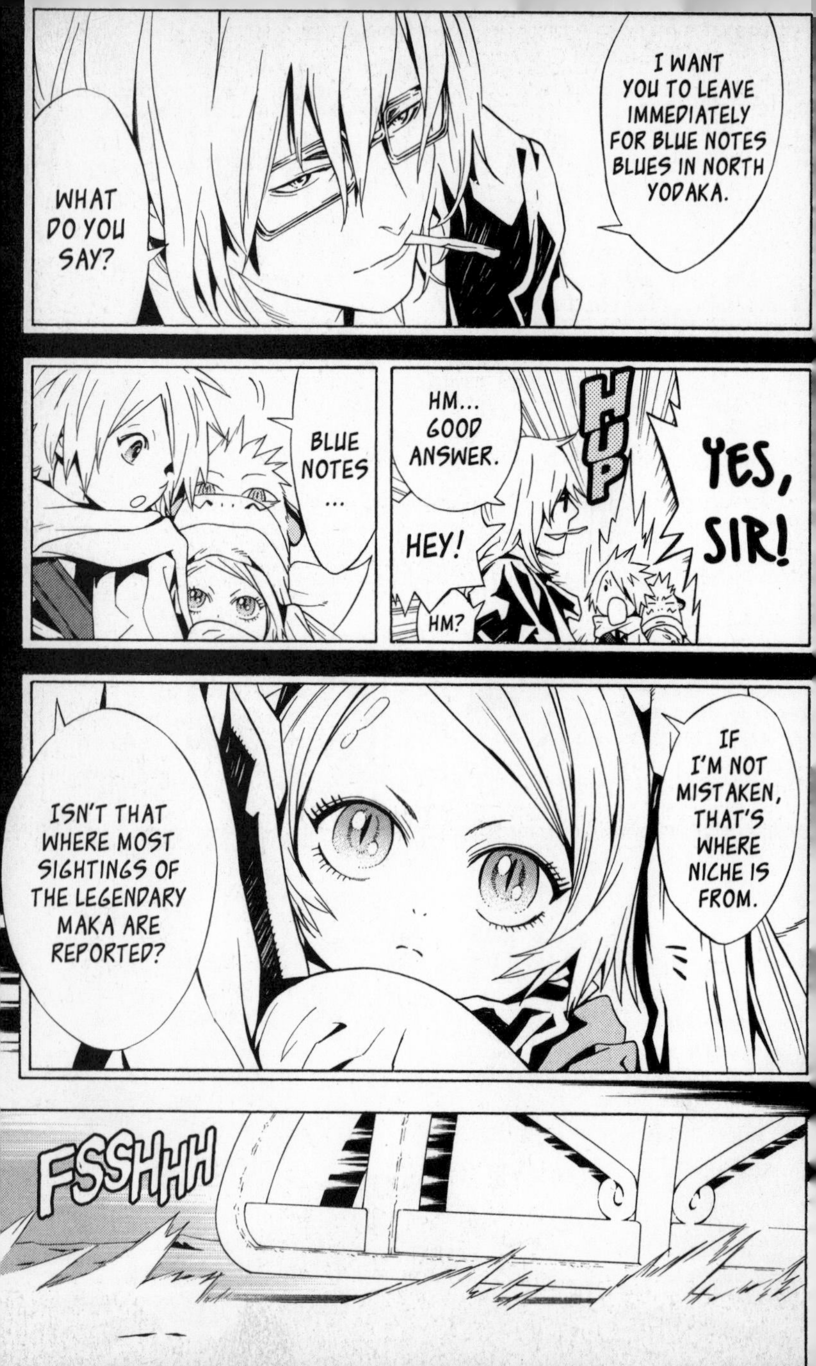
I WANT YOU TO LEAVE IMMEDIATELY FOR BLUE NOTES BLUES IN NORTH YODAKA.
WHAT DO YOU SAY?
YES, SIR!
HUP
HM... GOOD ANSWER.
HEY!
HM?
BLUE NOTES ...
IF I'M NOT MISTAKEN, THAT'S WHERE NICHE IS FROM.
ISN'T THAT WHERE MOST SIGHTINGS OF THE LEGENDARY MAKA ARE REPORTED?
FSSHHH

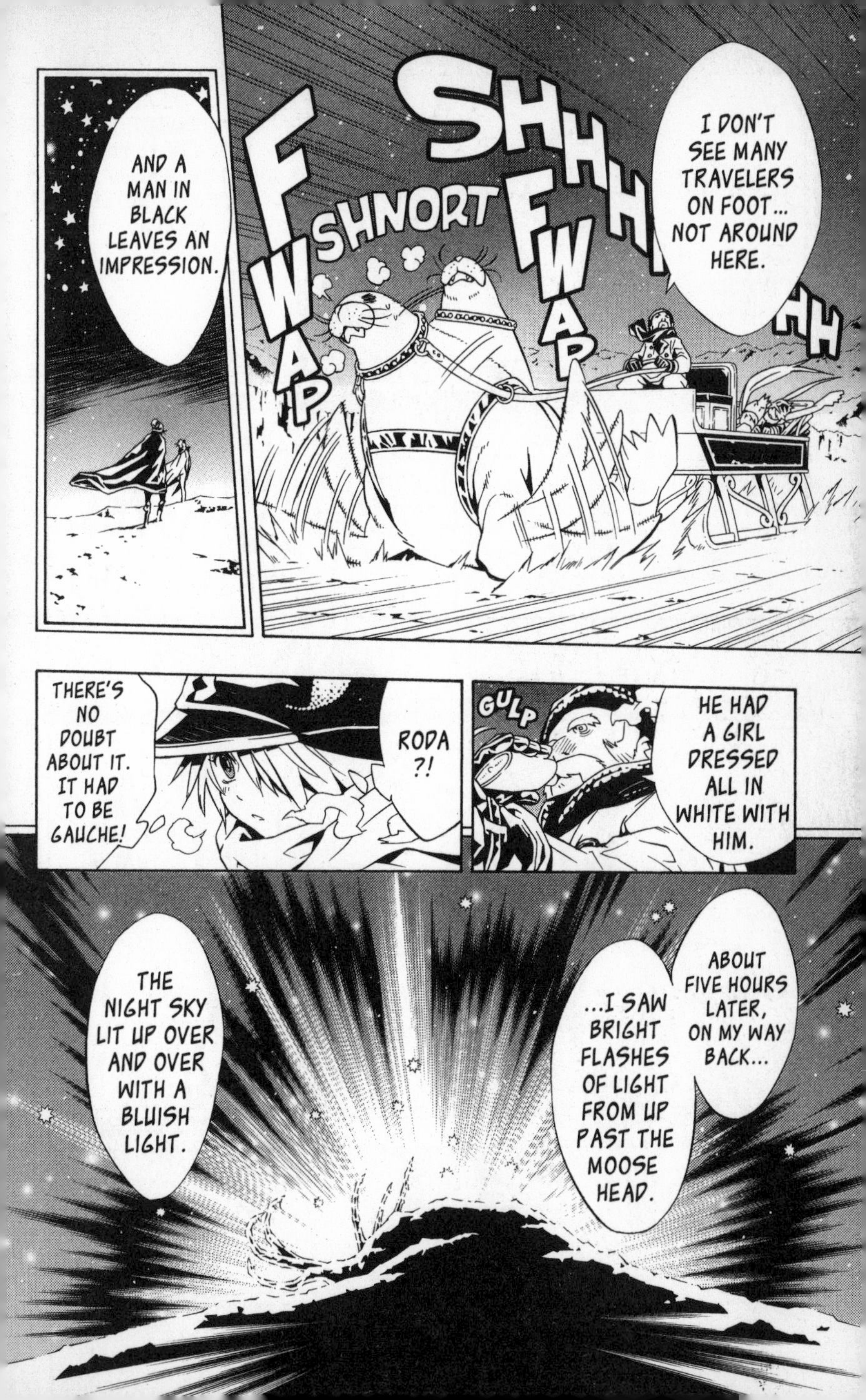

I DON'T SEE MANY TRAVELERS ON FOOT... NOT AROUND HERE.
FWAP
SHNORT
FWAP
AND A MAN IN BLACK LEAVES AN IMPRESSION.
GULP
HE HAD A GIRL DRESSED ALL IN WHITE WITH HIM.
RODA?!
THERE'S NO DOUBT ABOUT IT. IT HAD TO BE GAUCHE!
ABOUT FIVE HOURS LATER, ON MY WAY BACK...
...I SAW BRIGHT FLASHES OF LIGHT FROM UP PAST THE MOOSE HEAD.
THE NIGHT SKY LIT UP OVER AND OVER WITH A BLUISH LIGHT.

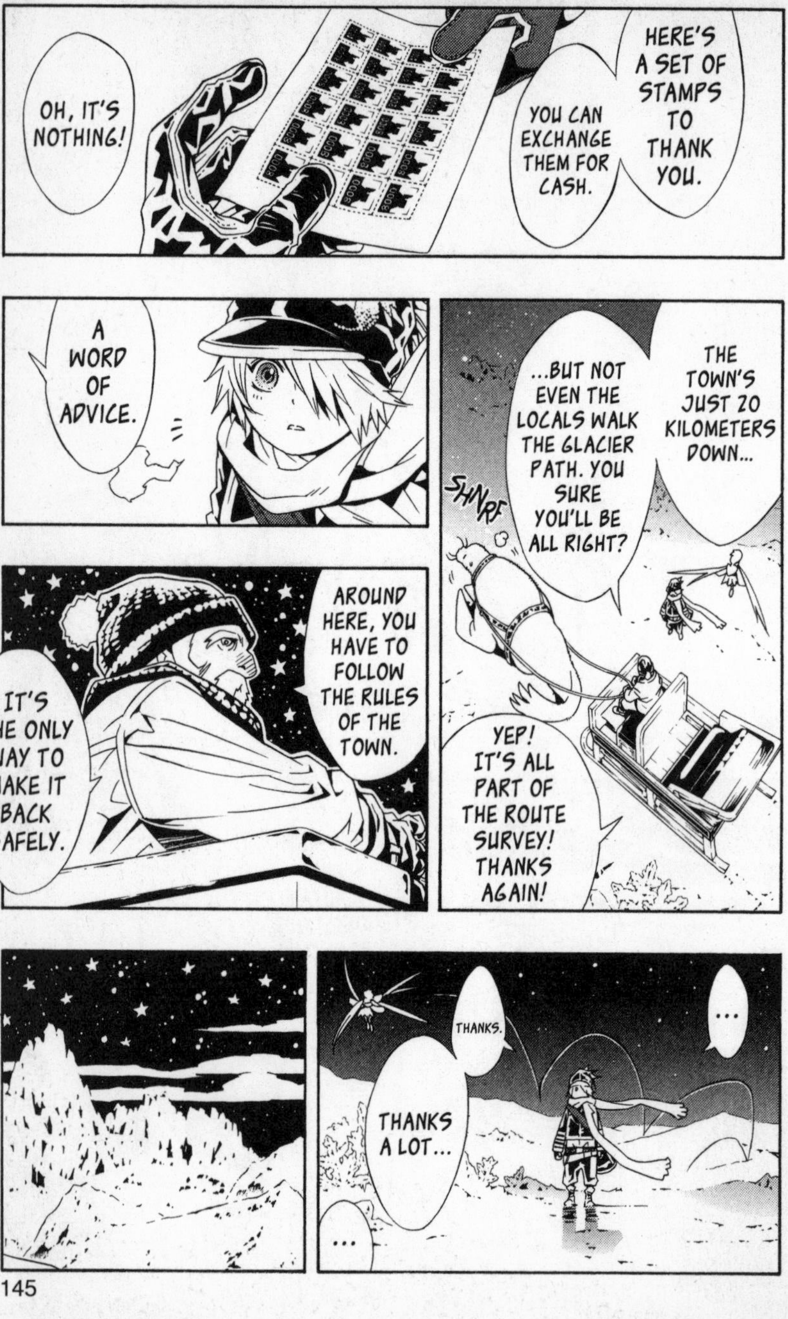
HERE'S A SET OF STAMPS TO THANK YOU.
YOU CAN EXCHANGE THEM FOR CASH.
OH, IT'S NOTHING!
THE TOWN'S JUST 20 KILOMETERS DOWN...
...BUT NOT EVEN THE LOCALS WALK THE GLACIER PATH. YOU SURE YOU'LL BE ALL RIGHT?
SHNRF
YEP! IT'S ALL PART OF THE ROUTE SURVEY! THANKS AGAIN!
A WORD OF ADVICE.
AROUND HERE, YOU HAVE TO FOLLOW THE RULES OF THE TOWN.
IT'S THE ONLY WAY TO MAKE IT BACK SAFELY.
...
THANKS.
THANKS A LOT...
...

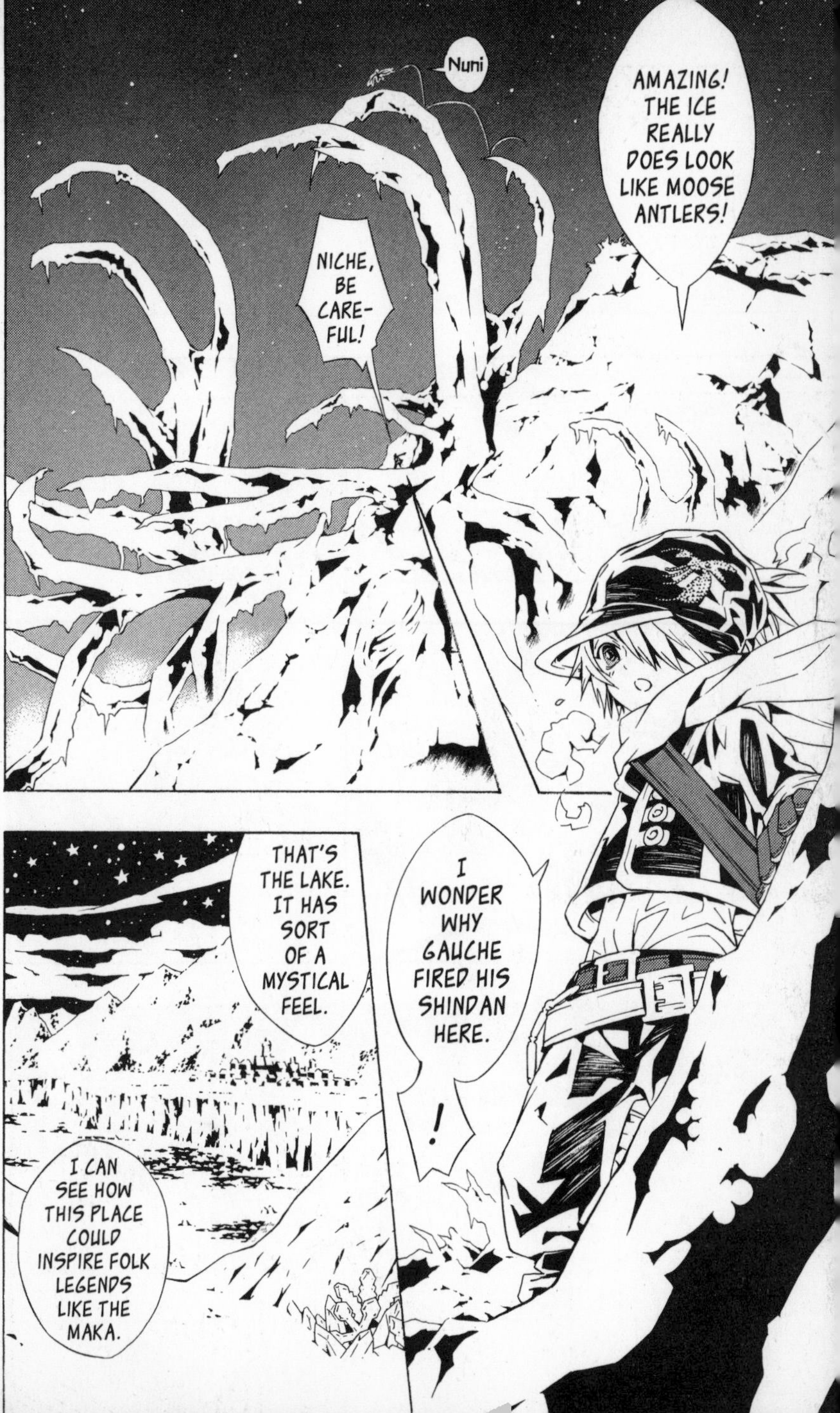
AMAZING! THE ICE REALLY DOES LOOK LIKE MOOSE ANTLERS!
Nuni
NICHE, BE CARE-FUL!
I WONDER WHY GAUCHE FIRED HIS SHINDAN HERE.
!
THAT'S THE LAKE. IT HAS SORT OF A MYSTICAL FEEL.
I CAN SEE HOW THIS PLACE COULD INSPIRE FOLK LEGENDS LIKE THE MAKA.

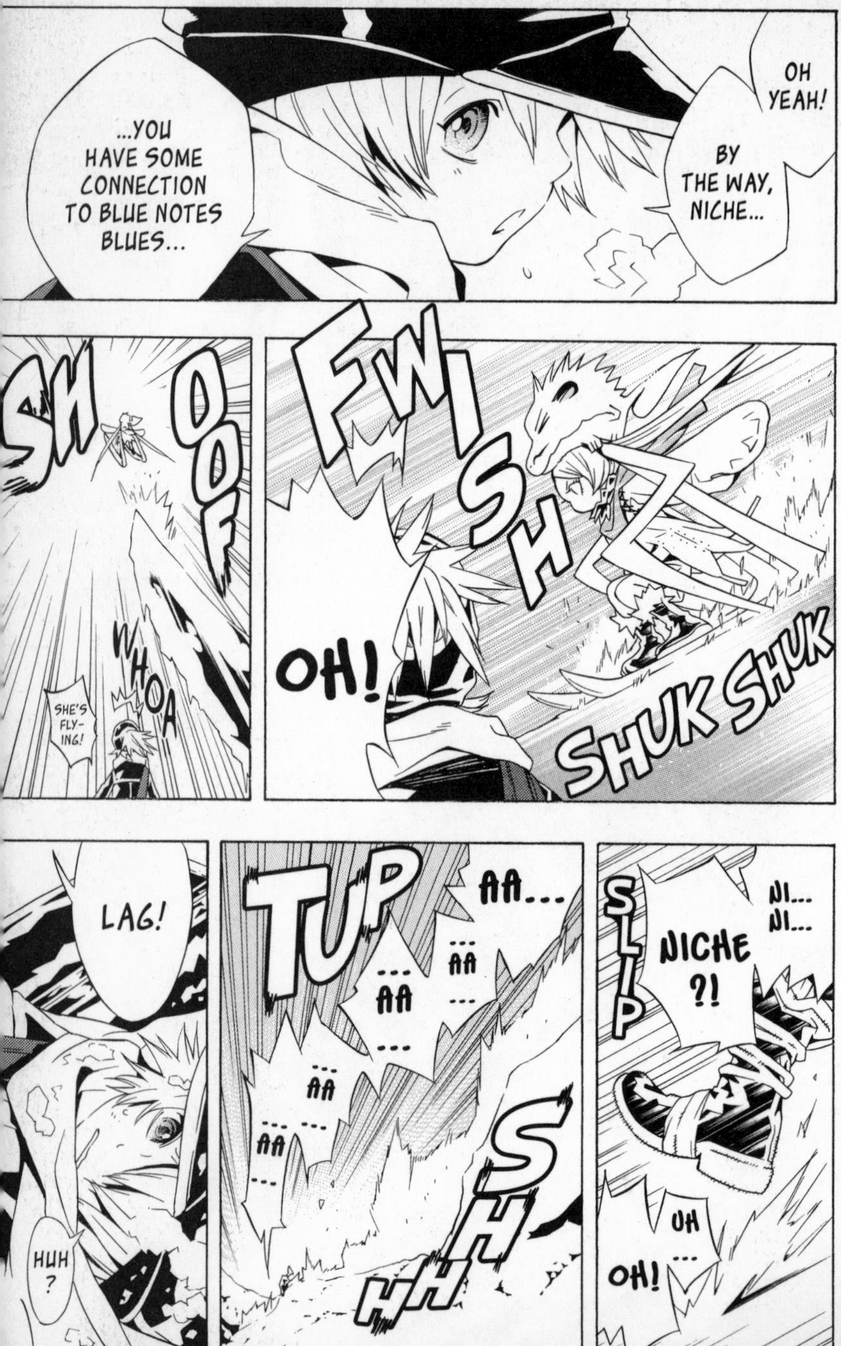
OH YEAH!
BY THE WAY, NICHE...
...YOU HAVE SOME CONNECTION TO BLUE NOTES BLUES...
FWISH
OH!
SHUK SHUK
SHOOF
WHOA
SHE'S FLY-ING!
NI... NI...
NICHE?!
SLIP
UH...
OH!
AA...
...AA...
...AA...
...AA...
...AA...
TUP
SHHHH
LAG!
HUH?

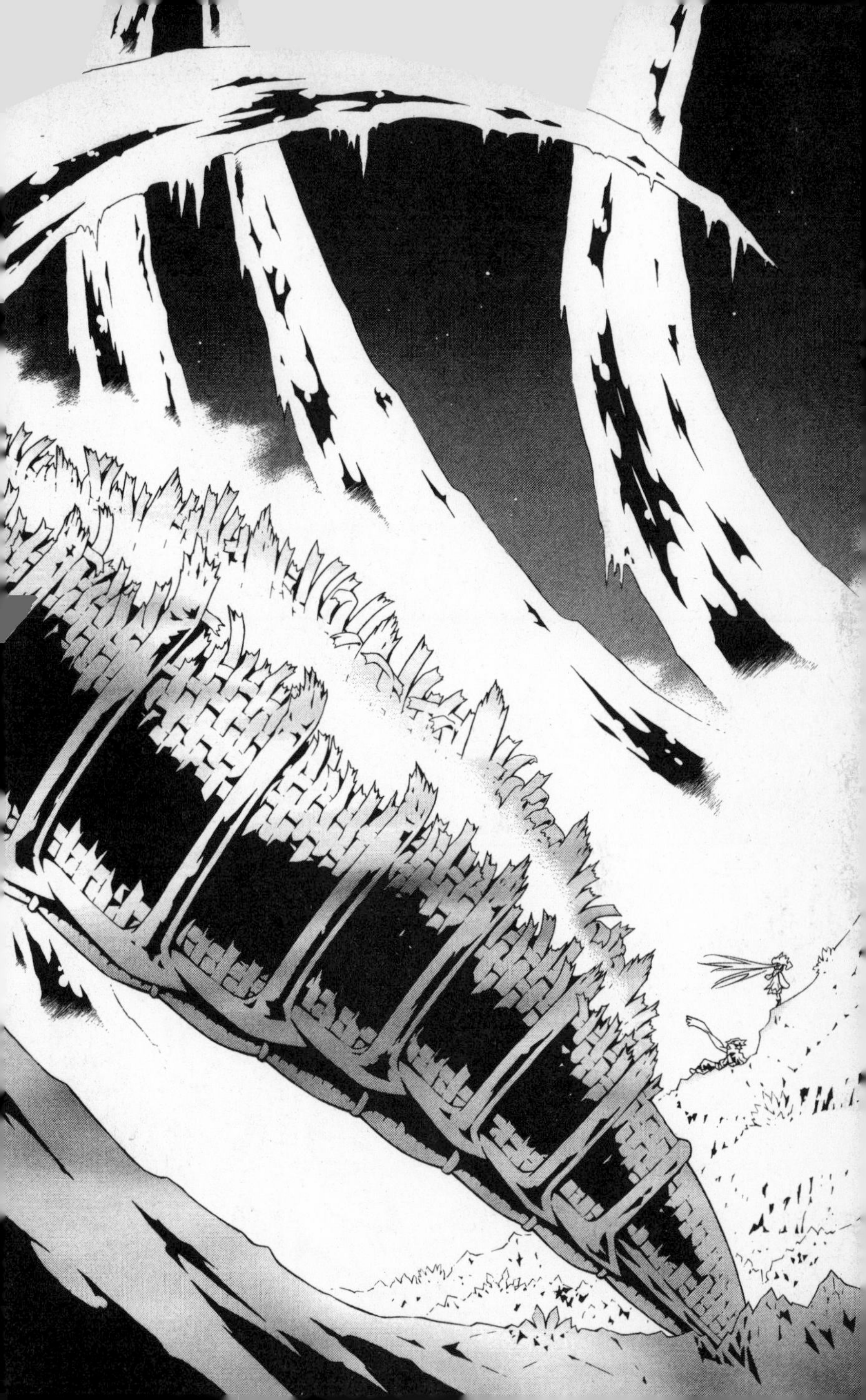

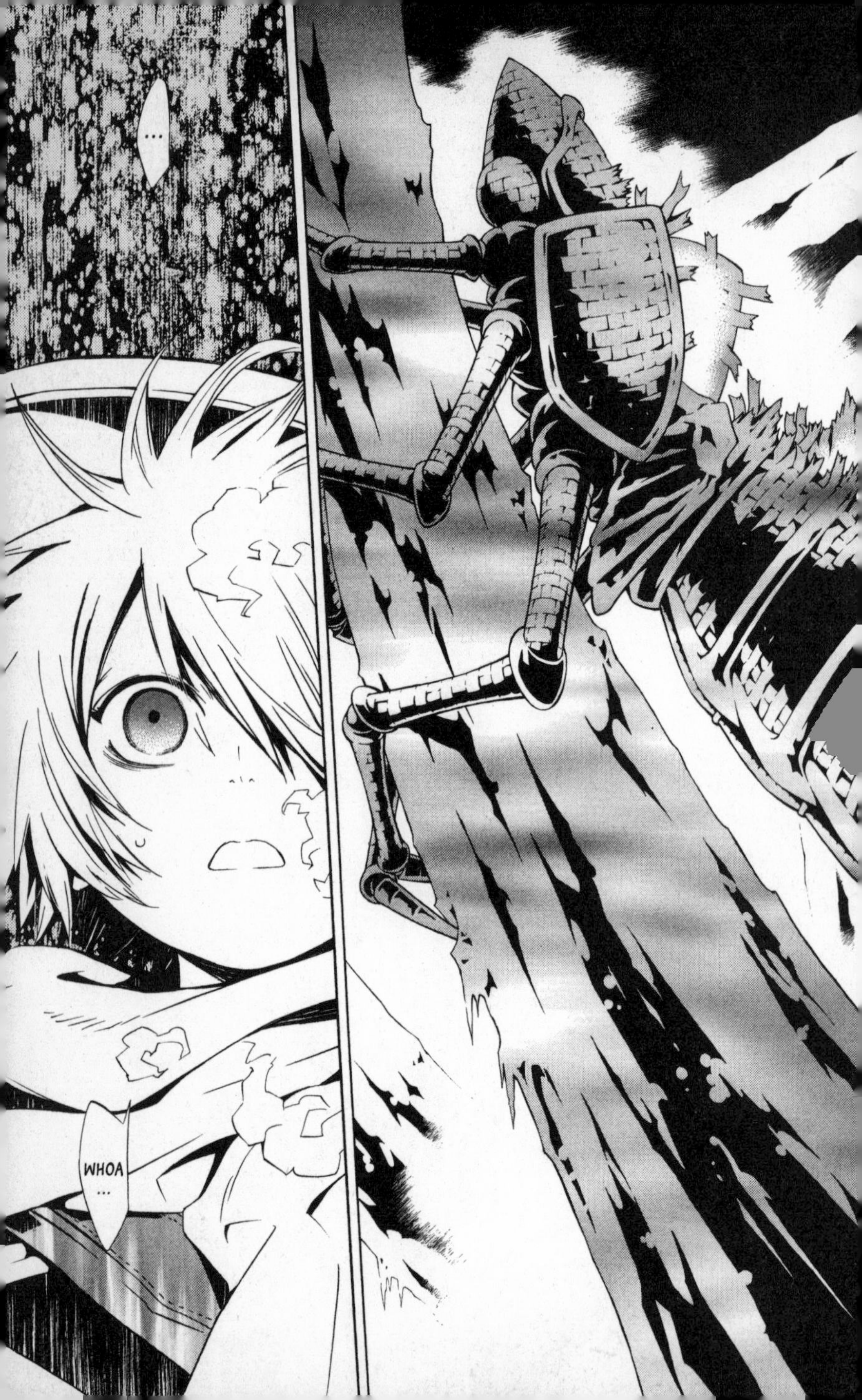
...
WHOA ...

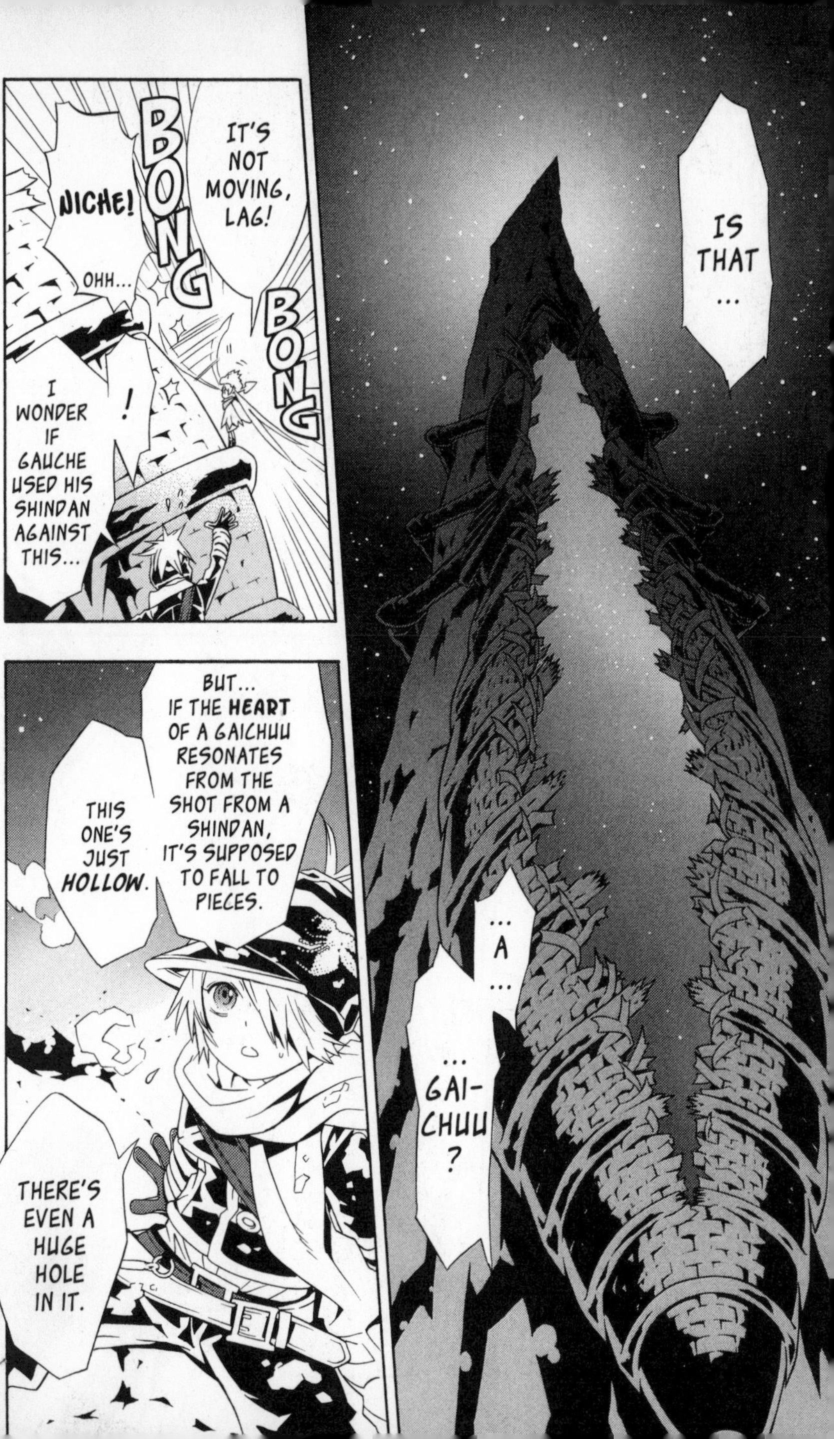
IS THAT ...
... A ...
... GAI-CHUU ?
IT'S NOT MOVING, LAG!
BONG
BONG
NICHE!
OHH...
!
I WONDER IF GAUCHE USED HIS SHINDAN AGAINST THIS...
BUT... IF THE HEART OF A GAICHUU RESONATES FROM THE SHOT FROM A SHINDAN, IT'S SUPPOSED TO FALL TO PIECES.
THIS ONE'S JUST HOLLOW.
THERE'S EVEN A HUGE HOLE IN IT.

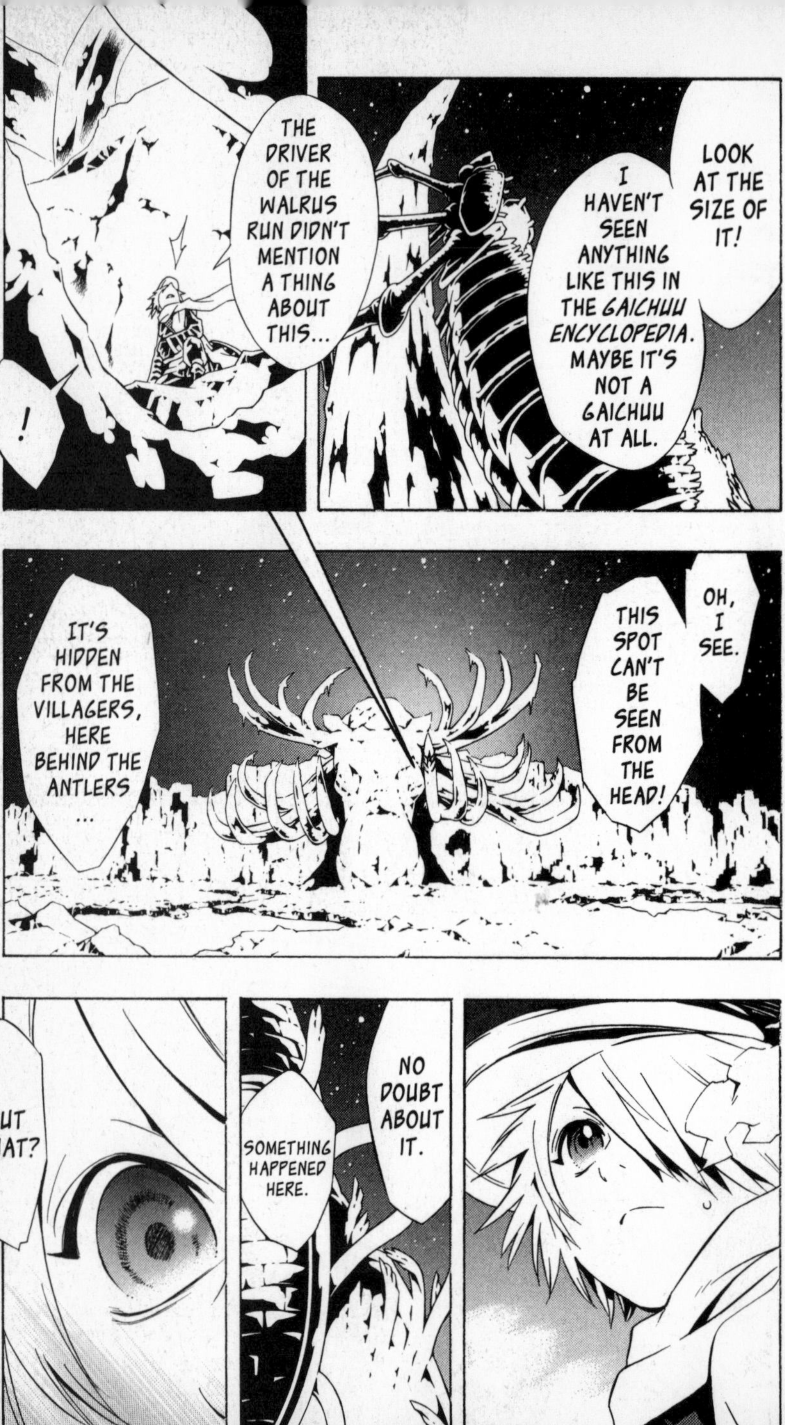
LOOK AT THE SIZE OF IT!
I HAVEN'T SEEN ANYTHING LIKE THIS IN THE *GAICHUU ENCYCLOPEDIA*. MAYBE IT'S NOT A GAICHUU AT ALL.
THE DRIVER OF THE WALRUS RUN DIDN'T MENTION A THING ABOUT THIS...
!
OH, I SEE.
THIS SPOT CAN'T BE SEEN FROM THE HEAD!
IT'S HIDDEN FROM THE VILLAGERS, HERE BEHIND THE ANTLERS ...
NO DOUBT ABOUT IT.
SOMETHING HAPPENED HERE.
BUT WHAT?

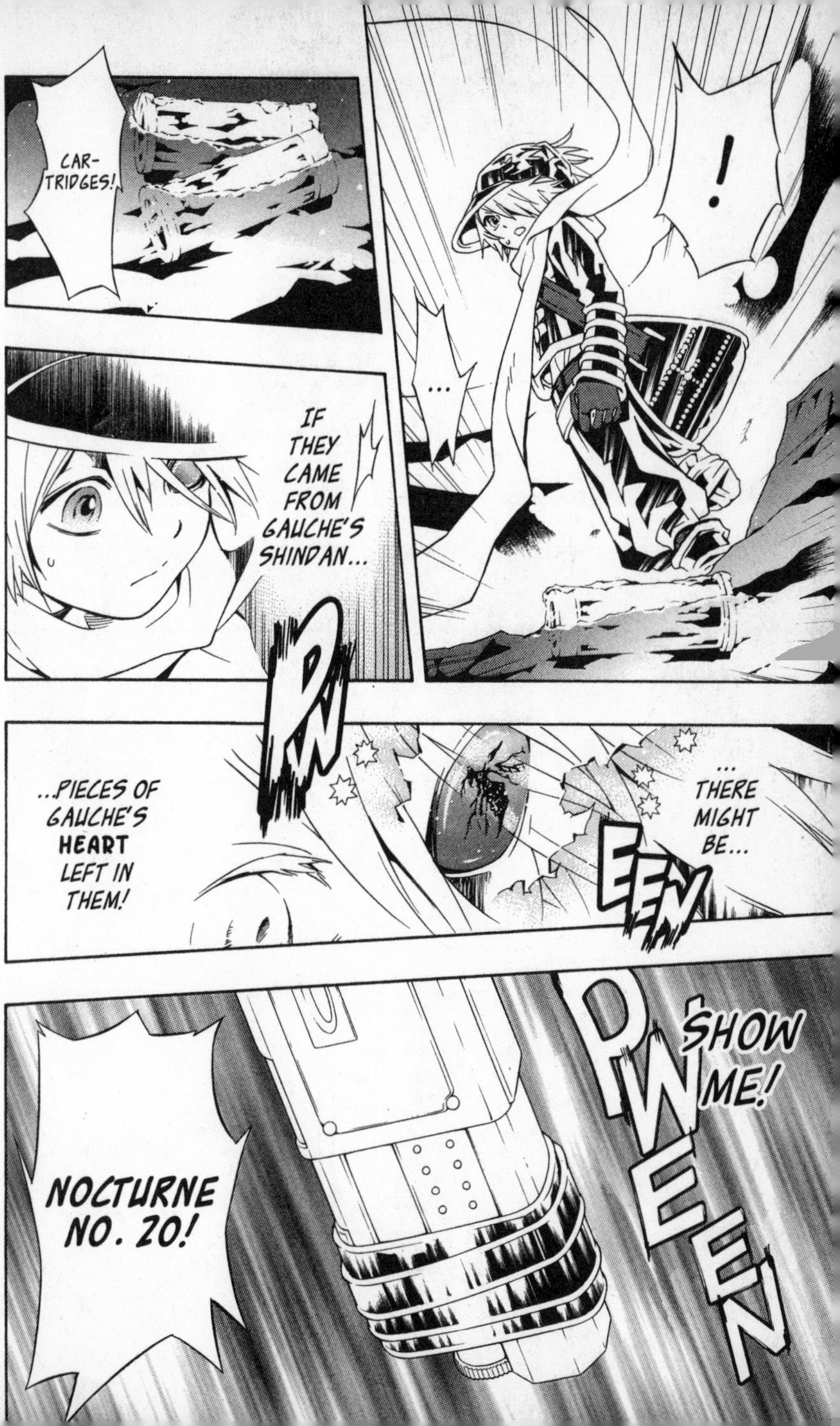
!
...
CAR-TRIDGES!
IF THEY CAME FROM GAUCHE'S SHINDAN...
DAN
...THERE MIGHT BE...
EEN
...PIECES OF GAUCHE'S HEART LEFT IN THEM!
SHOW ME!
DWEEN
NOCTURNE NO. 20!

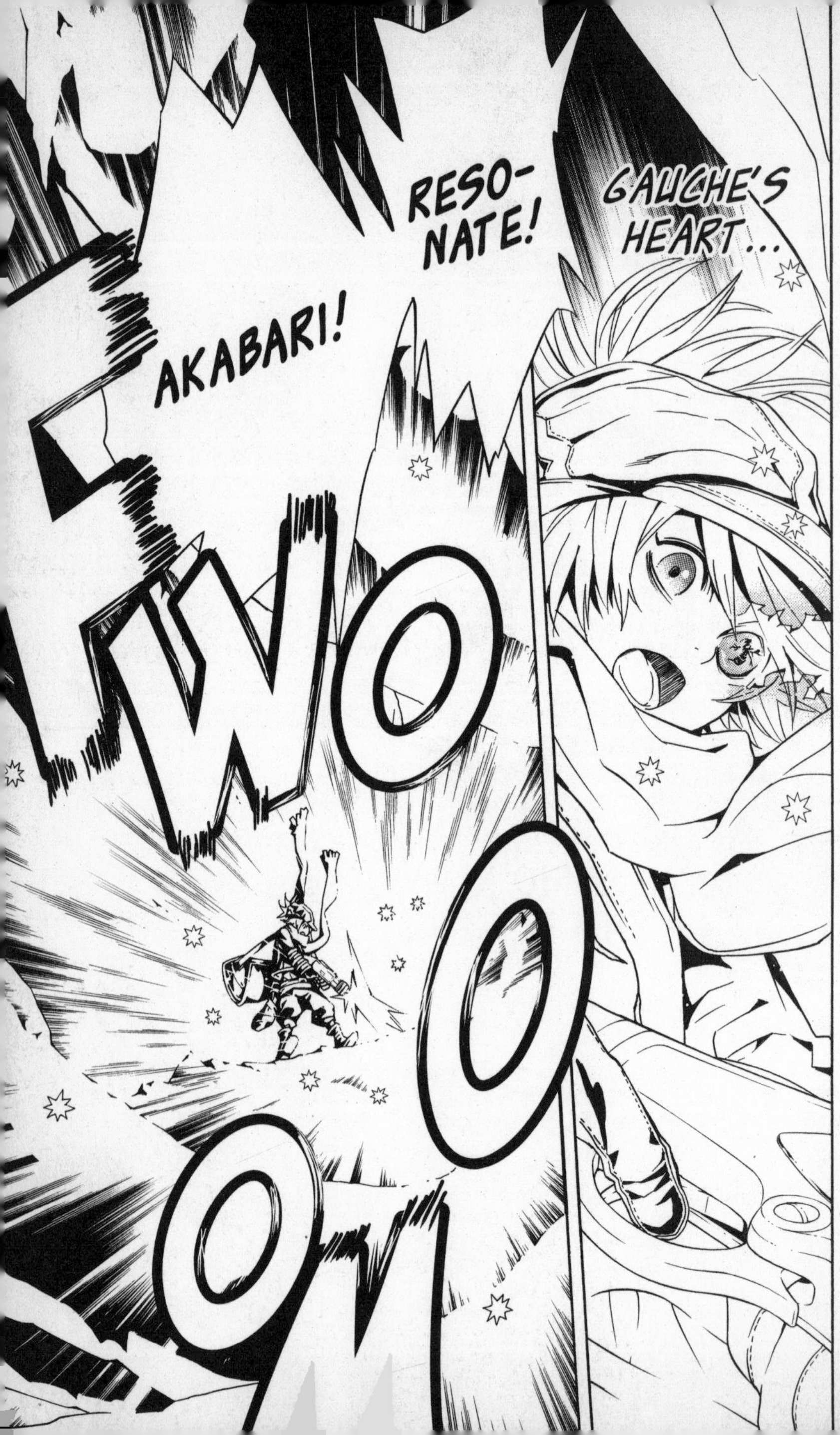
GAUCHE'S HEART...
RESONATE!
AKABARI!
WOOO

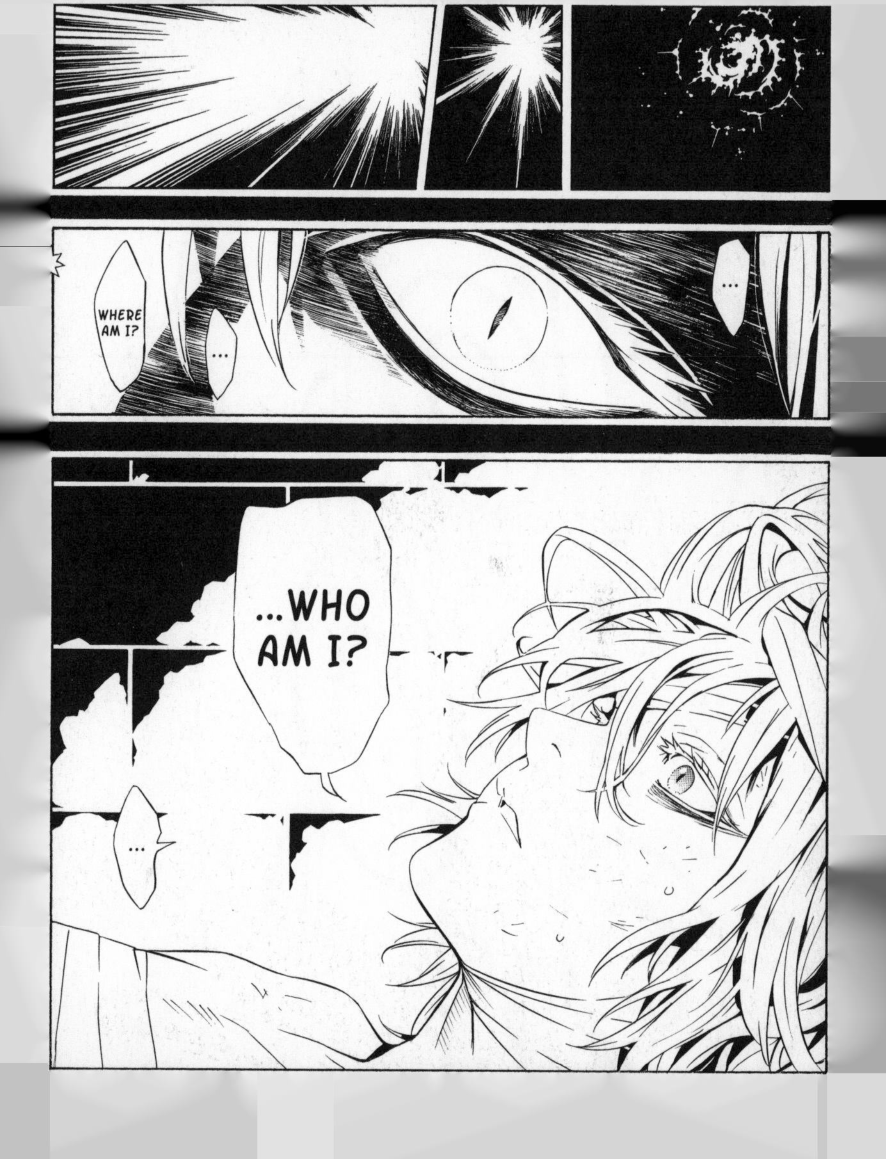
...
...
WHERE AM I?
...WHO AM I?
...

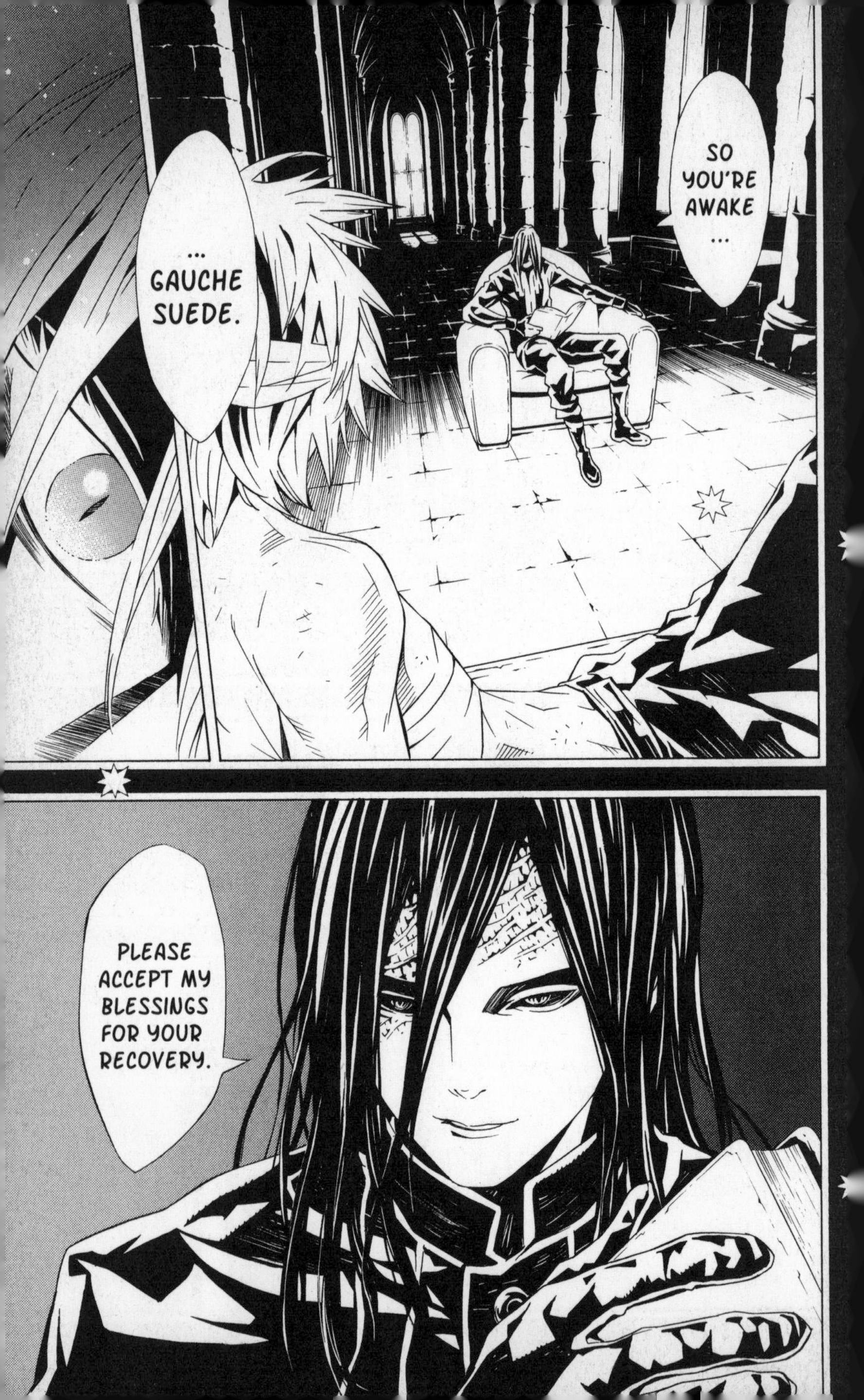
SO YOU'RE AWAKE ...
... GAUCHE SUEDE.
PLEASE ACCEPT MY BLESSINGS FOR YOUR RECOVERY.

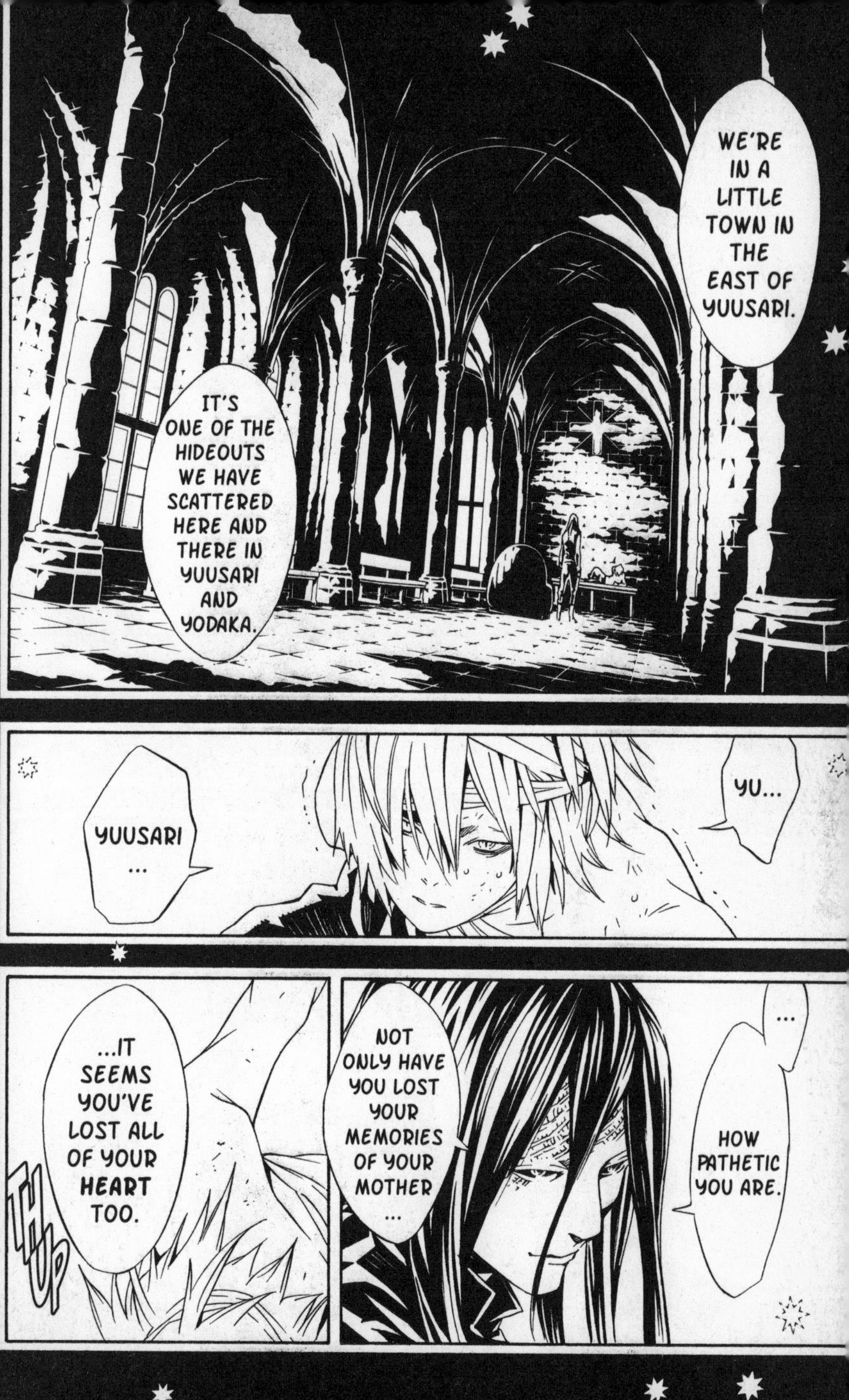
WE'RE IN A LITTLE TOWN IN THE EAST OF YUUSARI.
IT'S ONE OF THE HIDEOUTS WE HAVE SCATTERED HERE AND THERE IN YUUSARI AND YODAKA.
YU...
YUUSARI ...
... HOW PATHETIC YOU ARE.
NOT ONLY HAVE YOU LOST YOUR MEMORIES OF YOUR MOTHER ...
...IT SEEMS YOU'VE LOST ALL OF YOUR HEART TOO.
THUP

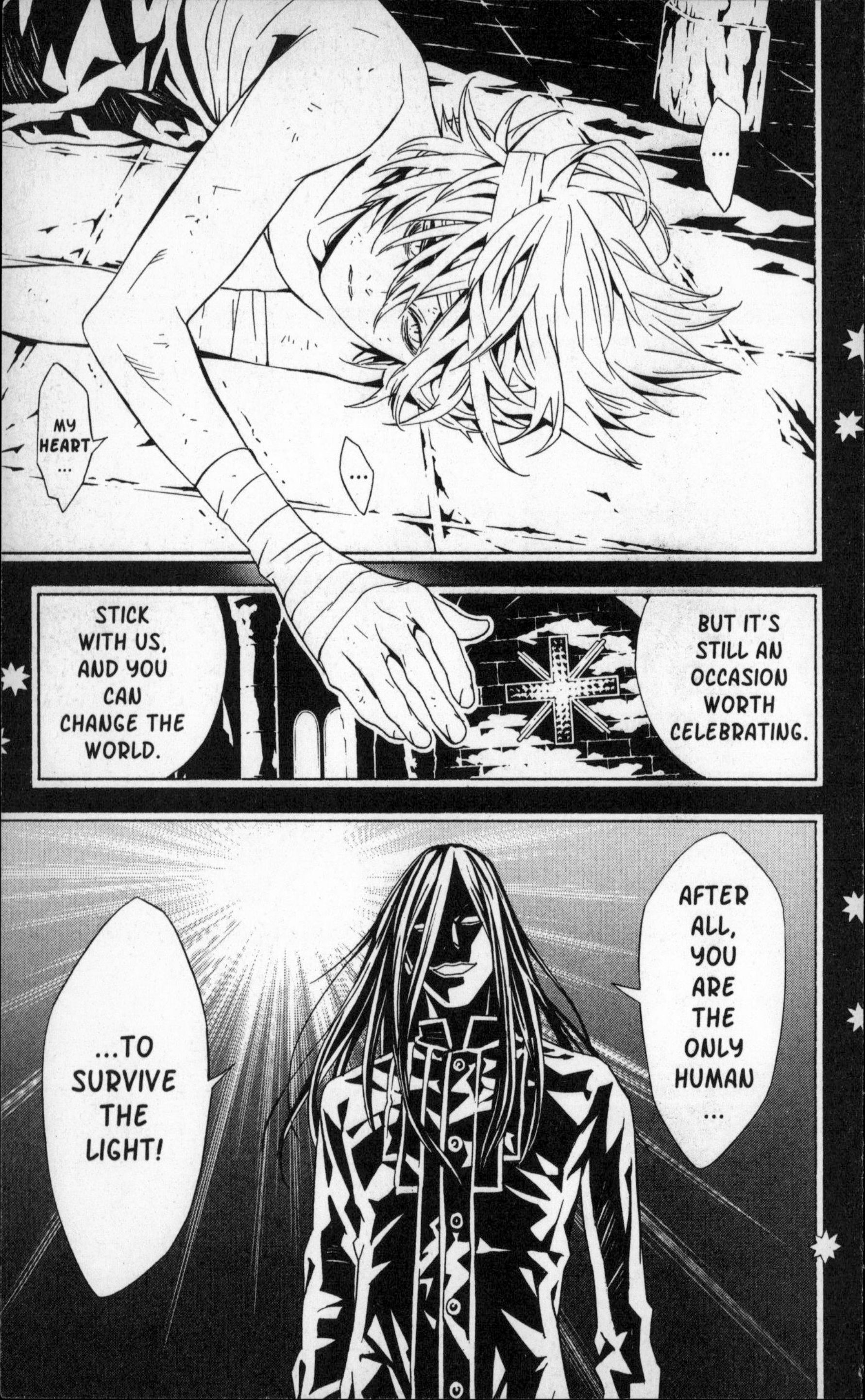
...
...
MY HEART ...
BUT IT'S STILL AN OCCASION WORTH CELEBRATING.
STICK WITH US, AND YOU CAN CHANGE THE WORLD.
AFTER ALL, YOU ARE THE ONLY HUMAN ...
...TO SURVIVE THE LIGHT!

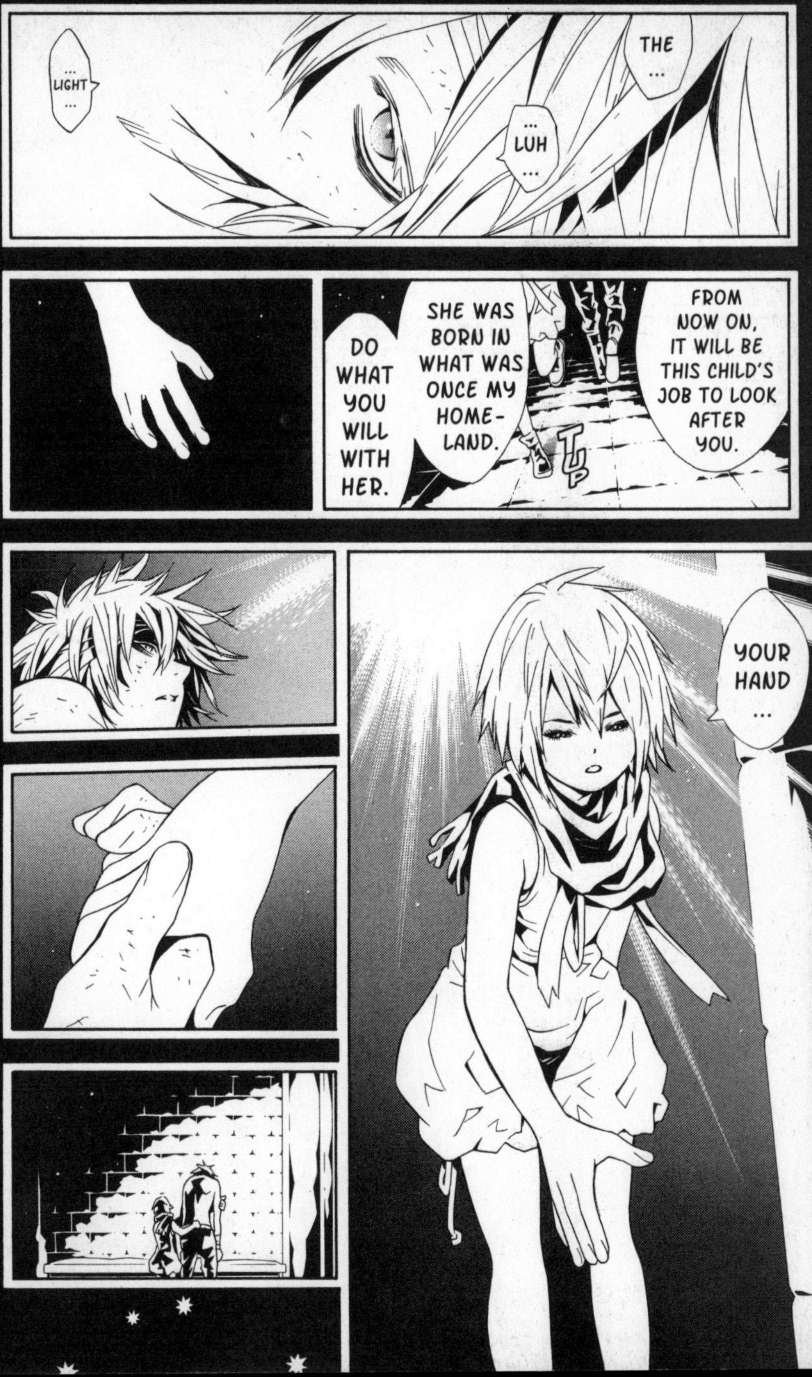
THE ...
... LUH ...
... LIGHT ...
FROM NOW ON, IT WILL BE THIS CHILD'S JOB TO LOOK AFTER YOU.
SHE WAS BORN IN WHAT WAS ONCE MY HOME-LAND.
DO WHAT YOU WILL WITH HER.
TUP
YOUR HAND ...

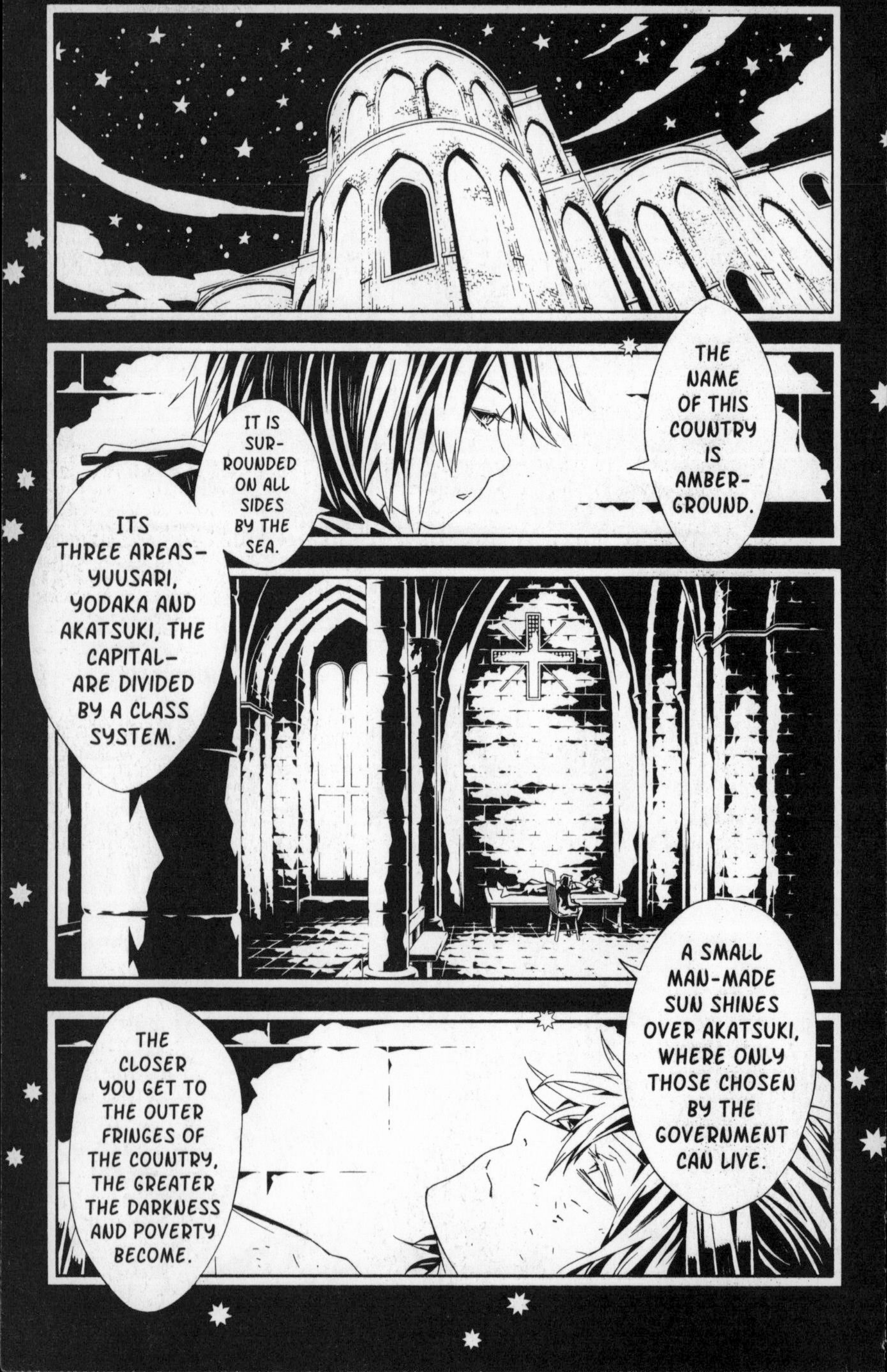
THE NAME OF THIS COUNTRY IS AMBER-GROUND.
IT IS SUR-ROUNDED ON ALL SIDES BY THE SEA.
ITS THREE AREAS-YUUSARI, YODAKA AND AKATSUKI, THE CAPITAL-ARE DIVIDED BY A CLASS SYSTEM.
A SMALL MAN-MADE SUN SHINES OVER AKATSUKI, WHERE ONLY THOSE CHOSEN BY THE GOVERNMENT CAN LIVE.
THE CLOSER YOU GET TO THE OUTER FRINGES OF THE COUNTRY, THE GREATER THE DARKNESS AND POVERTY BECOME.

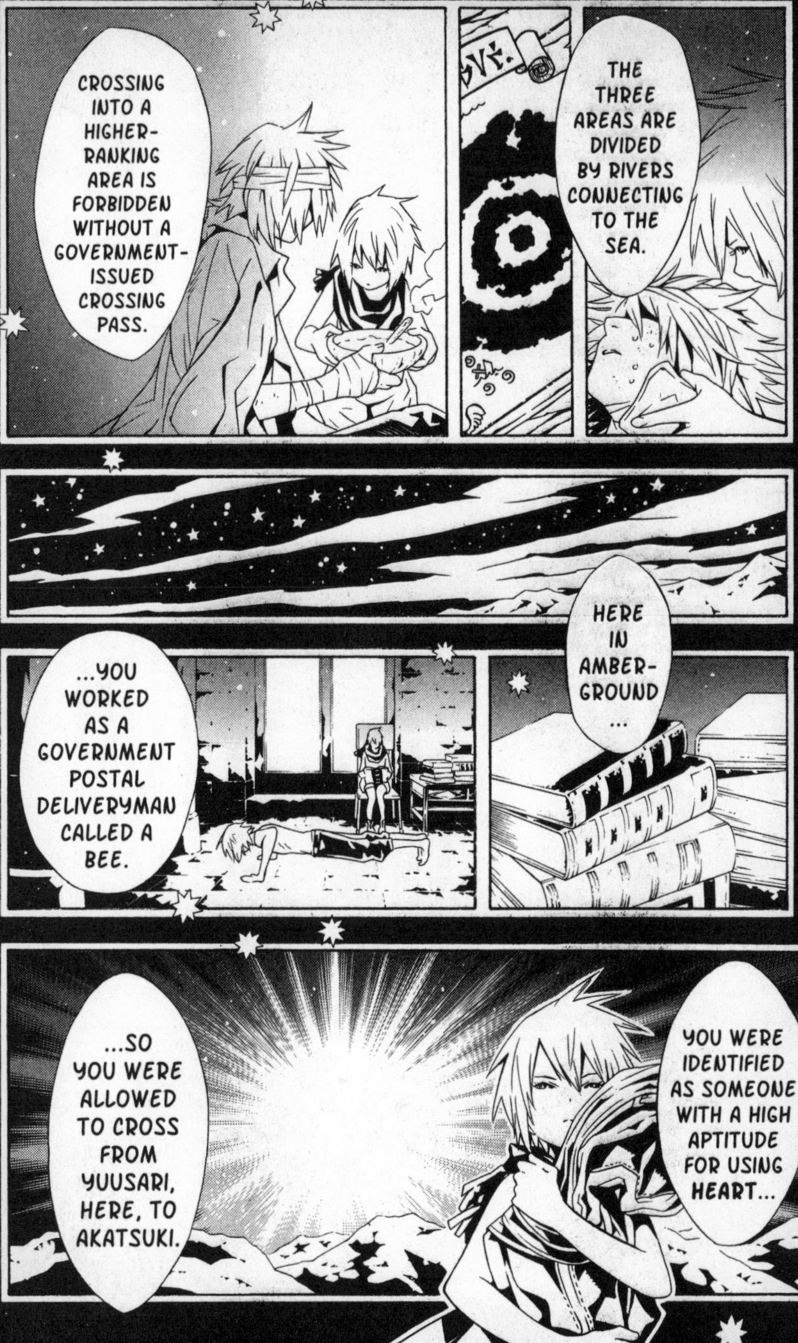
THE THREE AREAS ARE DIVIDED BY RIVERS CONNECTING TO THE SEA.
CROSSING INTO A HIGHER-RANKING AREA IS FORBIDDEN WITHOUT A GOVERNMENT-ISSUED CROSSING PASS.
HERE IN AMBER-GROUND ...
...YOU WORKED AS A GOVERNMENT POSTAL DELIVERYMAN CALLED A BEE.
YOU WERE IDENTIFIED AS SOMEONE WITH A HIGH APTITUDE FOR USING HEART...
...SO YOU WERE ALLOWED TO CROSS FROM YUUSARI, HERE, TO AKATSUKI.

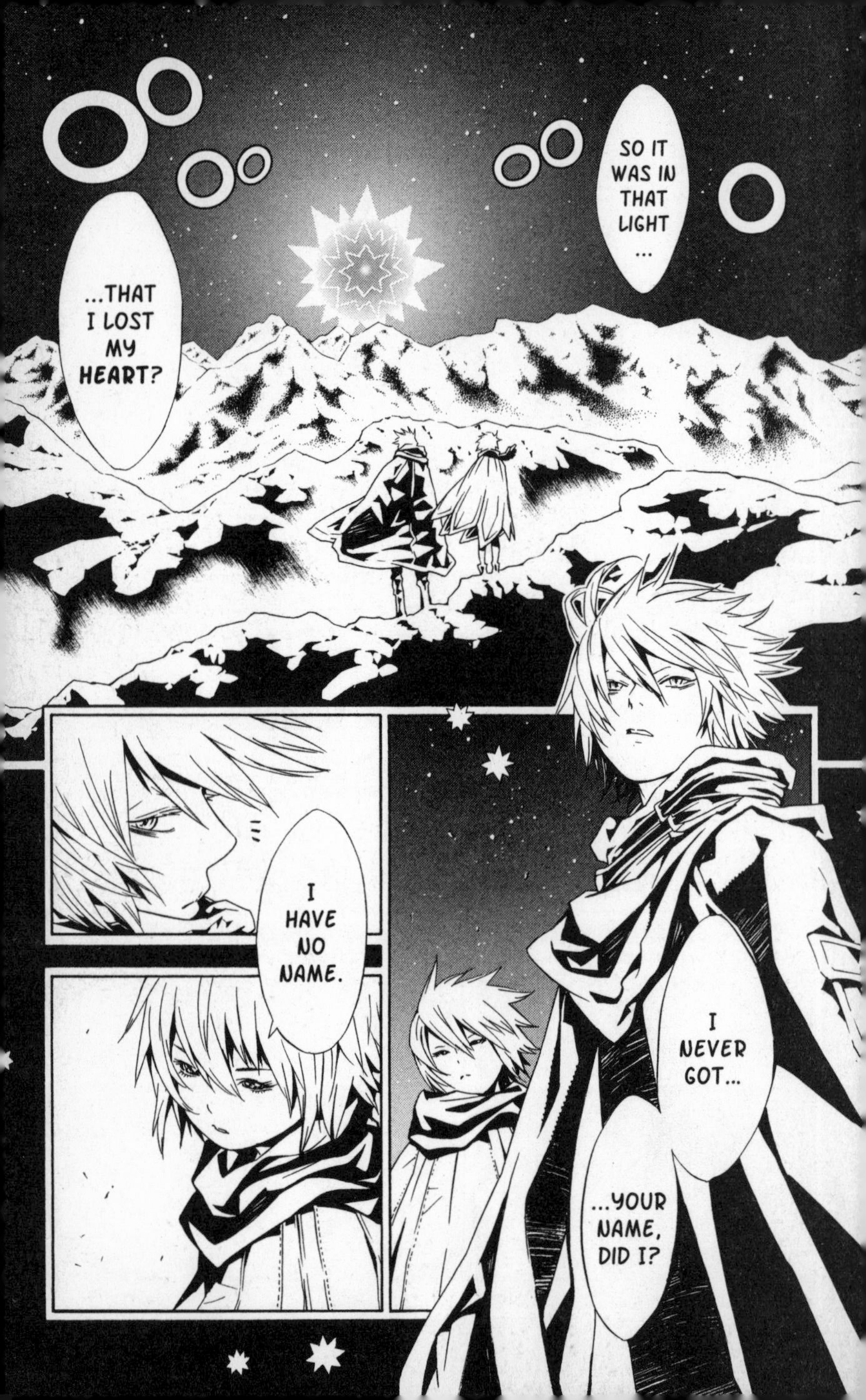
SO IT WAS IN THAT LIGHT ...
...THAT I LOST MY HEART?
I NEVER GOT...
...YOUR NAME, DID I?
I HAVE NO NAME.

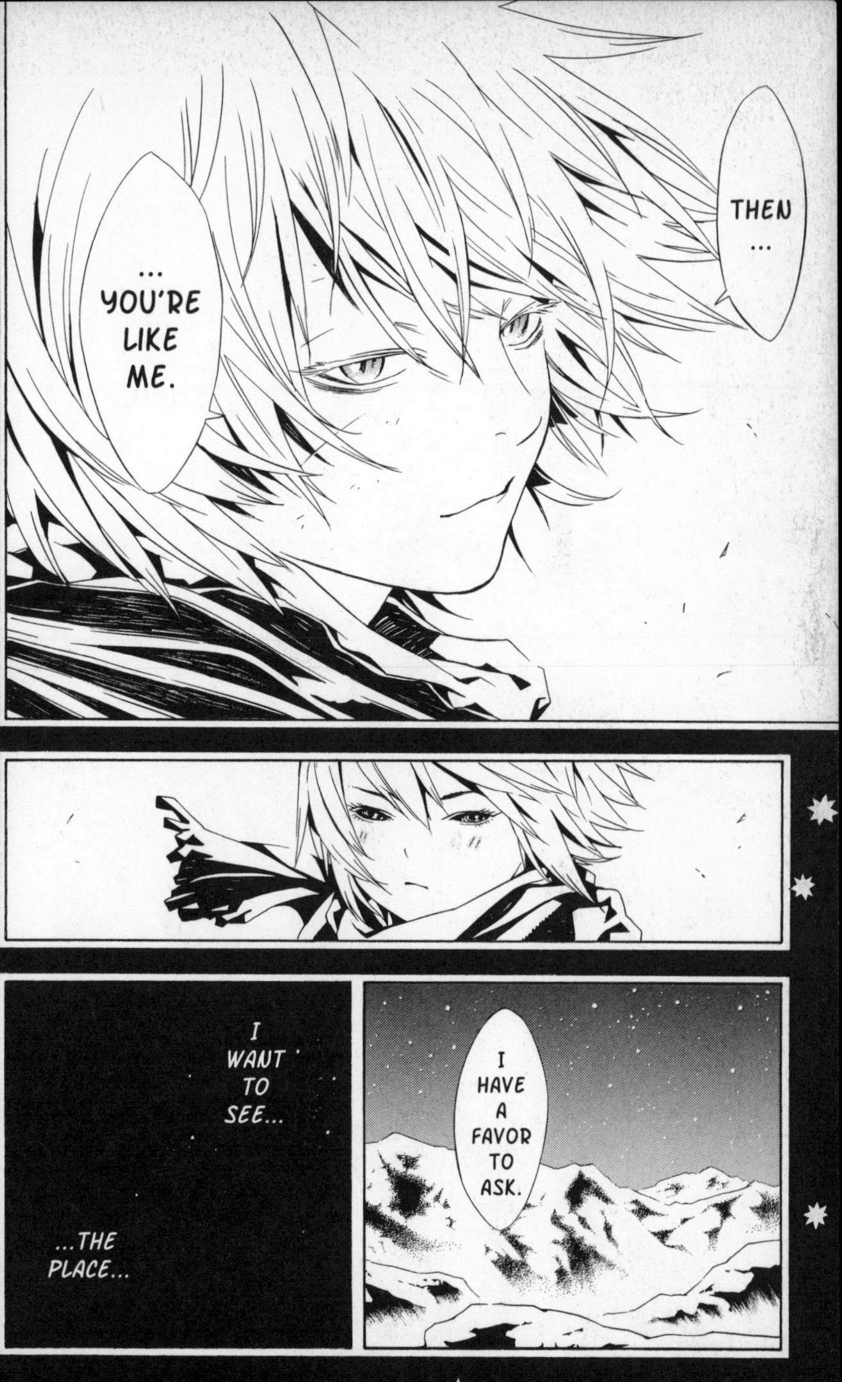
THEN ...
... YOU'RE LIKE ME.
I HAVE A FAVOR TO ASK.
I WANT TO SEE...
...THE PLACE...

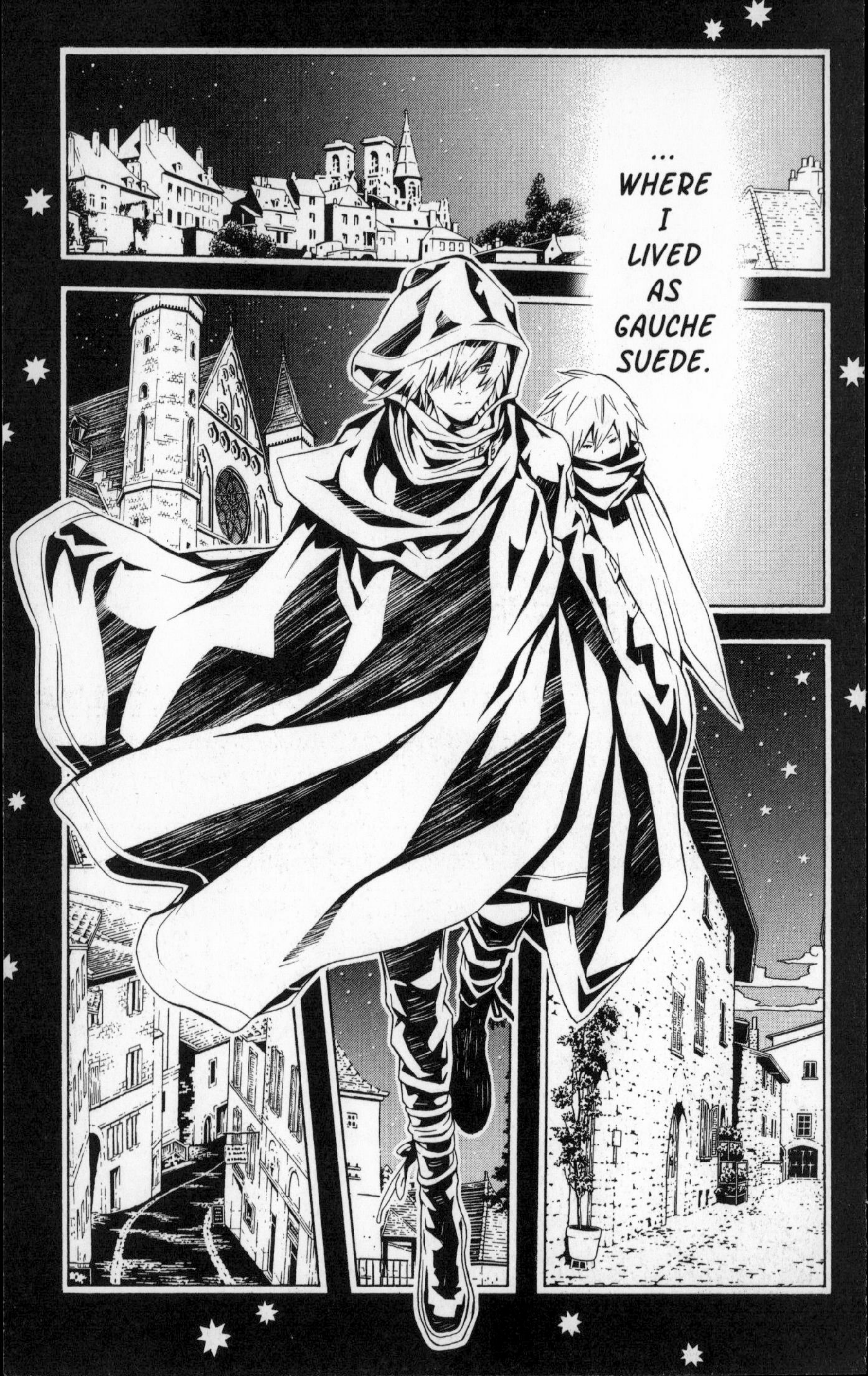
...WHERE I LIVED AS GAUCHE SUEDE.

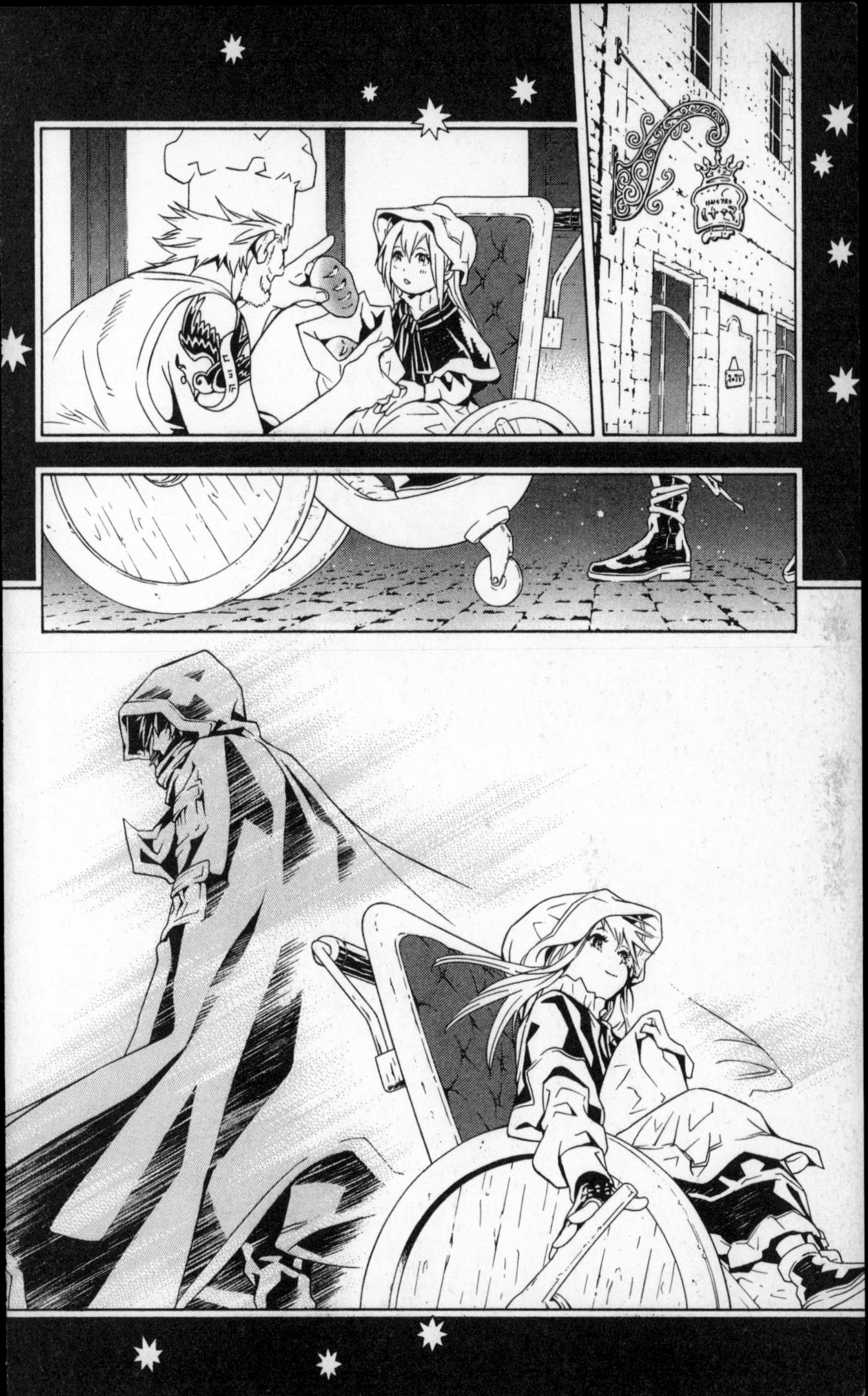

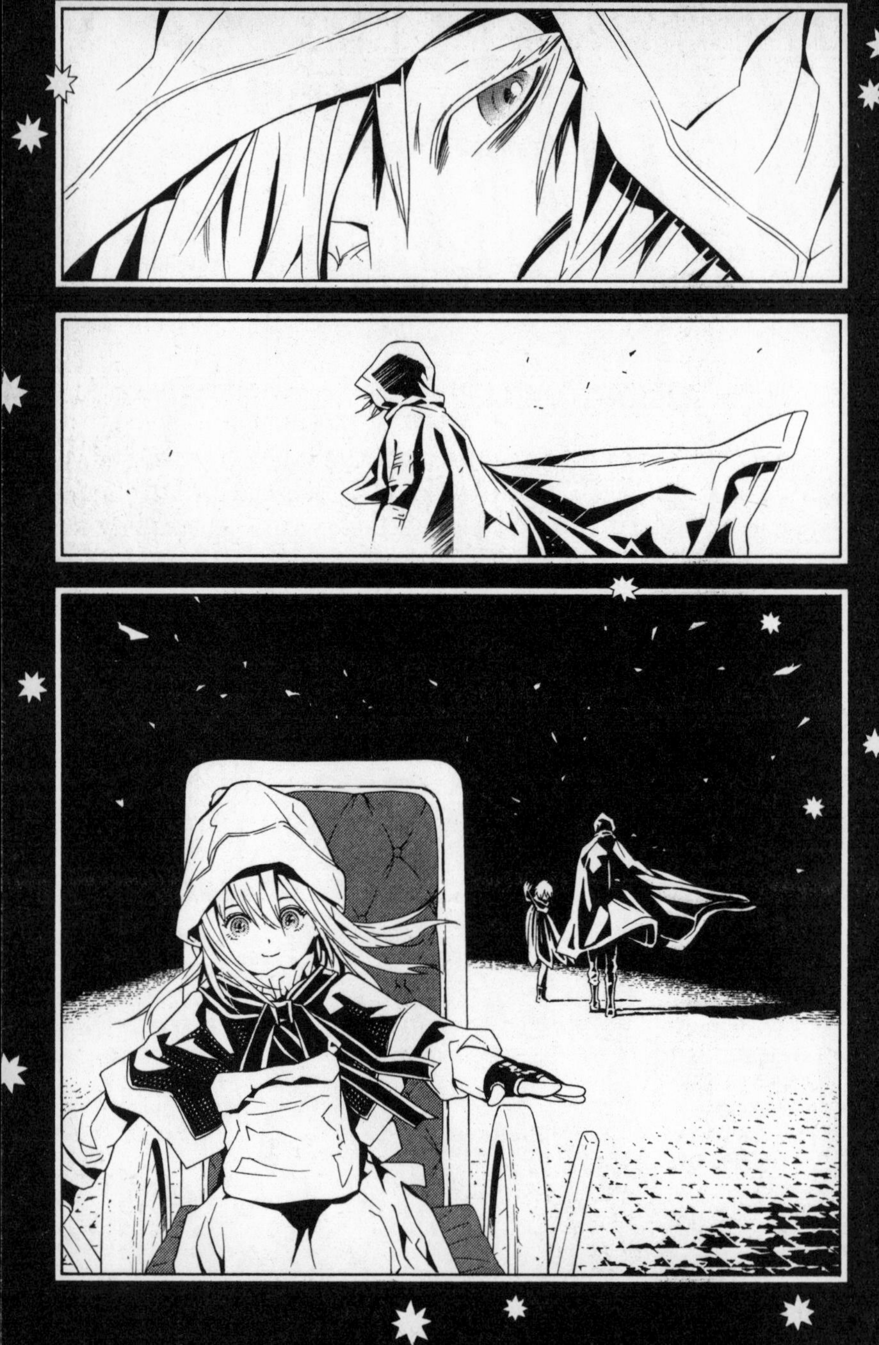

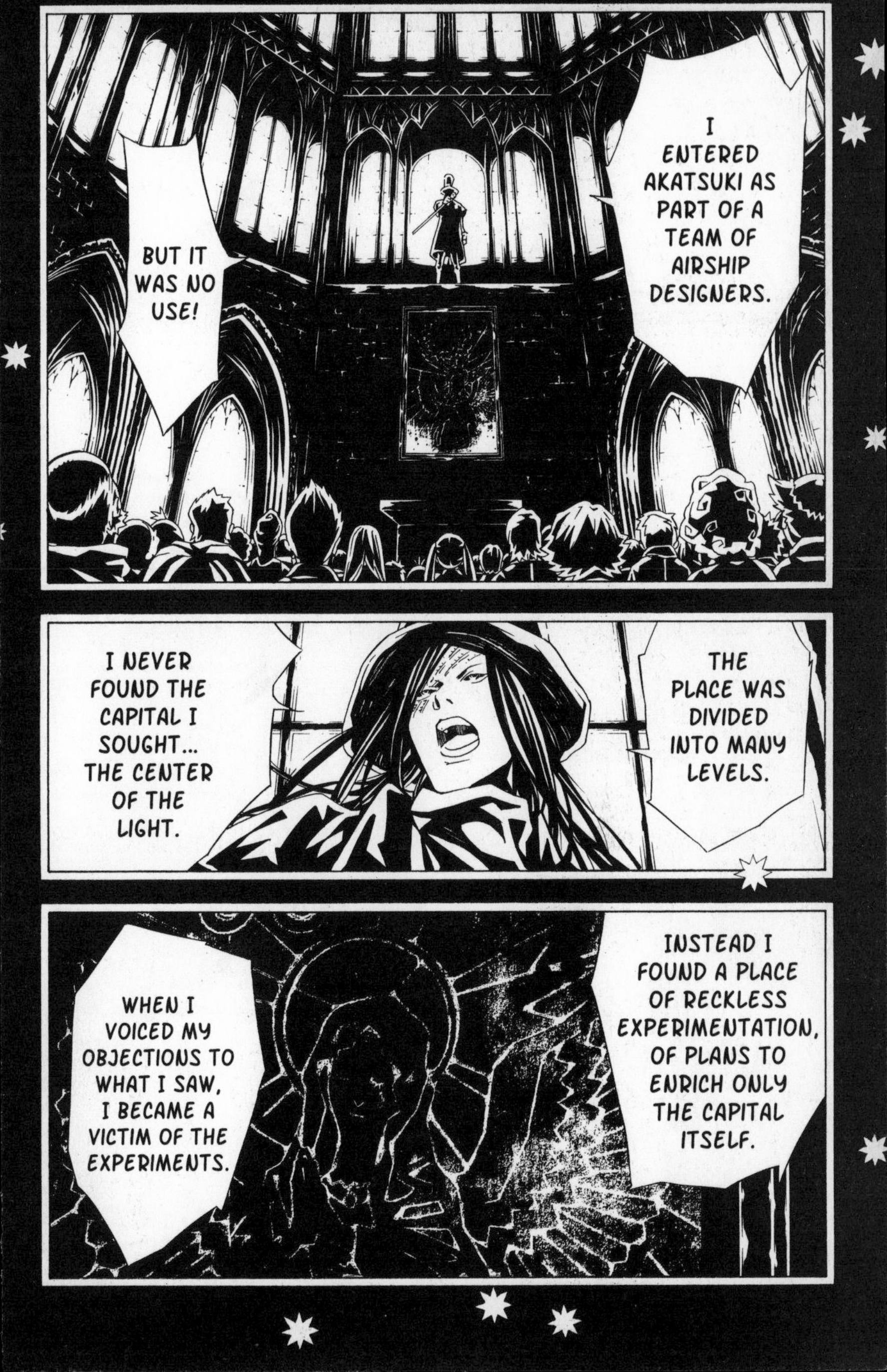
I ENTERED AKATSUKI AS PART OF A TEAM OF AIRSHIP DESIGNERS.
BUT IT WAS NO USE!
THE PLACE WAS DIVIDED INTO MANY LEVELS.
I NEVER FOUND THE CAPITAL I SOUGHT... THE CENTER OF THE LIGHT.
INSTEAD I FOUND A PLACE OF RECKLESS EXPERIMENTATION, OF PLANS TO ENRICH ONLY THE CAPITAL ITSELF.
WHEN I VOICED MY OBJECTIONS TO WHAT I SAW, I BECAME A VICTIM OF THE EXPERIMENTS.

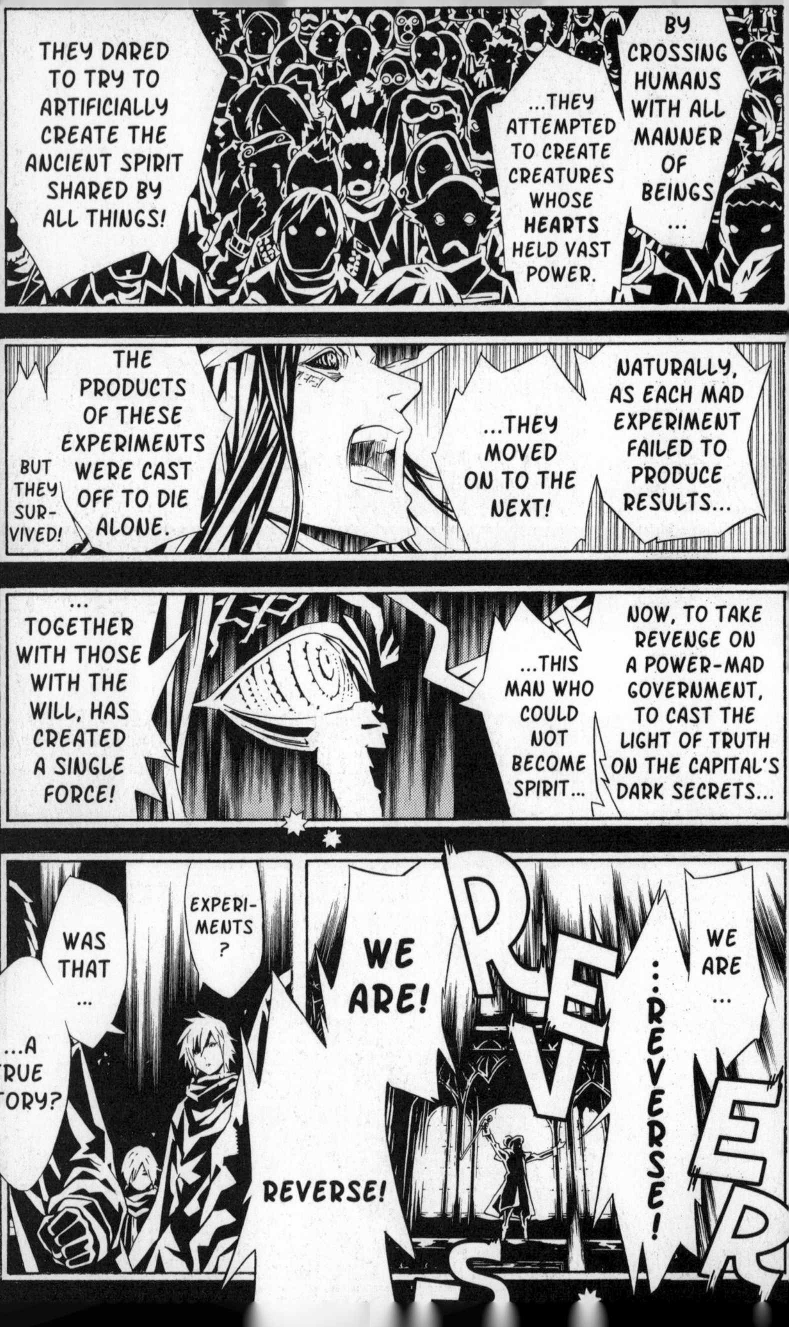
BY CROSSING HUMANS WITH ALL MANNER OF BEINGS...
...THEY ATTEMPTED TO CREATE CREATURES WHOSE HEARTS HELD VAST POWER.
THEY DARED TO TRY TO ARTIFICIALLY CREATE THE ANCIENT SPIRIT SHARED BY ALL THINGS!
NATURALLY, AS EACH MAD EXPERIMENT FAILED TO PRODUCE RESULTS...
...THEY MOVED ON TO THE NEXT!
THE PRODUCTS OF THESE EXPERIMENTS WERE CAST OFF TO DIE ALONE.
BUT THEY SUR-VIVED!
NOW, TO TAKE REVENGE ON A POWER-MAD GOVERNMENT, TO CAST THE LIGHT OF TRUTH ON THE CAPITAL'S DARK SECRETS...
...THIS MAN WHO COULD NOT BECOME SPIRIT...
... TOGETHER WITH THOSE WITH THE WILL, HAS CREATED A SINGLE FORCE!
WE ARE...
...REVERSE!
REVERSE
WE ARE!
REVERSE!
EXPERI-MENTS?
WAS THAT...
...A TRUE STORY?

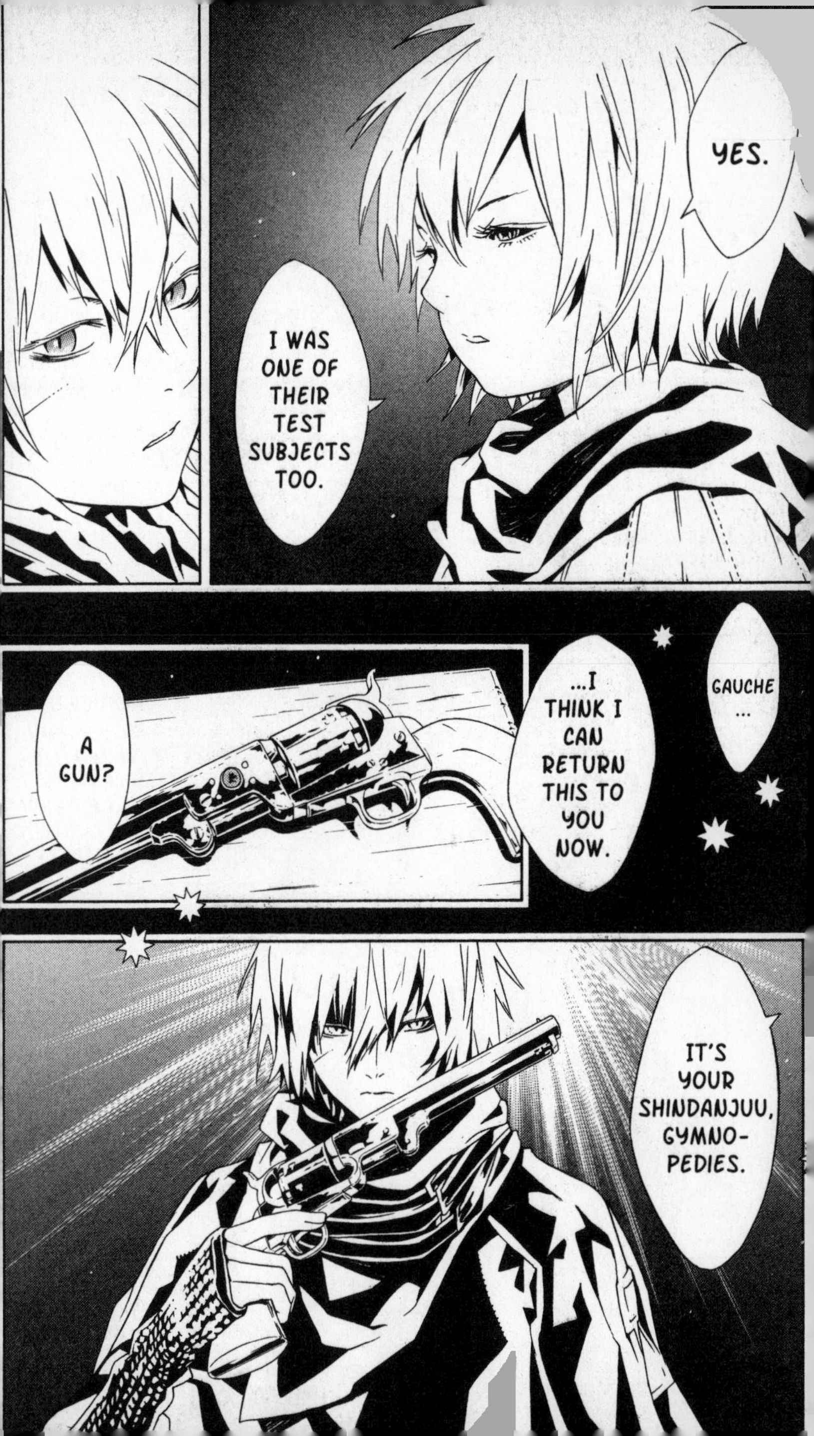
YES.
I WAS ONE OF THEIR TEST SUBJECTS TOO.
GAUCHE...
...I THINK I CAN RETURN THIS TO YOU NOW.
A GUN?
IT'S YOUR SHINDANJUU, GYMNOPEDIES.

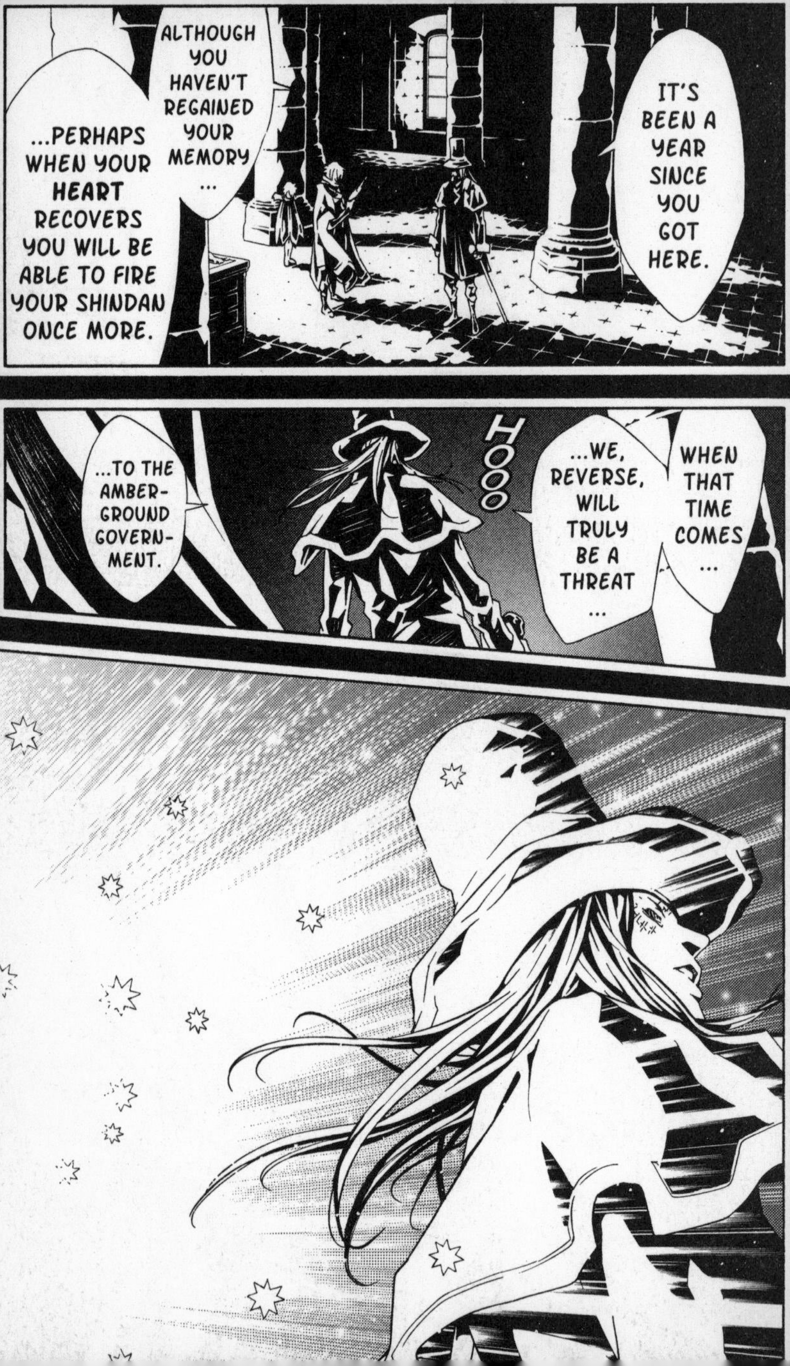
IT'S BEEN A YEAR SINCE YOU GOT HERE.
ALTHOUGH YOU HAVEN'T REGAINED YOUR MEMORY...
...PERHAPS WHEN YOUR **HEART** RECOVERS YOU WILL BE ABLE TO FIRE YOUR SHINDAN ONCE MORE.
WHEN THAT TIME COMES...
...WE, REVERSE, WILL TRULY BE A THREAT...
HOOO
...TO THE AMBER-GROUND GOVERN-MENT.

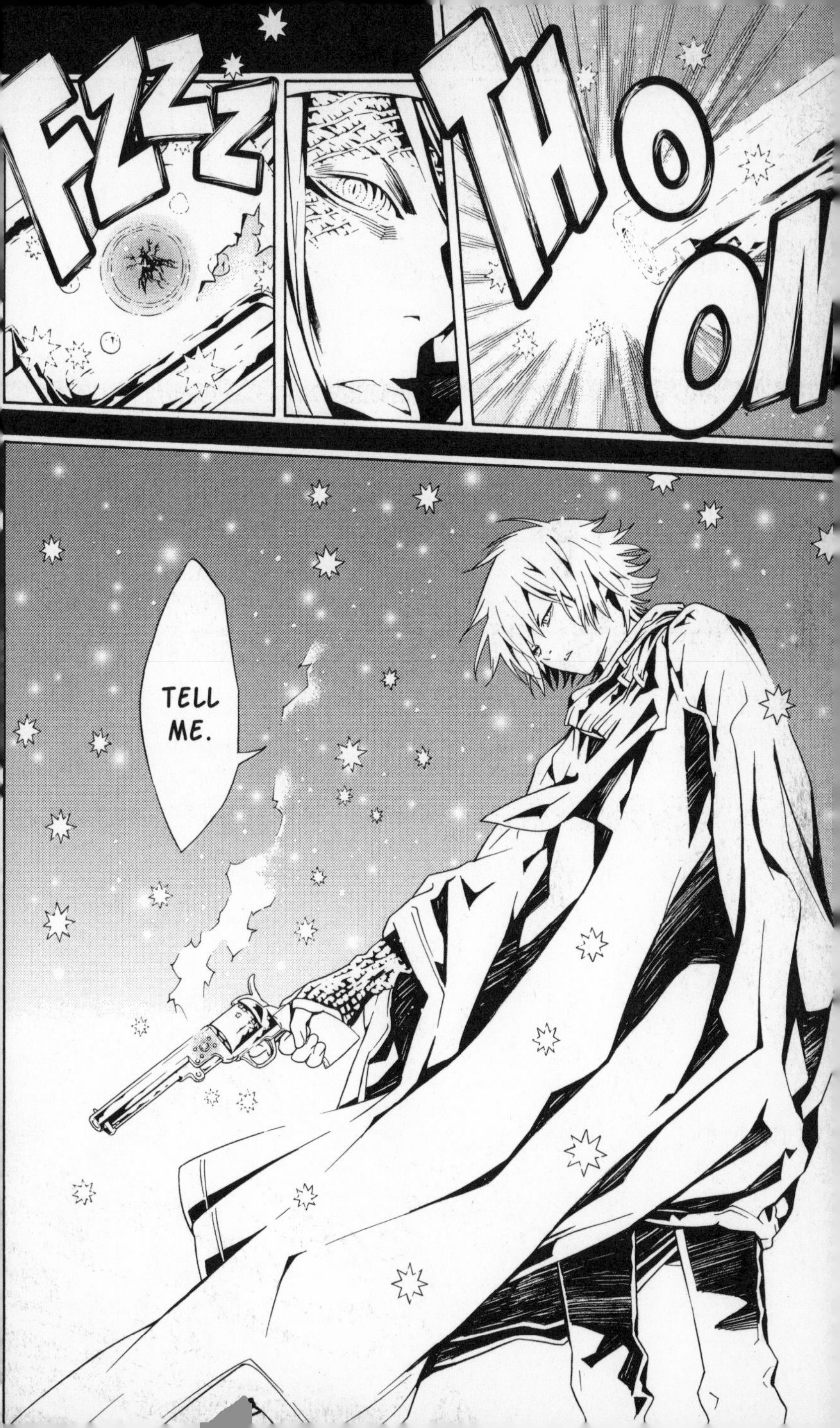
THOOM
FZZZ
TELL ME.

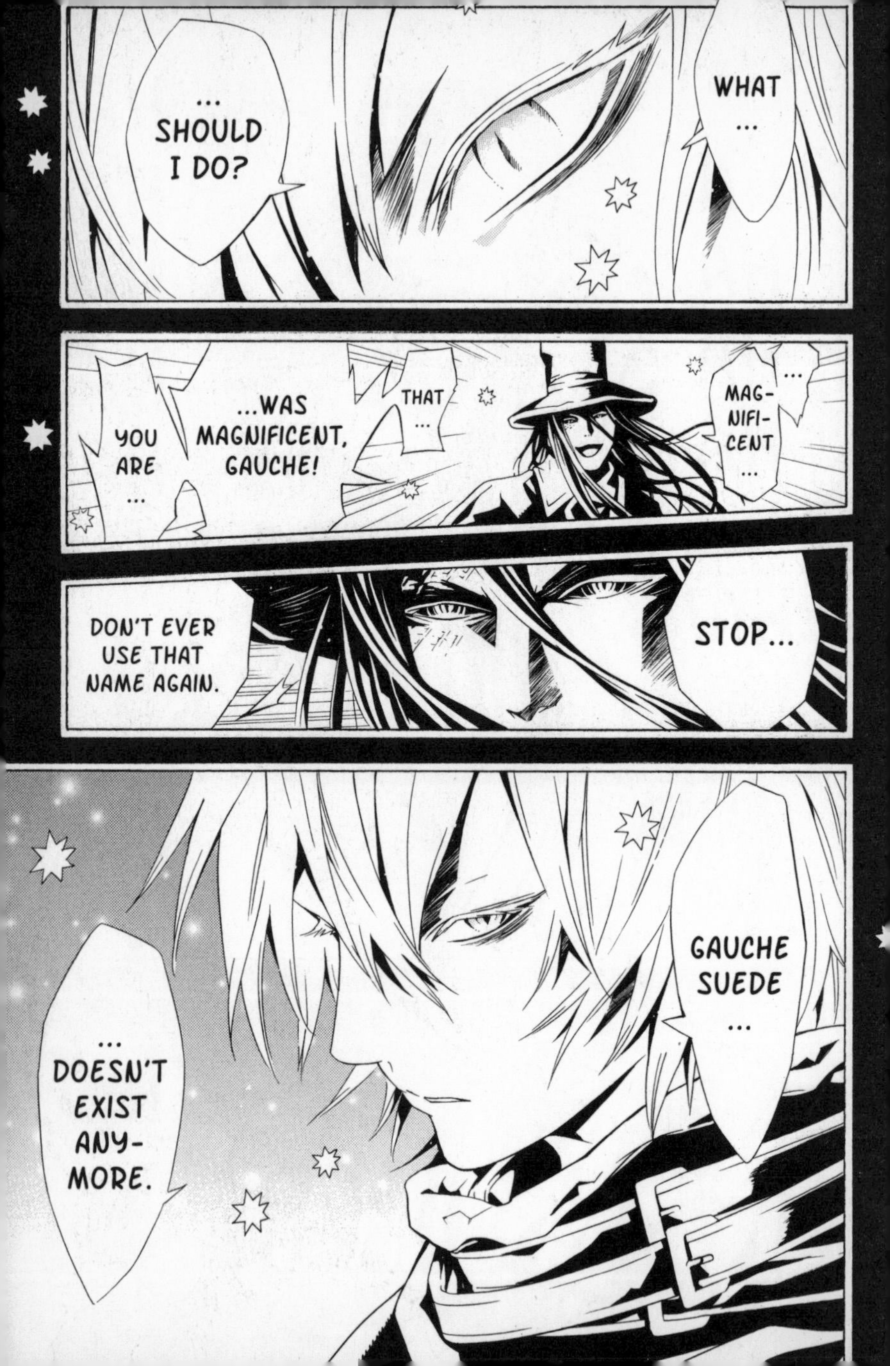
WHAT ...
... SHOULD I DO?
...
MAG-NIFI-CENT ...
THAT ...
...WAS MAGNIFICENT, GAUCHE!
YOU ARE ...
STOP...
DON'T EVER USE THAT NAME AGAIN.
GAUCHE SUEDE ...
... DOESN'T EXIST ANY-MORE.

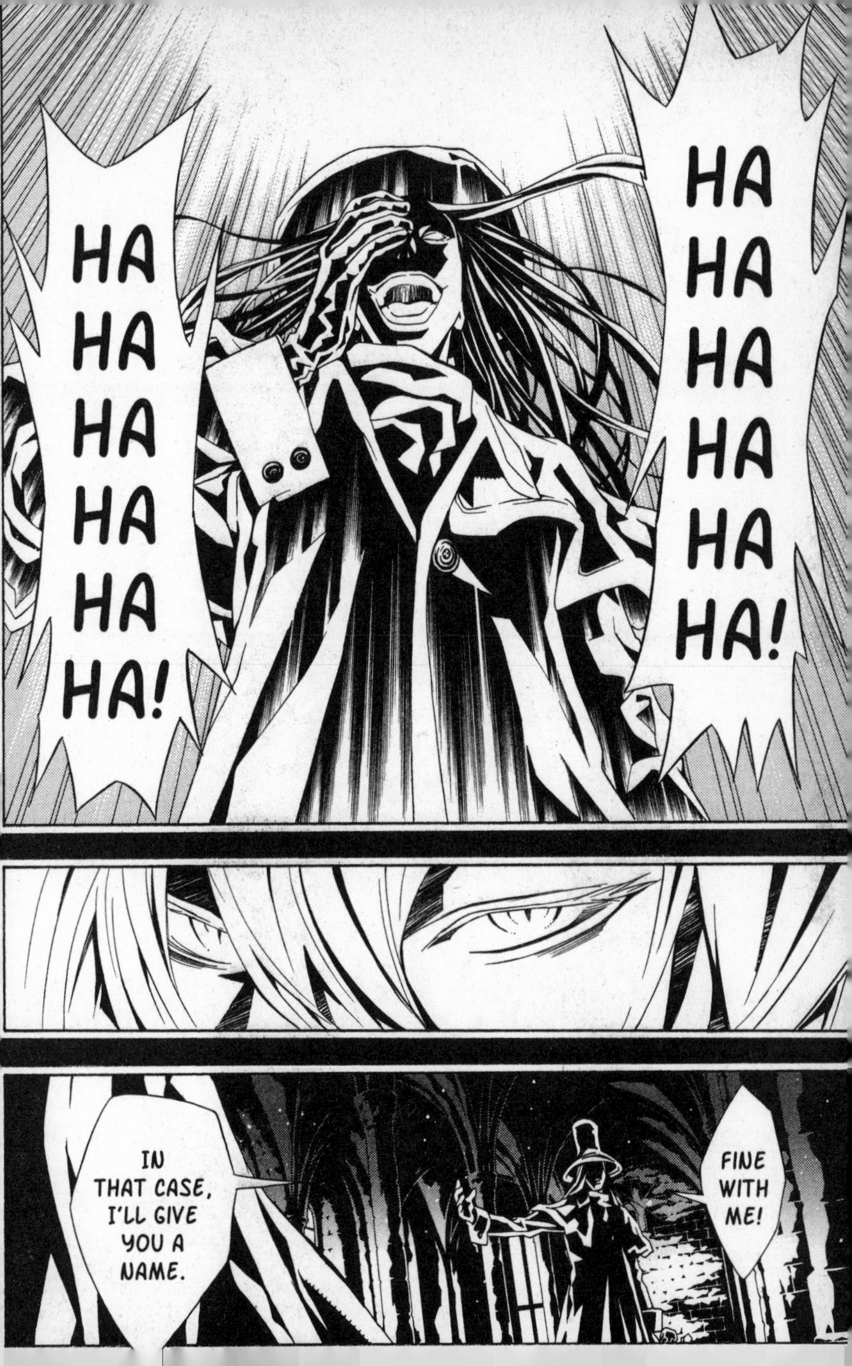
HA HA HA HA HA HA!
HA HA HA HA HA HA!
FINE WITH ME!
IN THAT CASE, I'LL GIVE YOU A NAME.

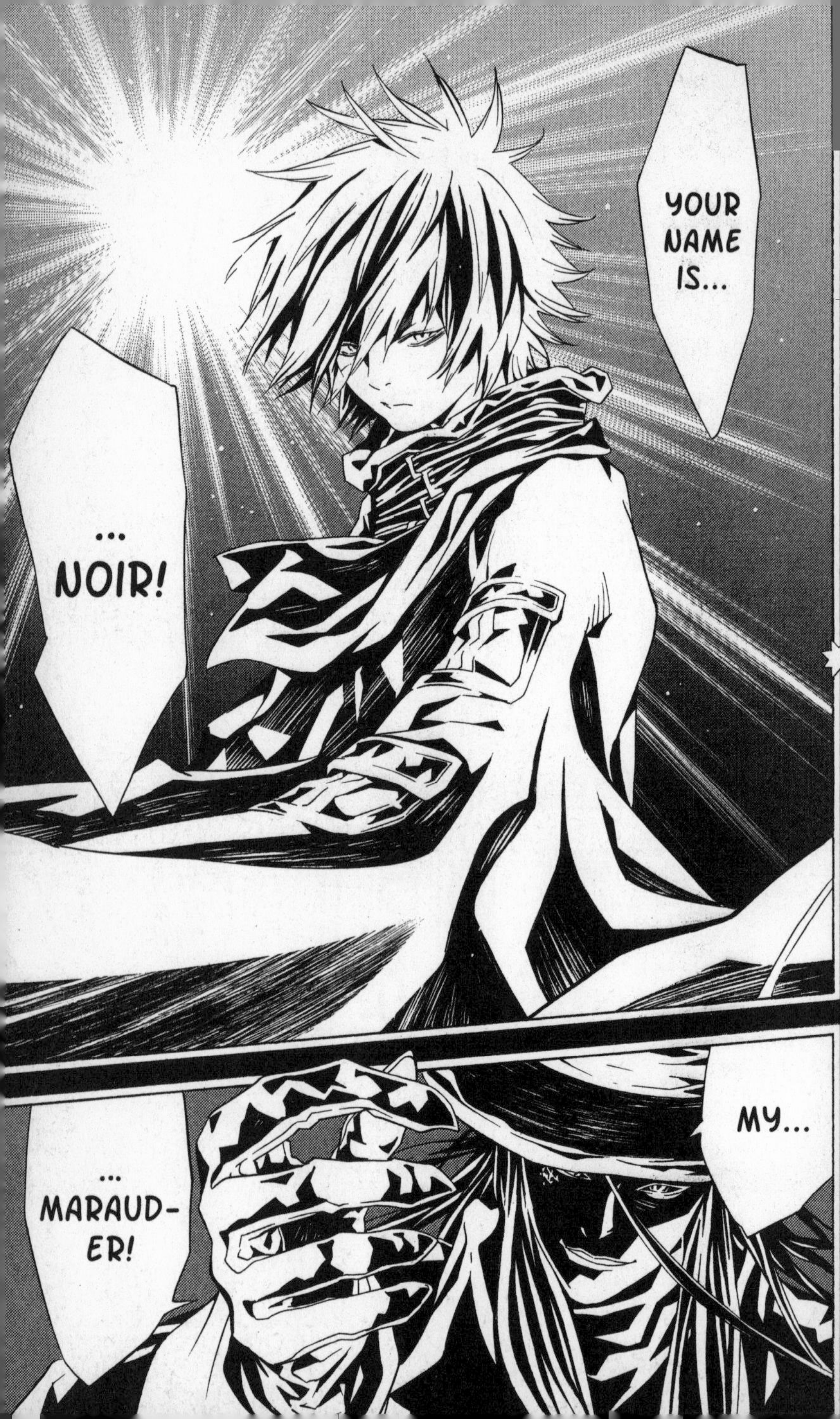
YOUR NAME IS...
... NOIR!
MY...
... MARAUD-ER!

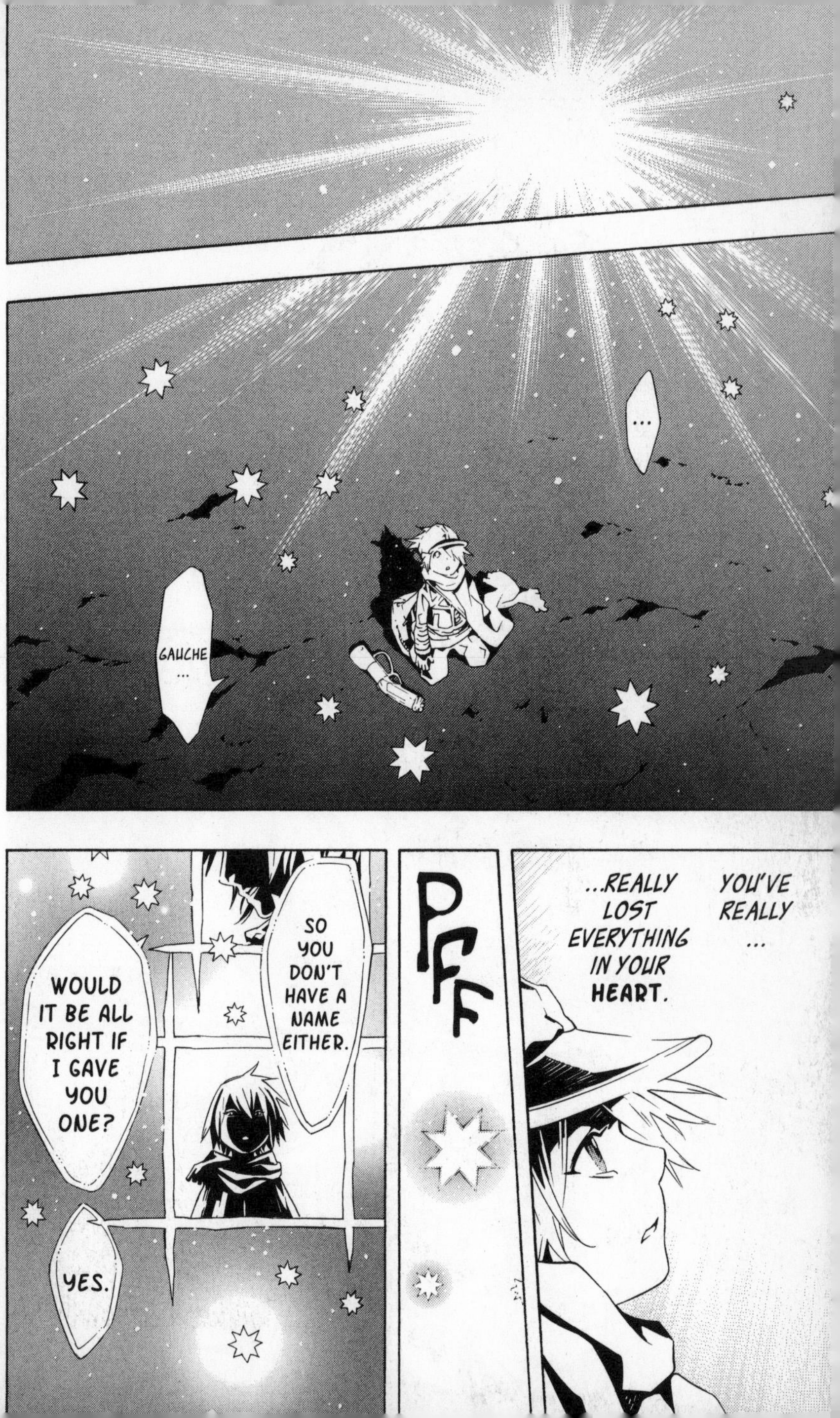
...
GAUCHE ...
YOU'VE REALLY ...
...REALLY LOST EVERYTHING IN YOUR HEART.
PFF
SO YOU DON'T HAVE A NAME EITHER.
WOULD IT BE ALL RIGHT IF I GAVE YOU ONE?
YES.

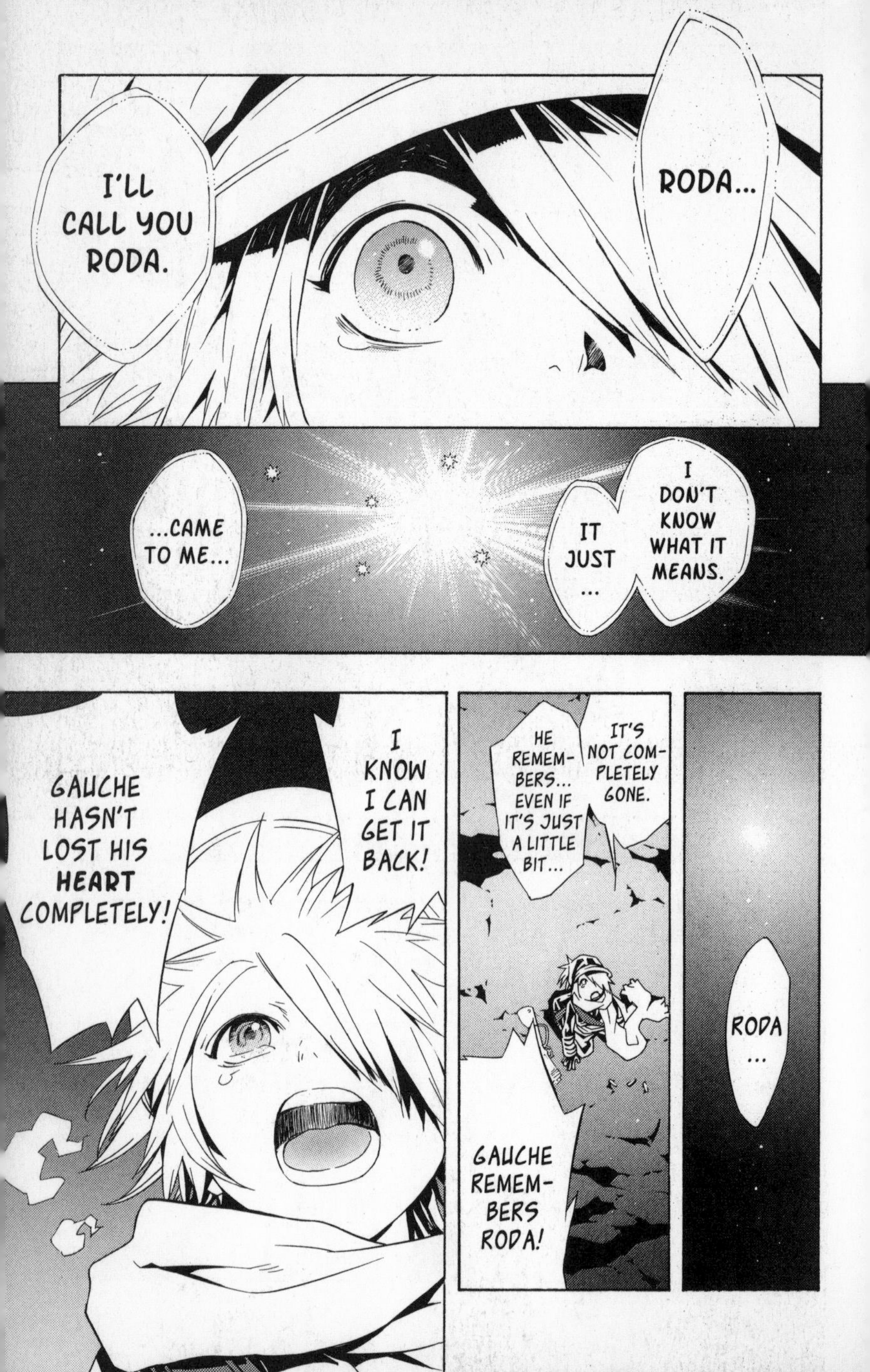
RODA...
I'LL CALL YOU RODA.
I DON'T KNOW WHAT IT MEANS.
IT JUST ...
...CAME TO ME...
RODA ...
IT'S NOT COM-PLETELY GONE.
HE REMEM-BERS... EVEN IF IT'S JUST A LITTLE BIT...
GAUCHE REMEM-BERS RODA!
I KNOW I CAN GET IT BACK!
GAUCHE HASN'T LOST HIS **HEART** COMPLETELY!

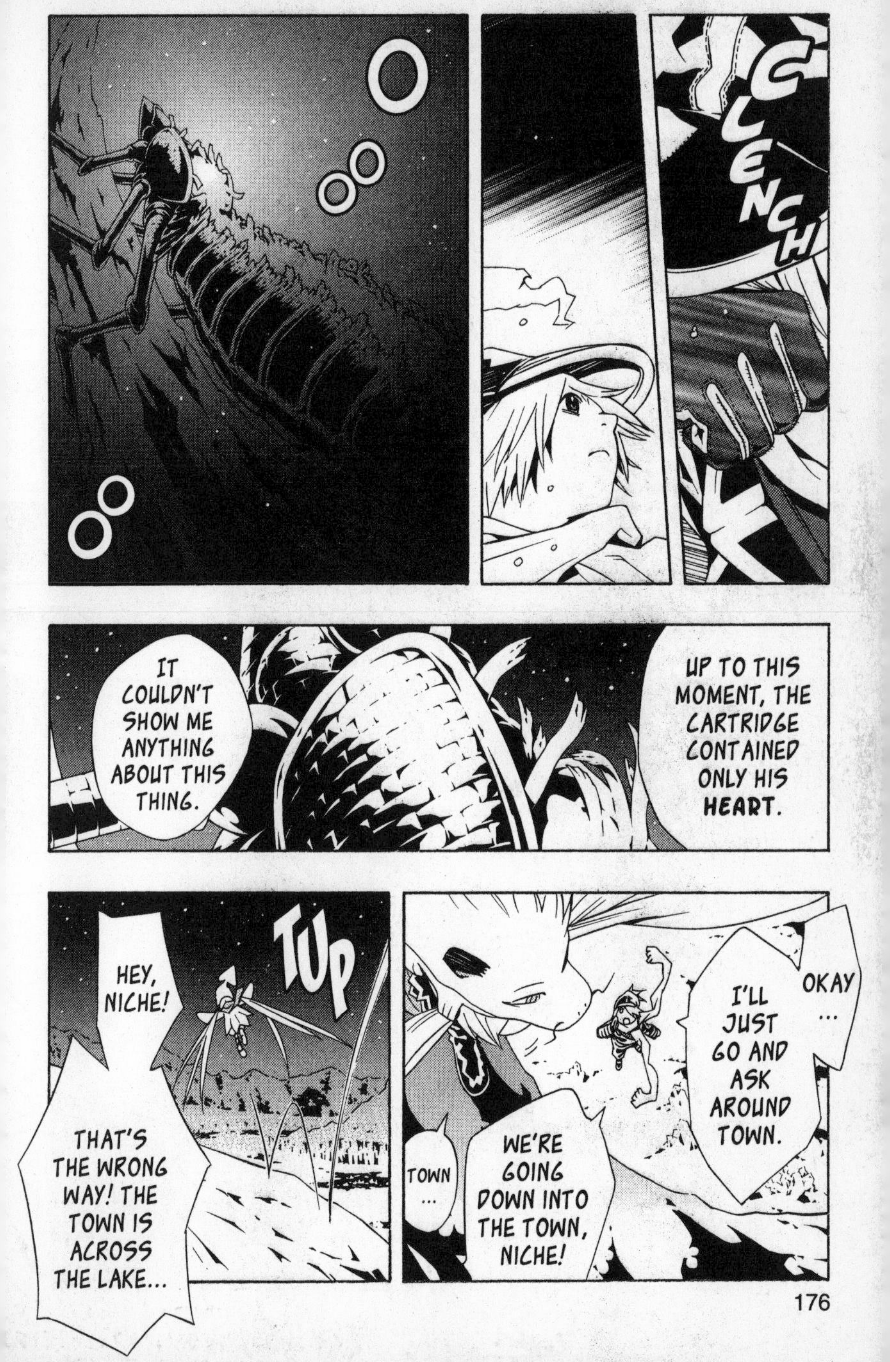
CLENCH
UP TO THIS MOMENT, THE CARTRIDGE CONTAINED ONLY HIS **HEART**.
IT COULDN'T SHOW ME ANYTHING ABOUT THIS THING.
OKAY ...
I'LL JUST GO AND ASK AROUND TOWN.
WE'RE GOING DOWN INTO THE TOWN, NICHE!
TOWN ...
TUP
HEY, NICHE!
THAT'S THE WRONG WAY! THE TOWN IS ACROSS THE LAKE...

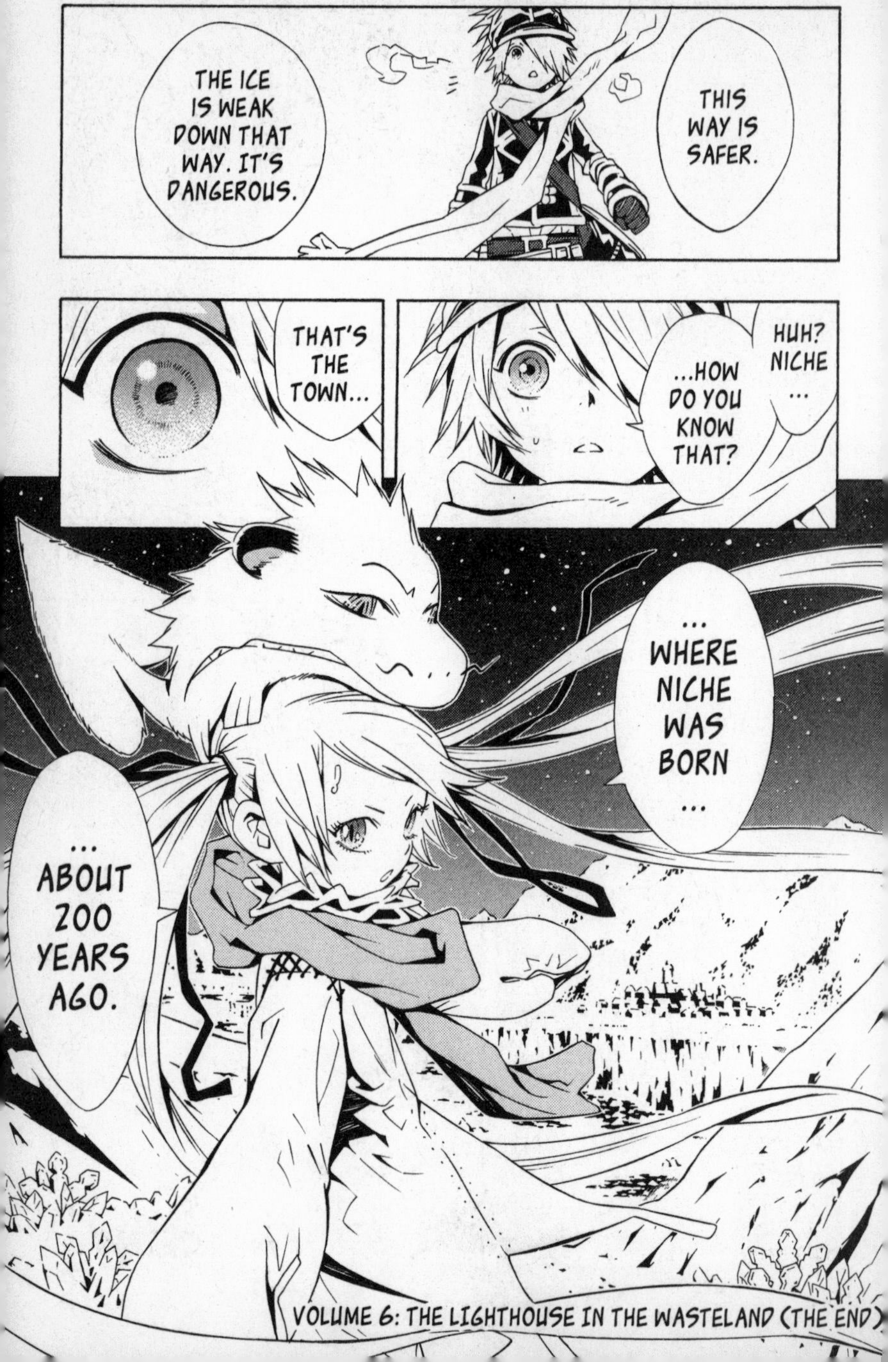
THIS WAY IS SAFER.
THE ICE IS WEAK DOWN THAT WAY. IT'S DANGEROUS.
HUH? NICHE ...
...HOW DO YOU KNOW THAT?
THAT'S THE TOWN...
... WHERE NICHE WAS BORN ...
... ABOUT 200 YEARS AGO.
VOLUME 6: THE LIGHTHOUSE IN THE WASTELAND (THE END)

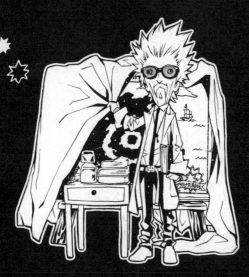

Dr. Thunderland's Reference Desk

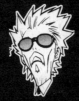

Hello, my little inattentive moppets. This is Dr. Thunderland's House of Vengeance. Why so angry, you ask? Why does the good doctor require immediate and inexplicably horrible revenge? It has come to my attention that YOU are not PAYING attention.

If you had been, you would have noticed that I still have not appeared in this book! You would have been outraged! You would say, "Why won't you show us Dr. Thunderland's work at the Yuusari Beehive?"

But no. And so I must seek...REVENGE! Through the power of education! Let us begin...

■ DEPOSITS OF SPIRIT AMBER

In this world where the sun barely shines, plants are able to grow and creatures thrive because of the Spirit Amber lying dormant underground, sustaining the planet's temperature and magnetic field... I believe I explained this all in volume 1, but we've already established that you haven't been paying attention! Ahem. And so, land rich in Spirit Amber supports life easily and is very valuable.

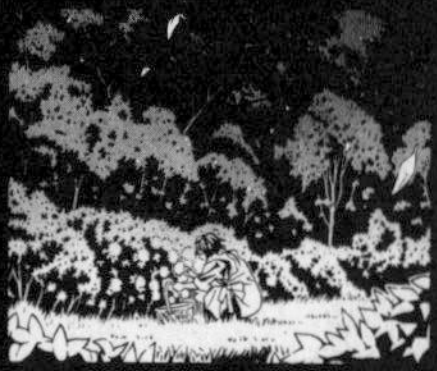

This type of land, which Colbasso asked Miss Rei to give her, is quite valuable. What a selfish woman. But at least she's in the story, whereas I remain— No, I mustn't dwell on the negative. Instead, I must have... revenge!

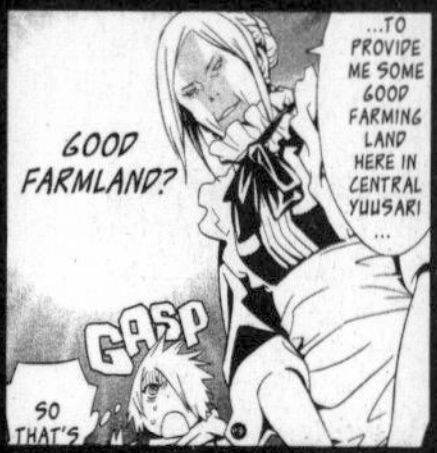
...TO PROVIDE ME SOME GOOD FARMING LAND HERE IN CENTRAL YUUSARI ...
GOOD FARMLAND?
GASP
SO THAT'S

■ GOD'S SINK

Astute readers will recognize this as a reference to the works of the ancient philosopher Socratetris. His books have come back into print and are all the rage among the women of Central Yuusari. Socratetris is famed for his pioneering use of dialogue. The work in question features an argument between a demon with filthy hands and the god of porcelain sinks. I have no idea how Niche learned of this book.

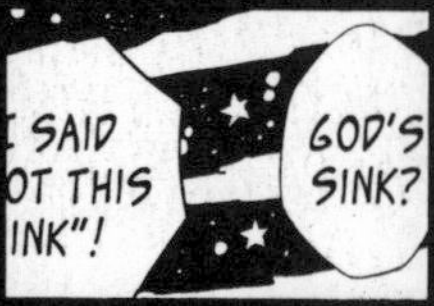
GOD'S SINK?
I SAID OT THIS INK"!

■ PAINT IT BLACK PAINT SUPPLIES

nb: "Paint It Black" / A song by The Rolling Stones, from their 1966 album *Aftermath*.

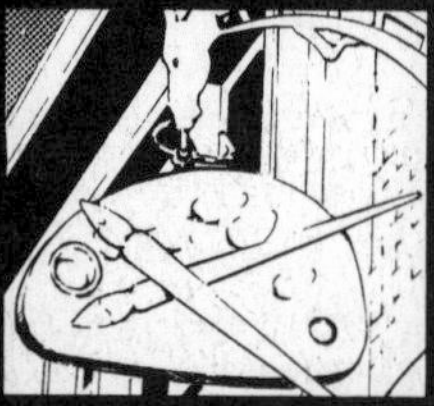

■ LIGHTHOUSE IN THE WASTELAND

There are so many fascinating machines, aren't there? The lubricant used in the machinery gets very hot and flows out like a river when discharged. Here in this world of perpetual darkness, the lighthouse seems valuable, but considering its environmental impact, it is a rather dangerous machine. An interesting quandary, don't you think?

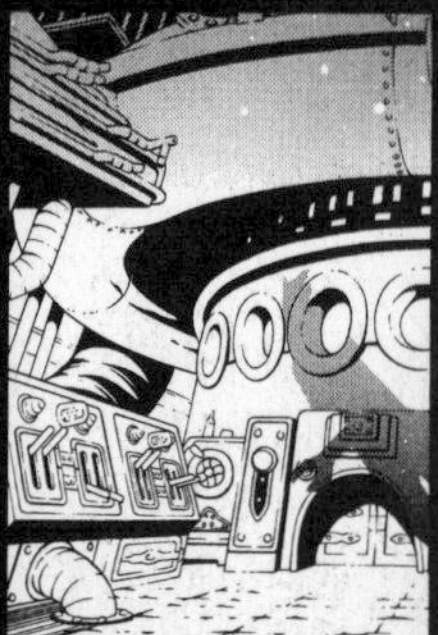

The water in the Liquid Sand River is viscous, so it cannot be used for drinking. The lighthouse uses it in great volumes as a coolant. Because of the danger it poses, the lighthouse is situated in a remote locale. Not much use, is it?

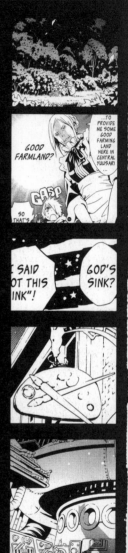

But who'd have thought Lag's bruises were caused by Niche slapping him? And still she gets to be on the cover?! Bah, I say! Bah!

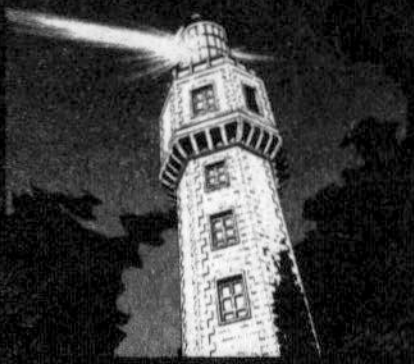

■ CARRIAGE SERVICE

The carriage service is much like the trains and buses in your own world, driven by animals suited to the different routes. It is much cheaper than renting a private carriage, so the general public uses this service as a means to get around. In Yuusari, many routes connect the city center to towns. However, routes are generally short, so to travel a great distance, you must transfer many times. Letter Bees often use them.

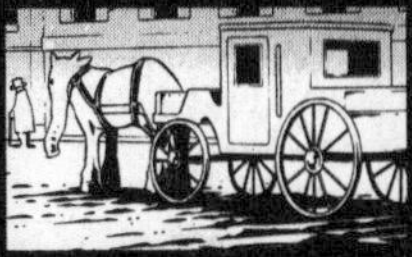

It's still strange to see a rhino-drawn carriage, I say.

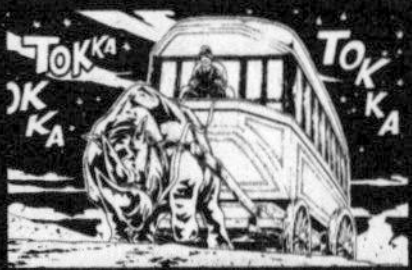
TOKKA
TOKKA

■ SYLVETTE'S WHEELCHAIR

Sylvette's wheelchair uses a complex hydraulic system: if the lever is pushed forward, the wheels will turn, and if it is pulled back, the brake is activated. The pressurized system makes the chair quite fast. A plodding rhinocerous carriage doesn't stand a chance against her wheelchair. And that power slide is not to be trifled with! One might describe Sylvette's driving style as both fast *and* furious, were one so inclined.

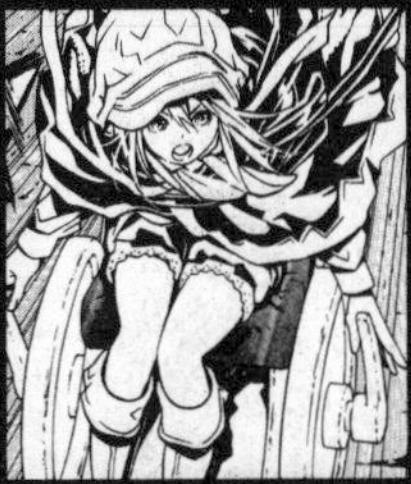

■ HOUSE OF DOLLS KATAN AND M. CROCE, THE GIRL WHO SENT THE LETTER

This shop, located in Yasomichi, specializes in dolls. Their main focus is a line of ball-jointed dolls, but they'll take anything with originality. For some reason, Sylvette's dolls seem to be very popular. They must like the funny faces.

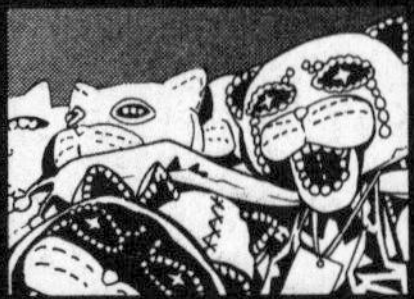

nb: Katan Amano (1953-1990) / Ball-jointed doll creator. The exhibition hall Maria Croce, where she held her exhibits, later became the Maria Cuore Doll Museum in Tokyo.

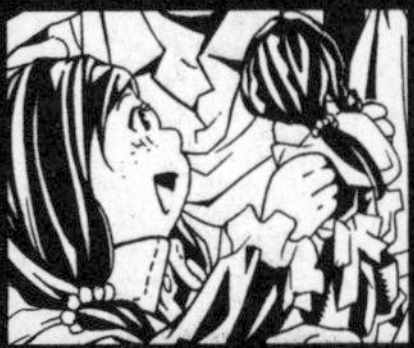

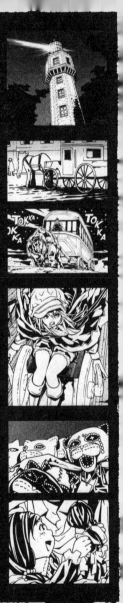

■ CENTRAL TIMES NEWSPAPER

This paper boasts the largest readership in Central Yuusari. They print only serious news, never the sort of fantasy novels like those written by Vincent in "A Letter Full of Lies." It's an important source of information for anyone living near Central.

I wonder if they wrote a story headlined "Autobahn Captured."

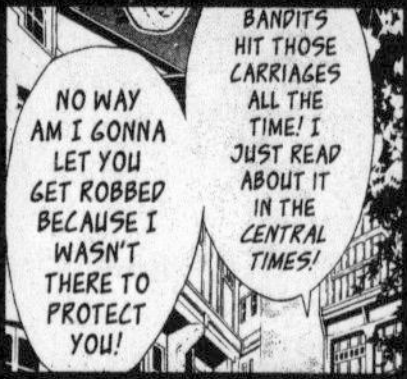
BANDITS HIT THOSE CARRIAGES ALL THE TIME! I JUST READ ABOUT IT IN THE CENTRAL TIMES!
NO WAY AM I GONNA LET YOU GET ROBBED BECAUSE I WASN'T THERE TO PROTECT YOU!

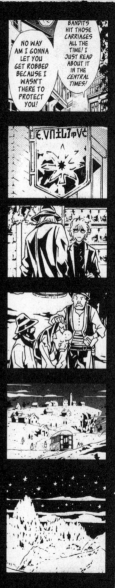

■ PINK ELEPHANT HERBS

You can get all manner of herbs from this specialist. He acquires his herbs from all over Amberground, so he picks up all sorts of information. This shop is a bit shady... It seems that the Beehive Director shops here not just for tobacco but also for information. The shopkeeper has some influence in the underworld as well.

nb: Pink Elephant / Slang referring to hallucinations had by those under the influence of liquor or drugs.

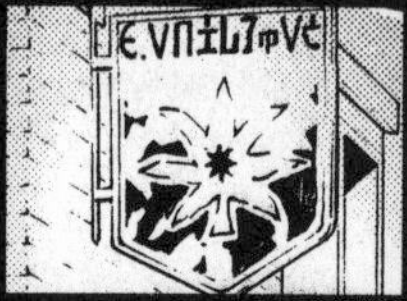

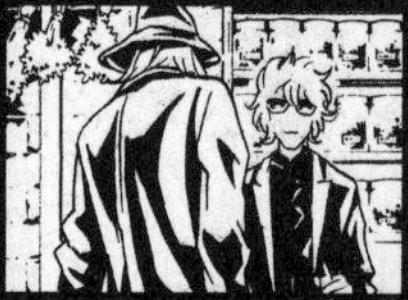

■ VIGILANCE COMMITTEE

There is no government-run police force in Amberground. Each town or district has their own civilian vigilance committee to protect their own areas and dispense justice. The government does get involved in some cases, and the vigilance committees of different towns may even work together. Justice in Amberground may not be swift, but at least it's tidy.

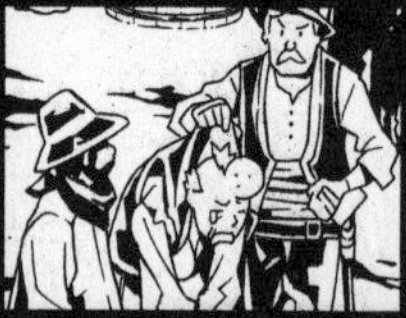

■ DOGURA TOWN

nb: *Kogura Magura* / Representative work of Yumeno Kyusaku (1889-1936), published in 1935. In it he writes, and I paraphrase, that anyone who has read through a book will, at least once, show signs of mental instability.

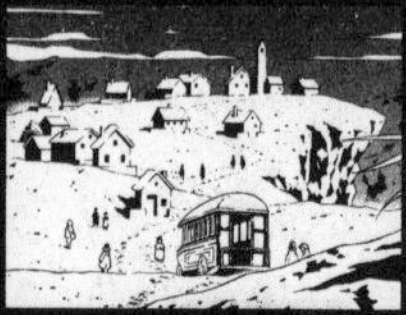

■ BLUE NOTES BLUES

In this world where the sun barely shines, plants are able to grow and creatures thrive because of blah, blah, blah. The Blue Notes Blues area, however, is a world of ice. There is almost no Spirit Amber here. No one knows if it's always been like this or if someone mined all the Spirit Amber. I'd like to find out, but I prefer sitting in front of the fire to digging around in the ice. Brrr!

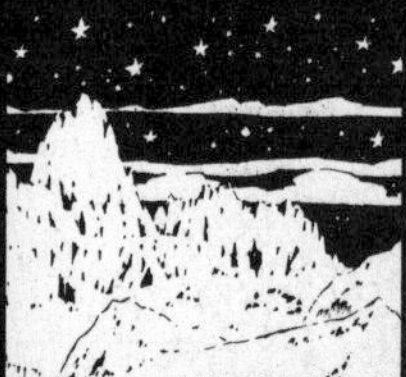

nb: Blue Note / A New York jazz club. Blue Note Records is a record label known for its novel record sleeves.

nb: Blues / Music that developed among African-Americans in the deep South during the late nineteenth century. It is the root of jazz and rock 'n roll.

■ SHINDANJUU GYMNOPEDIES

This is Gauche's—I mean Noir's—large-caliber shindanjuu. It's the one he bought from Gobeni's Sinners when he was still a Letter Bee. He may have lost his memory...his *heart*, but I guess he hasn't forgotten how to use his shindanjuu. How sad.

But the fact that he mentioned the name Roda means that some piece of his heart still remains—even if it is faint. Okay! I'll fix it! Team up with me, Lag! We'll clobber Reverse! Sounds like a good story, doesn't it? *Sigh*... Things would be so much easier if this comic were about science instead of adventure.

■ THE MAN WHO COULD NOT BECOME SPIRIT

Oh! This one seems to truly be a victim of the scheme to create man-made Spirit Amber. Yikes. And that girl Roda was one too. This was a complex plot—many layers to it. Slowly, we begin hearing descriptions of Akatsuki. And Gauche... Hmm... What is Reverse planning? Will it interfere with my revenge? And what about Niche's bombshell of an announcement? I can't wait for the next volume!

nb: Gymnopedies / Piano piece by Erik Satie, Erik Alfred Leslie Satie (1866-1925). Composed in 1888.

■ FILM NOIR

nb: Film noir / General term used to describe primarily crime dramas that emphasize light and dark, and tend toward pessimism, violence, nihilism, and decadence.

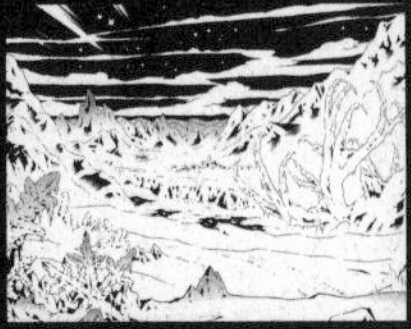

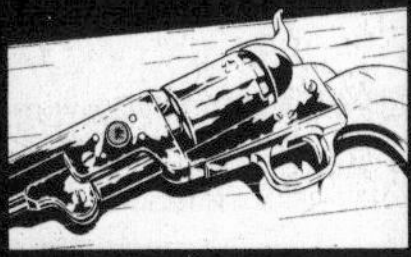

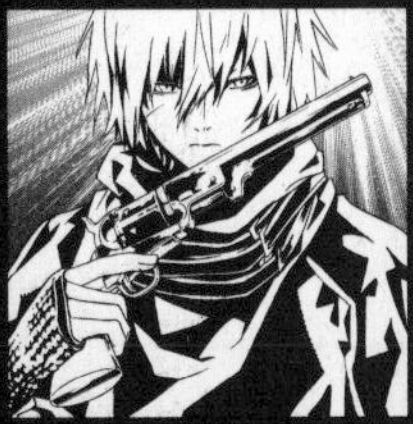

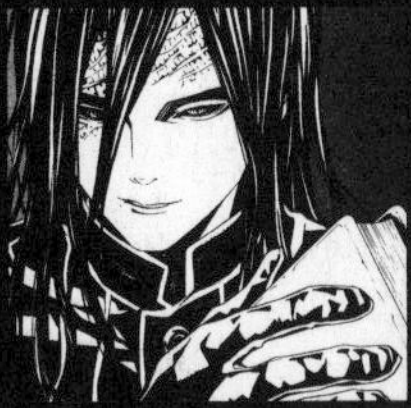

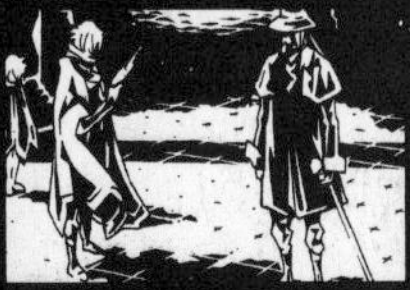

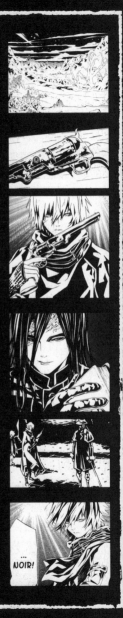

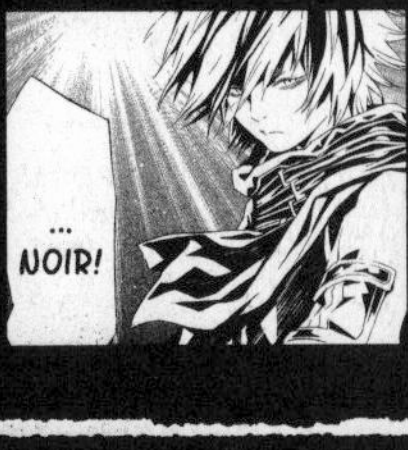
... NOIR!

Route Map

Finally, I am including a map indicating the route followed in this volume, created by the gentle souls at Lonely Goatherd Map Station of Central Yuusari.

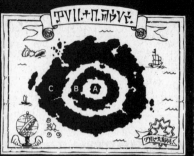

A: Akatsuki   B: Yuusari   C: Yodaka

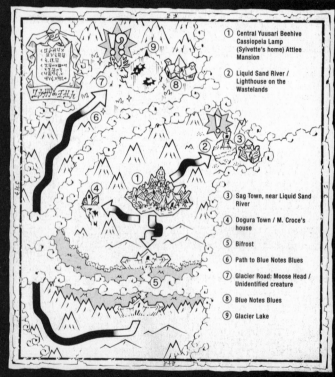

① Central Yuusari Beehive Cassiopeia Lamp (Sylvette's home) Attlee Mansion

② Liquid Sand River / Lighthouse on the Wastelands

③ Sag Town, near Liquid Sand River

④ Dogura Town / M. Croce's house

⑤ Bifrost

⑥ Path to Blue Notes Blues

⑦ Glacier Road: Moose Head / Unidentified creature

⑧ Blue Notes Blues

⑨ Glacier Lake

There? Have I had my revenge? Will you no longer ignore my plight? I'm not asking for much here—just pay attention to me! And maybe put me in the book! And…a cover spread wouldn't hurt either, now that I think about it. Can't you just picture it? Me in full color, leaping into action? Just give me a chance here!

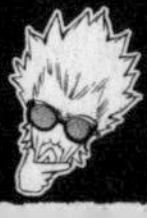

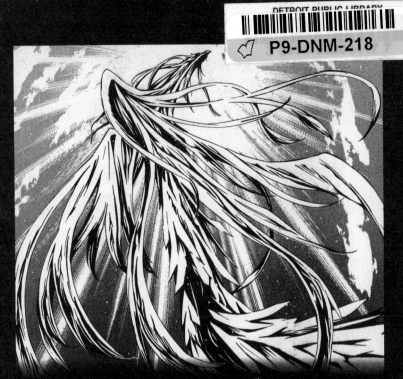

In the next volume...

Blue Notes Blues

Noir's trail leads Lag and Niche to the icy northern town of Blue Notes Blues. It just so happens that Niche was born here. Lag and Niche uncover her mysterious origins: a sacred underground lake...where her brethren still dwell.

Available November 2011!